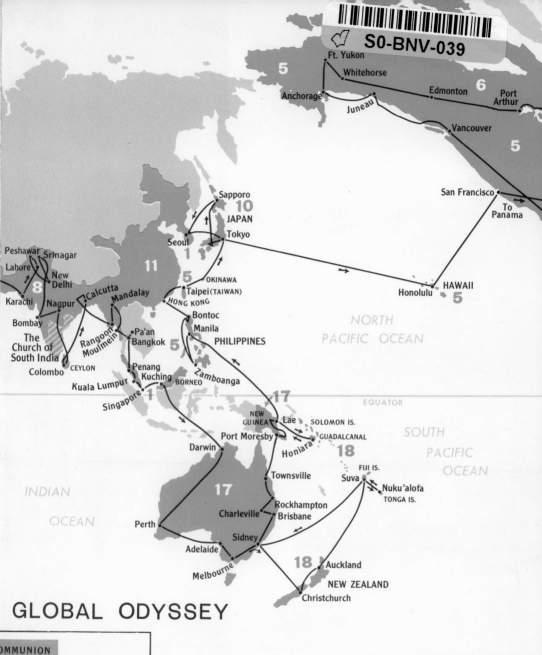

GLOBAL ODYSSEY

...OMMUNION

...glo- American chaplaincies

...as of the autonomous churches

10. The Holy Catholic Church in Japan

11. The Holy Catholic Church in China

12. The Church of the Province of Central Africa

13. The Church of the Province of South Africa

14. The Church of the Province of West Africa

15. The Church of the Province of East Africa

16. The Church of the Province of Uganda, Rwanda and Burundi

17. The Church of England in Australia and Tasmania

18. The Church of the Province of New Zealand

GLOBAL ODYSSEY

GLOBAL ODYSSEY

An Episcopalian's Encounter with the
Anglican Communion in Eighty Countries

by

HOWARD A. JOHNSON

Canon of the Cathedral Church
of St. John the Divine, New York

PHOTOGRAPHS BY THE AUTHOR

HARPER & ROW, PUBLISHERS

NEW YORK AND EVANSTON

FIRST EDITION

LIBRARY OF CONGRESS CATALOG CARD NUMBER: 63: 7606

TO
Henry Clark Smith
Albert T. Mollegen
and the late Walter Lowrie

— the three men most responsible
for having tried to make
an Anglican out of me

"High and low, rich and poor: one with another."
(Psalm 49:2 — from the Great Bible of 1539.)

This book is about the Anglican Communion. For anybody who needs to be told what it is, it has been defined by the Lambeth Conference as "a fellowship, within the One Holy Catholic and Apostolic Church, of those duly constituted Dioceses, Provinces, or Regional Churches in communion with the See of Canterbury, which have the following characteristics in common:

(a) they uphold and propagate the Catholic and Apostolic faith and order as they are generally set forth in the Book of Common Prayer as authorized in their several Churches;

(b) they are particular or national Churches, and, as such, promote within each of their territories a national expression of Christian faith, life, and worship; and

(c) they are bound together not by a central legislative and executive authority, but by mutual loyalty sustained through the common counsel of the Bishops in conference."

CONTENTS

ILLUSTRATIONS

A 32-page section containing 54 photographs, all taken by the author, appears between pages 160 and 161.

MAPS

A NOTE ABOUT MAPS

The maps, brilliantly executed by Lilli Mautner, seem to me to be
above reproach, provided one bears in mind their special purpose and
the limitations under which the cartographer had to work. To have
shown all provinces – and diocesan boundaries within each province –
would have been to render these small scale maps illegible. For the
same reason, it was decided not to try to indicate all of the places I
visited – the side trips, the incessant zigzagging. We attempt no more
than to show, in bold outline, those parts of the Anglican Communion
where geography is least likely to be familiar to the majority of readers.
These maps, although incomplete, are expertly drawn and, within the
restrictions imposed upon the mapmaker, accurate. Neither she nor I,
however, would suggest that you try to navigate by them.

H.A.J.

In this book I change *tyres*, pull away from *kerbs*, buy *petrol*, follow *programmes*, express *judgements*, visit *centres*, take recreation in *theatres*. My *behaviour*, in short, is that of an Englishman. But I am an *American!* My friendly and obliging publishers in England, where the type was set, do not yet acknowledge that the Fourth Day of July, 1776, brought into being an independent nation which developed its own idiosyncratic way of spelling the language.

H.A.J.

PREFACE

Christianity abounds in paradox. On the one hand, a text claiming dominical authority says of the Church that "the gates of hell shall not prevail against it". On the other hand, we are told that Jesus of Nazareth said, "When the Son of man cometh, shall he find faith on the earth?"

Only by faith can we cling to the hope that in historical time Christianity will not founder.

At the first Epiphany there were about two hundred million people in the world. Today there are eight hundred million *Christians*. From no Christians at all to eight hundred million of them! This looks impressive. But, lest we purr too contentedly about this phenomenal advance, we need to remind ourselves that there are fifteen times as many people to be converted to Christianity today as there were in the first century of the Christian era. Christianity has made progress, but the plain fact is that it is failing to keep pace with the growth of the world's population.

Human beings have never before multiplied as fast as they have in the twentieth century. The population of our planet passed the two billion mark in 1930. Experts calculate that the three billion mark will be reached this very year; the four billion mark by 1977; the five billion mark by 1990; and the six billion mark by the year 2000. Only thirty-eight years from now – if there is no catastrophic circumstance or other factor to change the growth rate – the world will be twice as crowded as it is today.

A report of the United Nations Economic and Social Council contains the startling information that the world population is currently increasing by more than 120,000 persons every day. One wonders how many of the fifty million people who will be born in this Year of Our Lord 1962 will ever so much as hear the Name of that Lord, let alone have an opportunity really to know him, love him, obey him. Not many. In most instances, it will not be their fault but ours.

These facts and figures, together with the prognostications based upon them, are profoundly disturbing. Christians are being outpaced, outdistanced, outbred.

Someone has called attention to the fact that, if on a map of the world you draw a triangle whose three points are Jerusalem, Tokyo, and Colombo, you have bounded but a small section of the globe, yet within this area live

more than half of the dwellers upon earth – and it is not a Christian half.
It is also the most prolific part of the world.

From a consideration of such themes – global in proportion and dark in
portent – it may seem a descent into the trivial to use the first person singular
and to write about a trip around the world which *I* made.

What claim have I to the reader's attention? Not much. But here are my
credentials, such as they are.   I am an American, an Episcopalian, a priest.
I have just completed a journey – a long one. I was seven hundred and thirty
days on the road. That meant living out of a suitcase for twenty-four months,
dispensing with electricity and running water for eleven months, and feeding
myself for four or five months without the help of knife, fork, and spoon. It
involved something like two hundred thousand miles, six crossings of the
Equator, two hundred and ten aeroplanes, two hundred and ninety-four
beds, and more mosquito bites than I could count.

What went I out for to see? The Anglican Communion, a small segment
of Christianity, of which the American Episcopal Church is a part. I wanted
to observe at first hand what response the Anglican Communion is making
to the emergencies of our epoch. And that is the subject of this book.

Four warnings must be issued:

First, the book is not systematic (all-embracing) but selective. Within
the covers of one volume, the whole cannot be told. I have had to be
guided by the principle of *pars pro toto*. A few examples must serve as
representing the whole.

Second, the book is not definitive but desultory – in the strict sense of
that term: it springs from place to place. A definitive treatise cannot be
written, thank God, for Anglicanism happens to be alive and is therefore
in constant flux.

Third, the book is not objective but subjective, impressionistic. While it
endeavours to report accurately what I encountered en route, it is only
an account of what *I* saw, which was far from the totality of Anglicanism,
and sometimes, it must be confessed, I was probably too travel-weary to
hear aright what people told me, too tired to see straight. For errors in
interpretation, I beg humble pardon.

Fourth, the book is unofficial, without authority. Although I travelled
with the knowledge, approbation, and support of the Presiding Bishop
of the American Episcopal Church and of his Advisory Committee on
Anglican Relations, I represented nobody except myself. If anything I
have said angers any readers, they are to be angry only at me.

HOWARD A. JOHNSON

Cathedral Church of St. John the Divine
New York
St. Bartholomew's Day, 1962.

GLOBAL ODYSSEY

I

WEST INDIES: The Topsy-turvy Province

ON THE MORNING OF SATURDAY, 24TH OCTOBER, 1959, NEW YORK
was a wind-whipped, rain-lashed city. The road leading to the International
Airport was often awash. Winter was soon to beleaguer the place. With the
instinct of a migratory bird, I was heading south – for the Bahamas and the
Caribbean.

When I laid my tickets on the counter, the airline clerk glanced up at me
and said, "That is the fattest bunch of tickets I have ever seen."

It was, I fear, with a trace of smugness that I replied, "This is but six
months' worth out of twenty-four."

Then he really *was* impressed. Spotting the camera equipment slung over
my shoulder, he said, "What are you going to do? Write a book?"

"You've guessed it," I agreed.

"What about?" was his comeback.

"About the Anglican Communion."

"What's that?" he asked.

A busy airport does not lend itself to theological precision, and so I told
him, in a rough and ready sort of way, that the Anglican Communion is
the Episcopal Church, as we have it here in the United States, in association
with the Church of England and similar Churches to be found in most parts of
the world, and that it would take me two years and more than two hundred
aeroplanes to make even a fleeting survey of it. Whereupon he jotted down
my name, the name of my publisher, and the probable date of publication.

"All right," he said, "I'll be looking for it."

I am hopeful that I sold the first copy of this book at the first airport.

Four fairly turbulent hours later I landed in Nassau, capital city of the
Bahamas. The sky was a faultless blue, the temperature, eighty-eight
degrees. I had entered a different world.

In this island paradise I had looked forward to having four care-free days, incognito and incommunicado, for basking in the sun. After the struggle with visas and vaccinations I needed time to recover my strength and recruit my spirits before announcing my presence to the Lord Bishop of Nassau and the Bahamas. But at Customs a man in a clerical collar came forward with a smile and said, "Aren't you Canon Johnson? We met at St. Augustine's College, Canterbury." There was no denying that. So the cat was out of the bag, and there went my blissful four days of anonymity and ease.

In this way I was plunged prematurely into a complicated part of the Anglican world called the Church of the Province of the West Indies.

I was not long in learning that the Caribbean is something more than a beautiful sea studded with picturesque islands, designed for sun worshippers, skin divers, and shutterbugs. It is more than a retreat for cruising Canadians and wealthy Americans escaping the rigors of a North American winter. It is more than free ports where Swiss watches, Danish china, and duty-free liquor are sold cheap. It is, in fact, a place where time means little, china is a luxury easily dispensed with, and rum is demon. It is an area where a lot of people are condemned to live the year round, in a climate which is enervating, and where the economic prospects for most inhabitants are poor. A great many of the people the tourist passes on the street are Anglicans – most of them devout, but unable really to read, and undernourished.

If your dazzling white cruise ship has anchored for a day at Kingstown in the Windward Islands, you should know (if it does not spoil your pleasure in this quaint place) that of every ten people you see (and are they not photogenic?), seven of them – by strict canonical standards – are illegitimate, and that four or five of these seven are Episcopalians. And if your ship or plane stops at Santo Domingo in the Dominican Republic – a city of broad boulevards, palatial homes, and lovely gardens – it may not be amiss for you to remember that over 50 per cent of the women you see coming home from Sunday Mass, whether they be Roman Catholics or Anglicans, will be consulting a spiritualistic medium before the next Sunday rolls around. One does not have to be a romantic or have extrasensory perception to feel how voodoo and related phenomena rest like a curse, an oppressive, stifling pall, over most of the West Indies. Christian inroads are few and short-distanced.

Santo Domingo was still Ciudad Trujillo when I was there in 1959, and I knew within a few minutes of my arrival that I had come to a police state. I can say this today because Trujillo, the "Transcendental Benefactor", has subsequently been assassinated and his régime overthrown. Conditions are vastly different now. At every street corner was a smartly uniformed officer,

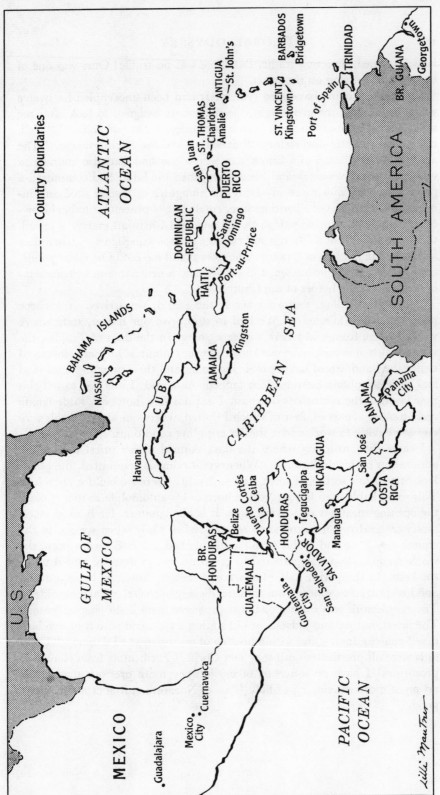

1. Central America and the Caribbean: the Province of the West Indies and missionary districts of the Protestant Episcopal Church in the U.S.A.

heavily armed, directing traffic. But there was no traffic! Ours was one of the few cars moving on the street.

I was taken to an abandoned rectory. It had been unoccupied for twelve years. In bidding me good-night, the missionary assigned to look after me said, "The last priest to sleep here was murdered. Do you mind?" "Well, no," I said a little uncertainly, "but what were the circumstances?" The account I then heard of a brave man who alone had had the courage to withstand the Transcendental Benefactor when the latter had committed a particularly heinous crime involving the slaughter of several thousand innocent persons was not a bedtime story conducive to peaceful slumber! However, I am proud to have slept on the bed of a Christian martyr – proud, that is, to be part of a Church still capable of producing martyrs when they are needed in the face of tyranny. The story is still too hot to be made public, but someday it will be known, and we will add a new name to be commemorated among the heroes of the Church.

The next morning, motoring across the island, we arrived at a check point every five kilometres. We had to stop, give our names, state where we had come from and where we were going. In the days of Trujillo, the whereabouts of every person was known at every minute. Our clergy laboured under the handicap of having their incoming and their outgoing mail read and their telephone conversations tapped. As I said, I am free to tell this now because the tyranny is overpast. I am not free, however, to designate certain other countries, four of which I visited, where our clergy to this very day are having to work under similar crippling conditions.

I came then to a city where the dark-skinned parish priest excited my admiration by his declaration. "Whenever a crime is committed, the police look first in this section of town, and so I said: 'Here we build a church.'" This remarkable man has rigged the horn of his automobile so that it plays the opening measures of a hymn tune. It is his signature. He honked incessantly as he drove me around to see the sights. Only when we got to the church (see Pl. 2 and 3) did I realize his method. Alerted by his horn, the whole congregation was gathered to greet me by the time we pulled up to the kerb. In the parish hall, after we had met in church to be introduced and had prayed together, I was shown a display of ecclesiastical embroidery. The needlework was exquisite. I was presented with a dozen purificators. The priest, not passing judgement but stating a fact, said with a superb lack of self-consciousness – and within hearing of unembarrassed donors – "Those girls were all prostitutes until they met Christ." Purificators from converted prostitutes! I have no souvenirs of my journey more precious than these, no proof more convincing of how Jesus of Nazareth still goes about doing good.

But if in parts of the Caribbean we can produce martyrs bludgeoned to death by evil politicians, I am worried that in other parts we have no martyrs at all. Some Latin American "strong men" have, in fact, been kind to our Church. The easy time we have had in certain countries is, I suspect, no compliment to us. The peace we enjoy must stem from the fact that Anglican preaching was far enough removed from political issues to ensure that we would arouse no animosity.

Is no Anglican yet willing to face the fact that "as Cuba goes, so goes the whole Caribbean"? Numerically, Anglicans are still large enough in the West Indies to make a difference. That on the whole we make no difference politically is my chief complaint. We are a huge ceremonially glorious political irrelevance.

In so saying I have laid it on the line and have made, I suppose, many enemies. But the "image" we have projected in the West Indian mind is that of ritual divorced from active concern for human rights. The more's the pity because in the Caribbean, unlike the rest of the world, we are big enough to count. There are exceptions. The Diocese of Guiana knows what it is to be socially relevant, and there are one or two others. I do not specify which . . . so that each of the many dioceses I visited can suppose that of course I am including it in my accolade!

The ecclesiastical Province of the West Indies is a sprawling affair. It starts with British Honduras in Central America, and then, following the great arc of the Antilles, it hops from island to island in a south-easterly direction until finally it latches on to the South American Continent at British Guiana. Seven of the eight dioceses which constitute the Province lie within the trajectory of the arc. They are from west to east: British Honduras, Jamaica, Antigua, Barbados, the Windward Islands, Trinidad, and British Guiana, where anchorage is found in the huge land mass of South America. It is a Province, therefore, which touches on two continents, while scooping into its sphere of concern many of the intervening islands. The one "eccentric" member of this provincial grouping is the Diocese of Nassau and the Bahamas. Geographically the Bahamas are in the Atlantic, not in the Caribbean, and they take a little pride in standing somewhat apart. In spirit, however, no matter what they may say, and in cultural patterns and economic destiny, they belong to the West Indies.

In the territories embraced by the Province the total population is about three and a half million, nearly a quarter of which is Anglican. For those who like statistics I can provide the following breakdown which I believe to be fairly accurate as of 1961, although some of these figures are only responsible guesses:

Guiana:

36 priests
97,321 baptized members
21,351 communicants
Total population: 540,000

Antigua:

24 priests
50,000 baptized members
10,000 communicants
This Diocese embraces over thirteen scattered islands

Barbados:

51 priests
Baptized membership: no statistics available
24,539 communicants
Total population: 239,000

British Honduras:

9 priests
No statistics available – all records having been swept into the sea by Hurricane Hattie in the autumn of 1961
Total population: 88,156

Jamaica:

86 priests
350,000 baptized members
44,500 communicants
Total population: 1,671,000

Nassau and the Bahamas:

24 priests
13,823 baptized members
7,274 communicants
Total population: 130,698

Trinidad and Tobago:

36 priests
175,000 baptized members
17,374 communicants
Total population: 817,000

Windward Islands:

17 priests
100,000 baptized members
8,500 communicants
Total population: 328,625

Three brief comments on these figures:

First, one at once notices a great disparity between the number of baptized members and the number of communicants. This probably has three causes: (a) with the high birth rate, there are bound to be many persons baptized who have not yet reached the age for Confirmation; (b) since discipline in the West Indies is strictly enforced, one cannot count as a communicant unless he has actually communicated at least three times in the year and has his "Church Dues" paid up; (c) many loyal Anglicans in the Caribbean area, who go to church with the utmost fidelity, do not communicate because they realize that in terms of canon law, their marriages are irregular.

Second, it is evident that the ratio of priests to people is low. This is a crippling circumstance enforced upon the Province by reason of its poverty.

Third, in most of these eight areas the Anglicans constitute the largest Christian group. Exceptions are the Bahamas, where the Baptists outnumber them, and Trinidad, where the Roman Catholic population is nearly twice the Anglican. It may come as a surprise to some to learn that in Trinidad and British Guiana Christian churches are often dwarfed by imposing mosques and Hindu shrines. The West Indies are full of East Indians, brought there as indentured labourers. For example, in Guiana, Anglicans – by far the largest Christian body – constituting 23.1 per cent of the population – live side by side with Hindus who make up 31 per cent of the population.

It is difficult to deal concisely with this complex of islands, for each is different from the others. The terrain is different, the colonial background is different. And then, from an ecclesiastical point of view, any sort of West Indian summary is made still more difficult by reason of the fact that present in these same Caribbean waters, interlarded between the eight British-born Dioceses of this Province, are five Missionary Districts of the American Episcopal Church. They are, from west to east: Cuba, Haiti, the Dominican Republic, Puerto Rico, the Virgin Islands. Cuba is extraprovincial; the others are attached, quite artificially, to the Second Province of PECUSA, i.e. the Protestant Episcopal Church in the United States of America. With the exception of the Missionary District of the Virgin Islands, which at present is cared for by the Bishop of Puerto Rico, each of the other four has its own bishop. Although these American-appointed bishops occasionally meet for consultation, they do not constitute an episcopal synod with legislative powers of its own. Rather, each bishop individually deals directly with the Overseas Department of the National Council in New York.

Friendly Jamaicans, intrigued by what they had heard of my Anglican odyssey, asked, "Where have you been so far?" "I'm barely started," I said. "First I went to Nassau and the Bahamas." Heads nodded in comprehension. An excellent starting place! "Then I went to Cuba." "But why Cuba?" I was asked. Immediately one of my interrogators answered his own question:

"Oh, of course, to change planes there for Jamaica." "No," I said, "I went
to Cuba to see our Church there." That we had in Cuba a Spanish-speaking
Church manned by Cuban clergy was news to him and to the Jamaican
Anglicans he had assembled to meet me in his home. "And where next?"
"Next to Haiti," I said – and knew in a trice that I was straining my hearers'
credulity. They had no idea that Anglicans were deeply involved in speaking
French and the Creole dialect. This was my first lesson in how little one part
of the Anglican Communion knows about the others. It was a lesson reinforced countless times before I had finished my tour. I myself experienced
the surprise of learning that not until recent years have the North American
bishops conferred with their British West Indian counterparts. We are still
strangers to each other.

A few facts and figures may help to give a notion of the size and strength
of the American-based Missionary Districts in the Caribbean.

Cuba, with a Cuban bishop, has twenty-three clergy, all of them Cuban.
This district claims a baptized membership of 74,059, of whom 8,651 are
communicants.

Haiti has an American as its bishop, and of its thirty-two clergy, nineteen are Haitians. It reports a baptized membership of 34,000, of whom
13,000 are communicants.

The Dominican Republic received its first bishop in 1960. An American,
he is assisted by eight priests, five of them Americans, and three of them
citizens of the Dominican Republic. Baptized membership: 2,557. Communicants: 1,164.

Puerto Rico, presided over by an American bishop, has twenty-eight
priests, of whom seventeen are Puerto Ricans. Baptized membership:
8,817. Communicants: 3,710.

The Virgin Islands are under the episcopal oversight of the Bishop of
Puerto Rico. There are eleven priests, none of them "home grown".
Baptized membership: 6,568. Communicants: 2,714.

To stop at this point would be to give a misleading impression. It would
make the American Church's endeavour in the Caribbean seem smaller
than it actually is.

Until now we have been speaking only of *islands* in the Caribbean. To
achieve a more accurate impression we would have to take into account
that Mexico's east coast is washed by the Caribbean Sea and that work
under auspices of the American Episcopal Church is carried on there and
as far "south of the border" as the Republic of Panama. Indeed, as we shall
see later, although this cannot be called a Caribbean enterprise, the Missionary District of the Panama Canal Zone has been extending its work down

the South American west coast into Colombia, Bolivia, and Ecuador. Central America and the Panama Canal belong ecclesiastically to the American Church's Second Province, and Mexico to the Seventh Province.

How exceedingly involved.

First, we encounter the British-born Province of the West Indies with eight dioceses, forming an autonomous member of the Anglican Communion and having to operate under the civil law of eight different British possessions, each at a different level of economic and political development.

Second, we have the five interspersed islands under the ecclesiastical jurisdiction of the American Church, forming no part of the Province of the West Indies and not a province on their own; and these are islands whose colonial background is not British. Cuba, the Dominican Republic, and Puerto Rico were Spanish; Haiti, French; the Virgin Islands, Danish.

Third, we have the three American-sponsored continental Missionary Districts: Mexico, the Panama Canal Zone, and the one called Central America, which, with audacity, encompasses El Salvador, Guatemala, Honduras, Nicaragua, and Costa Rica. Five separate republics within one diocese! English readers may need to be reminded that in all such places it is not an English Church ministering to English-speaking British subjects. Except for those Virgin Islands which are under the American flag, the Church came in as a "foreigner", a *Yanqui* intruder, and had to learn to speak Spanish or French and sometimes dialects too. It had to discover how to comport itself as a foreign body on the soil of an assortment of different sovereign lands. It has had to contend with figures like Castro and Trujillo. Add to these complications the consideration that the Episcopal Church was not always as welcome in its part of the West Indies as was the Church of England in territories assigned to its pastoral care, and one begins to understand how very complex this situation is. A bishop sent from America to Haiti, for example, could not expect to find that he and the President of the land both wore the same "old school tie". A bishop from Britain, by contrast, could look forward to a sort of class reunion; for if he and the Colonial Governor had not been classmates in their student days or "old boys" of the same school, they had at least attended the same type of school and could speak the same language. No gala affair in Government House was, or is, left ungraced by the presence of the Lord Bishop, seated in a place of honour. A newly designated bishop from Britain *has* status even before he arrives. The American bishop has to achieve status, if he can, after he gets there.

Anglicanism in the Caribbean area grew like Topsy. It should not surprise us overmuch that the result was slightly topsy-turvy, and it is quite uncertain how we are to go about achieving a concerted Anglican policy for the future. A single example of our disorganization will suffice. A man who resides on one of the Virgin Islands, which happens to belong to Great Britain and is part of the Diocese of Antigua, rises from his bed on a bright Caribbean morning and finds that by the canon law respecting marriage and divorce in the Church of the Province of the West Indies he is not permitted to make his Communion. He steps into a motor launch, as he does every working day of his life, and crosses a short stretch of water to another of the Virgin Islands where he has his place of business. This island belongs to the United States and is under the canon law of the American Episcopal Church. Here he *can* make his Communion, for the canon law is different. But this is chaos!

I have deliberately chosen a dramatic instance, but examples could be multiplied. I use it only to point out that our lack of co-ordination was perhaps tolerable in a day and age when people stayed put. Today, however, they move around. And we disconcert them by our failure to speak with a single voice.*

There are those who answer that the only logical step is for the American Missionary Districts to become incorporated into the Province of the West Indies, thus forming one mighty, consistent, well-integrated ecclesiastical whole. I myself believe that logic is on the side of this proposal. But logic has a way of tripping up on certain stubborn and sometimes absurd facts of life. All unreasonably, neither the English-born Dioceses nor the American-born Missionary Districts seem overfond of each other. Indeed, English missionary endeavour – I am going to put this bluntly – has produced a lot of "black Englishmen" in the West Indies; and these ebony Episcopalians, proud of England, are not in the least inclined to surrender their "Englishness" or give in to the Yankees – and they think this would be a consequence of linking up with the American Episcopal Church. Racism rears its ugly head also here, in a strange and puzzling form. Dark-skinned West Indians, many of whom speak English more perfectly than do most white Americans, do not resent the white who speak or even "butcher" English. They resent, because they fear, people of dark pigmentation who speak such "gibberish" as Spanish or French. The problem, I maintain, is more linguistic and cultural than it is racial.

The same insidious prejudice works in reverse, of course. Spanish-speaking, French-speaking, and even *Am-mur-ri-kan*-speaking West Indians who are

---

* Since writing the above, the instance I cite is happily obsolete. The Province of the West Indies has ceded to the jurisdiction of the American Church those islands which once were a part of the Diocese of Antigua, and the Americans have now set apart a bishop to care for this entire complex of islands.

Episcopalians are slightly contemptuous of their Oxford-accented Anglican cousins. But there is another reason for their disinclination to merge with an "English" province. They harbour affection for the land which mediated the Gospel to them. Christianity came to them via the United States of America. They have no intention of disavowing this inheritance. This is not blameworthy. But they received from America not only Christianity but also the American standard of life, a standard which can be maintained, if only on a reduced scale, by the constant influx of American dollars. Here the motives begin to be mixed. Opposition to the creation of one great overarching Anglican province in the West Indies stems from an extreme dislike of having to renounce the American dollar. American-spawned Episcopalians do not want to identify themselves with the desperate poverty of the Church in what has been called "the slums of the Empire".

For these and many other reasons, I cannot believe that the one great Caribbean province is a possibility at the present juncture – however logical, however desirable it would be.

If the ideal of a single province be beyond reach for the time being, what of an interim arrangement? The alternative, I think, is the formation of a new province embracing the American Missionary Districts to live as a neighbour alongside the already existing Province of the West Indies. I have no idea what it should be called. Province of the Caribbean, perhaps. It should be given autonomy, even though it would have to be partially subsidized from the United States for many years to come; and for this reason it might well have humility enough to admit to its councils, as advisers, liaison officers from the parent Church.

The two provinces co-existing, a council should then be formed wherein all the bishops of the Caribbean area, both from the Province of the West Indies and from the new province, would meet regularly – every three years at least. Their deliberations would not have the effect of legislation but would be of enormous interim benefit and would prepare the way ultimately for the formation of a concerted grand strategy and, perhaps, a single great province.

Need I spell out the advantages? In addition to the ones that even the most spiritual can perceive, I will note two that perhaps I alone am vulgar enough to mention: first, we would get Americans concerned enough to invest some cash in areas where this commodity is in short supply; second, we would free our Spanish work from the stigma of being simply a *gringo* intrusion.

Until such time as the Brazilian Church is constituted a province in its own right, its bishops should be invited to sit in on the meetings of this council. So also should be the Englishman whose cumbersome title is "The

Bishop of the Anglican Diocese in Argentina and Eastern South America with the Falkland Islands". These men from afar need the fellowship of a larger unit of the Church's life.

Gone are the days in which the difficulties of transportation made it easier for the Bishops of British Honduras, British Guiana, Jamaica, Barbados, and the others to assemble in London than anywhere within the Caribbean area itself. The whole Caribbean is now criss-crossed by daily plane service. There is no continuing necessity for these folk to be strangers to one another, no necessity for the infrequent rendezvous in faraway London. Within a matter of hours the Bishops can all be kneeling at the same altar at dawn, be "joshing" one another at breakfast, be locked in debate during the day, be thankful by eventide that they are all in the same wonderful boat, even though by night they may be in different aircraft heading home.

The Council I conceive, therefore, would be a kind of Lesser Lambeth, a *regional* consultative body. I will argue, before I am done, for the formation of many such conciliar groups throughout the world. We have not outgrown the need of a Lambeth Conference every ten years – there will always be value in that – but we have grown to such a size (and exist in a world where events happen so quickly) that the need is manifest for more councils, regional in nature, held frequently. There must be lots of Lesser Lambeths.

I have been speaking of a future for the West Indies. What of the present? What does one find when one goes there today?

I will tell you only what *I* found.

I found that sectarian Christianity (if indeed some of it can be called Christianity, even by courtesy) is running circles around the rest of us. The sects have, deceptively, the bounce, the joy, the ecstasy, about which we preach in measured, joyless accents. "The fringe groups get ahead," said one wise priest on the island of Antigua, "because they know, better than we do, who is going to hell." Precisely because he was a *wise* priest, he did not envy them their assurance, though he envied them their success. Certain of the sects are pernicious. The British always refer to them as "American sects". I must say, in defence of my own country, that some of them are attributed quite gratuitously to America. I try to keep informed, but I have never heard of some of them.

My next job as a reporter is to let it be known that parts of the Church of the Province of the West Indies have gone sky high. They press the ecclesiastical ceiling. "No Confession, no Communion" is laid down as the law in diocese after diocese. This is not pastoral advice, it is legislation. "The Society of St. John Bosco will meet on Tuesday and all men and boys *must* be there," announces the priest in authoritarian accents. Well, I have nothing against John Bosco, saint that he was, but I do object to the mandatory tone in which the announcement was made, and I do think we might find another saint within our own tradition. Benediction of the Blessed Sacrament is standard practice. To raise any question about it would be to label yourself a crank and an outsider. The Divine Praises at Benediction include references to the "Holy and Immaculate Conception" and to the "Bodily Assumption" of the Blessed Virgin. A side altar in an island church is ornamented by a placard setting forth "The Promises made by Our Lord through Our Lady to the Children at Fatima". I called the Bishop aside. "Really!" I expostulated. "This is too much." "Yes, I know," was his answer. "But what am I to do? This man, for all his exaggerations, is willing to come and work here. No one else will come for the meagre stipend the Diocese can offer."

I met many hard-working, high-minded priests in the West Indies, some of them sons of the soil, some of them imports from Britain. The Church in that province, however, in recruiting men for the Ministry from abroad, must be on its guard lest it become – because it is so hard-pressed for help – a repository for English discards. The poverty of a diocese can make it a breeding ground for ecclesiastical eccentrics who are willing to come "cheap".

The people of the Caribbean like colour, excitement, movement, drama – partly as a relief from the drabness, monotony, and uneventfulness of their own lives, partly because they share in a right and universal instinct for observing great things with due solemnity. Even the most austere Protestant is not immune to this taste for ceremony. The flourishing of fraternal orders with elaborate ritual in Puritan America is due to the hunger for ceremony and for fellowship which the Christian Church is meant to supply. It is not Anglo-Catholicism as such against which I am protesting, but I am prepared to wage war against a slavish imitation of certain late medieval liturgical excesses which the best Roman scholarship itself is striving to eliminate. It seems to me, in fact, that the liturgical movement, more than any other modern development, is drawing nearer together Roman, Anglican, Orthodox, Lutheran, and also Presbyterian and Methodist thinkers, and I regret that extremists in our camp should be opposing this movement of the Spirit. Why should Anglicanism be saddled with things from which Rome strives to be free?

In one West Indian diocese, where the only Churches of numerical importance are the Roman and the Anglican, an English-born archdeacon made this wry remark: "Here we have but two kinds of Christians: Papist and Ape-ist."

I deplore hateful names, no matter who calls them. For this reason I have called no man a "spike", but if I were pressed to define what a spike is, I think I would have to say that he is a man whose adulation and imitation of Rome stem from the fact that he has not kept up with Roman scholarship.

West Indians flock in droves to Benediction of the Blessed Sacrament. The attendance record makes quite an impressive statistic. One Caribbean bishop, himself by dedication a celibate, sincere and holy, exclaimed, as we came away from a Solemn Evensong with Benediction of the Blessed Sacrament, "Six hundred in the congregation! Wasn't that wonderful! And, oh, how I love Benediction! Isn't it the most perfect form of spiritual Communion?" Well, my dear Bishop, there was certainly a crowd of people present, and it warmed the heart to hear them sing. But did you notice how many more came to Benediction this evening than to Mass this morning? And does it perhaps occur to you what the reason might be for this preference for the evening hour to the morning hour? They were not here this morning in such numbers because fundamentally they are honest. Being honest, they admit in humility and contrition that for most of them their marital unions are irregular in the Church's eyes. By their own act, therefore, they excommunicate themselves. But this leaves them with a desperate hunger for the Holy Communion. Accordingly, in order to have some sort of sustaining relationship with the Communion, they come to Benediction. Here, at least, the life-giving Sacrament is exposed – and they can bask in its rays without having to expose to the public the irregularity of their marital arrangements.

Historically, there are excuses for the overpaternalistic, autocratic attitude which is characteristic of the Church in the West Indies. Young churches cannot abound from the first in vigorous lay leadership. Foreigners *have* to make the decisions which nobody else is yet ready to meet. Difficulties of communication and transportation in the Caribbean and the general poverty of the islands have restricted synods to the bishops themselves, and made those infrequent. An individual bishop, though not power-hungry, *had* to assume power. Moreover, his privileged position in the Established Church gave him prestige and disproportionate authority in British colonies. Understandable and excusable as it may be, however, this dependence on bishops alone for every decision affecting the corporate life of the West Indian Church has retarded most lamentably the development of maturity on the presbyteral and lay levels.

I would not have the heart to say all these brutal things if I did not think that there are signs of a better day ahead.

What are some of these better signs? First, nobody accepts with stoic resignation the bad features of the past; indeed, everybody was open with me in registering complaints, the College of Bishops being most vocal in the chorus of discontent, and the English missionaries themselves were no less vociferous than the West Indians. Second, the presbyters and the laity are increasingly being given a say in important decisions at both the diocesan and provincial levels. Third, the Province has just achieved a unified liturgy which, if followed, will go a long way towards eliminating ceremonial oddity. Fourth, the theological colleges, where British West Indians are trained for the Ministry, are now in responsible hands. This applies to St. Peter's Hall in Jamaica, an institution traditionally Evangelical, and to Codrington College in Barbados, traditionally Anglo-Catholic. The latter school is in the care of the monks of the Community of the Resurrection. What a difference they have made, even in the physical appearance of the place! One alumnus, singing the praises of what the C. R. Fathers had accomplished, exclaimed, "Why, in my day the College was so dirty that even the mice objected!" Today it is clean, swept and garnished, and a good spirit has taken up its lodging there. One does not usually expect to see the Community of the Resurrection cast in the role of bringing the level of churchmanship *down*. But this is precisely what the good monks are accomplishing in the West Indies.

In the American sphere of influence there are hopeful signs too. The creation in 1961 of *El Centro de Publicaciones Españolas* ensures that Anglicans are at last going to go to Press in one of the major tongues of the world: Spanish. This involves translation from English and other languages. But translation is not the whole of it. More to the point, we are going to commission and create *new* Anglican literature tailor-made for the particular needs, doubts, and queries of the Latin mind. The centre from which this will be done is in existence in San José, Costa Rica. It was made possible by a grant from the United Thank Offering of the Episcopal Churchwomen of America. The Forward Movement Commission has pledged its support to this programme which is under the leadership of the centre's first director, a Colombian-born priest, educated in the universities of his native land and of the United States, a man theologically competent and fluent in six languages.

A second ray of hope streams from Carolina, a suburb of San Juan, Puerto Rico, where we have built *El Seminario Episcopal del Caribe*. In 1959, before a spadeful of earth was turned, the Bishop of Puerto Rico (see Pl. 9) showed me the site and with evident pride said, "Here we will build the Seminary of the Caribbean." I was sceptical. I knew that Mexico had its own seminary which it would be reluctant to relinquish. I knew that Cuba was deeply committed to the Union Seminary of Matanzas, a joint venture with Methodists and Presbyterians. The present political situation requires that Cubans be trained in Cuba. And because both Cuba and Mexico incline to the Low Church school of thought it was more than likely that they would hesitate before entrusting their ordination candidates to a traditionally High Church Puerto Rico. I knew also that Haiti, having its own language, had its own seminary. (It has since joined forces with the seminary in Puerto Rico.) I knew that Portuguese-speaking Brazil was too far away. If it had money enough to send its candidates as far as Puerto Rico it could just as well send them on to the United States. I despaired, therefore, of Anglicanism's ever having a pan-Caribbean seminary.

It has been built, none the less, because people wiser than I are in charge of things, and I rejoice to say that I was present for its dedication in January, 1962. What gave me a change of heart about the project was not the splendid new buildings, the mortar hardly dry, nor was it the highly qualified teaching staff there assembled which won me over. No, my "conversion" was due to the skits presented by the seminarians after the buildings had been dedicated and a supper consumed. Here were young men of obvious talent, citizens of six different nations, swapping trilingual jokes. With ease they moved from English to Spanish to French, making puns and poking good-humoured fun at one another and "taking off" their professors in a kind, comic way. And I thought: Here are the Caribbean clergy of tomorrow – men acquainted with one another, able to speak one another's language, informed about the problems and opportunities of their neighbours, an international team ready to go.

My hope is that at least a few of these men will take an extra year at St. Peter's Hall in Jamaica or Codrington College in Barbados and that these two institutions will reciprocate by sending some of their men for an added year of study in Puerto Rico. In this way the foundations can be laid for concert and concord in the Caribbean. The day may yet come when we shall have a province devoid of provincialism.

Few parts of the Anglican Communion are more poverty-stricken than the Province of the West Indies. Small contributions dribble in from Britain and Canada. The American Church sends an annual token gift. But for the rest, the Province must support itself, which is a great deal to ask of a place where *per capita* income is so small. This means shamefully low stipends for the clergy, some of the bishops in shabby houses and even shabby cassocks, and here and there a magnificently proportioned Georgian church going to rack and ruin, plaster off and a playground for goats.

I have written more of Caribbean problems than of Caribbean achievements. The intention of this book is not to write a panegyric. Let me state, once for all, that wherever the Church is, *there* is healing. One shudders to think what life would have been like in the Caribbean if the Church had not gone to those isles.

In spite of my pessimism, there are exciting developments. With ease I could produce twenty of them. I mention but one – the Cathedral in Port-au-Prince, glorious in its murals. The story behind them is worth knowing. Haiti, a country incapable, it would seem, of self-government, chronically in crisis, destitute and diseased, came at last to have a low opinion of itself – one of the worst things that can happen to a nation or a person. Yet there were Haitian artists who tried to express beauty. They went to the Roman Archbishop and, showing him the cartoons, asked permission to transfer their vision of the Gospel to the Cathedral walls. They were rebuffed. "No, this building is pure fourteenth-century Gothic." And then the artists turned to our Bishop. He drew a deep breath. It took courage. "Go ahead and paint," he said.

More than once he must have asked himself, "What have I let loose here?" What he had let loose was a renaissance of Haitian art and a new self-respect among the people of Haiti. Artists now come from all the world to praise these primitives.

Imagine a whole transept given over to a depiction, Haitian version, of the Wedding Feast at Cana of Galilee. The father of the bride, spruced up and transparently happy in a double-breasted suit, sits in a rocking-chair, puffing on a cigar and nodding his benediction over the bridal pair and the friends who have come to rejoice. A uniformed policeman, a star on his breast to establish his authority, stands by, beaming approval. There is not much for him to do except enjoy himself. Nobody here is out of line. But Christ is in this picture too, heeding his Mother and busy with waterpots. All at once it is not Cana of Galilee where this happened, though indeed it did happen there. It is happening now in Port-au-Prince.

As your eye travels down from the mural, it comes to rest on the same people you found within that mural. There they are – hundreds of them, kneeling – in Sunday best, spotless white, although many of them, carrying their shoes on their head, have walked half the night down the mountains to get to the Cathedral. And why should they not walk? It is no small thing to receive a cup of wine which has become precious blood.

It is sad, however, to reflect that four o'clock in the morning is the preferred hour of worship. Darkness is for people too proud to show that they have had to come in rags.

2

SOUTH AMERICA: The Neglected Continent

SOUTH AMERICA IS THE CONTINENT ANGLICANISM DECIDED TO skip. This could easily be the saddest chapter in the book.

From the very start the Church of England had no intention of doing a missionary job in this vast, beautiful, incredibly complex land mass, for, "after all", she said in her characteristically too chivalrous, too unrealistic way, "all those people are Roman Catholics".

In point of fact, they are not.

A Jesuit scholar has made a scientific survey of the state of Roman Catholicism in Latin America. The findings are disturbing. His principal discovery is this: If the ratio between priest and people in Latin America were to be made comparable to the ratio in the United States and in many European countries, the Roman Church would immediately have to import two hundred thousand priests!

An honest Rome knows that it has barely scratched the surface in Latin America. It knows that with its present limited manpower it cannot hope to do an adequate pastoral job. Humbly it acknowledges that there are many thousands, particularly in the hinterlands, yet to be reached – and thousands more, particularly in the cities, who need to be recovered. It would be hard to say which figure is the more alarming: the number of Latin Americans still unevangelized, or the number of the lapsed. Several Roman Catholics were frank in sharing with me their anxiety. They are not unaware of the phenomenal growth of religious sectarianism, the fringe groups which sometimes are only slightly less frenzied and fanatical than their neo-pagan counterparts. Informed Roman Catholics see the danger signal, and many of them will admit that the very presence and popularity of the sects is, in some sense, a judgement on the Church. The sects would not be *there* if the ancient Church in these lands had been able to do all that the situation required of it. The sects have rushed in to fill a spiritual vacuum.

"Don't imagine for a minute that we lump you together with Pentecostalists and such in our thinking," said one Roman priest to me, a rueful smile playing about his lips, "but not even you Episcopalians would have had a *chance* in Brazil, for example, if somehow we hadn't muffed *our* chance."

I sympathize with the Romans! The sects are really offensive. Their raucous devotees stand on street corners and shout that "the Catholic Church is the Antichrist!" and that "Rome is the Whore of Babylon!" Is *this* the way to preach Christ? By their efforts they merely succeed in bringing the whole of Protestantism into discredit, thus impeding the work of every classical Reformation Church. Many South Americans have little love for their Mother Church, but when they hear her denounced in the public streets by a pack of *gringos* as a "whore" they get fighting mad. Who can blame them? The trouble is, it is hard to fight something daemonic without becoming daemonic yourself. Hence there is, to the detriment of everybody – Catholic, Protestant, and sectarian – an ever-heightening tension of recrimination and mutual distrust. Intelligent secularists, beholding the squabbles from the side lines, grow all the more scornful.

It would be folly to maintain that there are not a great many South Americans of imposing intellectual stature who are ardent Roman Catholics. Yet the unhappy fact is that the bulk of the intelligentsia, if not antichurch, has become anticlerical. University professors and people of like academic distinction are sometimes pathetically placed. They *want* to be Christians; their life is instinct with the Faith; but many of them have become disaffected with the Church; they are suspicious of a Church a bit too closely involved in power politics; they are perturbed by certain anti-intellectual tendencies of that Church. "I can no longer put the blinders on," declared one professor to me despairingly, "I *will* not do violence to the integrity of my own mind." There are many like him. They are men and women who are repelled by the obscurantist fundamentalism which sometimes mars the otherwise glorious mission of Rome, repelled by the too easy compromise with pagan superstition which occasionally is the mistake of Roman missionary strategy, repelled by a Church's dubious dabbling in the political struggle.

These people, perplexed by the Church and put off by some of its features, are at the same time so deeply imbued with the beneficent spirit of Catholicism that they could not possibly – either intellectually or emotionally – become, for example, Pentecostalists. Even to become Baptists or Congregationalists would be a psychological impossibility. Some will find, some have found, their way into Lutheranism, Presbyterianism, Methodism. But even here the psychological impediments are too powerful for the majority of these people. Catholics they are, and Catholics they want to remain . ..

but they cannot wholeheartedly do so when the only kind of Catholicism they know is the Catholicism in which they were reared – and which, in all charity, was Rome's worst foot forward.

Here, precisely, is a task for Anglicanism. It would be better, no doubt, if Rome could get its best foot (the Germano-Gallican foot) into the Hispanic door and thus accomplish on Latin American soil what Rome could do incomparably better than anyone else. Since there seems, alas, not much chance of this happening in our time, the finger points straight to Anglicanism. Our work is cut out for us. At this juncture of history only Anglicanism can convincingly show to Latin Americans that there is an alternative way of being a Catholic Christian, a way that understands, embraces, and embodies continuity and tradition, bishops and sacraments – devoid, however, of fundamentalism, obscurantism, intolerance, totalitarianism. On Latin soil, I repeat, Rome could do this better than we could. *But will Rome do it?* We cannot wait until a wavering Rome makes up its mind. For us, the duty is *now*.

Spectacular results cannot be hoped for. It will be a long, slow, patient labour. Fifty years, however, ought to make a difference. Our aim would not be to supplant Rome. This is neither historically a possibility nor ideally a desideratum. The Anglican job is none other than to try to preserve these lands for Catholic Christianity, to join in the efforts to save them from the seductions of paganism, materialism, communism, sectarianism. Not the least part of Anglicanism's reason for being is its potential ministry to Rome itself. Rome is healthy, wonderful, glorious – a boon to humanity – when held in check by powerful, sane, indubitably Christian minorities, especially if their claim to Catholicity cannot reasonably be questioned. It is for us to provide this check.

How to do it? First, by continuing in our accustomed ways, but with efforts multiplied a hundredfold. Second, by seeing to it that at each major South American university, so far as local law will allow, there is a student centre, presided over by an intellectually gifted Anglican priest. Third, by sending the most promising young students abroad to learn what the rest of the world is thinking.

Anglicans, adhering staunchly to their principle not to proselytize, excused themselves from having any concern with the continent of South America except for the English expatriates who had settled there for their health or their wealth and except, for conscience' sake, a few Arucanian Indians. The Gran Chaco, as a sound, has all the allure of a faraway place name, and the word "Arucanian" has drawing power too. They are exotic enough and romantic enough to loosen many purse strings in England when the missionaries to South America are home on furlough. These names stand for real places, and real people live there – primitive people, beloved of God and lovable even in themselves, but making no difference culturally or historically. One is grateful that the Church has a care for them. But what about the people in the cities in whose hands will lie the destiny of a continent? "It will be hard," one Englishman told me sadly, "to raise money in Britain for Spanish and Portuguese work in South America. People stemming from the Iberian Peninsula lack the magic contained in the romantic word 'Indian'. The English are easily worked up financially and even theologically about the 'poor Patagonians' (What about the Patagonian woman who never heard of Christ? Will she go to hell?), but few English can become exercised about the fate of, let us say, plain 'poor Peruvians' or the sophisticates of Rio."

Mother England does try to look after her own; and because Englishmen were attracted to the South American republics by the lure of economic gain, the English Church followed – but only to shepherd her dispersed sheep. She arrived with the avowed intention of ministering solely to persons of English speech, i.e. to the diplomatic corps and the foreign businessmen and their families. It was, in short, an embassy, not a mission.

To be fair to the Church of England, we should remind ourselves that in the nineteenth century these were still the lands of the Inquisition. The Inquisition lingered on in South America longer than anywhere else, and probably the English could not have got in at all had they come with missionary intention. So the Church of England signed concordats with the several South American governments by which she condemned herself from the start to being merely a chaplaincy, a foreign body in strange lands.

I have asked several lawyers their opinion of the legal force, the binding power, of the ancient concordats. Unhesitating and unqualified is the reply: None at all. The governments with whom they were contracted are no longer in existence.

Then there were rained upon the Church of England in South America three outrageous blows of history, for none of which the Church deserves any blame. They could not have been foreseen or forestalled.

The first blow was the digging of the Panama Canal, that marvel of engineering skill which promptly diminished the significance of all South American ports. The English business colonies suffered a tremendous setback, and this was of course reflected in the size and strength of the local English Church.

The second blow was the collapse of the Chilean nitrate industry. When a way of producing synthetic nitrate was discovered, the British-owned and -operated nitrate mines were doomed. We once had a handsome pro-cathedral in Valparaiso and a chapel in the near-by resort of Viña del Mar. The buildings are still there, and in good shape, but they are none the less a melancholy sight. I took the four-hour train ride from Santiago de Chile down to the coast to see them. I was met by our priest, a dedicated man if ever I saw one, and before the day was over I marvelled at his ability to stick the situation out. He showed me the Register of Church Services at Viña del Mar. Sunday attendance: Holy Communion, number of communicants – 2, 7, 5, 3; Matins – 17, 12, 9, 15. And so it read, Sunday after Sunday. Weekly services have long since been abandoned. The English simply are not there to attend them. There is a service now only once a month. After one such service, the chaplain asked me quietly, "What did you see?" He could have predicted my answer, for it was what this hard-working man himself had to see . . . and live with: "Average age of the worshippers, about seventy." "Add ten or twelve years to that," he queried, "and what do you have?"

But there it sits, this well-built edifice – its fabric intact because of its endowments – without much of a ministry to perform, although it is strategically located in the midst of a teeming city. Why no ministry? We cannot speak Spanish – or at least we will not.

The third outrageous blow to Anglican work in South America fell when, in country after country, dictators arose who nationalized the railways. The British for the most part had financed and operated the railways. Our Church in Argentina lost twenty thousand communicants in one day when the railways were taken over by the government and the British were told to "Go Home!" The inland port and railway centre of Rosario, to take but a single example, once had a resident colony of three thousand Englishmen. Today there are fewer than eight hundred.

Bit by bit, such work as we had was whittled away. The British still remaining are largely impoverished now, so impoverished that most of them can no longer afford to send their children back to England to be schooled. So they have to be educated locally. The result is that I met a number of attractive Anglo-Peruvian, Anglo-Chilean, and Anglo-Argentinian young people who speak English with a charming Spanish accent! And then the time comes for them to marry. Since there are few of them, they usually marry Roman Catholics and either become Roman Catholics themselves, or else sign away their children. In short, we have no future in South America unless, without delay, we learn to speak Spanish and Portuguese.

I have no hesitation in declaring myself an anglophile, because I really do believe that our dear English cousins are infinitely worthy of our love. But these hardy folk, to whom we owe so much, can be infuriating at times and terribly funny, all unconsciously. For example: In a train I found myself seated next to an English schoolmaster attached to the staff of a "posh" semi-Anglican school for the few English children in South America whose fathers can still scrape up the funds for tuition. Since he was an educator, I thought it might interest him if I told something of what I had learned about schools and the problems of education. "Did you know," I ventured, "that in Haiti 97 per cent of the populace is illiterate?" Frowning, he exclaimed, "Good heavens! Can't their parents do anything about it?" There'll always be an England, and for this I am glad. But the persistence of this kind of mentality will go far to explain some of the problems we are saddled with.

I had hoped to visit the Falkland Islands. I corresponded with the ecclesiastical authority there, a man whose unwieldy title is "The Bishop of the Anglican Diocese in Argentina and Eastern South America with the Falkland Islands". Here is the reply to my letter: "These islands are not served by air or by any regular steamship service. You would have to come by tramp freighter. Even if you were lucky enough to find a ship in Buenos Aires or Montevideo the very day you wanted it – a very big 'if' – and even if you were lucky enough to have the steamer sail straight to the Falklands – another big 'if' – and if the steamer were to unload and reload at once and sail back to any place you would want to be, it would take at least twenty-five days. And what would you find when you got here? Our one town of Stanley, with one thousand inhabitants clustered around our one-man Cathedral. No, I cannot counsel you to come."

Whatever was the Church of England thinking of – to place a man on the Falkland Islands and say to him, "You be Bishop to the whole of South America?"

Slender indeed have been our efforts in South America to minister to the peoples of the land. But to this rule three exceptions can be named.

The first bears the brand "S.A.M.S." – the South American Missionary Society, a freelance English organization, valiant, well-intentioned, but slightly eccentric. It is a society I denominate "the Anglo-Baptists", for they told me, without batting an eye, and as if no question of theology or ecclesiology were involved, that they had given up baptizing infants. As a disciplinary measure, an on-the-spot strategic necessity, this is something I can take in my stride. But it dismayed me that the society did not seem to feel that it was a theological decision of consequence. The S.A.M.S. is a missionary society to be praised none the less for its not having fallen for the line that Anglicans have no responsibility in South America because, "after all, they're all Roman Catholics". It has gone, heroically and healingly, to Patagonians in Patagonia and to Indians in the interior of several countries whose people had never before been evangelized by any Christian body. Moreover, it has exhibited its awareness of contemporary need by setting up centres in cities for ministering to Patagonians who are no longer willing to stay in bleak Patagonia and for meeting the spiritual hunger of Indians who have abandoned the interior for the exterior. They are coming to town. In the confusing cities, the Church is the one familiar thing they find.

The tragedy is that our Anglican efforts of this sort are on a minuscule scale. We reach hundreds where tens of thousands stand in need of help.

The second of our missionary efforts is, alas, a thing of the past, but it was bright while it lasted. On the outskirts of Buenos Aires was a tract of land, Palermo by name, tamer than a forest but wilder than a park. It was completely given over to lawlessness. Hordes of unwanted children roamed about, eking out a miserable kind of existence for themselves and getting into unspeakable mischief. There is the place to go to work, decided an English cleric named William Case Morris. So beneficial were his labours among the underprivileged children of the city that many hands, Roman Catholic and humanist, were open to the support of the schools Morris established. All Buenos Aires had reason to be thankful that by 1932, the year Morris died, there were twenty-five of these schools with some seventy thousand pupils enrolled.

This is what *can* be done – even though it was undone when the wife of a dictator, determined to be the Great Mother of the Poor, swept these schools into her own hands. That lady is no more, but even if the present government were inclined to restore the schools to the Anglican Church, the Church in Argentina is at present too enfeebled to receive them back. Moreover, the particular sociological need that Morris rose to meet is largely past. It is sad, however, for Anglicans to reflect that most of the children who were products of his schools had to become Methodists, simply because there were no Spanish-speaking Anglican churches for them to attend.

I have the utmost admiration for the English clergy I met in South America. A fine lot they are – but there are not enough of them! And I hated to eat the food they hospitably placed in front of me, for I knew that I was almost literally taking the food out of their mouths. Most of them simply cannot afford to have a guest. The rector of one Argentinian parish was, until recently, receiving a stipend the equivalent of twenty-four American dollars a month. He has it plush now: it has been raised to thirty dollars a month! Thirty dollars buys more in Argentina, of course, than it does in the United States. Yet the fact remains: this is bare subsistence. A priest who earns six thousand Argentinian pesos a month will have to plunk down four or five thousand of them to buy himself a new suit.

It came as a surprise to learn that of the seven hundred Americans residing in Uruguay, nearly half are missionaries – but not an American Episcopalian among them. We have left Uruguay to the English Episcopalians, and the most they have managed is a splendid Greek-revival temple in the heart of Montevideo's shipping and commercial district, a quarter where nobody *lives* any more. The three hundred English-speaking families who claim a relationship to this church have villas at a seaside resort so comfortably far from town that Sunday Evensong has had to be given up.

I was extended the courtesy of sitting in on a meeting of the Church Council. The men, mostly bankers, shipping magnates, or commercial agents, toyed for an hour with the idea of a daring experiment: Why not try saying Evening Prayer, at least once a month, in the living-room of one of their houses on the coast? A few thought it unseemly, too unchurchly. The majority, however, were willing to go along with the idea, but a dreadful uncertainty overtook them suddenly. *How* could word be got around to the effect that a service was to be held? The sending of postcards was suggested. "But it would cost twenty-two pesetas," somebody objected. (That is about $1.93 in American money.) "Couldn't we perhaps get Boy Scouts to take the notices around by bicycle and do it for, say, ten pesetas?" came one hopeful suggestion. I began to feel discouraged. I brightened, however, when one gentleman said, "We have an American present. Maybe he could tell us how this problem would be met in America; and perhaps he could also tell us how to interest some of the Americans living here in coming to our services." To me it was fantastic to see men who are accustomed to handling large sums of money sit and haggle over twenty-two pesetas. Is there no carry-over of talent, imagination, and technique from the business world to the Church? My first impulse (which, happily, I disobeyed) was to slam down twenty-two pesetas on the table and say, "Now come on! Let's get on with some important business!"

"The way to attract Americans to your services," I said, "is for you and your wives to put on your hats and go around to call on your American neighbours. Tell them about the services, assure them that they will be welcome even if they aren't Episcopalians."

The vestrymen were polite to me, but I could tell that I had failed to carry my point. A home, after all, is a man's castle. And if it is an Englishman's castle, it is impregnable.

The English chaplain, an admirable man, turned to me and said, "Well, now, Canon Johnson, where do you go from here? Where does your tour of Anglicanism take you next?" "From here," I replied, "I go to Porto Alegre in the South of Brazil." "Why do you go there?" he asked. "We have no work there." At this I bristled. "What do you mean we have no work there? We happen to have three large and flourishing dioceses there, manned mostly by Brazilian clergy, and we're already in our second generation of Brazilian bishops!" "Oh, that's right," he murmured after a pause. "I'm sorry. I was thinking of the *English* Church."

In my momentary annoyance, I may have exaggerated to some degree the size and prosperity of the *Igreja Episcopal Brasileira*. It has, as I am about to relate, its shortcomings. But, compared to our poor showing in the rest of South America, it looks good, and I include it as the third among my hopeful exceptions to the rule of our having done so little in the neglected continent. The American Episcopal Church, refusing to be intimidated by ancient concordats, learned Portuguese and went to work.

Porto Alegre, seaport city of Brazil's State of Rio Grande do Sul, did not at first impress me as a "happy port". When I arrived on the night of 23rd December, "Little Christmas Eve", no one was on hand to greet me and I do not speak Portuguese.

I made my way alone to a hotel. Its appointments were faultless, but no member of its staff could speak English. I sought help from the telephone directory. The Bishop of Southern Brazil was not listed, and the only number given for *Igreja Episcopal Brasileira* did not answer.

The next day the German manager, *gemütlich* and guttural, came to my rescue. He had never heard, he said, of *Igreja Episcopal Brasileira*, but he instituted inquiries which eventually involved the police and soon great machineries of detection were set in motion. At length I was given instructions for reaching the street address. I arrived to find that I was not expected and nobody knew what to do with me.

When contact with the Bishop had finally been established, I was enfolded in an *embraço* of Brazilian hospitality, and I took a more tolerant view of the whole situation. I soon began to understand the idiosyncrasies of the Brazilian communication system. When I attempted to send a telegram from Santa Maria to the Bishop of Central Brazil, who resided in Rio de Janeiro, a mere nine hundred miles away, it was eight days before it was delivered although extra *cruzeiros* had been expended to have it marked *urgente*.

After this frustrating experience, I fully exonerated the Brazilian clergy for all hitches in my travel arrangements.

Nor could I blame them for the plane and train failures which made mincemeat of my schedule. Of these there were many. A train for which I had a reservation never arrived, and the train which did arrive disclaimed knowledge of me and would not let me aboard. One of the two engines of the plane which was conveying me from Porto Alegre to Santa Maria coughed, gave up, and died, and we made an emergency landing on a makeshift airstrip between two cornfields. There was not one person aboard that grounded plane who could speak English, and I had scant success when I tried to communicate in other languages. This experience gave me a new appreciation of the theological concept of the *Word*, and of the miracle of Pentecost. In a critical situation one longs to hear a loosening word. One wants to know: Can the engine be repaired? Is help coming? When will it come? But nobody in that lonely spot could speak the word to me. So it is in the world at large. Is rescue in sight? Is help coming? This is the loosening, illuminating word the world strains anxiously to hear. And this is what the Church means when it says that in the fullness of time, in the crisis of history, God spoke his Word. . . . The word I needed in that Brazilian cornfield finally announced itself in the drone of motors and the descent of a plane. Thus I reached Santa Maria many hours late.

But I return now to Porto Alegre. The first day of the new year is, as even the lowest of Low Churchmen will admit, an important one. Since nothing was to be found in the newspapers listing services in the Cathedral Church, I rose early, walked to the cathedral at seven, and found it closed. I went back at eight, nine, and ten. Still no luck! But eleven, I thought, would reward my efforts. I returned with higher hopes at that hour. The doors of the cathedral were open; my heart leapt for joy. But the building was empty. Ultimately I found someone and was able to extract from him the information that there would be no service held that day. A Watch Night service, I later learned, had been held at midnight, but even so, it distressed me that there was no day-time celebration in a cathedral church, in a principal city, on a Prayer Book Feast!

Several times in the course of my stay here I had occasion to pass the cathedral in a taxi. Feigning ignorance, I utilized every passing to raise with the driver the question, "*¿Que edificio es esso?*"

Invariably the answer was, "*Igreja protestante.*"

"*¿Quel tipo?*" I persisted in my unprincipled Portuguese. "Methodista, Lutherana, Presbyteriana?"

With monotonous consistency came the reply, "*No se, Igreja protestante.*"

It seemed reprehensible to me that there was no sign in front of this cathedral to declare what kind of building it was, no notice board to indicate when services were held. If there were a law in Brazil, as there is in some countries, to prevent the posting of such signs and notices, that would be another story. But Brazil is different, enlightened, and tolerant. I would not bother to chronicle this little episode were it unique. I tell it only because I found the same reluctance to run up an ensign in country after country. Are we ashamed to announce our wares?

This was only the beginning of my dissatisfaction with Brazil. Our seminary there seemed to me a fragile effort, enfeebled by pluralism and nepotism. The same criticism would have to be levelled against many parts of the Church in Brazil.

Nepotism and pluralism are ugly words. They can be applied to the Brazilian Church only in a greatly diluted sense. It is true that every second or third highly placed cleric I met seemed to be the brother of this or that bishop or the nephew of this or that dean. This is not as sinister as it sounds.

We are dealing here with a small Church, a Church that is largely a family affair, an interlocking network of several families. A man who becomes an Episcopalian after having successfully bucked the passive or semiactive opposition of the surrounding culture may succeed, in turn, in persuading his wife to join him; then he, with her help, perhaps manages to win over his brother-in-law; and the brother-in-law, who is greatly looked up to by a nephew, perhaps convinces the nephew. This is evangelism chiefly following the ties of blood and of relationship by marriage. So far as it goes, this is unobjectionable. The only danger is that the few families that make up the Church may succumb at times to a proprietary feeling about *their* Church. It is as if they owned it.

Perhaps this pattern is inevitable in the case of a Church just getting started, an infinitesimal minority, whose handful of members must band together and cling to one another for mutual support. And because manpower is sorely limited, who *is* there to fill a vacancy or occupy a new post except the man whose only fault is that he happens to be cousin, nephew, or brother to the official who must appoint him?

Thus I refer to "nepotism" in this rather specialized meaning of the word. It is characteristic not of Brazil alone. The same would have to be said of, for example, Mexico and Japan – to name but two. Probably it is an inescapable early stage of development, a stage which will be outgrown. It is important, however, that the possible dangers be recognized and guarded against and that the familial, proprietary mentality be combated.

Pluralism is in all likelihood another unavoidable early phase of development. Why? Because the young Church, even when it is subsidized by an older Church abroad, is too poor to pay its clergy a living wage. When this is the case, a priest can be forgiven for taking on side jobs. He teaches school part time or puts to work his previous skills as a printer or lawyer, in order to supplement his income. Well, St. Paul did something of the sort . . . for a while, and rather prided himself on it. But finally he gave it up, not because it was beneath him, but because the Church's business was too urgent, requiring *all* his attention. The trouble with the part-time job is that, in altogether too many instances, it becomes the major job, and the man himself becomes, in effect, a part-time priest. The Anglican Communion has far too many men to whom this has happened. If economic need compels them to take this course, no blame attaches to their action. The blame must be laid at the door of a "headquarters" which apparently does not believe that the labourer is worthy of his hire. I cannot, however, shake off the disquieting impression that this is not everywhere a sufficient explanation. Necessity is surely not the only motive that drives clergy into taking jobs on the side. Just conceivably, more feathers for the nest may be the motivation.

Again it might look as if I were speaking of Brazil alone. On the contrary, if these remarks are true at all, their application is distressingly widespread.

I would not want it thought that I have in mind "worker priests". This is something entirely different. There are a thousand excellent reasons for urging that it may be sound missionary strategy in some situations to clothe a priest in overalls and put him in a factory as a worker alongside other workers – or vest a priest in an academic gown and place him in a graduate school as a student among students. In this way the Church has borne its witness and made an impact upon thousands it might not otherwise have been able to reach. Exempt from my strictures also are the "auxiliary priests" with which several dioceses are experimenting, the Diocese of Hong Kong having been the great pioneer. We shall come to this topic in due course. I am considering now only priests who for prestige or for profit take on extra jobs for which there is no economic necessity. Of these there are more than a few.

To its credit, the Brazilian Episcopal Church has lately begun to strive for "emancipation" – and by this is not meant getting free from the United States. It is the Brazilians' term for achievement of financial self-support. But the going is not easy. Bishop Stephen Neill and other counsellors keep urging upon the three Brazilian Dioceses the creation of a fourth Diocese so that a new, autonomous province of the Anglican Communion may be formed. This is a laudable aim. It is what most Brazilian Episcopalians themselves want. It may even come about before long. Yet there is little likelihood of economic self-sufficiency for the Church until such time as the country gets back on an even keel and, to be specific, shores up the faltering *cruzeiro*. In 1959 when I was in Brazil, the *cruzeiro* stood at 200 to the United States dollar. In 1952 it stood at 32 to the dollar. In 1962 it took 350 to buy a single dollar. Put in other terms: the Missionary District of Southwestern Brazil was able in 1957, to raise 80 per cent of its budget locally; the following year it was down to 48 per cent; in 1959 it dipped to a mere 30 per cent. "That," said a bishop grimly, "is inflation."

There is much in the Brazilian Church to excite admiration. The outstanding fact is that most of its clergy are "home-grown" and that two of its three bishops are Brazilians. In the same breath I want to say that it is also to the credit of the Brazilian Church that the third is *not* a Brazilian. When the time came to choose a new bishop for Central Brazil, the choice fell on somebody named Sherrill. He was chosen not because he bore a distinguished name nor because he had connections nor because, as a North American, he might have easy access to certain purse strings. He was chosen because, in the wisdom of the local Church, he was deemed to be the right man. Questions of nationality were not raised. They were known to be irrelevant. The inverse racialism or inverse nationalism which falls over backwards to be "nice" to people of other nations or races is a danger in our age especially. In its choice of leaders, the Church, while trying to meet the just aspirations of peoples for recognition and independence, must consider primarily the welfare of the whole body.

There is much else I could cite in favour of *Igreja Episcopal Brasileira*. I could tell of its schools, its four Boys' Towns, its two orphanages for girls, its three homes for the aged, its clinics for indigent people, its one hundred and eighty-five parishes (see Pl. 4), missions, and preaching stations – not a bad showing for seventy years of hard work. But since all of this has been told a hundred times before, I am free to tell things less well known – some of them unpalatable (for unpalatable things rarely meet the requirements for inclusion in standard missionary literature).

It should be known, for example, that our whole effort – fine as it is – is but a drop in the bucket. The smallness of scale came as a major shock to me. We have touched – and touched lightly – only one-third of Brazil.

It should be known that only six parishes in the whole of Brazil are "emancipated" – i.e. have achieved self-support.

It should be known that PECUSA has dollared the place almost to death. I mean, the American Church has habituated the Brazilians to an attitude of perpetual dependence. Our intentions were always the best, but there was unconscious arrogance in them. The early missionaries were all on the giving side. It did not occur to them that the Brazilians had any other role than that of receiving. Until recent years there was little teaching about tithing or stewardship. Our hand was open with generosity but was too full of "goodies" for Brazilians to be able to clasp it as a right hand of fellowship. Fellowship, after all, means *receiving* as well as giving. We were a long time learning that we had something to receive. "It is more blessed to give than to receive" is an utterance with dominical authority behind it. Kierkegaard, however, calling it "the little mystery", bids us take note of a "greater and more difficult mystery – that of finding blessedness in learning to receive".

Brazilian Episcopalians today are beginning, most encouragingly, to see that they must shoulder their own share of the load. This does not mean that fewer Yankee dollars should go to Brazil. It means only that the dollars should be devoted to extension, to the opening of new work, and not dissipated as a dole for the maintenance of old work which *could* learn to stand on its own feet. We cripple some work by our extravagant and over-protective concern to support it. The most difficult art in the relationships of human beings is that of learning to confer freedom.

It should also be known that there is grave discontent among the Episcopalians in Brazil over the inequality in wage scales. Missionaries from North America are paid, on the average, fifty x's per annum. (I am not saying what x stands for.) The Brazilian-born clergy average sixteen x's. The bishops, whatever their nationality, receive ninety x's! The disproportions are glaring. In justice, one must recognize that bishops have demands made upon them for which there is nothing comparable in the life of a parish priest. But still! The difference is too great. While the Bishops of Brazil do *not* live regally by any means, their stipend makes of them, by Brazilian standards, rich men, *grands seigneurs* – and their clergy resent it. And then, in fairness to the *Norteamericanos*, it has to be admitted that the missionary – he cannot escape this any more than he could escape his own skin – has commitments in the United States on a scale undreamed of in Brazil. That is, he has life insurance premiums to pay, he has children he feels he must send home for schooling, he may have relatives there dependent upon him, and a dozen other financial involvements all geared to a scale totally different from the Brazilian. He cannot help himself; he simply *has* to have more money than his Brazilian brother priest. Brazilian resentment against the missionary would be reduced if more Brazilians understood these facts. Even so, the disparity between the American's fifty x's and the Brazilian's sixteen is uncalled for and a breeder of the dark sin of envy.

The *facts* are clear to me. The solution is not. Ideally, each would receive according to his need. But we do not live in an ideal world. In time we can hope that the stipends of the local clergy will be raised. This will help. But I see little realism in the proposal that the stipends of the missionaries be lowered. They are not princely sums! In only two ways could missionary salaries be lowered equitably. One is by sending missionaries who will remain single. The other is by sending married men with their families who intend to stay, settle down, and identify themselves permanently with the people of the land. In this connection it should be noted that the foreign missionary is not resented in the mission field because he is a foreigner. What grates, rather, is his vocabulary, constant references to "home" and his recurring need to go home on furlough. "How long have you been out here?" one missionary asks of another. Why not say just "here", not "out here"? It is a great sacrifice to ask of a family that it settle in, put down roots, educate the children in the local schools; but, for a variety of reasons, both economic and psychological, the Church cannot afford so many short-term appointees. "Of course he never loved us," said a Brazilian to me of one especially fine American missionary. "He stayed only twelve years."

Sharp things I have been saying of Brazil, and I have no intention of backtracking now in order to soften the blow. I am sorry to find that in the main, though probably not in particulars, the Bishop of Central Brazil seems to agree with me; for he is quoted as having said in a public address that the work of the Episcopal Church, not in Brazil alone but in all of Latin America, is "marginal and confused". Yet this Bishop is no pessimist. Neither am I. Because North Americans were willing to speak Portuguese, we got somewhere. Not far enough, it has to be conceded, but, if numbers mean anything, we can claim thirty-seven thousand Episcopalians in Brazil as over against the eleven thousand claimed by the British for the whole of the continent.

But does it give us any reason to boast that we have some seventy priests working in Brazil? Not when you take into account that the Presbyterians have two thousand ordained men at work in that land. They have a seminary there which rivals, in terms of equipment and scholarship, the best that Britain or America have to offer. Our seminary in Porto Alegre, when I visited it, boasted a library of four hundred volumes – to not half of which I would afford space in my own personal library. And there was not one seminary professor who could afford to devote his full time to teaching; they all took side jobs to supplement their income.

Of all South American countries, the Republic of Brazil is the country most tolerant, most open to the work of non-Roman Churches. It is also the largest and most populous of these countries. The *Igreja Episcopal Brasileira* will not be found wanting when it comes to producing statistics to show that it too is growing. The figures are not unimpressive until one spends an hour with a slide rule and the population tables of a general census. Then it will be seen that although we have added to our numbers, we have not kept up with the population explosion. Such growth as we can show is due, for the most part, to the fact that Brazilian Episcopalians have children. Proportionately to the total Brazilian population, Anglicanism is no stronger than it was. Meanwhile, most other Christian bodies are growing absolutely, not merely relatively.

Weird syncretistic cults grow absolutely too. Compounds of Christian elements are all mixed in with ingredients borrowed from voodoo and primitive Indian rites. The Bishop of Central Brazil quite rightly insisted that I see a film called *Black Orpheus*. It is a terrifying masterpiece. He takes it seriously, as a harbinger of the horror to come. Most of his clergy, however, sleep on, oblivious to the dark urges that threaten to engulf the Brazilians. A reversion to semipaganism is a frightful possibility, more frightful than pure paganism, because a post-Christian, partly Christian paganism is always more daemonic, more destructive, than paganism unalloyed.

The work is started, it will increase. It would be an act of impatience on the part of the Church in the United States to expect of a daughter Church, as yet so young, so small, that she should have made a notable impact on the culture and life of big and busy Brazil. What can fewer than forty thousand Episcopalians be expected to accomplish among the seventy millions of Brazilians. Give them time!

Help has appeared from two unexpected quarters: from Germany and Japan. Brazil has given an open-armed reception to immigrants from both of these nations – with surprising benefits to all Brazilian life, that of the Brazilian Episcopal Church included. Within sight of São Paulo's dramatic skyline, two churches are in existence for Japanese congregations which are not yet quite at home in Portuguese; and within the city itself I attended services at a church whose congregation, though predominantly Brazilian, was bracingly laced with Germans, Japanese, English, Canadians, and Americans. It augurs well.

Other hopeful signs are not far to seek. To take a single example: my last day in Rio de Janeiro, which was also my last day in Brazil before flying off to Africa, I was present when news came that justified our holding a carnival of joy. The government, after deliberation, had given our Church permission to buy a sizeable piece of land in Brasilia, the new capital city. The location is ideal, facing immediately on the plaza where the parliament buildings are being built. For once in our lives we were in on the ground floor! We would be open and ready for business by the time the first session of parliament convened. That, alas, is not our customary procedure anywhere!

I gave thanks for the Brazilian priest, formerly an influential lawyer, who had the "savvy" to put this thing through. Strange how Providence can make use of every bit of knowledge and skill a person has acquired, even in preconversion days! When once we have seen the light, everything else we have seen, done, or known finds a place, comes in handy. Even our sins can make their contribution. For which reason St. Augustine cried, "*O felix culpa!*"

After such heavy considerations, let me introduce, for the sake of comic relief, something entirely irrelevant. All during my three weeks in Brazil I foolishly found myself recalling a scene from *Charley's Aunt*. The aunt, you remember, was returning to England from Brazil where she made her home (doubtless being ministered to by one of the English chaplaincies!). When she failed to show up at Oxford in time to chaperone a party, one of the students had to masquerade as the aunt. The deception was going well until the bogus aunt encountered at tea a don who knew something of Brazil. The don's questions taxed to the uttermost the student's powers of invention. "In what part of Brazil do you reside?" came the question. By a stroke of genius, the answer was, "The residential part."

Now, the residential part of South America's largest republic has hitherto been confined pretty much to the coastal areas. A formidable chain of coastal mountains blocked progress into the interior. The creation of Brasilia marks an arbitrary attempt to break through the mountain barrier, and it is encouraging that the Church is ready to go right along. The Church is there, even before the populace.

Although, unfortunately, I did not myself get to Brasilia, there was one excursion into the interior which I want to record. In company with the Bishop of Central Brazil I flew from Rio, via São Paulo, to Londrina, a city of eighty thousand people in the State of Paraná, which reminded me, somehow, of Omaha, Nebraska. There the Bishop took over the wheel of a jeep and we headed west. For four hours we jolted over fierce roads. The rains were torrential. Three times we skidded badly, making complete turnabouts, and once we were saved from upsetting only because a front wheel had lodged itself deeply in a soft bank of red clay. My heart was more often in my mouth than in its accustomed position. I began to wonder if we would ever get to the place where the Bishop was bent on going. The purpose of his trip was to explain to certain people that, as their priest was being transferred to another diocese and no successor was in sight, for some little time they would have to make out as best they could with the help of their own lay readers.

In the middle of what seemed to be nowhere we finally reached the house of a Japanese farmer. With his wife and seven children he extended to us all the exquisite courtesies of Nipponese etiquette. Then the Bishop and the farmer got down to business. Serious talk it was, in Portuguese. I looked on, amazed, at Portuguese-speaking Japanese in the midst of this wilderness. But that was only the beginning of my amazement. On a table in the living-room my eye fell upon a copy, in Japanese translation, of Emil Brunner's

Unser Glaube. I recognized the great Swiss theologian's picture on the cover. What a strange business altogether! Here we were, well inland in Brazil. My hosts were Brazilians now, though they were Japanese-born. They spoke Portuguese, yet in this remote spot they derived spiritual nourishment from a Japanese translation of a book written in German by a Swiss, a book they were willing to discuss with me, an American, to the extent of the few words I could command in a mélange of faked Japanese and pidgin Portuguese. Yet all of us were Episcopalians – except Brunner, who on the strength of what he wrote *ought* to be one! This is not the sort of experience one soon forgets. Perhaps never has my realization of our oneness in Christ been more vivid than in that rain-drenched isolated farmhouse.

This realization was reinforced the following day, Sunday, when, in Londrina, we rose early to celebrate the Holy Mysteries. Ankle-deep in reddish mud, we slogged our way to the church where we found waiting for us a congregation of seventy persons. Except for one Italian woman and her grown daughter, the rest of the congregation was Japanese! I have not the words to convey what I felt at that moment. An American bishop, assisted by a Japanese congregation, celebrated in Portuguese translation an English liturgy which, deriving ultimately from Jerusalem, had been mediated to us through Greece, Rome, Byzantium, the whole history of medieval Catholicism, and the needful purgations of the Reformation. It was all so right and so unmistakably the Christian religion. And suddenly, in this remote city of red mud, I was seized with two overwhelming emotions. Anglicans have become in fact what they have always been in essence: *catholic.* That was the first. And second, why should Church Union be such a difficult matter?

In conclusion, there are at least five justifications for Anglicanism's continued presence in South America:

First, the continent still teems with people of English speech, British, American, and others, who have long-term or even lifetime commitments to South America, and who stand in need of spiritual ministrations.

Second, all kinds of ordinary folk, never reached by Rome or perhaps offended by Rome, await a liberating word.

Third, intellectuals in particular, though they may not know it, pine for our appearing.

Fourth, those Latin Americans who were hungry for the Gospel and sought it from the sects often suffered painful disillusionment there, and now seek it elsewhere.

Fifth, Rome itself, which does not realize it now, will someday recognize with gratitude that we offered a much-needed corrective which accrued, in the long run, to Rome's own advantage.

Here the case rests.

It remains only to record, with thanksgiving, that the American Episcopal Church has made up its mind to get down to business in Latin America. Its chief missionary thrust these next few years will be "south of the border". High time.

¡ *Vaya con dios!*

3

WEST AFRICA: Coasting on Inherited Capital

IT TAKES COURAGE TO WRITE ONLY A FEW SLENDER CHAPTERS and then label them "Africa". For the first thing to say about the "Dark Continent" – and perhaps the only true generalization that can be made with respect to it – is that Africa is BIG.

How big I did not realize until I received a lesson in geography from a slip of an African schoolteacher in Sierra Leone. She could not have been more than sixteen. (Part of the pathos of Africa today is that it is *children* who must teach children. There is no one else to do it.) She spread before me a map of the world. Then, applying her scissors to an identical map, she cut out China and Manchuria and placed them in Africa. She next cut out India, Pakistan, and Tibet and placed them in Africa. After that she cut out forty-eight of the United States of America, and for good measure threw in the forty-ninth State, Alaska. These, too, she placed in Africa. *And there was still room left over!*

This dawning conception of the size of Africa was reinforced when I actually got going on safari. I soon learned that in Africa one does not ask "How far is it from here to there?" but "How long does it take to get there?" African roads being what they are, one needs a time gauge more than a mileage chart. I remember one place in Zululand where the missionary was driving me across a boulder-strewn field to an outstation. As the Land Rover lurched and pitched in the most frightening way, despite the skill and intense concentration of my priestly chauffeur, I naïvely inquired, "When will we get to the road?" "This *is* the road!" was his retort.

I was in Africa just short of five months, January to May. The year was 1960. "You certainly knew how to pick your year for coming to Africa," was the comment of a Nigerian lawyer. As everybody knows, 1960 was "Africa Year", that tumultuous season wherein the "winds of change" blew with sudden force, toppling empires. "Freedom" was everywhere the cry, and everywhere I went people had just got it or were preparing to get it or were getting fighting mad because it appeared there would be delay. Yet a discussion of the political developments in recent African history lies outside the purview of this present book save in so far as they alter the climate in which the Church must work.

Dakar was my first point of contact with Africa, after an all-night flight from Rio de Janeiro. Senegal was not at all the Africa of my imaginings. In fact, surprisingly little of Africa corresponds to the stereotyped notions most of us have. Here were no naked savages. Either people were enveloped from head to toe in flowing robes in the Arabian manner, or else were chic in the Parisian manner. Instead of mumbo jumbo they all spoke faultless French. And where were the steaming jungles with vegetation so dense that one must hack one's way with a machete? Such jungles do exist in Africa, but Senegal is bone dry – as is much else of Africa. Indeed, lack of sufficient rainfall is a major problem in vast reaches of the continent, south of the Equator as well as north. In Dakar the nearest thing to a "Jungle Jim" I saw was a smart "Jungle Gym" – slides and swings and overhead ladders and horizontal bars – in the yard of an ultramodern schoolhouse. In sum, this was not the Africa of Tarzan. It was French and Arabic. It was Islam.

Hugely irrelevant to this part of Africa are many cartoons and jokes (the lion piously saying Grace before devouring the missionary; the one cannibal explaining to another that it would be a mistake to boil a Franciscan for, after all, he is a friar!). Demolished too is the cherished picture of the missionary as a pallid Englishman sitting under a palm tree telling Bible stories to unclad blacks who look up to him adoringly, tears of love and gratitude streaming from their eyes. Today's missionary has to deal with university graduates who perhaps can speak more languages than he can. Today's missionary is often a black, brown, or yellow man. The "White Man's Burden" is increasingly being shouldered by many men and women who are not white at all – and this puts quite a different complexion on things!

Ecclesiastically, the African continent is divided into five autonomous Provinces: West, South, Central, East, and – newest of the lot – Uganda. I visited each of them in that order and now will try – though of necessity sketchily – to describe them in the same order.

The Province of West Africa, formed in 1951, embraces Gambia and the Rio Pongas, Sierra Leone, Ghana, and Nigeria. It has nine dioceses. I

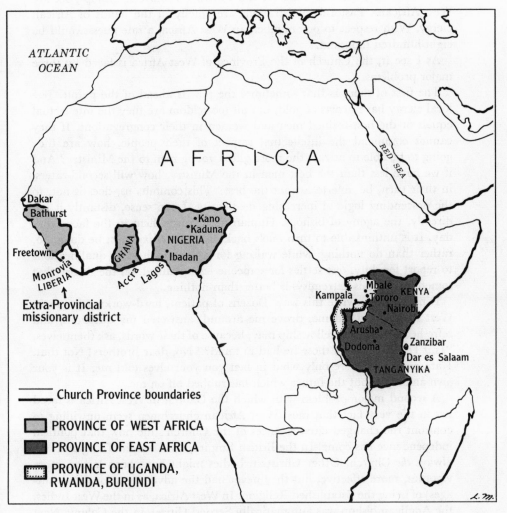

2. Three of the five Anglican Provinces in Africa: West Africa; East Africa; Uganda and Ruanda-Burundi

managed to get to six of them. Three Nigerian dioceses had to be omitted because I had grievously underestimated the time it would require to make the rounds in a land so vast. Of the Province's fourteen bishops, six are West Africans. Pastoral ministrations are chiefly in the hands of African clergy. With respect to our numbers in West Africa, a safe guess would be eight hundred thousand.

As I see it, the Church of the Province of West Africa is faced by three major problems.

The first of them is that sometimes the pew is ahead of the pulpit. The local clergy have hearts of gold, but all too seldom are they the intellectual equals of the best-trained men and women in their congregations. If they cannot command the intellectual respect of their people, how are they going to be able to attract the more gifted young men to the Ministry? And if we have less than the best men in the Ministry, how will second-raters, in their turn, be able to attract the best? This commits us, does it not, to the descending logic of increasing mediocrity. I can sense, distantly if not directly, the agony of bishops. Human need stares them in the face every day. It is unthinkable to turn one's back on it. *Something* must be done. So, rather than do nothing, while waiting for a man with ideal qualifications to report for duty, one settles for someone less qualified, on the theory that something, in this extremity, is better than nothing.

It pains me to write this way. Dozens of patient, hard-working priests in West Africa who fed me, drove me around, answered my questions, and refreshed me by their fellowship may, because of these words, ask themselves, "Is it I? Am I one of those he had in mind?" No, dear Brothers! Not that. I am expressing here only what in fact you yourselves told me. It is your own anxiety about the future which has rubbed off on me.

A second major problem with which the Church in West Africa is faced lies in the very fact that most West African churchmen seem unwilling to confront the changed circumstances of the Church's life now that political independence has come. In the British Empire, the Church of England was always *the* Church. Other Christian bodies might have been larger, more vigorous, more effective, but they never had the advantages (or disadvantages) of being the Established Religion. In West Africa, as in the West Indies, the Anglican bishop was automatically Second Citizen in the Colony. Next to the Governor, there was none more exalted than he. The Bishop participated in the British *Raj*, the prestige of the ruling power. The Governor flew a standard from the fender of his car. So did the Bishop. The Governor got snappy salutes from soldiers and police. So did the Bishop. In most cases the Governor combined, with his other excellencies, the excellency of being an Anglican. Or, if he was not that, he was, at the very least, a cultured despiser of the same; and since both men were *cultured* they usually got along. In any event, the Church had a favoured position.

I am not being cynical. I am stating a fact. The Anglican Communion owes an incalculable debt to the British Empire. It was the Empire, quite as much as missionary zeal, that carried us into all the world.

But that is gone now – or nearly so. The new tenant in Government House is probably a Baptist, black but comely. Even more likely, he is a Muslim.

This is the new look of things in West Africa, and I found no indications there to assure me that Anglicans, white or black, are prepared to face this new fact realistically. Perhaps the confrontation would be too painful. Instead, in Ghana's capital city of Accra (to take but one example) laymen come to the Cathedral Church decked out in striped trousers and cutaway coats. Edwardian attire! There is a pathetic clinging to the past and a fearful confusion between Christianity and European civilization.

The Cathedral in Accra is a handsome Gothic edifice. It has narrow slits for windows – in a climate that is blazing hot. The story told locally is that plans were sent out from London on the same day for a cathedral in Accra and a cathedral in Newfoundland. Inadvertently, the plans intended for Newfoundland got into the envelope addressed to the Gold Coast, and vice versa. It is a joke, and not a notably funny one. Its humour is dimmer still, from my point of view, when you realize that Anglicans of the Gold Coast, now called Ghana, fell in love with this English export to such an extent that nothing can be accounted a proper Christian church unless it resembles this structure. It is, I repeat, a handsome building, but it is a sweatbox. Are cutaway coats and Gothic slits of the essence of Christianity?

Not many years ago a new chapel was built a few miles distant from Accra at one of Ghana's finest schools. Ancient imitative mistakes were not repeated. The architects knew a thing or two about Ghanaian climate. They knew that circulation of air is a chief requisite. The building they designed is perfect for the climate in which it is situated. It is unmistakably a Christian church, one of the most beautiful in the world. Seeping eaves keep the rain out. The sides are open to catch each vagrant breeze. The natives hate the building. "It is not a proper church" because it doesn't look like the fortress which is the Cathedral. "This is *apartheid* architecture," they argue. Something cheaper than the Cathedral, something scaled down. It does no good to tell these people that this is a prize-winning design, that architects in Europe and America admire it and are sometimes guilty of plagiarism in reproducing it wherever the climate calls for a similar solution. The white man can argue until he is black in the face. The black man will still tell him that this chapel in a contemporary style is a cut-rate way of giving the African something "second best".

Say what you will, our African brother can sometimes be a difficult customer. In the midst of all his laments about this particular chapel he drove me out to the new university buildings. There, with a pride entirely justified, he pointed out a modern complex of buildings on a scale so grandiose, so opulent, that I blurted out a word which seldom escaped my lips: "Fabulous!" He did not seem to notice, however, that the style of the buildings and the materials which went into their construction are none other than those which created the chapel he had so recently abominated. This is an example of how the Church, as Church, is out of step with the times. We shall never be catholic until we succeed in being something more than English.

The third major problem in West Africa is Islam.

For every one West African who becomes a Christian, ten become followers of the Prophet. It is as simple as that and as drastic as that. Already we are outnumbered. Shortly we shall be overwhelmed. I see no way of arresting the trend. I can only recommend ways of adjusting to it – and it worries me supremely that the West African Church seems so little aware that adjustments will be called for.

However erroneous or incomplete they may be, I will set down here my explanations for the smashing successes of Islam. I note them with particular reference to West Africa, although they are not without validity in some other parts of Africa as well.

First, Islam stands for a pure and simple monotheism, uncomplicated by the necessary but subtle Trinitarianism of Christianity. To people just emerging from the quagmire and terrors of animism and polytheism, the sheer, naked, arithmetical unity of the God of the Prophet is singularly attractive. It exercises enormous power. Christianity, by contrast, seems to equivocate. It says "One" but names "Three".

Second, Islam sets before its followers an ethical standard which is unambiguous, easy to understand, and easy to live up to. There is no talk here, as there must be in Christianity, of an "impossible ethic" which introduces judgement and prepares the way for repentance, grace, and faith. The simplicities of Islam form part of its appeal. From a certain point of view, it is the religion of the natural man.

Third, Islam permits polygamy. This makes eminent good sense to the African. He has the greatest difficulty in grasping the reason for Christianity's insistence on monogamy. Our African brother is not more lustful than the rest of us. His entire heritage, all the traditional social patterns he has been brought up to respect, the economy on which the life of his community depends, were predicated on polygamy. Christ, apparently, is opposed to this. Mohammed is not. So Mohammed wins – at least for the time being. There is reason to suppose that the institution of plural marriage will not persist for ever in Africa. Changing economic and social patterns make it increasingly difficult for a man to have more than one wife. He just can't afford it. Moreover, the African woman, as she becomes better educated, isn't going to tolerate it. But these developments will take time, and in the meanwhile polygamous Islam clearly has an edge over monogamous Christianity.

Fourth, Islam, driven today by the nationalistic aspirations of Arab States, accords perfectly and conveniently with the nationalism, the thrust for independence, which dominates the African spirit of our time. Christianity, alas, is identified in the public mind with the colonial powers which brought it to Africa. Revulsion against imperialism carries with it revolt against the religion of the imperialists.

Fifth, Islam, greatly to its credit, can make one boast which reduces Christianity to a shamed silence: there is no such thing as a segregated mosque. Muslims can be fiercely intolerant of non-Muslims, but if you are a follower of the Prophet, they couldn't care less about your race. You are a brother.

One Christian summed it up when he said, "Islam has all the cards."

Christianity, I believe, is in West Africa to stay. It is well enough rooted for that. But unless we change our tactics and treble our efforts, it may be doomed to play a diminishing role in the drama of African development. Christians brought hospitals and hygiene. They brought schools. By these gifts they greatly endeared themselves to the inhabitants of the land, and the Christian religion was commended to many. Those who were not won over as converts became (with few exceptions) friends of the Church, at the very least. Not only in West Africa but nearly everywhere I went in the world I was astonished and gratified to discover great reservoirs of goodwill towards the Church. People of other religions and people of no religion at all recognize that the Church has done, in Plato's phrase, a beautiful deed. There are those who hate us, to be sure, but we have more friends than enemies. Currency should be given to the fact that many non-Christian hands are open to the Church: that Zoroastrians in Iran contribute to an Anglican hospital; that Muslims in Jordan helped build a new church; that witch doctors in Africa, grateful for treatment received in an Anglican clinic, send their presents of eggs and fowl. It would be impossible ever to assess the contribution the Christian Mission has made to international goodwill. It is *there* as a background and basis on which statesmen and diplomats go to work. Not all of Christ's victories are reflected in the annual report of the number of persons baptized and confirmed.

This means that few are the countries where the Christian Church faces the prospect of ouster. The presence of Christians is not only tolerated. It is, generally speaking, welcomed. Secular governments make room for us, and in more countries than I had thought possible, they *assist* us. As an American I was long familiar with the principle that religious, educational, and charitable institutions should be tax exempt, but (again as an American) I was totally unprepared for the discovery that governments tend to be liberal with grants-in-aid to Christian schools and hospitals. In some places, of course, not a penny comes from government. But these places are in the minority.

Here is the point I want to make. In West Africa we are coasting on an inherited capital of goodwill. It is a legacy left over from Christianity's pioneer benevolent efforts and from Great Britain's generally beneficent colonial policies. Britain's prestige has soared anew because it did not wait too long before granting independence to several of its West African colonies. But the question is: How long will this legacy last? How much longer can the Church count on it? Have we not, perhaps, counted on it too long already?

Most of the schools in Sierra Leone are still in Church hands. They are schools to be proud of. Muslims send their children to them because the great desideratum is to have "an English education". These Muslim pupils must attend daily chapel, all strictly Prayer Book, and are obliged to take the prescribed courses in religious instruction. If exposure to Christian worship and Christian teaching is the "occupational hazard" involved in getting the coveted "English education", most Muslim parents are willing to take the risk and pay the price. A child enrolled in a Christian school must be expected to accept the school's total discipline.

I had the privilege of attending chapel several times and of sitting in on some of the classes, all of them excellent. But then I raised this question with headmasters and headmistresses: "Are any courses offered to Christian children which will enable them to understand what it is that their Muslim neighbours hold dear?" The question was asked in innocence. Not until the moment of asking it did I realize I had dropped a bombshell. There was a stunned silence. Then, by delayed action, an explosion. *"What?"* The tone was incredulous, as if the questioner could not have heard aright. "That we should teach Mohammedanism in a Christian school!" They looked at me as if I had said something indecent.

When the splutterings ceased I attempted to clarify my meaning. "It is wonderful that you have this opportunity to present Christianity to hundreds of Muslim children, but what about our own Christian children? The family that lives across the street from them is probably Muslim and so, in all likelihood, are the people next door to the right and to the left of them. These are the people they are going to have to live with, trade with, vote with, get along with the whole of their lives. Shouldn't something be done to help them understand their neighbours? Without understanding what it is that the Muslims next door revere, how can the Christian ever hope to witness effectively in their presence? And even if the witness should fail, these are the neighbours Christ has given you, and they are yours to live with."

If the earlier silence was a stunned one, the new silence was stony. It was broken at last by an African priest-headmaster who said, "This is a Christian school. We exist only to proclaim the Gospel of Jesus Christ. We could never raise money in England for the teaching of Mohammedanism."

I went away from this conversation sick at heart.

I tell this story in detail because it was not an isolated experience. Similar conversations were repeated many times throughout West Africa – and in scores of places all over the world. Almost nowhere did I find any disposition on the part of Anglican educators to lift a finger to interpret to Christians the religions by which they were surrounded. Is this evangelism? Is it the task of the evangelist to remain ignorant of the insights and aspirations of people of other religions – and to perpetuate this ignorance in the name of Christ? I myself have a double interest here. In the interest of sound evangelism, I want Christians both to know what they are up against in approaching the adherent of another religion and to appreciate what points in common the two religions may happen to have, in order that dialogue may begin. And failing that, I have a civic and irenic interest in exploring the possibilities of co-existence. Does Christianity really want to seal itself up in a cultural ghetto?

More likely sooner than later, the Church in West Africa is going to be stripped of its schools. Colonies now free will fall more and more under Muslim control. They have the votes. I predict that soon there will be a clamour to secularize the schools. After that may come the Muslimization of the schools. One of these days, when government grants are no longer forthcoming, Anglican schoolmasters will have to shut up shop. Christian children in search of an education may find that the Koran is the required textbook. In itself, that will not do them any harm, but they will be harmed by the increasing scarcity of Bibles and Prayer Books.

An inevitability broods over all of this. Why not step forward bravely to meet the inevitable instead of waiting dumbly until it overtakes us? We could, *right now*, buy and store up against the future tremendous quantities of goodwill if, *right now*, on our own initiative, we would interpret Islam to the children in our schools – to the Christian children in order that they might better understand the predominantly Muslim environment in which their life is set, to the Muslim children in order that they might better perceive the glories of their own heritage and (who knows, since they are not stupid) some of its inadequacies. Before being *forced* to do something, why not do it willingly and graciously – and get some credit for it? And perhaps set a pattern which Muslim-controlled or Muslim-inspired schools might themselves follow one day with respect to Christianity, if and when we have lost the hegemony?

Reverting to the five reasons I gave for Islamic successes in West Africa, there is nothing we Christians can do about points one and two save to teach our doctrines far more coherently than has been our wont. Trinitarian monotheists we are and remain. We cannot abandon belief in the Triune God without ignoring facts which have been persistently disclosed to the Church in the long history of its spiritual existence. Nor can we lower the ethical requirements, since they were not set by us but by God. If the severity of the divine imperative cracks our pride and drives us to the throne of grace, that is hard on our pride but good for our souls. The acknowledgement of sin opens the way for the discovery of the Saviour. Points one and two, then, stand fast.

Is there anything that can be done about point three – the problem posed by polygamy? Most churchmen, particularly those from monogamous cultures, say No. Frankly, I wonder.

I wonder what would have happened if the Apostle Paul had headed south instead of west? Would he – the author of what theologians call the *Privilegium Paulinum*) (cf. I Corinthians 7) – have been willing perhaps to offer in the special African situation some adaptation of the canon law respecting marriage?

What should the nineteenth-century missionaries from Europe and North America have done on arrival in Africa? Was it sensible of them to seek to introduce into a pre-Abrahamic type of culture a standard of marriage which required centuries for its emergence in the Judeo-Greco-Roman world, a standard which even on European and American soil – despite centuries of our being nurtured in the community of grace – is as much honoured in the breach as in the observance? Africans believe in simultaneous polygamy. Our preference, apparently, is for successive polygamy. But in this discussion, it matters not what our preferences and practises are. The one question at issue is: What does Christianity require? We approach it not as sociologists but as religionists. Only at our peril would we tinker with divine law. This recognition, however, does not rule out considerations of missionary strategy . . . and of compassion.

Go around the world asking, as I did, in polygamous societies this question: "If a polygamist, on hearing the Gospel preached, presents himself to you for Baptism, what do you say to him?" With the answers to this question I could fill a book. Here I can give only a few samples.

"We tell him to choose the wife he likes best and dismiss the others. Then we can baptize him." This was the cruellest, most callous of all the answers. *The wife he likes best.* That's male arrogance for you! What happens to a wife dismissed? What is her status in society? Will her family receive her back? And a fine opinion this family will have of a Christ who begins by breaking up a family and spurning a daughter whose sin it would be hard to define! What of the children born to her? Does she take them with her? In that case they are deprived of a father's love, just as she is deprived of a husband's love. And how, then, does she provide for them? Contrariwise, if they stay in the father's household, they are deprived of a mother's love and are at the mercy of a stepmother who may suddenly find herself cruelly overtaxed by having more children than she can handle. Can this, I demand, be a *Christian* solution to the problem? Can this be what *agapé*, the love God has shown us in Christ, requires?

Fortunately, I found not many Anglicans making so insensitive a reply to my question. Some answers were a shade better. For example: "The polygamist must take his first wife and show evidence that he has made financial provisions for the others. Then we can baptize." Certainly an improvement on the first answer I heard, but it still leaves many problems unsolved.

In some dioceses the Church will baptize a woman who is married to a man with several other wives. After all, the argument goes, *she* is the wife of but one man. So in her case there is no problem. Her husband, however, though he might be as sincerely moved to repentance and faith as she is, is excluded – unless he will divorce her, for it just happens that she is not his *first* wife.

The thing grows more fantastic as we go. One diocese disclaims responsibility by saying, in effect, "We will wash none of you polygamists with the waters of Baptism. It's just too complicated. So we'll explain to you the doctrine of 'Baptism by desire' – and we'll just hope that the whole matter gets sorted out eschatologically." In other words, the Church in time cannot help you – maybe in eternity God can.

I now invite your attention to a graduated scale. One diocese will baptize a polygamous man but will not confirm him or admit him to Communion. Another diocese will baptize and confirm but will not let him come to the altar. Still another diocese will baptize, confirm, and communicate him but disbars him from ever being a churchwarden! What kind of theology is this?

Not for a moment do I suggest that there is an easy solution. Nor am I suggesting that the Anglican Communion should have one, uniform, inflexible policy. Different localities may require different decisions. But I do submit that what I have been describing is chaos, and that the most perturbing aspect is that many Anglicans in positions of leadership fail even to recognize it as a problem.

In Anglican circles there are three basic attitudes. The first is: The early missionaries could have done no other than they did, and we can do no other. We must maintain without compromise the Christian standard of permanent, indissoluble monogamous marriage. Any other approach is unthinkable. The second is: It is easy to be wise after the event, but we can now see (without criticism of our predecessors) that they made a mistake. They should have incorporated polygamous families into the Church by Baptism and then have trained the children in the principles of monogamy. But the mistake was made. The die was cast. It is too late now to make any change. Change would only introduce confusion. The third is: How can it ever be too late to tackle a problem which has never really been tackled? But the third, as the reader will readily perceive, is a radical attitude. It can claim support only in minority circles. Moralists, legalists, and all other persons content with answers which exempt us from all need of thinking will have little difficulty in shouting the opposition down.

The Lambeth Conference of 1958 was notable, among other reasons, for its Report on the Family in Contemporary Society. It contained one brief paragraph which began with the words, "And now a word about polygamy." After the reading of the Report, a Nigerian bishop of noble mien rose to his feet and with a scorn and irony perfectly under control began, "And now a word about polygamy." With that he really let them have it. Doesn't the semimonogamous, semi-Christian world know that great parts of the earth are neither monogamous nor Christian? Is it not perhaps a dubious circumstance that most of the canon law respecting Holy Matrimony was written by celibates? Are celibates alone competent to legislate for married men? Has Christ no word for men who, long before they met him, took more than one wife in accordance with the time-honoured custom of their nation? And are women to have no say in the matter whatsoever?

It was a great moment. But it was lost; lost, as such moments always are. For the legalists are adept, as prophets are not, in swinging elections.

My question about the Church's relation to polygamy was usually allowed as "interesting but academic". "In point of fact," I was told, "the question seldom arises." But what can this mean? It means, I fear, that the Christian

Church in many parts of the world, West Africa among them, is engaged almost exclusively in ministering to *Christians*. We are speaking to converts of an earlier, more vigorous phase of evangelism and to their progeny. We are not making many new converts, new inroads. A church once was gathered. Now it settles back and consolidates itself. Outreach is slight.

I come back once again to the five points I listed in explanation of the allure of Islam for Africans. My fourth point had to do with nationalism. Mohammed and Nasser (with apologies to the former) are seen today as a perfect match. A religion can be used as a foil in helping to dislodge a hated overlord. It is a technicality beneath our notice that the overlord was not really so very hateful. It is also convenient to forget that Arabs proved their competence as businessmen by lucratively cramming the slave ships with human cargo. Remembered now in Africa is the sole fact that Arabs love black men and are at one with them in their desire for freedom.

What can the Church do to dispel the confusion which prevails in the African mind between imperialism and the Church, colonialism and Christianity? Not much. It is too late for effective action. This, however, does not leave us with nothing to do. If I were an Anglican Pope (things would go very well then!) I would take out of West Africa most of the English missionaries; I would replace them with Mexicans, Brazilians, Filipinos, Japanese, Melanesians, and Arabs. In this way I would try to show the Africans that Anglicanism is something more than, and something totally different from, the ecclesiastical arm of an imperial power. Incidentally, the Englishmen thus released would be dispatched to, for example, Mexico, where the Episcopal Church labours unjustifiably under the onus of being nothing more than a Yankee outfit.

With respect to point five, there is little more to do than strike the breast with a *"Mea culpa"*. Yet there *is* something we can do even short of the integration for which most Anglicans long. We can at least get the word around that Anglicans are exercised by the problem and are joined in the fight for racial justice. That the Church's position is clear and that the Church does battle is *not* widely known. Nigerians politely inquired where I would be heading after I left West Africa. When I told them South Africa, faces fell. Most West African Christians know nothing of our Church's heroic stand in the Union of South Africa. They suppose the Church down there is part and parcel of the whole South African setup, consenting to it all or at least raising no voice in protest. They listened incredulously to my recital of the facts. "Why has nobody told us these things before?" I was able, I think, to impart to more than a few West Africans a new confidence in their Church and a new pride.

The lines of communication between the various provinces of the Anglican Communion are shockingly skimpy. Not even the bishops are in frequent touch. The year 1958 was the first time in history that the Anglican bishops of Africa met for consultation. It wasn't that they had not *wanted* to meet long before that. There was no money. When one thinks of the problems these men have in common and of the advantages for the whole African Church that would come of their taking counsel together, one wonders if the Church can possibly *not* afford to make such gatherings possible. There are too many lonely bishops having to make difficult decisions in isolation. What strength it would give them if they had the encouragement of fellowship! They would be benefited if opportunity were given for testing their own thinking periodically in a company of their peers. They need, the Church needs, more opportunities for the *consensus fidelium* to come to expression.

Provinces are partly the answer. Yet even provincial Houses of Bishops are too seldom convened. And when, as in Africa, several provinces must wrestle with similar problems, the provinces require one another. Provinces are fine. They are indispensable working units of a group of dioceses. But with the coming of the aeroplane, even so huge a continent as Africa has shrunk. It is small enough and, in a sense, unified enough to be plagued, throughout its length and breadth, by exactly the same problems. My point is: If we have continental-sized problems, we need continent-wide gatherings of the bishops to cope with them.

Provinces are in no wise to be eliminated. But as the universe grows smaller, local problems become more universal. The Church must learn to take entire continents in its stride.

It is notorious that ecclesiastical provinces in the United States are something of a joke. They exist, eight of them. They meet on schedule, i.e. infrequently. The talk is usually good. Friendships are formed. But what actions can be taken? The synods have not the power to legislate. The result is that they are something of a bore. To ask a busy layman to serve as a delegate to the provincial synod is to exact of him a big sacrifice . . . to little purpose. This used to worry me. I once argued for the strengthening of the American provincial system – giving each province legislative power, gracing each of them with an archbishop. Yet I think that way no more. I think, rather, that America stumbled into an anticipation of the future. By accident, not by design, it anticipated the day when modern means of communication and transportation would render the provinces superfluous, an unnecessary piece of legislative machinery intermediate between the diocese and the national Church.

In other sections of the world the requirements were different and the development was different. Probably it is premature to be thinking about transcending provinces when we are still in the stage of forming them! Two provinces are yet to celebrate their second birthday! It was a supreme achievement in the direction of greater co-ordination that these were brought into being. The number of dangling dioceses has been greatly reduced. All to the good. But will it be good enough, unified enough, for the future?

I have strayed from West Africa, but it was there that I first began giving serious thought to what a province is – because I was troubled by the fact that Liberia does not belong to the Province of West Africa, for reasons I fail to grasp. Liberia is a Missionary District of the Protestant Episcopal Church. It has historic ties with the United States, for to it went many emancipated slaves from America, just as slaves emancipated in the West Indies went to Sierra Leone. Sentiment, as well as a sense of loyalty to the Church which reared it, may dictate Liberia's clinging to the American Church and resisting the many friendly overtures from the Province. The Province is a bit too "English" in its ways to suit Liberians accustomed to American "get up and go", not to mention American dollars. But why should the flow of these dollars have to dry up if Liberia were to join the Province? There lurks at the back of my mind the thought that where American dollars go, American control would like to follow. This is not an unreasonable attitude on the part of Americans. Churchmen should see to it that funds raised at home are responsibly used abroad. But I have a theory about that too. It seems to me that if you give money to something – a church, a school, a cause – you should give the money, not in order to control the enterprise, but because you trust the people at the head.

I have another theory. The American Church has a bad conscience about the fact that it has done almost nothing in Africa. Therefore it is loath to surrender the one tiny piece of African work it can claim. From one point of view, this bad conscience is founded in no actual guilt. After all, the Church of England said in effect (and quite properly), "There must be a division of labour. Africa falls to us. You Americans take other parts of the world as your missionary responsibility." That is why we went elsewhere: to Central and South America, to the non-British parts of the West Indies, to Alaska and Hawaii, to the Philippines, Japan, and China. Except for Liberia, Africa was to be Britain's responsibility. That was the understanding – and not a bad *modus operandi* for the time in which the agreement was made. Things are different today. An England battered and impoverished by the catastrophes of this century, an England shorn of much of her Empire, now recognizes, with infinite humility, that from a missionary point of view England has bitten off more than she can chew. No guilt attaches to the English in this respect. History has not dealt kindly with Great Britain in our times. But in spite of all she has suffered, she still runs circles around the opulent United States of America when giving to missions. Ours is a paltry performance by comparison. It is not to her shame, therefore, that she must now look to us for help with the many missions she launched in Africa. The American Episcopal Church need have a bad conscience *only* if she does not respond heroically to this appeal. Our response should not take the form of trying to take over the management. No, leave that to the British. They have the experience which we lack. Our task is to put men and money at their disposal and let them deploy them – because they can be trusted.

Two sharp warnings, however, to the Church of the Province of West Africa: First, American Episcopalians, by and large, do not take kindly and do not give generously to churches in which the Cup is denied to the laity (this I found in one cathedral church in West Africa); and second, their charity and generosity are in short supply when they learn of a large church in a major West African city where there is no celebration of the Lord's Supper on Christmas Day unless the Feast falls on a Sunday.

Warnings such as this betray, I suppose, the incurable disease of wanting to control. On the other hand, I see no call upon us to encourage ecclesiastical eccentricity.

I ramble. It is because I have such a wealth of impressions that I do not know how to marshal them in proper order. Yet perhaps my very lack of methodology, my helter-skelter presentation, may succeed – better than any systematic treatment – in conveying a notion of how overwhelming Africa is, how variegated, how kaleidoscopic. I tell you nothing about landscapes, little about politics. Other books can do that for you. I tell you only something about one small Church – one among many – and even that is more complicated than I can deal with adequately. But the Church is people. It is of them I write.

First, there is the Lord Bishop of Gambia and the Rio Pongas. I begin with this rugged Irishman solely because he was the first bishop in Africa I met. Dressed in white duck shorts and shirts with soft collars, we went for a drive inland in the Land Rover. The country was quite wild. Suddenly, about a hundred feet ahead of us, down the rutted road, there emerged from the bush the first African I had seen whom Hollywood would even consider for a part in its next Tarzan picture. By his attire – or, rather, virtual lack of it – the Bishop knew he could not be from these parts. He had a bandana to cover his head and a breechclout to take care of the rest of him. He was carrying a spear, a smoking flax, and a kind of hula hoop. The hoop was to enable him to shinny up the trees. The flax was for smoking out the bees so that the honey could be gathered. (See Pl. 11.)

The Bishop, having alighted from the car, tried several dialects out on him; when these availed nothing, the Bishop's steward brought his linguistic skills into play, but with no greater success. All we could make out was that the unclad searcher for honey was far, far from home. The Bishop then said, "Christian? *Chrétien?*" and put the question in several African dialects. The man looked blank. The Bishop then made the Sign of the Cross upon himself and folded his hands in an attitude of prayer. A broad smile irradiated the face of the African, who promptly threw down the spear, the flax, and the hoop, took off the bandana, made the Sign of the Cross in return, dropped to his knees, and folded his hands. This was but my second day in Africa, and I was not yet accustomed to strange meetings in bush and jungle. It moved me indescribably that these two strangers, unable to converse, should be able to recognize each other by means of the Sign of the Cross. We said the Lord's Prayer in English. The Bishop gave his blessing. The man picked up the tools of his trade, gave a smile which melted my heart, waved his farewell, and disappeared into the bush. "I'll never see him again," I said sadly as we drove away. "Oh, but you *will!*" said the Bishop. "In heaven!"

I later told of this encounter in an exceedingly Low Church West African diocese. When I noticed that it visibly affected my hearers I added, with a touch of malice, I fear, "But of course it couldn't happen here; you people don't make the Sign of the Cross."

This malicious streak in me has a way of cropping out occasionally. When in that same Diocese Anglicans taxed me again and again with the charge that Christianity, after all, is a *Western* religion, and that because it is so Western we just can't expect it to make much headway in places like Africa, I retorted, "Western? Where was Christ born? And from what quarter do we expect his reappearing? And why do you suppose," queried I, hoping thereby to clinch my argument, "that we turn to the East for the Creed?" I thought that this last sally was an inspired bit of *ad hominem* argumentation, but all my cleverness failed of its effect: in that diocese nobody turns to the East!

Something happened in Liberia which I would like to record. Transportation is not easy in that land. In the time I could give to Liberia it was clearly impossible for me to visit both our Cuttington College and the Mission at Bolahun which is conducted by the monks of the Order of the Holy Cross. Yet the Bishop was determined that I should see both. At the merest hint from him, the Lutheran Mission sent its plane and flew me gratis from the one Anglican institution to the other. We landed by permission on the Baptist Mission's airstrip. I was picked up by a Roman Catholic who for the purpose had borrowed a car from the Methodist Mission. This is what I call "applied ecumenics".

I saw many examples of it in the mission fields where, somehow, the problems of Church Unity do not loom quite so large as they do when argued in plush offices in New York, London, Berlin, Geneva, and Rome. Christians of all kinds were good to me everywhere, interested in my errand, eager to assist me.

The next two stories are told because they illuminate our problems and should alert us to dangers.

Christians at the Holy Cross Mission at Bolahun,* in the isolation of their situation, knew only one type of Churchmanship – that which had been taught them by monks. It was High Church. Word reached the mission some years ago that preparation should be made for the arrival of the new Bishop of Liberia. He was Low Church. The monks of the Order of the Holy Cross, with instinctive good taste, wanted to arrange for the new Bishop a reception in which he would feel comfortable. Hence, the monks spoke to the villagers and said, "When the Bishop gets here, don't genuflect and don't kiss his ring." (For all the monks knew, the Bishop might not even be wearing a ring.) This, I say, proceeded solely from good taste and charity. In all their thoughtfulness, however, the Fathers overlooked one thing. They did not explain to the people that the new Bishop was a Negro. It never occurred to the monks to mention any such thing, for a bishop is a bishop – who cares about his race? Then it happened. The Bishop came. The villagers looked upon him, then muttered to themselves, "Ah, ha! You don't bow down to a black bishop. Only to a white one."

This is a sickening story. Should the Bishop and the monks who figure in the episode chance to read my account of it, I know they will take no offence. We are dealing not with personalities but with problems. If Africans are sensitive about race, the whites who would minister in their midst must be, if anything, more sensitive still.

I match that story with another. The Bishop of Accra, vested in cope and mitre, wearing a pectoral cross and an episcopal ring, and holding a crozier, was catechizing a group of Ghanaian children. He had come as far as "What orders of Ministers are there in the Church?" and had been given the proper answer. Then, departing from the Prayer Book's printed page, he

* The Bolahun Mission is one of forty evangelistic centres maintained by the Order of the Holy Cross, founded in New York in 1881, the first religious order for men of the American Church. The Holy Cross Fathers also have a hospital and seven schools in Liberia, continuing work begun in 1922 and greatly strengthened in 1925 when one of its members, Father Robert Campbell, became Missionary Bishop of Liberia. Work among the native women and girls is directed by the Sisters of St. Helena, an American order of nuns who observe the Holy Cross rule.

asked, "Now, children, how can you tell, by looking at me, that I am a bishop?" A little ebony hand shot up in the back row, and the answer came, "Because, sir, you're a white man."

Let nobody suppose that I enjoy telling stories like these. There is pain concealed in these anecdotes. But a kind of humour there is too, and I pray that one day, if not already, we may all be mature enough to laugh a little at the mistakes we have made, and still keep making, white and black alike, in our dealings with each other. When one hardly knows whether to laugh or weep, it is usually better to laugh – for it is not an unkind laugh. It is a laugh that makes bearable the bitterness of repentance and can perhaps clear the decks for action.

Nothing entertained me more in West Africa than the way in which one Nigerian bishop introduced me to his clergy. There I stood, pallid as usual, and there he stood with forty of his priests, all splendidly black. "Now, Americans are largely ignorant about the Anglican Communion," he said, "so Canon Johnson is being sent around the world to write a simple book that Americans can be expected to understand." Charming, charming! And how right he was! We understand, in fact, *nothing* about the Anglican Communion until we have been grasped by the wonder that God has wrought. Some of the priests who sat before me that morning in Nigeria had ritual scars upon their faces. Others had pierced ears where rings had been. Some were tattooed from head to foot. Yet these were the men who, besides coming to hear me, were met that day to discuss how more effectively to use radio and television for proclaiming to West Africa the Gospel of Christ. (See Pl. 27.)

We begin remotely to understand the Anglican Communion when we begin to glory in the fact that these people, who look so unlike us, are the brothers of whom Christ has made us a present, that they need us, and that we need them.

4

SOUTH AFRICA: A Land Turned in upon Itself

IF WEST AFRICANS NEEDED TO BE TOLD THAT ANGLICANS IN
South Africa have distinguished themselves in the struggle against the racial
injustices of their present government, then many other parts of the Anglican
World need reassurance on quite a different point.

Names like Scott, Huddleston, Reeves, and de Blank have been so
conspicuous in the world Press that it has occurred to more than one
Episcopalian to ask: "Is race the only thing that these fellows can think
about?"

Let us have a look at the record. In the ten years that Ambrose Reeves
was permitted to be Bishop of Johannesburg, seventy new churches were
constructed in his Diocese. This one fact should suffice. In other words, the
work of the Church in the whole of South Africa has been going patiently
forward. Old work has been consolidated, new work begun. The Word is
preached, the Sacraments are duly administered. The pastors tend their
flocks. Schools are operating. Hospitals carry on. Orphans and children
from broken homes are cared for. The iniquities of apartheid have been
fought with prophetic zeal and sacrifice but without detriment to the other
tasks which the Church is there to perform.

That enemies were made has to be admitted. A principal Capetown
newspaper, for example, in January, 1960, could get itself into such a rage
that it emblazoned across the front page a two-inch headline reading: "THE
ARCHBISHOP SHOULD BE HANGED." It should, I think, encourage us
that in our secular, indifferentist age, archbishops and their opinions can still
create as much stir as that.

To suggest the stature of Ambrose Reeves, the now exiled Bishop of
Johannesburg, it is perhaps sufficient to say that he saw to it, the second
night of my stay in his Diocese, that I should dine with a prominent layman,
owner of a mine, who happened not at all to share his Bishop's views on

problems of race. A lesser man would have surrounded me with "Yes-men".
Dr. Reeves deliberately exposed me to his opposition.

My host, I hasten to remark, was not an English Dr. Verwoerd. He was a
man whose conscience had long been pricked by the Anglican Church of
which he is a loyal communicant. As such, he had laboured hard, against
stubborn resistance, to better the housing conditions of mine workers. His
great desire was to increase salaries and to improve health and insurance
benefits. But he was revolted by the thought of fraternization. Put another
way: he sincerely desired that Africans should have better houses, but he did
not want them in *his* house – except, of course, as minions. In a beautiful
drawing-room we had come as far as after-dinner coffee. The conversation
had taken a serious turn. "Yes, I know," he said, "there's something wrong
about my racial attitudes. But for the life of me, I can't help it. I imbibed it,
as it were, with my mother's milk. Wrong it may be, and I realize it is
irrational, but I just couldn't accept the Cup from a black hand." This
from a devout churchman who, unaware of a dramatic coincidence then
happening, was receiving at that moment a cup of coffee from a black hand.
It scandalized me that he even talked this way in the presence of an African
domestic. Essentially, so far as his consciousness was concerned, the black
butler was not even present. But if coffee from a black hand, why not the
Chalice? Had I not been a coward, and a guest mindful of my manners,
I might have ventured to point out the incongruity.

Going back to my hotel, I thought of all the lectures I have given on
Original Sin.

South Africa, beautiful and tormented land, helps me to understand
what idolatry is. It is a land turned in upon itself. It is a land that, all
unconscious of what it was doing, has absolutized itself. A South African of
English descent, one of the finest human beings you ever met, will say to
you, "But you, as a foreigner, have had no experience of a multiracial
culture, and therefore you cannot possibly understand our situation." With
variations, this was said to me sixty times while I was in South Africa. The
real tenor of white South African speech is: "Our situation is so unique, so
unparalleled, that nothing in Holy Scripture, nothing in philosophy, nothing
in the experience of the rest of the human race is relevant to our problems,
nothing can shed light on our path." In other words, we must be a law unto
ourselves. But this is idolatry. It is not wicked exactly. It is not calculated
or wilfully pernicious. It is just tragically mistaken.

I would not let pass unchallenged, however, the allegation that I had
had no experience of a multiracial culture. "May I remind you," I said,
"that I come from a city named New York? It happens to be the largest
Jewish city in the world. Since the destruction of Warsaw, more Jews live

in New York than in any other city in the world. Their numbers exceed the population of Israel itself. It is one of the principal Spanish-speaking cities in the world. Spanish is the mother tongue of eight hundred thousand New Yorkers. From Cathedral Heights I overlook Harlem wherein dwell more people of African descent than in the whole of Johannesburg. Newspapers are published every week in my town in nineteen languages and many more foreign language newspapers are imported. When you ride in the subway you see the people jammed side by side, some reading their newspapers from left to right, some from right to left, some up and down. And they all get along fairly well. If you stand on the steps of the Cathedral Church of St. John the Divine and draw a circle thirty miles in diameter you will encompass an area in which dwell more human beings than the total population of your tremendous country. So don't tell me, please, that I've had no experience of a multiracial, multicultural society." This was intended as a conversation-stopper, the "perfect squelch", and usually it had this effect.

Yet, with all that said, it has to be admitted that the American racial problem is a simple matter compared to that which faces South Africa. To begin with, American whites are a secure majority; in South, Central and East Africa the whites are not. I must tell you also that it took me nearly five months in Africa to learn a lesson so elementary that you will blush for me when I announce it. It finally began to dawn on me that the African African is *not* an American Negro. The American Negro was never very advantageously exposed to European-American culture, but at least he was exposed to it. The result of that exposure was to make of him a being far more sophisticated than his African cousin, a person far better equipped to function in a mechanized, industrialized society, a citizen far more prepared to vote intelligently. I went to Africa expecting to meet hordes of people like the American Negroes I gladly receive in my home. I did not imagine that the Africans would all be Ralph Bunches or Marian Andersons or even postulants who could successfully apply for admission to the seminaries of the Episcopal Church. Yet it came as a surprise to find, in many places, people whose language I could not speak, whose food I could not safely eat, and who were so painfully shy that they could not be put at ease in my presence.

In the United States, all residents are Americans, whatever their race. In South Africa, a white man refers to himself as a "European"; only the black man is an "African". In America there are instances of friction and shameful discrimination, but we all acknowledge that all of us are here to stay and that, although it will take a lot of working out, we have a common destiny. In South Africa, the common destiny is denied and the battle is on to see which race can outstay the other.

I interrupt my discourse to tell two stories.

South Africa defaces its parks, as it does everything else (except the cash registers), with two sets of everything: drinking fountains, lavatories, park benches. Everything is clearly labelled "Blacks Only", "Europeans Only" – so that nobody may suffer the embarrassment of making a mistake. The aggressive American Bishop of West Virginia was to address the Rotary Club of Johannesburg. He was late and apologized for his tardiness by saying, "But you see, I lost five minutes looking for the non-European entrance to this building."

When Dr. Malan was Prime Minister of South Africa he was received in Buckingham Palace. It was a small party, as informal as things ever can be in the presence of majesty. The Queen herself (now the Queen Mother) was pouring out after-dinner coffee. "How will you have your coffee, Dr. Malan?" "Sweet and pure, Ma'am," he answered fatuously, "like our South African maidens." "White or black, Dr. Malan?" came back the acid and regal retort. As with many a good story, this is probably apocryphal – something too good to be true. But I believe that Her Majesty the Queen Mother was fully capable of such a barbed rejoinder. And it was deserved.

South Africa is hung on a dreadful, multiple cross. It is split many ways. The first split is between the whites themselves. There are the English-speaking whites and the Afrikaans-speaking whites. Nice people both, but apparently never the twain shall meet. Business concerns occasionally oblige them to speak to each other, but that, except on the very highest levels of society, is the end of it. Only sophisticates, it would seem, can refrain from fighting the Boer War over again. That is the first tragic split.

Next, each of these white groups is tragically split within itself. The speakers of English range in racial attitudes all the way from the courageous liberalism of their Archbishop to the reactionary bigotry of a Verwoerd. But the Afrikaners are similarly split. The Dutch Reformed Church has long since ceased, by tortured exegesis of the Scriptures, to find a theological justification for apartheid, and many of its leaders have spoken out boldly against the policy of the government in power. Moreover, many university professors of Dutch extraction have declared their unalterable opposition to the whole business on which Verwoerd & Company are so intent. So there are two white groups, mutually antagonistic, at war within themselves.

Now we come to the next tragic split. In South Africa it is nothing so simple as a two-way split between blacks and whites. There is a triple split: black, white, and coloured. "Coloured" in South African nomenclature is a technical term for persons of mixed race. The mixture may be anything. It could be English-African, Dutch-African, Indian-African, Chinese-African or any other possible combination. For purposes of law it has now been ruled that pure-blooded Indians and pure-blooded Chinese shall also be reckoned as "Coloured". The "Coloureds" are the persons most to be pitied in South Africa. They fall with a thud between two stools and get the worst of both worlds. To them come neither the benefits of being white nor the benefits of being black. They get no benefits at all. In a place like South Africa they know not, from day to day, what their fate the next day will be. Of all peoples, they are the most precariously poised. Blacks woo their political support, yet despise them. The whites woo them too, and likewise despise them. The picture is not pretty.

This brings us to another tragic split. The black Africans are not themselves united. They are divided by all manner of tribal feuds, jealousies, and enmities whose origins I could not trace even if I had the heart to. These differences – cultural, linguistic, historical – have been a comfort to the régime in power. The most has been made of ancient rivalries by a government whose prime design is to prevent African unity. Apartheid, I learned, does not mean simply that whites live in one neighbourhood and blacks in another. It means that one black tribe lives here, a second black tribe lives there, and a third somewhere else. Divide and conquer! This policy has worked before. The government is counting on its working now.

The whole story has not yet been told. The blacks are also divided between the tribalized and the detribalized. A city-bred, detribalized African takes tea with me in Capetown from eggshell-thin cups, and later in the day he is quite particular about the ingredients which shall go into the making of a dry Martini. Yet five days later, out on a Bantu reserve, I am sitting on a cow-dung-packed floor in a wattle-and-daub hut, eating with my fingers out of the same dishes with other South Africans. It is easier for me to make this abrupt transition than it would be for him. I was trained for it. He was not. The African reared in Capetown, Johannesburg, or Durban is no more at home or at ease on a native reservation than a Manhattan man-about-town would be among American Indians cooped up in South Dakota. To this we must add one more factor: the split between the educated and the uneducated. The educated African, no less a sinner than the rest of us, sometimes exploits his uneducated African brother unmercifully.

These are the multiple splits, the cross on which South Africa is hung. Had I understood all this earlier, some of my "prophetic" sermons would not have been preached, some of my fiery utterances would have been tempered. For all of which I still would have combated apartheid as something of the devil.

It is an instance of the Church being the *Church* – fearless but not fanatical – when it authorizes its Archbishop and Metropolitan (who at that time was Dr. Clayton) to dispatch the following letter:

Dear Mr. Prime Minister:

We Bishops of the Church of the Province of South Africa are approaching you rather than the Minister of Native Affairs because we believe that the issues raised in Clause 29 (c) of the Native Laws Amendment Bill cannot be regarded merely as Native Affairs. . . .

The Church cannot recognize the right of an official of the secular Government to determine whether or where a member of the Church of any race (who is not serving a sentence which restricts his freedom of movement) shall discharge his religious duty of participation in public worship, or to give instructions to the Minister of any congregation as to whom he shall admit to membership of that congregation.

Further, the Constitution of the Church of the Province of South Africa provides for the synodical government of the Church. In such synods, Bishops, Priests and Laymen, are represented without distinction of race or colour. Clause 29 (c) makes the holding of such synods dependent on the permission of the Minister of Native Affairs.

We recognize the gravity of disobedience to the law of the land. We believe that obedience to secular authority, even in matters about which we differ in opinion, is a command laid on us by God. But we are commanded to render unto Caesar the things which be Caesar's, and to God the things that are God's.

There are therefore some matters which are God's and not Caesar's, and we believe that the matters dealt with in Clause 29 (c) are among them.

It is because we believe this that we feel bound to state that if the Bill were to become law in its present form, we should ourselves be unable to obey it or to counsel our clergy and people to do so.

We therefore appeal to you, Sir, not to put us in a position in which we have to choose between obeying our conscience and obeying the law of the land.

A temperate but not temporizing document like this can give an Anglican, whatever his race and wherever he may reside, reason for pride in his Church. It takes nothing away from that pride to find in Capetown that the notice board in front of the Cathedral Church reads: "This Cathedral is open to welcome all men and women of all races to all services at all times."

Sober realism, however, requires us to acknowledge that not all services can be integrated. It is magnificent, as an act of witness, that great diocesan services are held occasionally in which members of all races are present. But by the nature of things, this cannot be a steady Sunday diet. Since Anglicanism rightly believes that the liturgy must be in a language "understanded of the people", different language groups have to worship apart – at least normally. There are geographical considerations too. Since the present government of South Africa has shunted people about to such an extent that nobody of one race lives near anybody of another race, worshipping together is out of the question. The black African simply has not the price of a bus ticket to carry him into the vicinity of a white African church, and only with difficulty can the white African with his car obtain a pass to enter the African township.

I must now make a confession about the most criminal Sunday I ever put in. From the comforts of Bishopscourt in a beautiful suburb of Capetown (the Archbishop's house had been the gubernatorial mansion in Dutch days), I was driven by limousine to an African housing development (the name of which has figured prominently in the world press since the time of my visit). It was quite illegal that I should be there, but with six hundred Africans I assisted at a flawless celebration of the Holy Eucharist in a language whose explosively glottal "clicks" nearly blew me against the east wall. Afterwards I ate with the priest and his leading laymen – a procedure forbidden by law. In the late afternoon I was taken to Evensong at a church in District 6, a coloured section of Capetown, a hotbed· of restlessness, famous or infamous – depending on your point of view. On the statute books, I had no right to be there, but not for the world would I have missed that big-hearted, big-voiced outpouring of prayer.

The service over, I felt the pangs of hunger. But where does one eat on a Sunday evening in Capetown? English-inspired Sabbatarianism and unionism being what they are, hotels and restaurants are all shut down. The Archbishop's Chaplain and I canvassed the field diligently, consulting the Directory's Yellow Pages and making several telephone calls in vain. Finally we saw that the alternative was either to eat illegally or else go to bed hungry. We elected illegality. This took us to a splendid Indian restaurant where by law we had no right to be. Fortunately, we dined undetected.

Then we decided to pay a mid-evening call on an Indian Christian. He and his wife received us kindly. To celebrate our arrival they produced a bottle of Scotch. Here was a double illegality: by law they were not supposed to be in possession of liquor, and by law they were forbidden to drink with "Europeans". But this was a Sunday in which lawlessness was rampant, so drink we did, discussing all the while the socially unacceptable topics of politics and religion. I fancy I have a way with children, and it pleased me that the four-year-old daughter of the house had taken something of a liking to me. When she came in to bid her parents good-night with a kiss, she also came up to me – and in an excess of sheer affection, to include me in the family circle, she climbed on my lap and gravely planted a kiss on my cheek. My Indian host, handsome father of this adorable child, chuckled quietly. "You realize," he admonished me with restrained bitterness, "that you have just broken the Immorality Act." Thus ended the most illegal, the most criminal of all my Sundays.

Facts I could give you, statistics and graphs, in the approved sociological manner. I cling, however, to the notion that my confession of a single day's criminality in Capetown may be a superior medium for conveying to the outside world an impression of how insane the whole South African picture is.

Frequently I found myself wondering how the clergy who are not South African born are able to stick it out. I have tremendous admiration for the Church of the Province of South Africa. How so small a Church could have accomplished so much! The patience and the dedication required to go on working when she is hemmed in on every side with crippling regulations! The urge to wash one's hands of the whole business and go home must be a daily temptation. Outsiders should try to think of the situation in the alto-gether human terms of a cleric who has his wife and children to consider. Dare a Christian expose his children to the contaminations of such a culture? Or his wife to the uncertainties of such a future? Yet, with clerical stipends what they are, he cannot afford to send the children to England for schooling. Nor can he guarantee his wife security tomorrow.

Imagine a white priest not allowed to enter an African location to attend the ordination of a deacon, his friend. Yes, the Bishop could go in, for police officials understood that without a bishop there can be no ordination. The presence of an extra priest, however, could not be said to be essential. Of course this refusal of permission was the result of an office error. Papers had not come through on time. In such cases, after due application, permission is normally granted. But just that it should be necessary to seek such per-mission! – this is South Africa today.

Apartheid will not last for ever. Someday South Africa will come back to itself and come back into the community of nations from which it has alien-ated itself, and the Anglican Church will have had an honourable role in helping restore a nation to sanity. Yet it is not the Church, not the university, not even humanitarianism, that will have been the chief agent in the restoration. That which will break apartheid eventually is big business, the irrecusable facts of high finance. South African economy cannot prosper without a supply of cheap African labour. A benevolent government moves these Africans far from town, far from the factories and the mines. The houses it builds for them are far superior – let it be conceded – to the slums from which they were forcibly evacuated. And the rents, by English and American standards, are fantastically cheap. Yet they are high for the African – and he has no choice in the matter – and so much of his pay check must go out in rent that the breakfast he eats is skimpy. New African housing units, the pride of the government, mushroom everywhere, but the transportation system has not kept pace with this development. Thus, vitamin-deficient, calorie-starved labourers stand for hours in line for the bus or train that is late in coming or else hike or cycle to the distant place of employment. They are tired and hungry when they get there. As such, they are not good producers. Efficiency is lowered. Nor are they good consumers: when the rent is paid they have not much left over for anything else. South Africa's African millions are a marvellous potential market for secondary industry, but that industry can barely move so long as Africans have little in their pockets and still less in their bellies. All of this, in addition to the growing contempt of the world and the scepticism of international high finance, leaves its mark on the Johannesburg stock exchange and affects adversely the inflow of foreign capital. A government that will not bow to God may presently have to bow to Mammon – but it will be bowing to God none the less, in spite of itself. For God is not stymied. If the Church cannot accomplish God's will, he wields a Rod of Assyria, or else raises up a Cyrus to do it for him. Not all South Africans recognize that apartheid is evil, but an increasing number of men of money are willing to say: It just will not work.

Meanwhile, there is nothing for the Church to do but bear its witness sanely against an insane régime and continue peaceably its works of charity, education, and healing. Of these works the Church of the Province of South Africa has many. Having climbed the steps of I know not how many schools, and after having inspected every ward and test tube of countless hospitals, I can testify that the Church in South Africa has reason for humble pride. But if the day of deliverance should be long delayed, and if in the meanwhile the government should turn more repressive than it already is, I think I should register my conviction that the work of the Church in the Protectorates is of supreme importance. I refer now to Bechuanaland, Basutoland, Swaziland, and other parts of the Church of this Province which politically are not included in the South African Republic. They are important in their own right, of course, but if things should take a turn for the worse in South Africa – and we should be prepared for that – the best possible preparation for the future is to make ourselves strong in the adjacent Protectorates. Here a Church frozen out of South Africa might consolidate itself for a renewed approach to South Africa as soon as the thaw sets in.

Swaziland was the only one of the Protectorates I was privileged to visit. I speak, therefore, only of it – in accordance with my strict policy of not describing what I have not seen and of not trying to explain more than I have understood. The moment you cross the border into Swaziland you can sense the difference. The air is no longer charged with the acrid scent of impending catastrophe. Public buildings have only one entrance, and everybody may enter by the same door. Even in the best restaurants, you may eat with whom you wish, and nobody thinks it strange that whites and blacks might enjoy each other's company.

Big things are afoot. The Usuthu, largest river south of the Zambesi, is soon to be dammed and put to work for irrigating the fertile soil and for generating hydroelectric power. Iron has been discovered. Pulp mills are being built. Gigantic projects of reforestation are in process in the high veldt. In 1960, when I was there, the bulldozers were busy. Today the main new tarred road goes right past our Usuthu Mission. British companies are investing heavily in agriculture, lumbering, and mining – all the more so now that economic prospects for South Africa are uncertain. The future will bring an increased population and better living conditions. Forewarned by the unhappy experiences of the Rhodesias, British companies are determined to employ white *and* black skilled workers right from the start. But where are the black ones to be found? Few are available, and Swaziland has not a single technical high school. Big business looks hopefully towards the Church. Could we not expand our already existing schools? And big business is smart enough, self-regarding enough, to be willing to pitch in and help us, if only we were in a position to move. But we are not. We can barely maintain the work already begun. If our effort were but a shade more imposing, more confidence-inspiring, we would have big business on our side.

What is it that we have at Usuthu at the head of the Malkerns Valley? For one thing we have a primary school just short of four hundred pupils, plus seven more schools in outlying districts with a total enrolment of about fourteen hundred children. We also have a secondary school, St. Christopher's, with slightly more than a hundred boys enrolled. All of this is the work of but ten years. (A crying need, by the way, is a secondary school for girls. I suspect that African women, in the long run, when once they are educated, will do more to raise African standards than will their menfolk.) The fees St. Christopher's charges are certainly moderate, but even so it requires heroic sacrifice on the part of Swaziland and South African parents to have their sons trained there. Grants from the British Government help. And now aid has appeared in the form of an annual subsidy from a voluntary American association called Episcopal Churchmen for South Africa. All very fine. But still there is a deficit. For the next few years the sledding will be tough for the school until the financial situation of Swaziland is sufficiently improved, as it will be, to make possible the charging of more realistic fees. By 1965 the school will almost certainly be able to pull its own weight. But can it survive the intervening years?

Remember, if you please, the Usuthu Mission in your prayers, but you cannot remember it with sufficient intensity unless you know that it is manned by five priests – all unmarried, for who here can afford matrimonial bliss? – who live ascetically, teach the children, manage a 250-acre farm to keep the pupils from going hungry, and minister to the spiritual needs of people in twenty-eight outstations. Include in your prayers, too, the Lancashire layman whose episcopate, whose overseership, involves no mitre other than skill with the indispensable tool which carpenters call a mitre. This excellent man excels in carpentry, in making concrete blocks, in designing earth closets. He is but one of the hundreds of laymen I met for whom the only adequate characterization is the English phrase "total Christian". A clergyman myself, I have the arrogance of my Order. I sometimes think that the clergy *are* the Church. It comes as a salutary reminder to reflect that the Church is 98 per cent laity. The Church's Mission is not carried out by priests alone. The better part of it is done by laymen in possession of such difficult and useful skills as that of medicine, nursing, teaching, printing, architecture, boat-building, carpentry, and plumbing. In Swaziland I met a layman who for the glory of God builds latrines. For him, God be praised.

I try to fall as seldom as possible into clichés. But will the reader forgive this lapse? The Usuthu Mission shines as a beacon. Clergy and laity, black and white, living together, praying together, fighting like mad sometimes and working like mad always: if that isn't the Church, then I don't know what the Church is. The sole check on my optimism is that they are so few among so many.

Also from a medical standpoint Swaziland is strategic. In South Africa itself, schools are more and more being taken out of the Church's hands. Church hospitals may be the next to go. If the schools go, where are African leaders in Church and State to come from? If the hospitals go, where are doctors and nurses to come from? If Dr. Verwoerd has his way, English will be as well understood in Bantu schools as French is by an English schoolboy.

In a hundred African places I asked about hospitals. Is it an area in which the Anglican Church should be involved? A useful missionary strategy, perhaps, in a bygone age, but one that the Church might be well advised to abandon at the present time, since governments are increasingly taking over?

The answers I received are not without interest.

Christian hospitals there yet must be, was the majority answer, provided we do not look upon them primarily as "conversion mills" – factories where the patient goes in heathen and sick and comes out Christian and well. The success or failure of the Christian hospital is not to be measured in terms of the number of converts it can produce. The Christian hospital exists, first of all, in obedience to a command of its Lord: "Heal the sick." The blind must see, the deaf must hear, the halt must walk – and we are not to be overconcerned if only one in ten returns to give glory to God. God is glorified in health, even if no one remembers to give thanks. Healing is a sign that the Messianic Age is breaking in, the Kingdom is coming. The Church must mediate the healing power of God, whether it results in conversions or not. That is the first thing to say.

A second, less loftily theological thing to say is that Christian hospitals represent more adequately than do most secular hospitals in Africa "honest medicine". That is, Christian nurses and doctors are not out for money. Their acts of mercy point not to the superstitious but to the supernatural. The patient pays for what he gets. He is not rooked. Actually he gets, from a medical standpoint, far more than he pays for. The Church hospital does not exploit his illness. And the crucifix above his bed points him to a motivation which is new in his experience. I would remark here, in passing, that Anglican hospitals deserve special commendation for their not taking advantage of a sick person's debility and "low threshold" to foist upon him the religion of his doctor. The Gospel is offered, not imposed. Beyond that, the Christian hospital produces a type of nurse the African has never known before. She has more than hygiene and scientific "know-how" (which the patient understands most imperfectly); she has something the simplest patient recognizes and gives thanks for at once: the quality of compassion. That which mission hospitals cannot rival in technical excellence, in competition with government hospitals, is more than offset by the gentleness and integrity the Christians supply. (See Pl. 25.)

There is, in addition, a fourth factor. Christian hospitals – of which the Charles Johnson Memorial Hospital at Nqutu in Zululand is an outstanding example – make their greatest witness simply by the example of their corporate existence. They exhibit a community in which people of different races pray, work, and eat together, enjoying each other's company and discovering that, after all, people are pretty much alike – a community of doctors, nurses, orderlies, laundresses, cooks, gardeners, all intent on ministering in Christ's Name to the sufferings of mankind. Such a communal life is a visible manifestation of Christ's power to break down the middle wall of partition. If a Church builds just another hospital, there is not much point in that. Such work might better be left to secular agencies. But if the staff of a Christian hospital can actually live together as a Christian fellowship, then truly this is a sign that the kingdom is beginning to appear. (See Pl. 24.)

Dr. Anthony Barker, who is in charge of the Charles Johnson Memorial

Hospital, enriched Ash Wednesday of 1960 for me by obliging me to reflect along the following lines. Inescapably, the white man in Africa is "able to do good". He has the education, the techniques, and the money to found schools and hospitals. This separates him from the black man and casts him in the role of a "do-gooder" . . . from a "superior" standpoint, even if he seeks personal communion with the people of the land. Add to this the fact that he is white, cannot ride in the same bus, cannot go to the same cinema with even his African medical colleague; add further the distance created by his different background and his superior training. The sum of our addition is that, even in the very act of literally doing good, he is resented. However humble and modest he may be, however desirous he is of identifying himself with this people, his very power to confer a *benefaction* alienates him from the people, for the benefaction itself, though thankfully received, comes as an unwelcome reminder of inadequacy on the part of the recipient. It is not easy to be perpetually on the receiving end. White missionaries have not always understood the inevitability of their being both loved and resented. But this *can* be understood by the white man and must be borne as part of the price of his being there at all.

I hope I have correctly reported the gist of Dr. Barker's conversation, for it leads up to an important point. The justification for mission hospitals (as distinct from government hospitals) is that they do create levels of personal communion. The white doctors and nurses may be prevented by law from eating together with their black counterparts at a public restaurant, but they do eat together at the same altar and at an *agape*-like breakfast in the staff dining-room afterwards. In such ways, and by being engaged together in a common Christian enterprise, the Christian hospital or school can partially countervail the tendency of benevolent activities in and of themselves to add to the resentment and deepen the gulf. On this level, an inferior Christian hospital is better liked and more trusted by the African than is the technically superior secular hospital.*

But what is to become of mission hospitals? The running of hospitals is nowadays highly technical and expensive. Can the Church afford it any longer? Ideally we would have ten thousand more hospitals, and still not all human illness could be cared for. Yet secular governments are increasingly shouldering the burden, and they have the money for it. The Church is hard up. Would it be better, then, for the Church to hand over its hospitals to government and deploy its manpower and money into channels that are

---

* Since my visit to the hospital at Nqutu, Dr. Barker has brought out a book which is an account of the fifteen years he and his wife, also a medical doctor worked there. The British edition is entitled *Giving and Receiving* (Faith Press), the American edition (Harper & Row), *The Man Next to Me*. There is no book like it anywhere. It ought to be read.

perhaps more directly evangelistic, more likely to produce immediate results? Some people say Yes.

My own answer – after visiting more mission hospitals than I can count – is that the question will have to be answered differently in different parts of the world. Always the local political and social situation must be taken into account. In lands where the government is either too young, too poor, too irresponsible, or too benighted to do the job of caring for the sick, the Church must do it. In other lands, where the government is both willing and able, I think the Church would be well advised to retire from the field – which it could do with honour – and devote its slender resources to other types of service. I can see no reason, for example, why we should have expended enormous sums of money on a great new gleaming hospital in Manila. That city is *full* of hospitals. It would have been far more strategic, in my so often clouded judgement, to build ten or fifteen humble clinics in the southern islands and in the northern mountain districts where the arm of the government has not yet reached. My hunch (and I hope I am wrong) is that we Anglicans built in Manila and a hundred other places solely for the prestige value of having a hospital. To put it plainly: because Rome had a hospital, we felt we had to have one. Personally, if we cannot have the many clinics in the hinterland, I would far rather help support the already existing Roman or Presbyterian or Lutheran hospital in a capital city. One should not overlook, I suppose, the importance of prestige. "Status symbol" is a term of recent mintage, but it describes an ancient reality. In the Orient it is called "face". Maybe the Church must have big hospitals in order to have "face". If so, this is a decision which must be taken locally after due thought has been given to what the local climate of opinion requires. I cling stubbornly, however, to my notion that the wonderful new hospital in Manila can accomplish for Christ only a fraction of what fifteen outlying clinics could accomplish at a fraction of the cost.

And the great St. Luke's Hospital in Tokyo. What are we to think of that? For many years it was, unquestionably, the finest hospital in the Far East. It deserved every dollar that Episcopalians and others poured into it. That hospital accomplished at least three things: first, it alleviated human misery; second, it made many friends for Christianity and doubtless many converts to the Anglican form thereof; third, it quickly taught the Japanese – an intelligent people – the excellence of scientific medicine. Well and good. A splendid achievement. But why continue it now? Having learned from the Church the benefits of Western therapeutic science, the state proceeded to build its own hospitals and is doing a first-class job. The state exceeds us on a scale so staggering that I have my doubts about the "prestige value" of a single Anglican hospital in Japan, despite its being, as it undoubtedly is, an institution of the utmost excellence. In a way, this is a purely academic argument, for I know that St. Luke's Hospital is there to stay. It has proved itself in Japanese eyes and is as largely self-supporting as any great hospital can ever hope to be. As for myself, however, I would not contribute a penny to its support. It did its work – a great work. But that is a stage in Christian missionary endeavour which has passed, at least in Japan. Let the government do it now. We must intensify our efforts in new directions that speak, as hospitals no longer do, to a contemporary Japan. If in modern Nippon a hospital can do little to point to the uniqueness of Christ, since it says no more than what every hospital is saying, the Church should devise new strategies. But of Japan more will be said in due course.

South Africa presents a special case. Christian hospitals there, I maintain, have their sufficient warrant in the fact that they are oases of Christian neighbourliness in a desert of apartheid. Which brings me back to my earlier point about the strategic importance of a Protectorate like Swaziland. Here doctors and nurses, schoolteachers, and seminarians can be trained without hindrance. While continuing to work as best we can and as long as we can in South Africa itself, we ought also to multiply our efforts in the Protectorates, not only for the peoples of those enclaves, but also in preparation for a day that may come when in South Africa our hands will be tied.

The whole discussion may seem less academic, less remote, if we actually pay a visit to a particular hospital. North-east of Grahamstown, which in turn is north-east of Port Elizabeth (places you can easily find on a map), you come to St. Matthew's, a mission station in the hills of the Ciskei Native Reserve – a beautiful region but a sad one. Young people with get-up-and-go have all gone. They have gone to the towns in search of wages, for there is little to earn here. Left behind are the old people and the very young and the unenterprising and wives without husbands, who worry about what is happening in town to husbands without wives. And the young married couples who have gone their separate ways into the towns to find work have left behind their infants in the care of aged grandparents, who have barely the strength to fetch water from the river, collect firewood, tend the few skinny cattle or sheep, and cultivate the eroded land. When taxes are paid, the few remaining shillings they have scraped together are spent at the store – often not very wisely. But people whose lives are comfortable ought not to be too severe in judging people who make the mistake of thinking that beer is the only available means for making life bearable.

Much of Africa is overgrazed, which results in erosion and infertility of the soil. Of this beautiful Native Reserve it might well be said, as it was said to me of another, "The Europeans got the farmlands, the Natives got the scenery."

The valleys are racked with coughing. Malnutrition is the No. 1 enemy and, as a simple consequence, tuberculosis is Enemy No. 2. (See Pl. 23 & 24.)

What does the Church do to meet a situation like this? It builds a central church, flanks it with fifteen district churches, erects schools, builds a hospital, trains nurses, sets up clinics at a trader's store and at a forest sawmill, puts on "shows" at night in the rays of ambulance headlights; anything, anything at all, to teach these people that Christ is the Saviour and that among his gifts are skimmed sour milk and fish powder.

And with what results? Only a few years ago few patients were brought to the hospital and even fewer were persuaded to stay. Today they come in droves and are bitterly disappointed when we cannot accommodate them all. In 1952 the Hospital of the Divine Compassion at St. Matthew's Mission had an outpatient attendance of 2,000. By 1958 the number had climbed to 25,800. Some, but not all, of the persons treated had a glimmer, at least, of the distinction between magic and medicine, and more than a few learned, to their joy, that Christ is something more than a competing witch doctor.

Only by breaking off arbitrarily can I end my treatment of South Africa. So here I set a period, although I am fully conscious of how much more should be said. I take leave of this valiant Province of the Church with one word of criticism. How is it that a Church, otherwise so admirable, has sent not a single missionary to work beyond its own borders? I know it will be answered, in self-defence, that so much of South Africa is itself a missionary area that nobody can be spared for work "overseas". *Concedo.* Even so, is it not a dubious circumstance when a Church concentrates solely upon itself? Should not the Church of the Province of South Africa, if only as a token, send two or three of its sons and daughters to "foreign" fields? Might it not be that the Province's failure to concern itself beyond its own boundaries is the ecclesiastical counterpart of the isolation in which South Africa, to its own detriment and that of the world, has wrapped itself?

5

CENTRAL AFRICA: Too Little Time

BABOONS DARTED ACROSS THE ROAD AND TOOK TO THE TREES IN alarm at the approach of The Most Reverend The Lord Archbishop of Central Africa.

"*Basta!*" His Grace had exclaimed to me that morning. "You have had enough of churches and such for a little while." And that was true. For three days he had driven me around to splendid churches, schools, orphanages, and homes for unwed mothers. "To make good your claim that you are a *bona-fide* tourist, let's take a picnic lunch and go see some sights." So off we drove on two narrow ribbons of asphalt from his Metropolitical See City of Bulawayo up into the craggy, boulder-strewn desolation of Matopos where the body of Cecil Rhodes lies buried.

As we jounced along, we fell for a while into a companionable silence which the Archbishop broke presently by prompting me to comment on the strange wild beauty of that lonely region. He was hoping, I think, that I would exclaim that I had never seen anything like it in all my life. I must have disappointed him when I remarked that actually I had used our silence to compose the letter I would write that evening to my parents who live in California and that the letter would begin: "To know what kind of terrain I've traversed today all you have to do is climb into your car and motor from Santa Paula to Castaic Junction and then north-east into the desert, but you will have to imagine that stretch of road teeming with baboons – and Englishmen."

As we picnicked, we had an audience of creatures simian, reptilian, and avian, all sitting at a respectful but intensely hopeful distance. The lunch was good. No one could blame them for their interest in possible leftovers. The silent ruggedness of our picnic spot bore no resemblance to the commercial and industrial bustle of Bulawayo on the plains below. When Rhodes brooded from these lonely heights hardly more than half a century ago, could he – visionary though he was – have foreseen the great city, the broad, tree-lined boulevards, the mansions, the formal gardens, the skyscrapers, the factories, the gigantic cooling towers, the slums? Most of the country which now bears his name was unsettled wasteland in his time. Much of it is settled today – though profoundly unsettled in another sense.

Despite an archiepiscopal declaration to the effect that that day was a holiday, we drifted into serious conversation while picnicking. "There are many Europeans in Southern Rhodesia," I remember him saying, "who persuade themselves that we have plenty of time. These same people are not slow to say that both in West Africa and in the West Indies some three hundred years have elapsed since the first contact between races. The implication is that we shall need a similar period of time before anything can be achieved here. These people are unaware of the pace at which events move in these days and they are also blind to the possibility that world events may easily take charge of the situation here." Then came the Archbishop's most alarming remark. "He would be an optimist who thought that we had even as much as thirty years in which to do what has to be done here."

The Archbishop, a man of courage, did not limit his forthright speaking to the baboons and me in a deserted place like Matopos. More than three years ago he was expressing himself vigorously from pulpits and in direct conferences with prime ministers.

Southern Rhodesia is one member of an uneasy Federation, the other two members being Northern Rhodesia and Nyasaland. From the start Nyasaland wanted no part in this Federation. Nyasaland is a region so unpromising economically that few Europeans were a tracted to it. It remained, thus, a black man's country, and the black men there wanted to keep it that way, especially when they saw that the Europeans who dominate Southern Rhodesia were only a shade better in their racial attitudes than their cousins in South Africa. Nyasaland's fear of the Federation, whether well-founded or not, was twofold: first, its inclusion within the Federation would impair its aspiration to eventual self-government as an independent African state; second, the discriminatory legislation existing in Southern Rhodesia would ultimately extend to Nyasaland and Northern Rhodesia as well. Neither of the latter two countries drew much comfort from the vague talk of both the Federal and the Southern Rhodesia Governments about removing "pinpricks", i.e. some of the discriminatory legislation that is a constant source of irritation to the Africans. "Unfortunately," commented the Archbishop, "these are not 'pinpricks' but injustices which Europeans would never tolerate for themselves."

The clergy have more to do than recite the Daily Offices, administer the Sacraments, and call on the sick and shut-ins. They also have to preach and teach. Christian preaching and teaching must be addressed to the situation in which the hearers stand. Such preaching is not easily achieved in any part of the earth, but there are especial difficulties in this Central African Federation which deliberately and laudably has set itself the task of creating a multiracial society – out of ingredients which do not readily mix.

There is Southern Rhodesia, most of whose white citizens think as do the advocates of apartheid in South Africa. As a result, the country is cordially disliked by the Federation's other two members. There is black Nyasaland, an unwilling partner in a Federation which it regards as a threat to its chance of becoming an independent African nation. There is Northern Rhodesia where the whites own the mines but need the blacks to dig out the copper. However, the blacks are not oblivious to the fact that the Copper Belt, by putting coppers into their pockets, has greatly lifted their standard of living; hence, two races in Northern Rhodesia, in spite of friction, seem determined to make a success of their partnership, since it is for mutual advantage; and they are united in dislike of Southern Rhodesia, the administrative centre of the Federation. Taxes to support the Federal Government and to assist the more densely populated south and virtually to underwrite the greatly impoverished Nyasaland are a source of friction. As one mine owner in the Copper Belt put it: "The Federation is like a cow. Its head is here in Northern Rhodesia, but the udder is in Salisbury [capital of Southern Rhodesia and seat of the Federal Government]."

Here, then, in merest outline is the kind of complexity with which an archbishop of Central Africa has to cope.* He is the umbrella which must shield from storm the many different types who huddle close to him for protection. In addition to the care of all the churches – which is the headache, backache, and heartache of every Father in God – he has the delicate, dynamite-laden task of interpreting Church to state and state to Church. To impatient Africans he must find reasons for urging patience. To recalcitrant Europeans he must show just cause for haste.

Central Africa suggests a location in the geographic heart of the continent. But, as the foregoing discussion has indicated and a glance at the map will confirm, the Province lies in the south-east, and the waters of the Indian Ocean wash the shores of two of its dioceses.

There are four dioceses in all. Two of them, Matabeleland and Mashonaland, divide between them the entire expanse of Southern Rhodesia. The other two, Northern Rhodesia and Nyasaland, cover the territories whose names they bear. In short, the Province of Central Africa is conterminous with the Federation of the Rhodesias and Nyasaland. In only one instance

---

* The Province of Central Africa has a new archbishop, the one who was my host having been translated in the meanwhile to Trinidad.

does the provincial border extend beyond that of the Federation: Bechuanaland, a British Protectorate, belongs ecclesiastically to the Diocese of Matabeleland. Formed in 1955, two years after the Federation itself, the Province
is new and still relatively small in numbers. Though we have only about
160,000 members out of a total population estimated to be 8,432,000, still
we *count*. Anglicans count in government. When the Church puts its foot
down, the Governments of the Territories take notice, the Federal Government too. The Church may seldom get its way – or all of its way – in secular
affairs, but it can claim a measure of success in helping to liberalize white
attitudes towards blacks and to inculcate in the blacks principles of non-
violence, while yet encouraging them and enabling them to press forward.

One of the Church's best contributions to the region is to speed the whites
up and slow the blacks down. White intransigence has to be softened; black
fury moderated. In the present touchy situation, it is not easy to be the
Church of the blacks *and* the whites. Invariably the Church is misunderstood
by one side or the other, and commonly it is under fire from both races at
the same time. Anglicanism could make progress more quickly if it addressed
itself exclusively to the one race or the other. Were it willing to be the White
Man's Church with perhaps a Black Mission on the side, it would surge
ahead. Contrariwise, if it were to conceive itself a Native African Church,
all black, and then import a few British parsons to set up independent
chaplaincies in the cities for whites, the going would be easy. But the
Province of Central Africa has rejected these simple solutions for the reason
that if the Church were to pursue either of these policies it would cease to
be the Church. To dot the cities and mining communities of Central Africa
with all-white chapels would reduce the Church to the status of a chaplaincy,
a foreign body. To minister to blacks alone, when there are also whites in
the land, would be to render the Church simply a mission. Even to do both
simultaneously but separately would falsify the Church's essential nature.

A church can well have chaplains *and* missionaries, but they must be
ministers sent out by the *one* Church in a particular land if that Church is to
have any claim to the title of being the Church *of that land*. Despite obstacles
and discouragements, Anglicans in Central Africa qualify for the title.
Whatever their race, they kneel together at the same altar, drink from the
same Cup, vote together in synod. This is not to say that there are not
individual Europeans, indeed many of them, who draw back from this
freedom with which Christ has made us free. Nor should it be concealed
that there are Africans, many of them, who out of resentment of the white
man draw back. But in the main, churchmen of both races get on well
together.

Race relationships in Southern Rhodesia are better than they are in South

Africa. But the best that either of the Rhodesias can offer is still none too good.

An example: European children in Southern Rhodesia are educated free of charge in the government schools; African children must pay. Not much, of course. But thirty shillings a year is quite a bit, given the earning power of an African father with many children. The government seeks to justify its policy on the ground that white people are paying income tax, whereas most Africans, not being registered as voters, pay only a head tax. Worth noting is the fact that some Africans do not register as voters even though they have the economic qualifications to do so, for then they would have to pay income tax and *also* the school fees! An African in Southern Rhodesia does not find it easy to be both a voter and the educator of his children. Apparently the government did not intend to make it so. That, however, is conjecture on my part. So let me limit myself to saying that in this part of Africa, in schools run by the government, there is no free education for Africans.

Also here, just as in certain states of my own country, there is a tremendous disparity between what is spent on the education of a white child and on that of a black child. The disproportion is criminal. Moreover, most schools for blacks go only to Standard III (i.e. to the age of twelve). The government would think me most ungenerous to complain about this, for in fact it represents a great step over anything attempted in the past, and the government means business; it really intends to make such education universally available, which is an ambitious and humanitarian plan when it is remembered that at present the existing schools can house only a fraction of the children of school age. Why then do I take issue? It is because I question the wisdom of the whole procedure. For the government to take children only as far as Standard III is to produce a vast horde of people who are not actually *literate*. Read they can, but there is little guarantee of their being able to comprehend what they read. Given the African veneration for the printed page ("If it's written it must be true"), the situation is fraught with danger when education cannot do more than spawn a mass of semiliterate people. It makes them vulnerable to every sort of demagoguery. Illiteracy is bad, but from a wider point of view it may be even worse when the populace, secure in the knowledge that it can read, has no very mature criteria for judging the reliability of the matter read. People who have newly learned how to decipher a type face are all too prone to take things at face value.

What is the relation of all this to Anglicanism in Central Africa? The answer is not far to seek. Since financially the Church is in straits, we had better abandon our primary schools (except in Nyasaland). The government, tardily awakening, is now ready to shoulder this burden. So let us concentrate on higher education. We ought to work intensively rather than extensively. Strategy requires that we lay a hand upon the most promising young students and see them through, take them to the very top.

Once upon a time the Church alone was concerned about universal education. All right, that served its purpose in its day. But the government has finally taken its cue from the Church. This frees us to go a step beyond, where the government is not yet prepared to follow. Secondary schools and colleges are where we should lay the stress now, not alone in Central Africa but wherever in the world governments are no longer asleep to their responsibility for primary education. I loved the toddlers in church nursery schools and the rambunctious youngsters in Katholick Kindergartens. But we cannot afford such institutions nowadays in those parts of the world where somebody else is willing to take over. So long as the sandbox is the chief medium of instruction I cannot see that it matters greatly that the sand is secular. We should hold our fire until it will score a hit. I maintain that this is *after* Standard III, or, to speak in terms that Americans are familiar with, we ought to bear down on junior high school, senior high school, and college.

One European educator in Southern Rhodesia maintained in my hearing that "the only way to preserve 'white civilization' is to share it. Instead, the whites seem bent on building a 'protective' wall higher and higher. But it will one day collapse," he prophesied, "inward, not outward, and crush that which it was designed to protect."

His pessimism was shared by an archdeacon who railed against the policies of most missionary societies. "The societies," he said, "have a way of taking all large legacies and putting them in endowment funds, thinking that this will guarantee a nice steady income one day. But 'one day' doesn't do for Africa. *Today* is the day – if it isn't *already* too late. Do they imagine that we have time unlimited? Endowments for the future may be futile. There must be capital outlay immediately. Otherwise we're finished."

The same archdeacon, warming to his subject, lashed out against the whole procedure of the Church of England for getting missionary support. "Here's a dear little black boy who doesn't have a blanket. Wouldn't it be nice if the Sunday School at Upper Piffledon would give him a blanket? A blanket costs thirty shillings." Irony, yes. And a caricature. Yet a trifle too close for comfort. It is good that a little black boy, whether he is dear or not, should have a blanket if he needs one, and I hope he gets it; but the Church in Central Africa has to think of thousands of black men to whom a blanket more or less is the least of their worries. After all, it is a warm climate. The problem is, the law debars Central Africans, by reason of their colour, from doing certain types of work which would earn them the salary that would enable them to buy their own blankets and would lift them from the slums and squalor which undermine their morale and corrupt their children.

Not for a moment am I so blue-eyed an idealist as to imagine that every African is noble. He perhaps was not at pains to marry in the way we understand marriage. Almost certainly he has begotten too many children. The lure of cities was for him the El Dorado which enticed him from the village just as it caused our European forebears to set sail . . . and beget many children in foreign parts, in proof of which are the peoples of mixed race today. Our forebears, however, had this advantage. They went from an advanced culture to a more primitive one. The African, by contrast, moves from a simple culture to a complex one.

What astonishes me is not his slowness in making an adjustment but rather his speed. The industrial revolution was a gradual process in Europe and the United States. To Africa it came in a rush. "Do give our souls time to catch up with our bodies," is the way one African layman has stated the case.

In 1899 Bishop Hine gave expression to a notable ideal for Central Africa: "What this Mission has always proposed to aim at is the building up of a native Church . . . native in the true sense of the word; the Church of the people of the land, irrespective of European influence, and adapting itself to the special circumstances of the race and country in which it exists." He was not alone in holding this view. All the early missionaries hoped, prayed, and built for a great *African* Church. What they could not have foreseen was the tremendous influx of Europeans who came for financial reasons when copper was discovered, and with this the missionaries were not prepared to cope. Now there must *not* be a special *African* Church; there must be a multiracial Church – a catholic Church – *one* Church. There is no possibility any more of a Church "irrespective of European influence". For better or worse, the European influence is there to stay – even if one day, in violent upheaval, the Europeans themselves should be ousted. Millions of Africans are already partially "Europeanized", and it is their ardent desire to become more so, however much they may boast of vanished African glory and seek for its revival.

The Universities' Mission to Central Africa has played a heroic role in the evangelization of much of this region, (see Pl. 20–22 and 25) yet to me there is something pathetic, out of date, smacking of nineteenth-century romanticism in the policy of the U.M.C.A. missionaries I encountered in Nyasaland. Because the people of the land go barefoot, the missionaries themselves went barefoot – all on the principle of *kenosis*, the self-emptying of the Son of God who, although he was rich, for our sakes became poor. Our Christian calling to the *imitatio Christi* was heard by them as involving the missionary's total identification of himself with the people to whom he had come to minister. If they had no shoes, he must have no shoes. If they had no electricity, he also must sit in darkness. In the manner of a minor Incarnation, the missionary must divest himself of glory and enter completely into all the conditions and limitations of life as it was lived on the shores of the great lake, Nyasa.

This is a magnificent idea. It evoked from many men and women a sacrifice so great that I can only bow before it in reverent admiration. The love they expressed in saintly and unboasting self-abnegation created a Church in Nyasaland, a great Church. But today, suddenly, this technique is wrong, though the principle is eternally valid. In private, Africans expressed to me their consternation that the missionaries went barefoot. "Englishmen pretending to be what they are not!" is the way one Christian chieftain voiced his displeasure. But he followed this by something more fundamental: "What we want is *shoes*! Why don't the missionaries show us how to make them? They must set a standard. They keep coming down to us, but we want to go up to them."*

This desire for shoes (and for all they symbolize) is usually stigmatized by white Christian commentators as "materialism". It is easy for the "haves" of the world to accuse the "have nots" of materialism. I myself prefer the less abusive term "realism". I happen to believe that God wills that "all God's chillun" should have shoes – perhaps especially in Africa where fearful parasites enter the human body through the toes of unshod feet to destroy the health of men, women, and children.

None the less, when I was offered the privilege of the altar at Mpondas, where the Bishop of Nyasaland makes his headquarters, I had no intention of being a nonconformist. If they celebrated barefoot, so would I. This was fine, except for my having overlooked the fact that it was Palm Sunday. Suddenly a Victory Palm was thrust into my hand and we formed a procession to make an ambit around the church. The path was lined with burrs. "All glory, laud [ouch] and honour," I sang. Tenderfoot that I am, it was the most penitential procession in my life.

At a settlement called Likwenu, south of Mpondas but north of Zomba, I visited Malosa, a fine co-educational secondary school run by the Diocese

* Slyly, it might be suggested to proponents of this type of "incarnational" missionary tactics that the Athanasian Creed maintains emphatically that our redemption was accomplished "not by conversion of the Godhead into flesh: but by taking of the Manhood into God".

of Nyasaland. Co-educational secondary schools present difficulties, especially in Africa, because of disciplinary problems. Boys will be boys and, quite delightfully, girls will be girls. But Malosa is helped by reason of a rushing mountain stream which neatly cuts the campus in half. Boys' dormitories are on one side, girls' on the other. Fortunately, the stream is a favourite resort of evil spirits at night, and no African boy or girl would dare to cross it. "This is one pagan superstition," said the English headmistress with a twinkle in her eye, "which we have no intention of trying to dispel."

Diffidently I expressed – in my brash way – surprise that the rushing mountain stream had not been harnessed. It would be easy to generate electric power for the school on the heights above and for the Anglican Leprosarium in the valley below. But such a proposal has always been met with a negative response. "The people round about have no electricity. *Ergo*, we should have none." This seems to me the height of romanticism. Africa has changed – and wants still more change. It does not befit the Church to cling to a bygone age. The methods of that age are too reminiscent of a colonialism and paternalism now resented.

Nyasaland was one of the places I liked best in my whole tour – and not solely or even primarily for the reason that everyone there received me with extraordinary courtesy. It is undeveloped country. Zomba must be one of the few capital cities of the world which is served neither by air nor by rail. There is no radio station. Roads are not plentiful, and it is more often a hand-drawn ferry than a bridge that conveys you across the rivers. Periodically the motorist must drive himself into a shed to be fumigated against the tsetse fly.

Compline by the light of Coleman lanterns on the mud floor of the great church at Mpondas is the prelude to a quiet night whose silence is broken only by the strange nocturnal utterances of the hippopotami. The kneeling figures who at that service cast fantastic shadows against the walls will be in their accustomed place again next morning at daybreak for the Breaking of Bread. Even on a *feria* it causes no comment that there are as many as two to three hundred persons present to communicate. They know no better beginning to a new day – nor do I, except that they are much more given to practising what they preach than I am.

Many of these folk are already second- and third-generation Christians. They will occupy themselves after Mass in a great variety of ways. Some will be pupils in the Church's schools, some will be teachers. Some will be nurses in the Church's hospital, some will be patients, many of them having come from afar. Some will fish that day, some will farm – and a share of what they catch or harvest will be offered next day at the Eucharist to help feed the many hungry mouths. And almost certainly one or more of the persons present in the Church on any given morning will be dead before the Coleman lanterns are again lit for Compline.

I love these people. I have only one thing against them. They seem to have little concern for the people who are not Christians. They accept it as the order of the day that half of the ten thousand inhabitants of Mpondas are Muslims and that the villages roundabout are largely heathen, healed (if at all) by "village medicine". The one disagreeable trait about the otherwise excellent Christians of Nyasaland is an attitude they have in common with the Christians of New York: "Why should we take our religion to these other people? After all, they have their *own* religion." When a society matron of New York says this, it betrays a degree of ignorance and callous insensitivity which shocks. One hardly knows whether to laugh or to weep. But when one hears the identical remark from a Nyasalander, who "loves" his Church in exactly the same way that a New York *grande dame* loves hers, it is enough to convince one of the truth of Article IX in its nasty insinuation about Original or Birth-Sin. "This infection of nature," it claims, "doth remain, yea in them that are regenerated."

I have said nothing about the small but significant work carried on among Europeans in the urban centres of Blantyre and Zomba. I have said next to nothing about schools and hospitals. I have not even mentioned Likoma Island, the centre and showpiece of the Diocese. Likoma is not easy of access. The difficulty of getting there has been increased by the fact that the woodburning mission steamer which for fifty-two years proudly puffed up and down the lake, serving all mission stations, is now out of commission. She grew uneconomical in her old age and has been honourably discharged. Alas, there are no funds to find a successor for her.

There were good historic reasons for putting the Cathedral, an enormous edifice, and the big primary school and the theological college on an island in the middle of Lake Nyasa. Yet one wonders if withdrawing to an island all our own was not part and parcel of the "compound mentality" that seemed to govern so much of missionary strategy in the last century. In too many places, Christians huddled together behind compound walls or took refuge in a detached place like an island. The missions tended to do what their Lord did not do: take the Christians out of the world. Christianity became a religion to be enjoyed among the initiates rather more than a life to be lived in the world. There must be a connection between that, our earlier method, and today's singular lack of missionary zeal on the part of good Christians who are themselves products of recent missionary endeavour. When Christianity becomes something for Christians alone, the point has been missed. The salt has lost its savour. I speak here not of Nyasaland, as if somehow it were a more grievous sinner in this respect than other places. I speak of it because it is, unfortunately, typical.

Reculer pour mieux sauter, I may be reminded by somebody who does not agree with me. I have nothing against the withdrawal, provided it issues in a leap.

Although the day is hot, I invite you to bestir yourself, come out from under the shade of the baobab tree, and accompany me by Land Rover to Malindi Station. Ferrying across the river is sheer delight for the passenger because the men who toil at the ropes attached to the cable that will carry us across chant as we go and lighten their labour by stamping rhythmically on the steel deck. The opposite shore reached, we have to be fumigated before we can proceed. Then it is a short but bumpy run to the lakeside where we are greeted by a sight we had not counted on: a man in a kilt. He is entitled to wear it, for this is Dr. Stevenson, a Scot, young, friendly, criminally overworked. This kilted medico from the Episcopal Church in Scotland has Malindi Station as his home base, but he is there less than a third of the year because he must serve ten other stations as well. It is expected of this one physician that he shall be a specialist in every ailment to which the human body is heir and that, at the same time, he shall do practically all the administrative work. It is the least of anybody's worry that he is buried in paper work by feeble and flickering lamplight when everybody else has gone to bed. He cannot get through a single night without being summoned to a ward, usually more than once. Yet at daybreak you will find him in church.

The government helps him. About 50 per cent of his hospital costs are shouldered by the government. The Africans by their fees can contribute about 10 per cent. The rest must be provided by the Mission, i.e. by friends in Great Britain.

Not far from the hospital is St. Michael's Teacher Training College, another Anglican institution, where sixty men are in training to be teachers in primary schools. The library is pathetically small, but will grow now that the government, with unaccustomed largesse, has allotted to the library the munificent annual grant of £25. There is, I admit, sarcasm in what I have just said; and yet, by an additional admission, I have to report that *in these circumstances* even the paltry sum of £25 – less than $75 – makes a world of difference. I hope that at least one American Episcopalian will cancel next Lent's cocktail party which, for the merriment of one hour, would have consumed in caviar and champagne a sum of money equivalent to the total annual appropriation for the library of a strategic school. Blessed be God who has given wine to make glad the heart of man! Puritan I am not. But the next time, before ordering my second drink, I ought, perhaps, to have second thoughts about ways and means of making glad the hearts of other men – the eager men on the shores of Nyasa, for instance.

A Nyasaland government official confessed to me that Britain was reaping no more than it had sown. "Do you realize," he said, "that the government did not lift a finger here with respect to public education before 1950?" To this day, I learned from him, 90 per cent of the schools are in Church hands, with government subsidies. My conversation with this highly placed official caused me to raise several queries. Except for the fact that the British churchman who teaches in these schools does so at very great personal sacrifice, to what extent, I wondered, can we claim these schools as *Church* schools redounding to the credit of the Church? True, such schools give us an opportunity to have chapel services and teach the Faith. But when, at home, to raise money and make an impressive show, we claim all of these as *Church* schools, we build up a falsely inflated conception of the real size and strength of the Church's contribution. To pronounce in an English parish church the word "Kotakota" and to explain that there we have a big senior primary school with eighty "feeder" schools in the hills is equal, in magic power, to saying "abracadabra". People open their purses. But is it honest? These are schools that might more correctly be described as government schools which are Church-aided. The government looks upon the Church as a source of cheap help. Being espoused to the principle of sacrifice, the Christians can be hired "cheap". In a sense, the Christian readiness to live sacrificially is exploited. And actually, the government grants are far from adequate for creating good schools. The Diocese is unable to contribute much, the government gives only a little, and we end up with a poor Church school, inferior in equipment and staff to the secular schools.

Should the Church allow herself to sponsor what is clearly second-rate? Africans soon recognize that the Church schools are a poor show vis-à-vis what the government now offers. Here we limp between two sides. In one of our moods we want the many schools, aided by government, in order to reach in a minimal way many children and to amass the statistics that will open pocketbooks at home. In another mood we want to "go it alone", without government help, and strive for quality. But we hold back, for without assistance from the government, we are too poor to attempt anything.

At the risk of offending those pupils in our schools who may chance to read this passage, I will say what already they know: With exceptions, they are there because they are not from the top drawer. A government which looks out for itself has already seen to it that the youth of greatest promise are corralled in the government's own schools. The Church rarely gets a chance at them. What, then, ought we to do? Would the government take over if the Church bowed out? Probably not. At least not now. At the present time the government has not the money and could not find the recruits. Only Christians are willing to serve for a pittance. To pull out, however, would leave the less promising totally unprovided for educationally. Christianity obliges us to be concerned about the poor, yet I hate the identification in the public mind of the Church with the mediocre. Equally I hate the feeling that somehow the Church is being "had", exploited as a source of cheap labour both in schools and hospitals. What would happen if the Church were to call the government's bluff?

I have dwelt overlong on Nyasaland, economically and culturally the weakest and most unwilling member of the Federation, but I confess I have a special fondness for it. It is time now to turn our attention to the Rhodesias.

Let me take you to Ndola in Northern Rhodesia. It is a place name you might never have heard of had not the great Dag Hammarskjöld perished there. Ndola is the commercial centre of the Copper Belt, the world's second largest copper-producing area. In record time the Copper Belt drew to itself a population of thirty thousand Europeans and three hundred thousand Africans. Attracted by higher wages, the latter came streaming in from Uganda, Angola, Mozambique, the Congo, Tanganyika, Nyasaland, Southern Rhodesia, and South Africa. With over seventy tribes represented, there has been a Babylonian confusion of tongues. Although English is rapidly coming to the fore as a lingua franca, it is still a problem for the Church to know in what language or languages to minister. The situation is also confused culturally. Many peoples from many lands – lands at different stages of development, lands with different patterns of race relationships, and lands where memories of ancient tribal wars die hard – are suddenly lumped together in close quarters. A stable community cannot be created overnight. And none of the Churches is present in sufficient force to do the sort of pastoral job that ought to be done.

In much of history Christianity has been predominantly an urban affair – too much so. But in great stretches of Africa, and especially in Northern Rhodesia, the Church began its work in rural areas. No cities existed. Rural "islands" of Christianity emerged. With a few exceptions, the inhabitants of a particular "island" were fairly insulated against day-to-day contact with non-Christian Africans, and almost the only Europeans they had ever seen were Christian missionaries. What is more, for the most part they were acquainted with only one expression of Christianity (i.e. they knew but one denomination), and if they were Anglicans they had been exposed to only one school of churchmanship.

By no stretch of the imagination, I suppose, can any of us from the Older Churches intuit the severity of the traumatic shock every African sustains when he first comes to town. What is he to make of the cars, the riveters, the hiss of escaping steam, the cacophony of a mine in operation? He meets people of other religions or of none. He encounters a church which, disappointingly and puzzlingly, is not a bit like the church back home. At least in church one had hoped to find the old, familiar, the well known, and the greatly beloved; but here too everything is so strange. ("Why is there all that smoke in church?" Alternatively: "Why isn't there any smoke?") And, most confusing of all, there are *Europeans* who apparently do not go to church at all! And there are Europeans, even Christian ones who go to church, who do not seem to like us.

In rapid succession – indeed simultaneously – the African has to meet at least four factors new to him: one, twentieth-century mechanization and urbanization; two, the scandal of divided Christendom; three, the secularism and irreligion of many whites; four, race prejudice and social discrimination. I do not know when in history a race has ever been put to so severe a test and has passed it with such a measure of excellence. Such is the resilience of the African spirit and the intelligence of the African mind.

Not that the time of testing is over. For all the promise contained in a clumsy beginning, the possibility of failure and expensive defeat lies close at hand.

When I was in the Copper Belt in March, 1960, a white pastor exhorted his congregation of Europeans to think more realistically about the speed with which events were moving and to consider more earnestly their responsibility as Christians in the whole process. It was a good sermon, moderate and reasoned; but it came in for heavy criticism because it contained such a passage as this: "Do Europeans really understand what it means for their own future that there will be a black government twenty miles up the road in three months' time? [He was referring to Elisabethville.] That Tanganyika will have independence under black rule in six months' time? That by the end of the year, one hundred and fifty million people, seventy-five per cent of the total non-white population of the continent, will be ruling themselves? . . . Now there is nowhere in Africa to which one can run to evade the challenge of relationships [with Africans]."

The Federation is a state still in a rudimentary and unintegrated condition, facing grave danger of violent disruption and characterized by a great lack of contact and confidence between the major groups of its citizenry. Christians are called upon to make a sacrificial effort, in all areas of human encounter, to exercise their ministry of reconciliation in the interest of developing such confidence.

But consider even a few of the obstacles.

In Northern Rhodesia nine-tenths of the indigenous people still sit on nine-tenths of the land, whereas in Southern Rhodesia nine-tenths of the people sit on only three-tenths of the land. When the Monckton Commission made its celebrated inquiry, the members travelled together in Northern Rhodesia without interference; in Southern Rhodesia, however, it required two special acts of the Legislative Council for the Commissioners to be able to travel together as a unit, for otherwise the African members would have had to spend their nights in the Native Locations while the European members were air-conditioned in the best hotels. At the time of my visit there was not a single black man on Southern Rhodesia's Legislative Council. In the light of facts like these it is not difficult to understand why Northern Rhodesia and Nyasaland were apprehensive from the first about the idea of federating with Southern Rhodesia.

The Province of Central Africa is well aware of these facts and is fully abreast of current events. But how much can the Church in Northern Rhodesia, for example, be expected to accomplish when its total trained leadership numbers no more than fifteen African priests, twenty-two European priests, and five nuns? "What are they among so many?" Actually, by the operation of the Holy Spirit, they count for much.

I marvel at their stamina – and can find for it no purely naturalistic explanation. By way of illustration, I choose almost at random a single instance: The Reverend John Houghton, Priest-in-Charge of St. Peter's Church in Lusaka, the city which since 1935 has been the capital of Northern Rhodesia, but only since 1944 has begun to grow markedly. St. Peter's embraces twenty congregations within a radius of 130 miles. Seven of these congregations have their own buildings. For the rest, the Anglicans assemble in homes, school classrooms, and the exercise yard of a jail. Somehow or other, the one priest manages to visit each congregation at least once a month and still keeps the wheels humming at St. Peter's, Lusaka, which in itself is an operation so big that in an American parish of comparable size the rector would be clamouring for a second curate.

Father Houghton shares with other clergy in Northern Rhodesia a concern about urban evangelization. In the earlier phase of the movement to the cities, the African from the country was a short-term visitor, a "target worker". That is, he went to town to work just long enough to buy a bicycle, a brideprice, a sewing machine. Then he returned home, triumphant in his new possessions. In those days, very little provision was made for a man to put his roots down in the town.

Later it was different. Country folk came to town to stay. A surprisingly large percentage were already Christian. In the second phase, the Church addressed itself almost exclusively to these "ready-made" Christians. Little was done in direct address to the non-Christian Africans who also had gone to town. Not until almost 1950 did the Church wake up to the necessity of evangelizing *in* the towns.

Which brings us to the third and current phase: an attempt at urban evangelism. John Houghton is a pioneer in this respect, willing to experiment in any way he can think of. Attached to St. Peter's Church and under his direction is a fine Community Centre with its suppers, dances, cinema (called locally a "bioscope"!), discussion groups, Little Theatre Group, and night school where people who currently must labour at menial jobs by day enrol eagerly in commercial classes and pound typewriters late into the night. There is no means of calculating how many conversions may result from this oblique approach. But I wonder if the statistics of conversion are the all-sufficient measuring stick of the Church's success.

Father Houghton manages to find time to write illuminating articles for English and American publications, and to lecture regularly on *pastoralia* at Lusaka's Theological Seminary. In after hours, whenever they are, he supervises the seminarians as they practise the delicate art of being pastors to persons enrolled in the schools, inducted into the army, incarcerated in jails. I know not when he sleeps. We all owe it to him to wish him *Bon Repos*.

I could not think of leaving Lusaka without having paid a visit to the Seminary of St. John the Baptist which, along with the Seminary in Nyasaland, is responsible for training Central Africa's clergy of tomorrow. I found two full-time and two part-time instructors teaching fourteen engaging young men. But only relatively speaking are they young. Their average age on entering seminary is thirty. Their late arrival has a double cause. All of their preliminary schooling got off to a late start, and before they are enrolled as postulants for Holy Orders the Church requires them to perform acceptably in a secular job to test their stability. This training is necessary, I suppose, but since the course lasts four years, a man is thirty-four before he can be made deacon and thirty-five or thirty-six before he is advanced to the priesthood. Precious years can never be recovered.

Only four of the fourteen students when I was there were unmarrried. The ten married men had had to leave their families behind in the villages. I protested against this. It is wicked and senseless to separate husband and wife, father and children, for as much as four years. In school and in city the man matures. One day he returns home, ordination certificate in hand, to find his children strangers to him and his wife a simple country girl, unable to have spiritual comradeship with him on the highest levels. The splintering of the family in this fashion is the result of the poverty of the Seminary. Yet perhaps I am asking for the moon when I request that the poverty-stricken seminary at Lusaka take on wives and children as well as ordinands. But especially in Africa, it is a paramount necessity to show forth the example of a Christian home.

This is the seminary that had only twelve books in its library when the present Warden arrived nine years ago. And this is the place, one among many, where instruction proceeds by endless hours of dictation. Teachers drone while students like drudges laboriously copy down what their mentors give out. "Why not mimeograph the lectures?" I said. "Let the students read them in advance and then come to class prepared to discuss them." "We have no mimeograph machine," was the answer to that suggestion. "Well, with only fourteen students, why not do it by typewriter with carbon copies?" "We have no typewriter," was the answer to that. Americans will not believe me. Their wealth precludes them from understanding.

Also, the lectures thus dictated must be translated into Chibemba, Chinsenga, Chilala, Chitonga – the four native languages in which the Diocese of Northern Rhodesia has to operate. As someone has said: "The tower of Babel casts its long shadow over Africa."

Both in Bulawayo and Salisbury, the two See Cities of Southern Rhodesia, I was kept hopping for several days to make even the briefest inspection of churches, schools, hostels, nurseries (see Pl. 15 and 26), orphanages, refuges for unwed mothers, and other charitable institutions. It would be unfair to the Southern Rhodesian Government to make no acknowledgement of its generous contribution towards most of these institutions. But because some of them are for whites, some for persons of mixed race, and some for purest Africans, a Church fully prepared to integrate is yet held back by the segregation policy of the government on whose grants it largely depends. Americans, brought up on the principle of the separation of Church and state, are quite unprepared to understand the degree to which the Church is helped by government throughout the British Empire and Commonwealth of Nations; and American preachers are totally unrealistic when, in prophetical zeal, they demand that the Church in Africa take up an uncompromising stand on the race issue. Take that stand – and at once we shall have to close down three-quarters of our eleemosynary institutions – institutions, be it noted, which benefit all races. Would it be worth it? I doubt it.

Salisbury Cathedral, dedicated to St. Mary and All Saints, is a beautiful Byzantine structure. To a naïve outsider such as I who does not expect to find a lofty edifice in Central Africa, the surprise is even greater when one discovers, only one block away, a six-story reinforced concrete parking lot, with circular ramp and every other appurtenance of modernity, to relieve the congestion of city traffic.

This is a cathedral where thirteen hundred persons communicate on Easter Day and at least six hundred return for Low Sunday. The Cathedral runs a night school and there was no night life I enjoyed more on my trip than a visit to the Cathedral cloisters to watch one hundred and ninety African men – many of whom had bicycled or walked as much as eight miles after a day of hard labour – learning reading, writing, arithmetic, and religion.

When the Lord Bishop of Mashonaland had shown me his Cathedral Church and the other churches and institutions of Salisbury, he was eager to get me out into the country. But we proceeded gradually. We went first to the suburbs, to St. Michael's in an African township. Ultracontemporary in style – successfully so – was the church building, a gift of the granddaughter of David Livingstone. A flourishing parish, it looks after thirteen centres of worship roundabout, in addition to having oversight of near-by St. Nicholas, a large nursery where working mothers can confidently leave their children for the day.

Then we headed for the country. For eight days the Bishop and I toured this highly favoured region. There is beauty on every side – like the best of California, except greener. We visited three great "islands" of Anglicanism. St. Faith's, Rusape, was one of them. Here, with twelve thousand acres to dispose of, the Church is involved in co-operative and scientific farming. Six hundred farmers, Anglicans all, work the soil. In near proximity to the Church are a maternity hospital, a dispensary, a clinic for cripples, a convent, two schools for children, and a community centre for adult education and "town meetings". From this centre the staff works out to about one hundred outstations, with forty-five schools. I must remind you once again not to let the word "school" suggest to you something "grand". Yet grand it seems to the people of the land whose sole hope for education is enshrined in these miserable huts.

St. David's, Bonda, is another such "island". With its twenty-two schools it reaches over two thousand children. Its hospital, pitiful by Anglo-American standards, is the consolation of this entire mountainous and pain-racked region. The eagerness of young girls to learn the arts of healing is revealed by the fact that in 1960, of the three hundred applicants who by examination qualified, only sixteen could be admitted to the training course for nurses. There was no dormitory space for more. At the risk of boring my reader, I repeat that there is no limit to what could be done if only we at home would limit our appetites. I never really believed in fasting until I made my Grand Tour of Anglicanism. Now I see the point of it – not as an ascetic exercise to cultivate holiness or gain "merit", or even to slim the figure, but as a means for getting on with the Church's mission.

"The learning child and the sick person represent two of the Church's biggest and best opportunities for evangelism," is the message which the free bondservants of Christ at Bonda charged me to bring to the rest of the Faithful. As best I could, I have now obeyed their bidding (see Pl. 20).

There is a surprise in store for the tourist who motors eastward in the direction of Penhalonga. You achieve a summit and there, opposite you on another height, is the great Italianate church dedicated to St. Augustine of Hippo. You would think you had come to Siena. Clustered in its shadow are schools which cater to everything from childhood to second childhood, the whole gamut of life being lovingly superintended by monks and nuns. One remembers gratefully that 70 per cent of Mashonaland's clergy are "old boys" of the central school and its forty "feeder" schools. Gratefully too one thinks of the Prior who has been there twenty-one years, incessantly obliged to make bricks without straw, and of the "trekking priest" who for twenty-six years has trekked the mountains to supervise the schools, catechize children, hear confessions, celebrate the Lord's Supper, solemnize marriages, succour the sick, bury the dead. They are not venerable patriarchs, unapproachable in their sanctity. They are men who sweat when it is hot and who laugh when you tell them a joke. Moreover, they are sometimes homesick. No Englishman can forget England. Did they not seek a better country, that is an heavenly, seeking it even in Africa, they would never have abandoned their green and pleasant land.

6

EAST AFRICA: A Province is Born

EAST AFRICA TODAY IS NOT AS I REMEMBER IT, EVEN THOUGH I was there as recently as 1960. Politically, parts of it have since become independent. Ecclesiastically, a new Province has been formed. All that follows, therefore, is hopelessly out of date. There must be newspapers, not a book, to keep pace with East African current events.

I visited East Africa in the spring of 1960, the rainy season, which made many difficulties for me. At that time, each of the dioceses was an independent unit. Each bishop severally was holding jurisdiction under the Archbishop of Canterbury.

For many years there had been talk of forming a Province, but it was slow in coming. By a stroke of luck, I was present the very moment it came to birth. A guest in the house of the Bishop of Mombasa, I sat glued to the radio to hear whether he or another would be elected first Archbishop of the new Province of East Africa. Mombasa won. It was a victory in which all took pleasure.

But what an achievement! That elements so disparate could ever come together! American Episcopalians are well aware of the distinction between High Church and Low Church, but they have had little experience of anything as High as U.M.C.A. and as Low as C.M.S. American Highs are rarely that High, and American Lows are never that Low. What had to be fused together to create a province were the U.M.C.A. Dioceses of Zanzibar, Masasi, and South-West Tanganyika and the C.M.S. Dioceses of Central Tanganyika and Mombasa (Kenya). If ever – without reason – there was mutual distrust, this was it. It is touching to read the documents which led to the merger. The impediments loomed larger, ludicrously enough, than if Constantinople and Geneva had been seeking union. I never knew how deep the cleft between Catholic and Evangelical was in the Church of England until I watched East Africa agonize before it could become a

Province. That it eventually did become a Province, on the most amicable terms, gives me more hope for and confidence in Anglicanism than I have ever had before.

In its struggle to be born the new Province had to contend with political as well as ecclesiastical impediments. Tanganyika, overwhelmingly a black man's country with expectations (that have now been realized,) of self-government, looked with little favour on Kenya, where the whites in the White Highlands held the reins of government firmly in their own hands. Uganda, which originally was to have been included in the Province, resisted for the same reason. Kenya was the *bête noir* – because it was so white. Part of the solution was to be found eventually, as we shall see, in making Uganda a province in its own right. Uganda was big enough numerically to be a province on its own, and the Anglicans of Tanganyika and Kenya finally proved big enough in a spiritual sense to realize that their political fears had nothing whatsoever to do with the life of the Church, and that an altar, whether it had a crucifix and six lights or none, was still the one Holy Table around which they already were united.

Spread upon the minutes of an Ordinary Session of the Mombasa Diocesan Synod, held in Nairobi in October, 1958, are the words of the Bishop of Mombasa (Dr. Beecher): "[In 1955, after several fruitless attempts to form a Province], it was the Members of Standing Committee of Synod, without difference or distinction of race or colour, who got up one after another and spoke to me as their Chairman. 'In the years of the past we have sinned against the Light and against the Truth; we have allowed fear and we have allowed political considerations which have nothing to do with the Church to have a victory in our hearts.' They said, 'Will you write to the Archbishop of Canterbury as it would be our wish as Standing Committee of Synod to repent of the sins of former years. We would hope that we might be allowed to send an invitation to all the Churches in East Africa who will to join with us as brothers in Christ in a Province.'"

American Anglicans, as has been said before, have little consciousness of, or feeling for, a province, nor are they so well acquainted as Englishmen and Australians are with such ecclesiastical extremes as U.M.C.A. and C.M.S. Therefore, they do not readily understand the authentic, manly, and Christian pathos in the Bishop of Mombasa's next remark to his Synod: "I do not often shed tears. I was moved with joy and a deep sense of spiritual humility that brought tears to my eyes as that decision was made." History will one day show that it was a great decision, a great moment. Anglicans in East Africa now live in concord and act concertedly.

But I prefer to tell things in the order in which they happened to me,

From Nyasaland in Central Africa I flew to East Africa's Dar es Salaam. Then, almost without halt, I proceeded by plane to Zanzibar – Zinj, the Coast of the Blacks. The tiny Sultanate under British protection consists of two islands, Zanzibar and Pemba, and a strip of Kenya. I was intrigued by the following numerical coincidences: Zanzibar is 64 miles long, 640 square miles; 640 feet is its highest eminence, and 6,400 miles is its distance from London.

No, I will not cap the climax by telling you that there are 64,000 Anglicans. Actually the number is a discouragingly small 400 on the island of Zanzibar itself and about 17,000 in the Diocese as a whole.

The latest statistics available to me (1958) show that His Highness The Sultan, who has died since I was in his land, had just under 300,000 subjects, of whom 210,000 were Africans, 50,000 Arabs (the majority of whom were of mixed blood), 30,000 Indians, and 300 Europeans. In urban areas 80 per cent of the people are Muslims; in rural areas practically everybody is a Muslim.

There was something curious about observing Good Friday on the clove-scented Island of Zanzibar. We were about four hundred, gathered in the Cathedral to insist that Jesus really did die, really was buried, and really went into the place of departed spirits, whereas outside we were surrounded and overwhelmingly outnumbered by Muslims intent upon affirming that so great a man as Jesus could *not* have died. Poor Islam! Not knowing the Death, it cannot know the Resurrection. As a religion, Islam is a near – and tragic – miss. Is its very nearness what keeps it so far from us? And does not Judaism present a similar case?

A book exists, I believe, called *The Ritual Reason Why*. Never in my life did I feel more need of it than on the night of Maundy Thursday, 1960, in the vast coral-rock Cathedral of Zanzibar. But even that handy compendium might have failed me. I have a certain knowledge of liturgics and a personal preference for a fairly rich ceremonial, but in that service I was totally at sea. As a pageant, it was superlative in its showmanship, but it would take a practised eye to see what connection it had with a farewell supper in an upper room. Deliberately I exaggerate for the sake of emphasis. *Of course* it was the Lord's Supper, administered with devout intent to express, as best poor mortals can, the exalted significance of the Eucharist. But even an Irish Catholic from Boston would have been baffled. And the Orthodox of Istanbul, though impressed, would have been mystified. One begins to understand how great a venture in faith it was for the austerely evangelical Anglicans of Kenya and Central Tanganyika to link up with dioceses of this stamp.

The elaborate service over, I took a simple Lenten collation with the

Bishop and his Archdeacon and had a good time. Hardly could I recognize in the severe, clear-thinking, utterly devoted, totally evangelical men, my genial hosts, the liturgical personages who, overlaid with vestments, deep in skullcaps, for ever taking mitres on and off, and partially concealed by clouds of incense, had figured in the previous hour in a service I could barely follow. But the incongruity, I said to myself and to God before going to bed that night, is Anglicanism, and if people are not inclined to embrace such a reach they are better advised to seek a Christian home elsewhere. I believe in the Ecumenical Movement because I believe in Anglicanism. If Anglicans of such divergent tastes can get together, so can the rest of Christendom.

The Paschal Feast I celebrated on the mainland in the resplendent Collegiate Church of St. Alban in Dar es Salaam. There were services that day in three different languages, and the congregations were segregated not racially but linguistically. I was glad to note that between the services Africans, Indians, and Europeans mingled freely in the courtyard to wish one another a "Happy Easter". I do not suggest the total absence of racial tension. Here, as in many sections of Africa, tension exists between Africans and Indians, for the latter are shrewd traders who by dint of great industry have managed to get the lion's share of business under their control. Africans resent the greater prosperity of their Indian competitors, and Indians are sometimes at no pains to conceal their feelings of superiority. One of the surprises in store for me on arrival in Africa was the discovery of how *Indian* Africa is, East Africa particularly. And I found myself wishing that the Church in India were rich enough to spare many more priests to work among the *émigrés*. I imagine that it is easier for an Indian to become a Christian in Africa than in Mother India, just as it appeared to me that the Church is having greater success with Japanese in Brazil than it has in the Japanese homeland.

Returning to the problem of race relations, there are multiple stresses and strains: African-Indian, African-European, Indian-European. Yet relationships are far better here than in Kenya to the north and the Federation to the south.

Accidents of history have caused the Diocese of Zanzibar to be curiously set up. The Cathedral was built on an island long before anyone could have foreseen that the beautiful city of Dar es Salaam would become the seat of government. For this reason St. Alban's was elevated to the rank of a Collegiate Church, a kind of co-cathedral. But the Bishop himself lives neither in Zanzibar nor in Dar es Salaam. He believes it is expedient for him to maintain his residence at mosquito-infested Tanga upcountry, to the north, where most of the rural work is centred. The Diocesan Educational Secretary lives in still another place. One wonders how an organization so decentralized can be successful – but it is!

From the sophisticated beauty of Dar es Salaam it is but a short drive inland to picture-book Africa. Just west of town you come upon tall, slender men, their hair henna-red from the mud with which they have packed it, their earlobes weighted down by metal hoops in bizarre profusion. How is one to get a snapshot of these fiercely proud, shy, and suspicious folk? I know that it *can* be done, but it is a job for professionals. By the time I could bring my camera into play, my quarry had fled – but not before they had directed at me such glances that, if looks could kill, my safari would have ended right there on the plains of Central Tanganyika.

At Morogoro the car that had brought me from the coast turned back to Dar es Salaam, and at the appointed hotel I sat down and waited for the woman medical missionary to arrive by auto to take me on an excursion to several village hospitals and schools. She never came. By late afternoon we guessed the reason for her failure to appear. There were floods up the line, and the rains were continuing to fall. She had probably found the road impassable. My hope was that she was not bogged down somewhere. I used my enforced halt to confer with the Assistant Bishop, Yohana Majani Omari, a man of towering spiritual strength who has been an active leader in the East African phenomenon known as Revival, about which something will be said later. The Bishop's wife had so much light of interior beauty shining through her eyes that it gave me an ambition to learn Swahili if for no other reason than to be able to talk with her.

At six the next morning she and the Bishop and their many children and all the clergy of Morogoro were down at the station, despite the rain, to see me off on the train to Dodoma. I begged them all to keep their hats on, for one of the things an African most fears is to get his head wet. Feet and the rest of him don't matter in the least. Wet hair means, all too often, catching cold, and in the topics a cold is a hard malady to shake. Yet they paid me this tribute of standing bareheaded even though the train was late in coming.

The discomforts of the journey by rail from Morogoro to Dodoma pass almost unnoticed because one's attention is fixed on the scenery. Varied as the terrain is, the human inhabitants are even more varied. During a ten-hour run, the traveller passes through a whole series of tribal territories. Each tribe is distinct from the other in architecture, methods of earning a livelihood, dress and physiognomy, even in bone structure. It will take time to forge a genuine national unity out of elements so diverse.

An Australian bishop, who talks with the speed of a riveter and is charged

– in equal measure, I think – with holy zeal and high-voltage energy, met me when the train pulled into his See City of Dodoma at nightfall. He never stopped talking the entire time I was his guest – and all of his talk was informative and interesting. I learned from him the story of the Australian-supported Diocese of Central Tanganyika: In twenty-five years it grew from nothing to what it is now. Two-thirds of the houses of worship were not in existence ten years ago. Six hundred of the nine hundred are new. Until 1959 there were, in all of Tanganyika, only three secondary schools that could carry Africans up to pre-university standards. Three such schools for a country of ten million people! One was run by the government, one by the Roman Mission, one by us. (Therefore, how absurd it is to ask: "Where are the university graduates among the African clergy?")

The secondary school population is about four thousand, a considerable increase over the fifteen hundred of a decade ago. In the same period the number of children in primary schools has trebled. The Church on its own could not, of course, have achieved so much. The government lent a hand. It would take omniscience to assess what it will mean for the future that so much of education in Africa has been Church-inspired and Church-directed. But even a finite intelligence can divine that it will mean a great deal – indeed, already has.

Yet a new day is upon us. Future governments may be less inclined to leave education so largely in Church hands. The poverty of the Church is such that, even with grants-in-aid from the State, we cannot quite meet the academic standards the new Africa is demanding. My firm conviction is that, in a place like Tanganyika (although instances could be multiplied), the Church ought to hang on to the schools as long as it can – as long, that is, as governments are willing to help and the Church schools are able to do a creditable job, even though they may fall short of the very highest standards. It behooves the wealthier parts of the Anglican Communion to support these schools to the hilt in the hope of making them worthy of continuing government support. But what if we should fail to make the grade and one day find ourselves dismissed? My answer is that the Church, even while endeavouring with might and main to extend education and improve its quality, should be giving thought to other strategies of Evangelism. For the time being, the Church must work with Christians who are no better trained than our own schools have trained them. The Bishop has about eighty-eight evangelists who know no English. They know Swahili, as well as one or more of the local languages, but as yet there is no Swahili concordance to the Holy Scriptures! A marvellous opportunity for some scholar or some retired member of the diplomatic corps who has devoted many years to East Africa, or a similarly equipped businessman who has made his home in East Africa – a man who might find this very task his Christian duty and joy!

The knowledge of English in East Africa will increase, but the Church dares not wait until this happens. Bishop Omari never got beyond the seventh grade, for that was as far as the schools in his locality could take him. Yet he is able to preach in seven languages, which is what the Diocese of Central Tanganyika requires. His own home spotless, he uses his seven languages to labour not only for the eradication of sin but also for the extermination of bedbugs. Both endeavours stem from Christ. And veritably there was need for the latter, to say nothing of the former. Of the bedbugs I convinced my-self by the simple empirical method of turning back the covers and lifting the mattresses in several of the diocesan schools I visited.

The Tanganyikan success story must be accompanied by an ominous note. Breathtakingly speedy as the development of our Anglican work has been the last twenty-five years, its effects will be lost unless in the next twenty-five years the pace can be accelerated. In this African Wonderland every Anglican Alice is learning the distressing lesson that you have to run twice as fast to keep in the same place.

I thought the Bishop was over-charitable when he said of the "Older Churches" – by which he meant those of Britain, the United States, Canada, Australia, and New Zealand – that they could hardly be expected to give more. *They could.* Even so, I liked the spirited way in which he said, "The attack, therefore, must be along new lines." The radio was the first new line he urged. "Once it was the age of tracts," he said, "but ours is the age of the wireless." (How refreshing this was in contrast to the withering comment of a highly placed, silken English prelate, whose experience beyond Britain was that of wintering on the Riviera: "The Church will touch mass media of communication at its peril.") The Bishop of Central Tanganyika wants literature in the vernacular – quantities of it – for he understands the venera-tion of the newly literate African for the printed word. Moreover, he wants the accent to fall on theological education. We simply have to take many more of the fine young Africans who are offering themselves for the Ministry and make it possible for them, while preparing for Ordination, to support their numerous offspring. If missionary bishops are to grasp new opportuni-ties and adjust their tactics to the changing local scene, they need a freer hand than most of them have been given.

It is hard to convince home missionary committees of the wisdom of deviating from patterns laid down in the last century. They rely upon a pattern which has proved relatively – and in some places even sensationally – successful in the past. What once worked should always work. Thus, with the devoutest of intentions they send out funds allocated and earmarked, irrevocably, for going through exactly the same motions. There is not enough leeway left to the discretion of men and women in the field. People send money not in trust but in desire to control, as though someone in Sydney understands better the needs of Dodoma than the people who have elected to batter their brains out and waste their health there. The Bishop, by the way, did not say this. *I* do. But I back him up on what he did say: "The first in the field wins." And a second observation of his is worth under-scoring: "Rightly planned, you can expect an increase of missionary workers to pay for itself in increased giving."

A typical provincial town of East Africa is Dodoma. It has sprung up in recent years, a commercial and governmental centre. Of its ten thousand inhabitants, twenty-five hundred are Asians, four hundred are Europeans, and the remainder are Africans. Woe betide you if you get a toothache. The nearest dentist is in Dar es Salaam, and it will take you a week to get there, be treated, and return. And I hope your drug and cosmetic needs are not too elaborate, for there is – or was – no pharmacy.

Who are the people in this town to whom the Church must minister? In principle, all of them. But who are they? First, but not in order of numerical or economic strength, the Europeans. The missionaries excepted, they are almost entirely government servants. A few are businessmen. To the Euro-peans falls, too exclusively but almost inevitably, the top supervision of modern institutions like the post office and the railway. Next come the Asians, more numerous and richer. They are the merchants, craftsmen, property holders, and clerks – in short, the middle class. They own, I was told, 61 per cent of the property in the town. Government owns 26 per cent. The residue for Africans can be ascertained by simple arithmetical computation. The African sector of the populace is widely diverse. It ranges all the way from African officers in government – surveyors, health inspectors, post office clerks – down through skilled and semi-skilled workers – fitters, carpenters, electricians, locomotive and truck drivers – to the majority who speak no English. These last must take the simplest jobs, and are in general strangely confused about the introduction of a type of life for which they have had no preparation. In outline, this is the kind of community to which the Church, with an equal duty to all, is called to minister.

Faced with a task of such magnitude, the Diocese conceived the idea of building a centre "designed to demonstrate the highest standards of Western professional skill enriched by Christian qualities of personality and mental attitude". The centre stands today, close by the Cathedral and second only to the Cathedral in beauty and straight lines. It is an ornament to a city which otherwise is characterized chiefly by formless Asian masonry and African indifference to the perpendicular. It is an honest building from which will be dispensed honest advice. The purpose of the project is to make available services *wanted* by the people, in the hope that this will open the way to personal contacts and friendships. Ultimately, if God please, conversions may ensue.

The plan envisages, and today partly realizes, having a doctor, a dentist, an optician, a pharmacist. Dreams have a way of soaring, so included also is the hope of obtaining a consulting architect and a lawyer. The three-story building was just being completed when I was there, but I saw the promise of the bookshop, the cafeteria, the library, the social centre, the conference rooms. It was beautiful, up to date and efficient. In addition to what the centre may contribute to East Africans, not the least of its usefulness will be in supplying to keen young Christians from abroad – professional men who yearn to serve yet feel no call to the ordained Ministry – a creative outlet for their idealism.

I had a thoroughly delightful drive overland by Volkswagen, chauffeured by the sharply intelligent young representative of the Continental and Commonwealth Missionary Society. It was no fault of hers as a driver that we twice got stuck. That was the fault of the roads in the rainy season. But neither can I give her all the credit, despite the eminent edibility of the sandwiches which she had prepared, for the most completely successful roadside picnic I have ever known. The success was partly the contribution of the twenty or more giraffes who from their grave height, standing at the respectful distance of a hundred yards, watched with interest our every mouthful. While motoring northward our sentences were frequently left dangling by reason of a sharp "Look!" For there were also that day plenty of ostriches to see and gazelles, and birds whose names neither of us knew. Despite these zoological interruptions, our conversation continued, and I learned how remarkable a work the Continental and Commonwealth Society is doing. To Britishers dispersed throughout the Continent of Europe and remote parts of the Commonwealth it makes available by post admirable Sunday School lessons, materials for the children, and guidebooks for the elders.

It broke my heart that when we came to Arusha, Mount Kilimanjaro was concealed from view. But touristic disappointments were characteristic of my trip. Was there ever another journey around the world so arranged that it was Arusha without Kilimanjaro, Lusaka without Victoria Falls, Cairo without the Sphinx, Delhi without the Taj Mahal, and – to mention the supreme instance – Jerusalem without Bethlehem? Ordinary tourist attractions had to be worked in as best they could *en passant*. Though I legitimately claimed to be a tourist, I had business in hand.

And so I came to Kenya, which at the time of my visit was but one Diocese with the name of Mombasa. Today, hardly more than three years later, it is the four Dioceses of Mombasa, Maseno, Nakuru, and Fort Hall. Two of their bishops are Africans – and *such* Africans! They are men who proved themselves, in fires of affliction, during the terrible years of the Mau Mau.

I wish I could convey some sense of the "feel" of a city such as Nairobi, seat of the first Archbishop of East Africa. A quarter of a million people now live in what, seventy years ago, was a tiny depot on the Uganda railway – a "lunatic line" that was built in the nineties to get British administrators into the interior, to end the slave traffic, bring peace, and drum up trade. Nobody realized then that the way station would one day become the economic and political backbone of a new nation.

Millions of good English pounds are invested annually in commerce and in buildings which rival the headquarters of the United Nations in sleek modernity (see Pl. 14). The equatorial sun, not nearly so fierce as I had supposed it would be, glitters on the glass of skyscrapers, and steel sinews of new construction assault the deep blue sky. The streets are a cosmopolitan joy. Few indeed are the races and nationalities not represented. You see astrakhan-capped men from the subcontinent of India, Sikhs unmistakably identifiable by their beards and turbans, English office girls smart in cotton prints, Indian women exotic in saris, Africans clad and semi-clad. Some pedestrians, without refurbishing or retouching, could adorn the fashion pages of *Vogue* or *Esquire*; others are the "primitive-picturesque" types greatly featured in television travelogues. If one African bank clerk comes towards you in Arrow Collar and Brooks Brothers suit, he may have striding behind him, close on his heels, an ochre-smeared Masai warrior magnificently nonchalant about his spear, his feathers, and the amount of skin he exposes to public view. After all, both he and the teller are headed for the same air-conditioned supermarket.

Nairobi is a great city, and it cannot be helped if it does not correspond exactly with the standard picture exhibited in magic-lantern shows and conventional missionary talks. It is *here* the Church must work, as well as in villages as yet untouched by the twentieth century. Tribalism is one part of the picture; trade unionism is another. In a crowded and cluttered section of the city the Diocese has rented a store building and established a Centre for working men. Here Christian and non-Christian, union and nonunion, white and nonwhite, can get together to thrash out their problems under the wise and watchful eye of an extraordinarily gifted English priest who knows his sociology as well as his theology. He knows, too, how to preside over a debate and guide a discussion without controlling it or attempting to pre-determine the outcome. He conducts what might be called a night school with courses on current events and brings in speakers who know their subjects. To university students it is a favourite forum.

A Centre of a different sort is run by the Church Army.* Wives who have newly come to town to join their husbands find the city baffling. It is no small service to them, therefore, that the Church Army Centre provides a course in domestic science. They are taught how to keep house in a dwelling very different from what they have been used to, how to cope with the supermarket, and how to cook with gas. Sometimes education has to start by explaining that there is no need to recoil in horror from the can on the supermarket shelf which shows a picture of a blond infant: "Baby Food" is food *for* babies, not adult food made *of* babies! A point worth learning! But what an easy mistake to have made. For in the shiny new store, shelf on shelf, the tinned goods are displayed in bewildering profusion. Tins with carrots in them are adorned by pretty labels picturing carrots. Tins of beets have pictures of beets. These pictures are reliable guides to the contents inside. If the next row of tins shows babies, what is one to think, even though it is a revolting thought? Are the Europeans still cannibals?

This actual case serves perfectly to illustrate the logicality of the African mind and the ease with which Europeans, all unwittingly, confuse it.

While the women are taking their lessons, they park their children in the Centre's nursery and kindergarten. Food prepared by the women is served in the canteen which is open from dawn until late at night. The canteen is much patronized by men working in the city who are separated from their wives until they can earn enough at their new jobs to send home for them. Some of the men who come to eat remain for evening classes, recreation, and prayer. What they pay for their meals helps to finance the whole venture.

The Church Army Centre does much else besides. Young Africans are trained here to become Lay Evangelists. Work is done in prisons, hospitals, and the big railway training school. The Centre is also responsible for making radio broadcasts in Swahili about forty times a year, broadcasts which are heard by an estimated thirty thousand persons in Tanganyika as well as in Kenya.

* The Church Army, it should be explained for those unacquainted with its beneficent tactics, is *not* the Chaplains' Branch of the British Armed Forces. Nor is it the Salvation Army, although it resembles it and has cordial relations with it. This "Army" began within the Church of England in 1882 and is unswervingly loyal to the doctrine, discipline, and polity thereof. The "Captains" and "Sisters" of this Militia Christi are to be found in many countries. Their chief intent is to win for the Kingdom of Christ people who stand outside organized religion and are seldom reached by conventional means.

Across from the Centre is the thriving St. Stephen's Church. I was moved on a Sunday morning to see a congregation of six hundred persons, each with Bible in hand, following carefully the reading of the Old and New Testament lessons, and then, during the sermon, turning with facility to each of the many texts the preacher quoted as he showed how concordant the Scriptures are in their witness to the great themes of judgement and redemption. It was a touching sight because most of these people could not read a short time ago. They really know their Bibles. No American congregation could equal them. But if this blessed familiarity with Holy Writ testifies to the Evangelical background of the work here, similar testimony is to be found in the bleakness of the church building. The lines are good, but the walls are bare. Not one dot of colour enlivens even the sanctuary. Is the Almighty ashamed of the colours he himself created? To me it seemed pathetically and pointlessly drab. The neighbouring Presbyterian Church, not a whit less Evangelical, has a fine eye for colour – and the Africans are not blind to it.

There is time for a visit to one more institution carrying on a specialized ministry in Nairobi and vicinity, the Pumwani Industrial Centre. As a vocational school it attracts many boys for whom a conventional curriculum has no appeal and for which they themselves have little aptitude. More important still, the Centre makes provision for those who have completed four or six years of school elsewhere but are unable economically to continue their education; yet by law they are not eligible for employment until they have turned sixteen. Adolescents are left with a gap of two or three years with nothing to do except roam the streets of a crowded city in which it is easy enough to go wrong. In 1957 (the most recent year for which I could get statistics) thirty-six hundred boys were picked up by police. That means nearly ten a day. Most of these youths are straight out of the native reserves, and many run straight into trouble. They are totally unaccustomed to mechanics in any form, and they share the notion which prevails practically everywhere in Africa that people with education do not do manual labour. Educated folk become clerks, teachers, and the like. But farming and trades are *infra dignitatem*.

The Church in Nairobi is making its small-scale but excellently conceived contribution to this complex of problems by taking one hundred and fifty boys under its wing at Pumwani. So far as possible, the policy is to have the boys live at home, if their home conditions are at all tolerable. Some come from very decent homes. Some are from remand homes (i.e. an institution where a boy who has had a brush with the law waits until his case comes up in court). The Centre could boast in 1960 that "so far not one boy out on probation to the Centre has gone back into court, and some of them are already out in employment". It should not be thought that all or even a majority of the boys are juvenile delinquents. The Director of the Centre sagely remarks that "there's not much point in putting a misfit in with too many other misfits. We try to surround a misfit with normals".

The workshop was ringing with the sound of hammers. In progress were classes in carpentry, plumbing, general mechanics, sign painting. A bunch of the boys were whooping it up with a spray gun, painting the jeep which they had carefully taken apart and then lovingly reassembled. The school cannot hope to turn out a finished craftsman, but it can introduce a boy to tools, to city life, and to the dignity and joy of manual labour. It inculcates punctuality and other "civic virtues" and quietly it instils an understanding of Christianity and of Christian standards of family life.

Industry has given magnificent co-operation to this venture. On our say-so it will employ a boy in spite of his police record. Government, however, contributes nothing. The Centre is so new in government experience that it fits into no recognized category of school eligible for grants-in-aid.

My tour of these four institutions has been recited in some detail because I want to stress the absolute need for more *city* work. Yet this is the work for which it is hardest to raise money. In the United Kingdom and the United States it lacks romantic appeal or monetary pulling power. Our phlegmatic missionary sense is stimulated, if at all, by the picture of preaching to semi-naked savages. The Community Centre type of approach with which Nairobi has been experimenting is looked upon a little askance by certain conservative missionaries coming out from Britain – and also by many African Christians. It doesn't seem "spiritual" enough. This method of evangelization, they claim, is too indirect. I disagree. It constitutes, at the least, a tremendously fruitful *praeparatio evangelica*; and when it is the Evangel that must be put through, no avenue of approach can be too roundabout, too arduous, so long as no shorter way can be found.

I should like here to give honourable mention to yet another Kenyan experiment: St. Julian's. A beautifully appointed mansion up in the White Highlands, it must one day have been the home of a wealthy gentleman farmer. It is operated today as a sort of rest home. By this I mean neither a convalescent home, in the usual sense, nor a retreat house in the usual sense. It is simply (and uniquely) a place where you go if you are tired or need some time to think. There is a chapel with daily services and occasional devotional addresses – but you do not have to attend. There is a well-stocked library, big enough to supply every legitimate taste in literature. Yet nobody requires you to read unless you want to. If you like, you need do nothing more than sun yourself on the terrace and take in one of the world's great views. Among the few house rules strictly enforced by the two exquisite Englishwomen who run St. Julian's is that of observing certain periods as quiet hours, and if a visitor should desire even more silence he is at liberty to retire to a wing of the house and a section of the extensive gardens where, by common consent, nobody ever speaks.

For the rest, if you want to talk, you can find good conversation at St. Julian's. Interesting guests are always on the premises, from all over the world, and the aforementioned Englishwomen are themselves proof positive that the art of conversation is far from lost. Guests pay according to their ability. They may stay as long as a fortnight. It would be cheap at any price. For the guest is well fed, luxuriously housed, treated to a panoramic view of surpassing beauty, tranquillized by silence (in the degree that he may feel a need for it) or stimulated by good talk (to the extent he desires that). I feel sure that in that gracious house many a person has learned how to pray again, many a knotty personal problem has been solved, many an impending nervous breakdown has been averted, many a good article has been written or a book conceived, many a lasting and rewarding friendship formed. There is only one respect in which St. Julian's could fail with certain people to live up to its claim of being a *rest* house. The house is "colour blind".

St. Julian's has a "branch office" in downtown Nairobi, but there the purpose is slightly different. In a charming apartment, there is chiefly talk. In this branch office the educated European, the educated African, and the educated Asian can meet, without any feeling of constraint, in a civilized, Christian, and thoroughly cultured environment, to discuss any problem whatsoever. The group on a typical evening will be small (for it is not a large apartment, and a big one might well defeat its special purpose), but it will be a brain trust and a powerhouse. Weighty matters are discussed, and understandings there reached are not without result in what these leading citizens of different races and religions do publicly later on.

My sole query: Why are there so few such places? Why is the idea so slow in catching on? Is this not a form of missionary activity par excellence for our century?

Not often in this account of Anglicanism will we be able to tarry so long in a single city. Nor is it necessary. *Pars pro toto.* A few examples must serve for the many. I chose Nairobi for more extended treatment, partly because prolonged rains and floods confined me pretty much to the city, and partly because it is my opinion that Nairobi has shown a good deal of imagination in the whole realm of urban evangelization.

A few general remarks before we press on to Uganda. The astonishing growth of Anglicanism in East Africa can best be indicated by resort to facts and figures. As recently as 1944 a book could be published called *Laws and Regulations of the African Church in the Diocese of Mombasa*, and everybody talked of British chaplaincies, on the one hand, and the African Anglican Church, on the other. Today there is but one Church, fast growing into unity. The races worship together in Nairobi's Cathedral and vote together in synod. The barriers are not so much racial any more as they are linguistic and cultural.

Here is proof of progress. In 1924 when the Diocese of Mombasa, territorially, was much greater than its present size, including the whole of what is now the Diocese of Central Tanganyika, it had a bishop, four archdeacons (all Europeans), three canons (all Europeans), thirty-six priests (of whom only ten were Africans), and one African deacon. The Clergy List of 1960 presents a different picture. Even with the Diocese greatly reduced in geographic spread, it had, in addition to its English bishop, two African suffragan bishops, 149 priests of whom 98 were Africans and one an Asian. And today (1963) the story is again strikingly different. What was one Diocese is five, with an archbishop (English) and four African diocesans. A far cry from the Equatorial East Africa which knew episcopal supervision for the first time in 1865 from the not very handy distance of Mauritius, some fifteen hundred miles out to sea!

There is, then, reason for thanksgiving, for progress cannot be gainsaid. Yet, to be frank, one has to confess disappointment over the smallness of our effort. The work we have done is of good quality, but it is so minute that it will bear no comparison with the achievements of other major Christian bodies. That remark applies to more than Kenya. It is true so universally that I almost despair of our own claim to universality. We Anglicans have achieved for ourselves a certain ubiquity, but it would be folly and self-idolatry to delude ourselves into thinking that we are not often thin on the ground.

It would, I suppose, be negligence on my part not to say something here about Revival and its relation to Mau Mau terrorism, yet I hesitate to venture an opinion about matters whose complexity exceeds entirely my best efforts to inform myself. Even so, a few points may be made without risk of contradiction from responsible observers.

In the early stage of missionary pioneering, it was tough going. Converts were few. They became Christians in the face of ostracism and persecution. This factor guaranteed depth and sincerity. But then, under the impact of Western civilization about the time of World War I, the structure of African tribal life began to crumble, and the missionary enterprise gained momentum.

There was a mass movement into the Church which continued until the middle thirties. But it began to show signs of decay as the Church – something now acceptable and even fashionable – passed into a second generation. The lesson was largely forgotten that the Church needs conversion in each succeeding generation.

It was against the background of spiritual decline in the life of the Church that the Revival Movement came into being. It was not a case of "hot" evangelists coming in from Britain or America to pitch tents and stir things up. It was strictly African in origin. Or, to put it another way, it arose as spontaneous work of the Holy Spirit in response to the prayers of African Christians who were desperate at the sight of the spiritual stagnation that seemed to be taking hold of the life of the Church. There was in Kenya and in other parts of East Africa an upsurge of spiritual vitality, a startling vivification, a new earnestness. But, like revivals before it and since, this movement was not without ambiguous features. It went first through a phase of exclusiveness and arrogance. The quickened, the Spirit-filled ones, in their supernatural exaltation sometimes succumbed to the very natural temptation of sitting in cruel judgement on fellow churchmen whom the Spirit had passed by untouched. But it can be reported, in praise of Revival, that it was followed by a second phase of correction and penitence. Pride in one's own spirituality, with its attendant intolerance of people less spiritual was repented of. And thus the movement entered into a third stage: that of humility, love, and service. To say that one phase *followed* another is too broad a generalization to be strictly accurate. Often, right down to this day (and more especially farther west, in Uganda, as I was to find) the three phases can exist concomitantly, in the same congregation, in the same person. In general, however, the movement is as I have described it: from a profound experience of vivification, to spiritual pride, to contrition, to a new spirit of love with desire to serve.

This manifestation of Holy Spirit was extraordinarily well timed, for there was, just subsequent to its advent, the appearance of another spirit – an evil one. This was Mau Mau. Dark fury, an uprush of a million resentments and frustrations, it sought to harness Satanic religion in the service of nationalism. It was a daemonic rampage, vicious and violent, a fact well known to anybody old enough to read this book. Nothing more need be said.

Less well known, however, is the fact that the Church in Kikuyu country, where Revival had had its greatest success, was the one great point of resistance to Mau Mau madness. In its turn, the Church was hated as something Western and white. Defections from the Church under persecution there were, but hardly from the Revival section of the Church. Revival Christians stuck it out though there were many martyrdoms. When the mania had passed, it was the Christians who had been touched by Revival who worked hardest for the rehabilitation and reconciliation of the Mau Mau followers. Absorbing these people back into the life of the Church has been the conspicuous achievement of the Revival Anglicans – black Christians, winning back for sanity and salvation black brothers who for a season went mad.

It is noteworthy that the Revival Church has been exceptionally free from the tendency to become separatist. There were a few extremists who in the early stages might easily have gone off on their own. Revival's having remained within the Church became a rejuvenating power rather than a divisive force because the clergy had identified themselves with this movement of the spirit.

I was driven to Fort Hall to see the new Church of the Martyrs. (Since the time of my visit it has become the Cathedral Church of one of the newly created Dioceses.) The architect should get full marks for his design – contemporary, functional, right for its setting. Worthy of a long hot drive are the murals executed by an African artist. They are, if I may put it this way, veritably African without any self-conscious striving to be African. In case I should be misunderstood, this is my way of paying a high compliment. The life of Christ is depicted in African terms, with an African background, and without a shred of African defiance. But can it be true, as I heard alleged, that certain government officials had exerted pressure to keep the building from being called the Church of the Martyrs, because the government dislikes being reminded that under its régime any martyrdoms could have taken place?

I could not tarry for an answer to that question. I had to press on to Uganda.

7

UGANDA: Our Best Foot Forward

IT WAS TUESDAY, 3RD MAY, 1960, THAT I WENT TO THE AIRPORT
of Nairobi to fly off to Uganda. I was worried because, although flight time
was imminent, so few people were around. Plane service to Tororo is only
once a week. I had no wish to be left behind. I went to the desk and inquired, "Is the one-o'clock flight to Tororo on time?" The answer was, "It
will be called in a few minutes." Shortly thereafter, in response to instructions blared over a loudspeaker, I wended my solitary way down the ramp at
the bottom of which was a young woman in airline uniform who, with a
wry smile, said, "You will find your aircraft, sir, just beyond that Comet."
All alone, I rounded the Comet, a sleek monster, and there was my plane,
almost a replica of Lindbergh's Spirit of St. Louis. Well, not quite that. But
a stranger outsized kite I have never seen. When once we were airborne I
shouted into the pilot's ear, "What are the merits of this aircraft?" Good-
humoured, he was ready with his reply: "One, extreme dependability; and
two, capacity to land in highly restricted areas – as you will have occasion
to observe four times this afternoon."

The mountaintops we barely brushed past were spectacular. Such country!
Lofty plateaus terminate abruptly in sheer drops. The land is green, rough,
uninhabited. We landed first at an airstrip, the diminutive size of which
fully proved the pilot's second point, at an elevation of 8,500 feet. Freight
and mail delivered, the pilot turned the switch; but when nothing happened
he, with deference to my cloth, limited the expression of his exasperation
to a mild "Oh, drat it! If at this altitude it doesn't go the first time, sometimes
it never goes." Twenty tries later, the fuel ignited and we went roaring down
the little runway. But all at once it was flaps down, brakes on, engines reversed. A promenading giraffe, which we nearly hit, temporarily cancelled
our flight.

Eventually we got to Tororo where, in the late afternoon, I was met by a merry shepherd, The Right Reverend the Lord Bishop of the Upper Nile, who since my time has been shorn of that enviable title. Today he is not "Lucian Upper Nile" but only "Lucian Mbale", his vast Diocese having been subdivided in the meantime.

Here again events have moved rapidly. The two Dioceses of the region which a careless and foreign-dominated geography called Uganda are now seven Dioceses, with their own Archbishop and Synod, an autonomous Province within the Anglican Communion. Also belonging to the Province is the Diocese of Ruanda-Urundi in the former United Nations Trust Territory which has now become two countries, the Republic of Rwanda and the Kingdom of Burundi – making eight dioceses in all.

According to the 1959 census, Uganda's population was 6,538,175. It is bigger now. Uganda grows fast! The 1959 figure, for example, registered a 31 per cent increase over the census of 1948. Indians, Pakistanis, Goans, Arabs, Europeans, and all other alien races number only 87,058, leaving 6,451,117 Africans in possession of the land. Uganda is definitely an African country. There are no White Highlands as in Kenya. There is no great city like Nairobi. The three principal communities are Kampala (46,714), Jinja (29,741), and Mbale (13,569); there are a few small towns; but in the main, it is a land of villages. The villages are simple, without paved streets or sidewalks, without plumbing or electricity. From an architectural standpoint, the only buildings with a claim to distinction are the church, the school, the police station or administrative headquarters, and the hospital or dispensary, if there is one. Even these buildings will be distinguished only if they are somewhat larger than their neighbours'. Otherwise they are constructed of the same materials: wattle and daub, with thatch or corrugated iron for a roof and packed cow dung or earth for a floor. And like every other building in town, they will be out of plumb.

Wattle and daub, it should be remarked, was actually a missionary contribution. Simple as it is, it represented an advance over any type of construction the people had had before. When the missionaries first came, there were no permanent houses, no money, no need to take any thought for the morrow.

Some critics of missionary endeavour have protested that it was wrong of the missionaries to introduce the permanent house, the strange abstraction of money, and the principles of thrift and prudence. The answer to that, I think, is that these things were to come in any event, and it is a mercy that the Church did what she could to prepare people for the coming of the twentieth century. But when money did come, it was always other people's money – spent often on the African's behalf, but not spent *by* the African. It should not surprise us, therefore, that, to this very day, Africans have

little sense about money and management. No graver problem faces the
African Church today.

One Bishop, an Englishman, desirous of building a Community Centre
to help meet the problems of the sizeable town which had sprung up around
his Cathedral, realistically saw that the way to finance the project was to
lease some parts of the extensive tract of land adjoining the Cathedral.
The Church owned many acres, far more than it could ever use itself, and
now – with a city suddenly under construction – Indian merchants were
willing to pay good prices either to buy or to rent lots in the vicinity of the
Cathedral which occupies a central location. But the Bishop found that
only the most advanced of his African clergy could understand what he
was doing in leasing some of this property. Most of his people believed he
was *selling* the land, which seemed to them sacrilege. Leases, loans, mortgages, etc.: they are all very hard to understand. At a clergy conference I
attended the Bishop tried to explain such matters and to explain, too, that
in addition to the revenue brought in by the rental of property, gifts were
coming from Britain and the United States and together these would
make it possible to proceed with the new Community Centre immediately.
The Bishop is an expert pedagogue, patient and plain-spoken. But when he
had finished his exposition, the first question from the floor was: "But who
then *owns* this building?" A barter economy does not quickly catch on to
the intricacies of a money economy. There is a lack of comprehension, which
is understandable, coupled – unfortunately – with suspicion.

Let no reader, African or otherwise, think I am poking fun. I am merely
reporting. In Tanganyika some of the appeal of the concept "Freedom!"
lies in the belief that freedom means freedom to walk into a bank and draw
out money. Whites do this; we will be able to do this as soon as the whites
are out of the way and we are free. That you have to put something into a
bank before you can take something out is a principle imperfectly understood.

Of the wife of the Bishop who would build a Community Centre I asked
this question: "Why, especially in this heat, do the men go around in
such tattered shirts?" The shirts or T-shirts or singlets were literally hanging
by a thread, more tatterdemalion than I can describe. The effect was
ridiculous. How silly to deck their splendidly proportioned bodies with
mere shreds of cloth! Her answer was that there is prestige value to wearing
clothes, no matter how tattered. As long as they have *something* on, the
people of the region need suffer no longer the taunt of the Buganda people
about their being "the naked ones". The prejudice of race against race is
almost nothing as compared to the snobbery of tribes or classes within any
given race. I did not need to go so far as Uganda to learn this lesson; it is

plainly seen at my home base, the island of Manhattan, in Harlem's rigidly
stratified society, where kettles are forever calling the pots black, not to
speak of Park Avenue society which prefers emphatically to be a breed by
itself. But coming back to Uganda, I remarked to the wife of the Bishop that
apparently the tattered and torn people don't believe in the adage that a
stitch in time saves nine. She agreed. "They can't see why on earth they
should spend good money for a needle and thread. As long as a garment
will cling to you, it matters not at all what it looks like."

From April to October every year one of the Bishops is on constant safari.
Each of the one hundred and fifty parishes in his jurisdiction is visited once
a year. It is no fleeting visit – a quick in-and-out to lay on hands suddenly.
He stays. He shares their food. A hand with episcopal ring dips deep into
the same mound of maize porridge from which his spiritual children draw
their sustenance. I was glad to be in on a bit of this, to sleep on a cot,
experience a safari bath, sit on the floor, share the same dishes, and to enjoy
the fact that there were fingers before forks.

My host and hostess at Aduku, a young African priest and his wife, were
as fine a pair of human beings as I ever expect to meet, but I was with them
for twenty-four hours before it even began to sink in that I was not an
Englishman. I was the first American they had ever seen. Avid for news of
the world outside, they repeatedly flung at me questions beginning, "Now
in U.K. is it so and so?" "May I remind you once again," I would reply,
"that I am not from U.K. but from U.S.A." When finally it dawned upon
them that I was an American, not an Englishman, and that I came from
New York, not York, the questions came thick and fast. For example:
"What do you grow in New York?" I can sometimes answer abstruse
questions in metaphysics or theology, but the difficulty of explaining to
them a place in which you grow nothing except people surpassed my meagre
talent as a teacher. They heard me but did not follow.

Because they had shown such interest, I produced, on the morning of
my departure, a map of the world. Spreading it on the bonnet (i.e. hood)
of the Bishop's Land Rover, I pointed and said, "You see this wiggly black
line? That is the Nile. And here is about where you live." We were but a
short distance from the banks of the river. "Over here is another wiggly
black line. That represents another river, the Hudson, and I live right
there," said I, laying an index finger on the island of Manhattan, "and I've
come all this way to see you." My sweet young hostess, after studying this
map intently, lifted her head and, with an expansive gesture indicating the
map of the whole world, inquired, "And where do you go today?"

The dear lady didn't have a clue. Yet people at home, since my return, ask me such questions as, "What do the people of Uganda think about the Berlin Crisis? and the United Nations?" – which means that people at home don't have a clue either. There *are*, of course, people in Uganda who ponder issues of world-wide importance, intelligently and urgently, and *they* must be ministered to by the Church. But the majority for whom the Church must care are like my hostess: intelligent, interested, but uninformed.

With the Bishop I went on successive days for Confirmations in places along the Nile with lovely names like Aweye, Cawante, and Inomo. The arrival of the Bishop is an event. The entire village is gathered, lining the road that leads into town, men and boys on one side, women and girls on the other. A welcoming triumphal arch, made of bamboo, has been erected, and the whole line of approach is studded with bamboo poles from which flutter bright-coloured pennants. At the arch the Bishop dismounts from his Land Rover to proceed on foot in order that he may shake the hand of every man, woman, and child. There is no genuflecting, no kissing of the episcopal ring, for it is a Diocese born of austere C.M.S. Evangelicalism. Even so, no prelate, no pontiff, ever had a more royal welcome. He is *papá*, and his children love him. His authority is absolute, but it is an authority won by his willingness to be a servant. In love to bend down to serve, with no trace of condescension, is something many (but not all) of our bishops have mastered in the School of Charity. I do not find this school on any list of accredited institutions, but it exists none the less.

The Confirmation (see Pl. 16), except for language, is little different from what it would be in Sheffield or Sydney or Cincinnati: The same questions asked, the same answers given, the same vows taken, the same laying on of hands, the same miraculous action of the Holy Ghost. But one difference an American did discern. The alms basin, instead of being stuffed with one-dollar bills (which bill in America has become the sacred symbol of sacrifice), was laden with hens' eggs and fruit of various kinds. Three live chickens, braced at the feet, were also – in obedience to the rubric – reverently brought to the priest who humbly presented and placed them upon the Holy Table.

At the conclusion of the service the joy of the congregation was so great that it issued in spontaneous dancing. We were barely outside the church before it began. Somebody grabbed a five-gallon tin, and with this for percussion the people, in perfect rhythm, jumped higher and higher, pulling their legs up under them. I threw myself to the ground and took a picture (see Pl. 17): a congregation of one hundred people in levitation, three feet from the ground! It all seemed natural and right, a typically African way of expressing happiness. I congratulate this part of the Province of Uganda on permitting it. In others it is strictly forbidden.

The Church in Uganda is one of Anglicanism's best achievements. Except in sparsely populated areas, it is impossible to go for more than five miles in any direction without coming upon an Anglican Church. Four of its eight bishops are Africans. Of the 354 clergy it had in 1960, only 42 were imports from abroad. At the end of 1959 there were more than 800 Anglican schools with an enrolment of just over 120,000 children. Our thirteen teacher training colleges have an output of about 485 teachers a year.

But there are weaknesses. In a strict sense, there is not much in the way of a pastoral ministry. The pastors have had to spend too much of their time on the road, getting from one preaching station to another. A great virtue of Evangelicalism is its emphasis on *preaching*, but a price has to be paid for it. Since we must preach far and wide, the preacher is forever itinerant. He seldom stays in a place long enough to function as pastor and priest. There can be no question that Uganda is short on pastoral and sacramental ministrations. The Bishops of the Province are well aware of this, but their hands are tied until more men offer themselves for the Ministry.

The need for settled pastorates is accented particularly by the emergence of cities and by the growth of villages into towns. Since most of the ordinands come from country districts, they are ill-equipped for an urban ministry. There is not much help to be had from theological colleges, themselves deep in the country. In the towns the newly ordained will meet, usually for the first time, Christians of other denominations and people of other religions. What should be our attitude towards them? What degree of co-operation is possible with churches bearing a different name? How does one approach the Muslim or Hindu? What about social welfare agencies, which were never known in the country districts? What about the restless youth in the towns for whom the old tribal patterns of family relationships and discipline have broken down? A youth club might be the very thing – but who on the backwaters of the Nile ever heard of a youth club? And really, what are we to make of the Clock Tower? It seems to dominate every African town of any size. Not only is it the highest structure in town and the one placed most centrally; it regulates and governs the whole tempo of the town's life. Say what you will, city folk are strange. They do not get up at sunrise and they do not go to bed when it gets dark. And they set great store by some thing they call punctuality. What's the reason for all the rush?

It is a good question, of course. When I was at Buwalasi, our Theological College situated magnificently in the mountains above Mbale, I pointed to my wrist watch and inquired of the English Warden, "Is it really necessary that we bring this along with Christ?" His answer was unhesitating. "Yes, we must shackle the African to our conception of time – and to the straight line as well – if he is to make progress." In no case could the clocks be put back. African primitivism is fast disappearing, and the Church would do the greatest disservice, would retard the African's development, were it to cling, in mistaken romanticism, to patterns obtaining in the days of Livingstone and Stanley. There is a sense in which the incomparably great Albert Schweitzer is the last of his kind. For a very long time to come Africa will have need of missionaries from the older churches and of technical advisers in every phase of life. But in the future they will be present on quite a different basis.

The Bishop of Mbale had a brainstorm the day he conceived the idea for St. Andrew's Fellowship. A brilliant project on a small scale, it commended itself without delay to the Inter-Church Aid section of the World Council of Churches whose grant will enable the Bishop to build a hostel for ten ordinands at Mbale. When their mountaintop training at Buwalasi has been completed, ten men will come down to the plain and meet the town head-on under expert guidance. A priest on loan from the Church in America has arrived to give a hand. Credit must go to the American Diocese of Delaware for having sent men as well as money both to Buwalasi and to Mbale – a harbinger, I hope, of a future in which the Episcopalians of the United States will have an increasing concern for their brothers in Africa.

The walls of St. Andrew's Hostel were rising when I was there. A jubilant Bishop showed me around and explained that it was but the first stage of a far more ambitious plan. He envisages the construction of additional hostels to provide housing for young men and women who have just come to town to try their hand at living in modern times. No moment in their lives is likely to be more critical than the transition from country to city. The Church loses them then or else gains them for eternity. Place them in a hostel under Church auspices, and you have a chance for the latter (see Pl. 18).

The Bishop also spread before me the blueprints of the cathedral he hopes to build. Inspired design! The building will be circular, the preferred African form, and constructed of local materials. The Holy Table will be in the centre. The church will look as if it belonged there – no oddity, no foreign importation, yet not simply a magnification of existing African styles, not an African hut writ large, but a thoroughly contemporary building which, when built, will, I predict, set the style for years to come. The Bishop with his plans meets some opposition. As a variation on a familiar theme one hears many African clergy say that it is not "a proper church", and by that they mean not Gothic. But younger clergy and younger, better schooled laymen are beginning to understand that the *imitatio Christi* does not necessarily obligate them to follow the Victorian era's imitation of medieval architecture.

When the first stage of the cathedral has been completed, the existing church will be converted into a community hall, and then the Bishop's dream of Scouts and sewing circles and forums and study groups will have a chance of realization.

Europeans in the last century found it difficult to give credence to the reports of pioneer explorers that on Mt. Kilimanjaro, so close to the Equator, there was snow. Nowadays everybody accepts such geographical anomalies. But it none the less took me by surprise, on my flight to Kampala, that so much of the high-lying territory – at an altitude of 6,000 feet – should be swampland. I had always associated swamps with lowlands.

Kampala is ringed by hills. Three of them dominate. The same three stand as symbols of the twisted and tragic history of the city. It was from one of these hills, Rubaga, that Stanley sent his famous message to England, appealing that missionaries be sent. That hill became, in time, the site of the Roman Catholic Cathedral. The next hill, Bulanga, is crowned by Government buildings and the Palace of the Kabaka. From this eminence was ordered the death by burning of twenty-two Ugandan Anglicans – but that is past history. The third hill, Namirembe, the Hill of Peace, supports the gigantic Cathedral of the Anglicans.

The struggles of the two cathedral-topped hills to have influence over the hill that lies between them supply the materials for one of the least edifying chapters in Church history. In the eighties pro-French forces rallied around the Roman Cathedral; pro-British, around the Anglican; and a bitter war was fought, ostensibly under rival banners of religion. When Uganda became a British Protectorate, the English Government wisely begged the Roman Catholic Church in Britain to send in English missionaries so that the people of Buganda might be disabused of their notion that Roman Catholicism is the "French Religion" and Anglicanism the "English Religion". Relations between the two Churches are, of course, infinitely better today, although there is still much room for improvement. It is even possible now to joke a little about something that was so painful in the past. When I had trudged up the hill to see the immense Italianate Cathedral of the Holy Romans, I identified myself to one of the priests. As we stood chatting on the steps outside, we both remarked on the extremely handsome silhouette the Anglican Cathedral makes against the sky. "Yes," he observed wryly, "it is often said that your Cathedral can best be viewed from our Cathedral" – a remark rich in tantalizing ambiguity!

Despite yesteryear's disgraceful failures in charity, the two Churches, between them, have done a fine job. Over half the population of Uganda is at least nominally Christian, which makes of it the most nearly Christian of all African countries. Further evidence of work well done is to be found in the fact that Uganda, almost alone on the continent of Africa, is remarkably free of splinter groups, home-grown separatist movements, and Christian deviations of local invention. It has proved to be infertile soil for such foreign importations as Jehovah's Witnesses, Seventh Day Adventists, Mormons, and Pentecostalists. These groups have lately attempted to make inroads, but for once they are not getting far. Catholicism, be it "French" or "English", is clearly superior.

The drums are beating from the Drum Tower on Namirembe. No bells here. The Church is speaking a language "understanded of the people". The drums say that.

The service, though too severe for my taste, is a moving experience because of the tremendous concourse of people and the incredible volume of sound when they sing. Africans fall easily into four-part harmony. It is not the harmony of any authorized hymnal, but it makes a merry noise, and for this reason there is wisdom in the decision of most missionaries to dispense with such costly incumbrances as organs and harmoniums. Half-tones present difficulties for African ears. The next time you sit down at your piano, try something like "Forty days and forty nights", but take a whole step instead of a half step whenever it occurs, sing nasally and as loud as you can, also as slowly as the capacity of stout lungs will permit, invite three members of your family to take the other parts, and imagine the sound amplified by a choir of one thousand voices. By this simple exercise you can give yourself an approximate notion of what it sounds like when Anglicans of Uganda gather to give thanks.

Evangelical Anglicanism has its perverse aspects. A new Bishop of Uganda almost had a riot on his hands when he introduced into the Cathedral a three-panelled stained-glass window commemorating the Martyrs of Uganda, the twenty-two young men who, rather than deny their Lord, suffered dismemberment until they swooned, being compelled to watch first a hand, then a foot, then an arm, then a leg roasted in the fire. Another window commemorated the English Bishop whose words to the warriors who speared him to death on orders from the Sovereign were, "Go tell your king that I am dying for the people of Buganda, and that I have purchased the road to Uganda with my life." Stirring moments of human greatness! Yet present-day Christians of Uganda could get really irritated over putting into the Cathedral of Kampala a stained-glass window representing, with great restraint, the heroic sacrifices of the past. "It is idolatry," they cried. "The worship of graven images!"

The iniquity of a weak and vicious king who, suspicious of white men and of their religion, ordered in the last century the murder of the English Bishop and his followers is but a small matter compared with the iniquity of our having foisted upon Africans to this very day the silly churchmanship squabbles of the nineteenth century. That we should have conveyed to Africans – and Asians too – the notion that candles are of the essence (alternatively: that candles are of the devil); that there is no Mass without a chasuble and the eastward position (alternatively it is all papistical and vain imagination unless it be in surplice and black scarf from the north end); that the essence of Christianity lies in externals: *this* is iniquity, this is sin. We have much to answer for. To have perpetuated among the Younger Churches domestic and outdated quarrels which only our selfish luxury at home could have permitted us, was perhaps an historical inevitability, but it was a sin, a sin of the saints . . . and that is the worst kind of sin. Is it not enough that Africans must come to terms with the twentieth century? Must we also make them relive the controversies of the nineteenth?

This Hill of Peace, Namirembe, is a great constellation of Anglican buildings. In addition to the magnificent Cathedral, there are homes for the Bishop and other ministers, the Mengo Hospital where the sick are cared for and where nurses and midwives are trained, primary and second-ary schools for both girls and boys, offices for the Diocese and the Mothers' Union, a bookshop, a printing press (with sixty employees), and the Sanyu Home for Babies. At this Home I saw adorable tots, unwanted by anybody but the Church; and the warmhearted, tough-minded Matron announced to me, with no intention of creating an effect, "We have milk and food enough until Friday. Where it comes from after that, God only knows."

Of the many establishments out of town that I was taken to visit, one stands out especially in my memory. It was the Gayaza High School for Girls. I realize that prize pupils were placed to my right and my left at lunch – not *all* can be that articulate and gracious – yet what prizes they were! A school that can produce even two such poised and well-informed maidens is a success. Gayaza, as a matter of fact, has produced many more than two. Its graduates are filling some of the most prominent positions in the social and political life of the vigorous and promising young country.

At present the girls worship together in a small, thatched, mud-walled building. It is, however, becoming more and more apparent that a chapel is needed in its stead, where services may be held regularly and the future mothers, teachers, and nurses of Uganda may fully realize that everything they do is for the glory of God. The girls themselves, the staff, and friends of the School have tried to raise money for such a chapel. But unless help comes from the outside it will remain a far-off dream.

In addition to services at the School, the girls go regularly – on their own initiative – to the church in the adjacent village, prompted by a desire to take a maximum part in village life. They teach Sunday School and act as parish visitors. Out they go, in twos or threes or fours, to call on the sick and shut-ins, to draw water for them, and to fetch wood. At first it required courage, but now they take in full stride their responsibility to visit the women's prison, the leper colony, and the mental hospital. That there are one hundred and ninety-nine such girls in a place called Gayaza evokes from the visitor the ancient words: "Blessed art thou, O Lord our God, King of the universe, for that thou hast put compassion into the hearts of men!"

8

EUROPE: Matins and Mountain Climbing

BY ONE PRODIGIOUS JET-POWERED LEAP I WENT OVERNIGHT from Africa to Europe, from Uganda to Italy, from Entebbe to Rome.

Scandalously short was the time I had for Rome, indeed for the whole of Italy – less than one day. I could *not* have endured this were it not for the fact that I had been privileged to visit Italy several times before.

In Rome I paid lightning-swift visits to the two churches, one maintained by the English Church and one by the American. But there was no point in tarrying. They serve a useful purpose in ministering to the large Anglo-American colony resident in Rome, as well as to those Italians who elect to come in. There is no ministry to the people of the land, except indirectly and incidentally, and that is why I had no mind to linger.

Europe is dotted with such chaplaincies. It is good that they are there, not only for the sake of the inveterate hordes of tourists from the British Isles and the States but also, and more importantly, to meet the needs of the long-term British and American residents who are engaged in commerce and diplomacy. Indeed, I wish that tourists went less to our churches in Europe and more to the churches of the lands whose guests they are.

Once in my life, for four months during an illness of the English priest, I had the honour of being His Britannic Majesty's Chaplain to the British Embassy in Copenhagen. I was glad to see American tourists in St. Alban's English Episcopal Church,* but I was disappointed to find that so few of them had had the courage or curiosity to worship in the Church of Denmark. And although this will be strictly anathema to the Episcopalians of Scotland, as a tourist in that land I much preferred to go to the Kirk. It is still my conviction that it is best, when in Rome, to do as the Romans do. But I

* Its principal donor is memorialized in a plaque to "Alexandria, Princess of Denmark and Queen of England".

speak now only of tourists. For the long pull, for the steady diet, a man needs his own Church.

Bishop Gore once made a remark to the effect that thanks to the English-man's love of mountain-climbing and of Matins, we have more than one hundred chapels in Switzerland alone. Yet few are the experiences I would exchange for my having worshipped on a Palm Sunday, several years ago, with the Roman Catholic villagers of Zermatt who skied to church, waving pine branches and filling the valley with the echoes of their yodelled "Hosannas" as they raced down the snow-covered slopes. Why exchange that for a few wilted palm branches imported from Italy and psaltery wheezed out in Anglican chant by eighteen expatriate dowagers from the de-luxe hotels?

But the matter is not so simple as I make it. I lived long enough in Denmark to know that many Danes are far from content with the Church of Denmark, Lutheran in theology and established in law. Not many of them are attracted to the Roman Church, and most of them are positively repelled by the Baptist Church which is practically the only other Christian alternative. During World War II, when Denmark was occupied, numerous Copenhageners, including many who had not been greatly addicted to churchgoing, showed up at St. Alban's English Episcopal Church regularly – just to let the Gestapo know how they felt. But people who come for one motive often remain for another. And word gets around. The Church of England in Copenhagen, without making any attempt to proselytize, has none the less – just by being what it is – attracted a very considerable congregation of Danes. With variations, this story could be repeated all over Europe. And we are often begged to send a mission. "Why don't you come in force?" has been asked me more than once. "There is need of you."

Take the Netherlands, for example. Sixty per cent of the membership of our churches in Holland is Dutch. We went to the Low Countries with no intention of competing with either the Roman Catholic Church or the Dutch Reformed Church, but solely to take care of our "own". After all, we would "get in Dutch" with the Dutch if we closed our doors to them. It is a public service we hold, and if certain Dutchmen want to come, we cannot very well debar them. Strangely enough, some of them seem to like us. Their liking for us goes so far as to express itself in impassioned calls to "come over and help". But what are we to do? We have to consider our relationship with the Old Catholic Church stemming from Utrecht. It is a Church we believe in, are in communion with, and support. Ticklish and touchy is the ground upon which now I tread, but the plain fact is that many Hollanders, desiring neither Rome nor Dutch Calvinism, have just as little desire for the Old Catholics. Perhaps the people I met were jaundiced in their views, but they find that body too "High Church" in an old-fashioned way, too inbred, too much a "family affair", too static. "It adds few members," was the comment of one group I talked with, "and we have no intention of adding to it our numbers."

What to do about the Netherlands? Even today Sunday Schools are having to be conducted in Dutch for the sake of children of English mothers and Dutch fathers. These children ask nothing excessive when they inquire why the services have to be in a foreign language – namely, English. To the credit of the Old Catholics it must be reported that in some places their assistance is invaluable. Out of love alone they come and conduct Confirmation preparation in Dutch, celebrating once a month according to our rite in Dutch translation. We owe them much for this service. But is this a totally desirable permanent arrangement? Approximately one hundred Anglican congregations are involved.

And what are we to do about Continental Lutherans? Hundreds – nay, thousands – of them would flood our churches if only we did not make such difficulties about Confirmation. Testifying out of the depth of their own spiritual experience, they have *already* been confirmed – usually by beloved pastors – and great as their desire is to become Anglicans, they have no inclination to go back on the validity of the Christian ministrations they have already received. I can hardly blame them for that. In fact, I would despise them if too easily they would disown and undersell the tradition which had first given them Christian nurture.

The standard Anglican policy of refusing to proselytize from other Christian bodies and of declining to set up churches in lands already claimed for Christ by some other denomination is unquestionably right. Our record in this respect is blameless, a fact that has frequently been given grateful acknowledgement by other Churches, particularly the Orthodox and the Roman. But can we help it if people in several European lands happen to want what we happen to have? Would that be proselytism? Our normal procedure, in face of invitations to make Anglicanism available, is not to enter the lists in competition but rather to assist some existing indigenous Church with which we have theological and liturgical affinities. Examples are the Lusitanian Church of Portugal, the Spanish Reformed Church, and the Old Catholic Church in Holland, Austria, Germany, Switzerland, Yugoslavia, and Poland. Assuredly here is the Christian way of conducting ourselves. To set up a rival "show" would be wicked. But this presupposes the presence in a land of a Christian body which, with integrity and good conscience, we can latch on to. What, however, should be our stance if no such body exists or if an existing body with proper credentials happens to be a poor "show"?

These are not hypothetical questions. They are actual. And not raised by us. More continental Europeans than you might suspect ask these questions of us. In view of Europe's widespread secularism, scepticism, search, and wistful glance in our direction, we may yet – and in the not too distant future – have to reassess our traditional policy towards the Continent of Europe. Whatever else we may be, we are not just an *English* religion. The world-wide Anglican Communion is the standing refutation of that earlier attitude. It is not inconceivable, since we hear so many Macedonian cries, that we are responsible for some kind of mission to Europe as well as to other continents.

At present, however, our "occupation" of Europe is limited to the following: one, British and American chaplaincies to take care of tourists, business-men and diplomats; two, Europeans who have found their own way to us despite our reticence and reluctance to receive them; and three, a ministry to men in the armed forces who are still stationed there to preserve the peace. Privileged information, which I am not at liberty to divulge, shows that Anglo-American military personnel stationed in Europe, together with their dependents, adds up to a staggering total. I can report only that our Church is there to minister to these people – and need not be ashamed of the job it is doing.

It is, for example, something more than a trifle that four hundred American G.I.'s at a time are willing to give up three days of their hard-earned leave to go to Berchtesgaden for a teaching mission as tough and demanding as any military briefing they ever underwent. Many such sessions have been held under the leadership of chaplains who are Episcopalians.

In the parlance of the present day, the Anglican approach to the Continent is "unstructured". Military chaplains, being men under authority, have their own Chaplains-in-Chief to answer to, some of them British, some of them American. Seven congregations (in Paris, Frankfurt, Munich, Geneva, Nice, Florence, and Rome) make up what is called "The Convocation of American Churches in Europe". Oversight of these is a responsibility of the Executive Officer of the Anglican Communion, Bishop Bayne. The English Chaplaincies in North and Central Europe look to the Bishop of Fulham, who is Suffragan to the Bishop of London, for shepherding. English Chaplain-cies in southern Europe and the Mediterranean have for their Father in God a Bishop of Gibraltar, who holds jurisdiction under the Archbishop of Canterbury. His diocese stretches from Madeira to Moscow! Obviously there is overlapping. It is an untidy arrangement, and typically Anglican.

But that there once should have been three Anglican churches in the city of Florence, one for the Americans, one for Low Church Englishmen, and one for High Church Englishmen, seems a bit too much. Not one of these could pay its own way. Could we not have found a cleric human enough to make himself *persona grata* with both English and Americans and flexible enough to minister both to High and Low? Such senseless duplications occur to this very day in Rome, Geneva, and Paris.

None the less, chaotic as our structure is, I am glad that we are on hand. Tourists and expatriates quite apart, we make friendly contacts with Calvinists, Lutherans, Romans, and Orthodox that may one day bear fruit. The long-range task is not to make Episcopalians out of everybody but to make the entire company of believers one.

9

ENGLAND: Second Reformation in Progress

TWENTY OR THIRTY YEARS AGO IT WAS FASHIONABLE TO SPEAK of "the moribund Church of England". Such a verdict, although it lingers on in some minds, is totally out of date. Moribund aspects there still are, and parts of the ecclesiastical machinery still creak. On the whole, however, the English Church is vibrantly alive. No section of the Anglican Communion is making more effort to adapt its methods of evangelism and its social work to changed conditions and to revise its ancient liturgy in the light of modern scholarship; none possesses more creative imagination.

Six years would hardly be long enough to study adequately an organization as large and complex as the Church of England. At my disposal were only six weeks, regrettably cluttered with the red tape of applying for visas at various foreign consulates scattered across the sprawling city of London. Yet I had time to appreciate a fact which seems still unrecognized by much of the secular Press, even in England – that the Mother Church of the Anglican Communion, after a period of lethargy, is now in the process of renewing her youth. She can still run circles around any of her athletic young daughters when it comes to missionary outreach. No aspect of current Church of England life is more instinct with promise than the fact that S.P.G. and C.M.S., laying aside their ancient rivalry based on High Church *v.* Low Church, began in 1960 to issue a joint appeal for missionary funds. The amounts that have poured in surpass anything the Church has known before. Each year a new record is set. A percentage of parishes that would put the American Church to shame contribute to missions as much as half their total income. There is, in much of England, a new awareness of the "immensity and urgency" of the Church's unfinished task. S.P.G. could report that in 1961 more than twice as many priests presented themselves for service overseas as had ever come forward in any one of the Society's two hundred and fifty previous years.

British and American approaches to missions differ. American Episcopalians have, since 1835, known that to be a member of the Protestant
Episcopal Church in the United States of America makes them *ipso facto*
members of The Domestic and Foreign Missionary Society of that same
Church. You cannot belong to the one without belonging to the other.
There is only the one official missionary society, and the direction of all
missionary work is in its hands. Centralization of control results. American
missions are the work of the Church *qua* Church.

The Church of England does not *as such* have any missions at all. Her
missions are the work of voluntary societies within the Church, but none
of them can claim the authority of the Church as a whole. There must be
at least a hundred such societies – "Friends of the Diocese of this or that".
Eleven of them stand out by reason of their size and the scope of their
activities.

There are two very different methods of tackling the missionary enterprise.
Each has its merits. The proponents of the American scheme advance the
claim that their way makes for co-ordination and greater efficiency. The
English retort that their scheme is better designed to elicit personal interest
and therefore greater willingness to give sacrificially. That is, an Anglican
family with relatives living in Sarawak might become enthusiastic about the
Diocese of Borneo, whereas an appeal for the Diocese of the Arctic might
leave them cold. A mother whose son served in the Korean War might be
greatly inclined to assist Bishop Daly in Seoul while remaining singularly
indifferent to the needs of the Bishop of Gambia and the Rio Pongas. The
human imagination has its limits. Neither emotionally nor imaginatively
can one embrace the universe.

Better, argue the British, to engage the natural tendency of the human
heart to focus on one concrete thing, to love it, pray for it, and give to it.
An English boy whose happiest pastime is to go down to the tracks and
check the trains as they speed by, keeping careful notes on the numbers
the locomotives bear, might quite easily find his imagination stirred by an
appeal from the Rhodesia and Nyasaland Church Railway Mission Society.
He is thrilled by the thought that the pence from his mite box should help
to keep going in Africa a caboose with bedroom and kitchenette, and with a
sitting-room that is converted into a chapel when the caboose is shunted on to
a siding! That three English priests, two African catechists, and two women
workers are constantly riding the rails, stopping at every station to bring
the Church to scattered English families and African gangers or plate-layers –
surely this is something to excite a boy and encourage him to fast and pray.
When the Church is more than a building – when it becomes trains and
ships and people you can visualize – then it is something worth supporting.

Oddly enough, American Episcopalians are beginning to think they ought to encourage the formation of particularized missionary societies, just when the Anglicans in England are beginning to think that they should centralize their organization. Coming from opposite directions, the two approach each other and may end up with a system which combines the best features of both.

As an American partial to the American system, I rejoice in the recent creation, by the Church Assembly of the Church of England, of an Overseas Council whose *raison d'être* is to try to co-ordinate the work of the manifold societies and to think imaginatively about long-range strategy. Its authority is slight. It can recommend but not command. Prestige born of its wisdom may, however, in time give it great moral force.

Since it is beyond my power to treat the Church of England methodically or systematically, I choose the haphazard way of spreading on the record, in rapid succession, those additional examples of creative vitality with which I have had direct contact.

The Society for the Promotion of Christian Knowledge is vigorously alive, its presses humming. Witness the monograph it issued in 1960 entitled "Literature for the Anglican Communion". There is about the publication – an analysis of what the various parts of the world need in the way of printed matter – a comprehensive outlook, a breadth of vision, a businessman's realism refreshingly new. And the recent agreement between S.P.C.K. in England and the Seabury Press in the United States is rich in promise. It is a liaison whereby the Church of England and her eldest daughter will share the wealth of their respective literary treasures. The difference between the dollar and the pound sterling has much to do with our literary estrangement, but the present concord between the chief publishing houses of the two Churches will help to surmount this difficulty.

Radio and television are strictly fair in their presentation of the Church, but the image of it projected by much of English journalism is outmoded, a prewar image which has scant resemblance to the Church's postwar vitality. In part of the press the Church of England is under attack for her regulations on divorce – and the attitude of the English Church *is* too inflexible, too legalistic. Another part of the press delights in playing up factions and dissensions within the Church, petty wranglings over liturgical questions – and I fear we get what we deserve. It makes good copy and serves us right. Even those parts of the press which are not on principle or out of avarice hostile to us fall easily into the habit of presenting parsons as namby-pamby tea drinkers, ineffectual, innocuous, gentle, otherworldly, unrelated to life as it is actually lived. The gossip press has a field day whenever a clergyman has fallen into sin. The more carnal the sin, the greater the journalistic carnival.

But changes are coming and even the Press is beginning to alter its tone. It has to. For the Church has a new look. The black beetle with its strange predilection for rotting church timbers seems to have been conquered and no longer claims so exclusively the attention of the curates. A new generation of clergy speaks with unaccustomed frankness about unpleasant topics such as bombs, alcoholism, and homosexuality. The English pulpit is again finding its voice on significant matters.

Almost gone, but not quite, is the type of Good Friday I endured in Surrey in 1947. A guest on a farm, I crossed the fields and went on foot by country lanes for several miles to reach a sturdy Norman church in the nearest town, which was of considerable size. Arriving at noon in expectation of a Three Hour Service, I was greeted at the church door by a notice that a service would begin at one-thirty. For the next hour and a half I occupied myself as devoutly as I could in the churchyard, reading tombstones. At the appointed hour, twelve elderly ladies and I, having taken our places in the pews, rose to our feet at the entrance of a reverend gentleman who, bidding us be seated, commenced the proceedings by saying, "Really it takes three hours to do the Seven Last Words, but since it didn't seem practical this year to have so extended a service, we'll start with the First Word from the Cross and just do as many of them as we can by three o'clock." Not a promising beginning, but at least we were started.

"'Father, forgive them, for they know not what they do.' How mean-spirited we are in our dealings with each other! How little inclined to forgive! How intolerant of other people's shortcomings and failures!" Et cetera – for a good twenty minutes. All true, but it did not contain one word about the stupendous act whereby God in Christ reconciled the world unto himself. Of Atonement there was nothing, only advice as to how nice it would be if people would be nicer to each other.

Fortified by the spiritual refreshment of a hymn, we then attacked the Second Word, the Word to the Penitent Thief. "'Today shalt thou be with me in Paradise.' Under the stress and strain of the war years, there has been, unfortunately, a decline among the general public of a sense of personal property. The incidence of theft is much higher than it used to be. It is impossible to pick up a newspaper without reading about several burglaries. One may no longer safely leave one's bicycle unlocked." And much more in similar vein. Of repentance or paradise or purgatory we heard nothing.

I had half a mind to get up and go but was halted by the recollection of

Kierkegaard's dictum that it is a Christian's duty to be edified by *whatever* happens in the house of God and by George Herbert's comment on sermons: "If all want sense, God takes a text and preacheth patience." We were nearing three o'clock, and I felt confident I could hold out a bit longer. It was a penitential exercise well suited to the solemnity of the Great Day. So I braced myself for the flagellation of a third sermonette.

"'Woman, behold thy son. Son, behold thy mother.' Family relationships have undergone grave deterioration since the end of the war and, in part, as the result of the war." It was on this note, without mention of ecclesiology, that we ended, the hour of three having struck. Liberation at last! I went away grateful that I had not succeeded in persuading my secularist host and hostess to accompany me. A performance like this would have added unnecessarily to the already sufficient fuel for their scorn.

Such homiletical inanity is not a fault of the English alone. During World War II, one of New York's most prominent rectors delivered himself on Trinity Sunday of a quasi-Athanasian vindication of Christianity's trinitarian monotheism. "The doctrine of the Trinity," he said, "is difficult to understand – how God can be One yet Three, Three yet One. But it may help us if we use the analogy of the Allies engaged now in this great war. There is, first of all, Great Britain. With its age, venerability, and great dignity, we might liken it to God the Father. America, young and vigorous, willing to roll up its sleeves and get down to work, suggests God the Son, active in the world. Then there is Russia. A new spirit seems to be abroad in the world today, dynamic, infiltrating into all ancient structures, stirring things up, turning the world upside down. By analogy we might compare this to God the Holy Spirit. Britain, America and Russia: three they are, yet these three are absolutely one in the mighty endeavour to put down the evil forces of Hitler. Now, of course, I do not forget our fourth great ally, China; but of China we will speak on another Sunday."

In the light of that farce I am sure to be accused of comic invention, but I assure the reader that the sermon *was* preached in the City of New York in a major church. I have in my files a handsomely printed copy of the sermon, on fine paper – despite wartime restrictions – and in two colours, to prove it.

Even conceding that these are egregious examples of fatuity, it has to be admitted that to the greatly gifted Anglican Communion there was not given, in conspicuous measure, the *charisma* of preaching. We can talk, but we seldom preach. In English cathedral churches we often produce theological essays of extraordinary erudition. But they are not *sermons*. Anglicanism hardly knows what a sermon is.

Yet there are encouraging signs that increasing numbers of clerics have a better conception of the specific requirements of a sermon. We have a long way to go, however, and it behooves us not to rely so heavily on our "incomparable liturgy" as a way of excusing our laziness when it comes to preaching. With other churches copying us right and left, and with some even improving on the Prayer Book, our liturgy is not going to be "incomparable" much longer.

From preaching let us move to population problems. I sought advice from several counsellors. "Where," I asked, "can I find a live-wire diocese which is meeting creatively the problems of post-war England?" "The Diocese of St. Albans," was the unanimous answer, "but in order to understand what's going on there, you'll need a bit of background." And here it is.

Even before World War II London had grown much too big. It was uncomfortably large, bursting at the seams. By the end of the war, when huge areas of houses and flats had been pulverized in the blitz and thousands of people were literally homeless, the situation was intolerable. To take the strain off the city, the postwar government in 1947 passed the New Towns Act by which it was decided simply to go out and create eight new towns at a reasonable distance from London. The Diocese of St. Albans was to contain four of these towns, including two of the largest.

The town planners conceived of the towns as entities. That is, each one was to be a place where people not only resided but also *worked*. In fact, houses could not be rented or purchased until the applicant presented evidence that he was signed up for employment where he was to live. The purpose was to avoid dormitory towns from which people would commute to London to work. Although the plan was for an eventual population of about sixty thousand for every town, the limit now appears too low. Today's best guess is that eighty thousand people will move into each development. It has proved impossible to enforce the rule about "No commuters". Many people who took employment in one of these towns have since reverted to old jobs or else obtained new ones in London. Many thousands, as I had occasion to see, fight the rush-hour traffic into the city every day. None the less, the architects of these modern communities hope to keep them self-contained with their own schools, churches, shopping districts, and industries.

New cities on a large scale are a novelty to these ancient British Isles. Not since the industrial revolution when a semisomnolent Church of England largely lost the working classes, have cities suddenly burgeoned.

I was therefore determined to go out to the Diocese of St. Albans to see if we had learned anything from past mistakes. The Diocese presents a study in contrasts. Arriving late one Friday night in June, 1960, I stayed in a thirteenth-century inn. I had no difficulty in believing that the hostelry was as ancient as that. It would require at least six centuries for even a poorly constructed building to settle so that all walls tilt crazily and the bottom of one's bedroom door must be sawed off at a thirty-degree angle in order to open and shut.

Early the following morning I walked the short distance to the top of Holywell Hill, where stands the great Abbey that now serves as a parochial cathedral. The oldest parts of the Abbey date from the eleventh century, but a church has stood on this site from at least the fifth century. On this hill was murdered the first British martyr, St. Alban. After exploring the Abbey, which is a strange hodgepodge of styles – though not without effectiveness – I sauntered down the hill to see the remains of a Roman wall and The Roman city called Verulam.

Antiquity, therefore, is the first note of this city. Yet radiating from it, in close proximity, are four satellite towns, brand new. The new towns have, however, as their core, an ancient country town.

I went that day to see two of them, so much alike that it will be sufficient to concentrate on only one. Bishops Hatfield, it was anciently called, and in law is so called to this day, because the Bishops of Ely found it a pleasant place to summer. Their Old Palace still stands, at a distance of eight miles from St. Albans. Where picnickers now disport themselves, Elizabeth I of England was incarcerated during the reign of Mary. The story is told that when she was sitting under a tree in the garden reading her Bible and came to the text, "This is the day which the Lord hath made; we will rejoice and be glad in it," messengers arrived to inform her that she was Queen of England.

We do not know the size of Bishops Hatfield in Elizabeth's day, but the census of 1930 shows that it had reached alarming proportions: 5,000! By 1949 it could boast a population of 9,000. Eleven years later, 1960, it had to report the soaring total of 29,000 – and it is bigger than that now, being well on its way towards its planned destiny of having six subcentres, each of which will be 10,000 strong.

The man I headed for when I alighted from the bus was the Reverend Canon R. D. Say, rector of the Parish Church. He stands six feet six inches tall – and in other respects too, I discovered, he is something of a giant. He has subsequently been made a bishop (a blow for Hatfield), but I shall continue to speak of him here as I remember him, rector of a parish in continuous existence since the thirteenth century, a man imaginatively busy in directing the work of five priests intent upon coping with the problems of a newly manufactured city.

It falls strangely on the ears of an American to hear that the first rector of the Parish was appointed in 1228, that the incumbent is only the fiftieth in the succession, and that three of his predecessors are still alive in various stages of retirement. That there should have been only a half-hundred rectors in the period from 1228 to 1960 shows how stable life used to be and how long clerical tenure once was. The Parish, dedicated to St. Etheldreda, recently celebrated the accession of Queen Elizabeth I. For the occasion Canon Say did some historical research. He uncovered the startling fact that there had been more rectors *before* her reign than since. With the passage of time, clerics – like everybody else – have lived longer . . . and have stayed too long. But in England they have to. There is no adequate pension scheme.

To get a panoramic view of Bishops Hatfield the rector and I did some climbing. The Parish Church itself is on a hill. Just behind it, a bit higher up is the Old Palace. Still higher on the hill is Hatfield House, seat of the Marquis of Salisbury, a vast Tudor establishment built, as the fancy of the period decreed, in the shape of an E. Whenever the present Lord Salisbury is in residence, it is the duty of the rector of Bishops Hatfield to conduct a service every morning in this residence. I go into this detail only to show that to be in Hatfield is to be saturated in history. Yet modernity has also put in an appearance. Where five years before there were only fields there is now a booming city, clamorous in demand, too "American" for easy acceptance by those who cannot get in, loved by those who are in, spiritually a pauper despite the glut of creature comforts dreamed of before but hitherto unobtainable. As I drove around the Parish with the rector, it seemed to me that the people doing the best business were the movers of furniture. Moving vans were ubiquitous. A public is arriving – numerically big, spiritually starved.

What, then, is the Church to do? How to go about it? What response should the volunteers in the *Militia Christi* make to an influx like this?

Most of the new towns, as we have noted, were built around the nucleus of a country town. That meant the presence of a fine church building which might have stood there for seven hundred years. It was a start. Usually, however, the building was too small, and sometimes the old vicar was too small – too bewildered, that is, to know how to take advantage of the opportunity which had been laid in his lap. Whenever the old parish was not able to meet the challenge, the Diocese came to the rescue. It sent in curates, paid their stipends, gave them a house, set up a hut that could double as a church and a workers' canteen. Thanks to systematic and incessant house-to-house visitation, a congregation was built up which, before long, was able to assume responsibility for the curate's stipend. In record time, the people began to build their own church and parish hall as a replacement for the canteen. The two churches I visited were admirable examples of contemporary architecture. Each was perfectly geared to the general style of the new town and strategically located right in the heart of one of the town's subcentres. The municipal councils, heeding the advice of expert town planners, saw to it that the church should enjoy a commanding position, facing on a large plaza or public square, around which was a shopping centre, with a town hall for community gatherings near by.

The pattern is familiar to Americans and Canadians, but in England it is exciting and new. It is a thrilling novelty to build a church in a land where, since time immemorial, churches simply *were* – a standard feature of the landscape, inherited and as much taken for granted as fens or fog.

The great thing is that the Church "prevented" the crowd. "We were here, on the lot, before the people arrived," Canon Say told me. "Not long after their arrival they were visited. Services were held in homes, in quonset huts, in shops, in community halls; and even that was a refreshing experience for people who hadn't supposed that worship was possible unless conducted in the refracted light of stained-glass windows with an organ sounding sonorously from some Gothic distance. It was no easy matter in the beginning," he continued, "to find the manpower and money which these new opportunities cried aloud for. The Diocese simply wasn't accustomed to having so many people to deal with."

Special appeals went out to individuals and agencies for support of the work. At the beginning of 1959, however, it was realized that the enterprise needed systematic organization. Bravely, the new churches were put into the comprehensive budget of the Common Fund of the Diocese. That caused the Diocesan budget to zoom overnight from £30,000 per annum to £60,000. Understandably, the Diocese of St. Albans staggered a little. Borrowing not dollars but ideas from the American Church, it launched out upon its first programme of planned giving. Through careful teaching, stewardship became much more than a hallowed New Testament phrase. To the everlasting credit of that Diocese, it came within 98 per cent of meeting its more than doubled budget in the fiscal year of 1959. Astonished and pleased, people said it was wonderful; but an innate scepticism caused them to add that it was a "flash in the pan", a "special effort good for one year". They were wrong. Each and every year the amount has been increased and the quotas have been met.

This striking achievement is having repercussions in the whole of England and beyond. It has encouraged many a diocese to make a similar bold venture. The Every Member Canvass is an institution so well known in the United States that I cannot imagine a time when it was not an accepted feature of the terrain. But in Britain, as in Australia and New Zealand, it is something new, hot, and exciting. English Anglicans have long laboured under the delusion that because of the Church-State relationship the expenses of the Church of England were all provided for by the government through taxation. Of course there is not a half-farthing of truth in this notion, though it persists to the present day. The Church of England does not receive a penny from the State. Its holdings are enormous, and from them it has quietly been drawing interest for centuries. But in England, as all over the world, endowment funds do not bring the sort of rates which once obtained. Costs are up, revenues are down. The purchasing power is no longer what it was. All at once the English laity are having to wake up to the painful fact that their Church is not subsidized by government and that its endowments are not sufficient any more.

In other words, England is now learning what frontier churches have long known: If you want a church, you have to pay for it. So now, at last, a Central Board of Finance has made room for a Department of Christian Stewardship. In April, 1959, it published a book called *The Christian Steward-ship of Money*, two copies of which were sent to every incumbent in England. The book had an encouraging reception and rapidly gained acceptance as the "recognized textbook" of the stewardship movement. There followed a spate of leaflets seeking to popularize the message. I read some of them: *Loaves and Fishes, How Much Should I Give?* and *The Stewardship of the Gospel.* And for children there were leaflets bearing such cheerful titles as *The Jolly, Jolly Sixpence* and *The Super Story of Sammy the Sixpence.* Some Englishmen hate all this as being too "terribly, terribly American", i.e. commercialized and high-pressured. American it may be, but it has been given, as you can see, a decidedly English twist. And in many places, I might add, it has met with better than American success.

But to come back to Bishops Hatfield and towns like it. The new churches have been on the giving as well as the receiving end. When the first new church was to be built, there was a campaign of systematic house visitations. It resulted in eight hundred families pledging contributions every week. Even if it was only sixpence, each pledge was collected every week by a team of devoted campaigners. Of these families only about two hundred are – even to this day – known as churchgoers. Why the other six hundred gave is something of a mystery. Yet we must remember that this is England, the land with an established Church, which still baptizes 66 per cent of the total population. People may not go to church, yet the Church still enjoys prestige as the Church of the land. It is what the book *1066 and All That* would call "a good thing". English people still want the Church to be there even if they seldom go.

Who are these people, the citizens of Bishops Hatfield? They come from everywhere but chiefly from North London. To come from North London is to come from the second of London's three ecclesiastical belts. Outer London is encompassed by a circle of churches, some pronouncedly High, some emphatically Low, that cater to people of comfortable means. This is suburbia, whose inhabitants have cars and can drive to a church where the churchmanship is to their liking. These churches have done a good job.

As we come in nearer the centre, we encounter London's second belt, a greater concentric circle all the way around the city. The area was fairly fashionable a century ago, but is now a bit down at the heel. Handsome old houses have been divided into small flats. Six or more families are living where once a single family dwelt in considerable splendour. The result is a great sprawling section, overcrowded, grey with soot. With too few exceptions, the parishes in the second belt are just as dreary and drab as their surrounding neighbourhoods.

The third belt or innermost circle is at the very heart of the city where there are some famous and highly effective churches, such as St. Martin-in-the-Fields and All Saints', Margaret Street. They exemplify Anglicanism at its creative best. Their congregations are drawn from all over, just as people still go long distances to Trinity Church, New York, although nobody nowadays lives anywhere near. Perforce, their best work is done on weekdays.

The people who have settled in the new towns around St. Albans have come, for the most part, from the middle belt, the drab and dreary belt, in which the Church, like a chameleon, assumed the nondescript colour of its environment. They are, therefore, largely lost to the Church. They arrive without any record of active churchgoing. If pressed, most of them would identify themselves as Anglicans, and they would look to the Church of England for water at christenings, rice at weddings, and earth at burials. Basically "nice" people, they turn to the Church only to be "hatched, matched, and dispatched". Now that they have left the city and found country homes, they regard themselves as having "passed into the middle class". Such residual religious impulses as they possess are not easily stimulated by the methods of Methodism. Having "come up in the world", they want something more than Nonconformity. Strange! An industrial revolution in the last century gave Chapels their great chance – which they seized magnificently. A new industrial revolution in our century gives to the Church her second chance.

The average weekly income per capita in Hatfield is £15, as contrasted with the national average of £11. One might think that these folk would be exceedingly grateful to the Labour Party which did so much to create the new towns and bring about higher wages. But precisely those who think of themselves as getting ahead in the world failed to support the Labour Party in the elections. Although that party had counted on them, it did not, in fact, carry a single new town.

How like America! It is true that these people are making more money than in the past. On the other hand, they pay high rents. They must furnish a new house; and many of them are rather desperately "keeping up with the Joneses", buying television sets or washing machines to rival their neighbours. With high rents, mortgages, and monthly instalments to pay, most men have to work on Sundays and their wives are doing at least part-time work as well. In addition, the English suburbia, too, has its population explosion. Stevenage, the new town bordering Hatfield, has the highest birth rate in all England.

All these factors, not to mention gardens to cultivate and babies to care for, often keep town families from attending many church services, or, for that matter, from joining organizations, church or secular, that involve evening meetings.

Realizing that for the first two years the new-comers are busy making their homes, the clergy concentrate on pastoral calling. If the home will not come to the Church, the Church must go into the home. It is a policy that has paid rich dividends in the form of tremendous congregations on a Sunday morning at nine-thirty for the Parish Eucharist, a service to which all members of the family, from grandmother to baby, come simultaneously. And afterwards they eat together a token breakfast of coffee and buns – the modern *agape*. Thus are communities built.

Other church services and organizations that used to splinter the parish family according to age and sex are reduced to a minimum. There is a new emphasis on the importance of preaching, and the clergy of Hatfield, realizing that great themes like atonement or eternal life or sacraments cannot be adequately dealt with in sermonettes, provide sermons at the Parish Eucharist. To the truth that we shall not have better sermons until we have longer sermons, the corollary is that nobody will listen to longer sermons until they are better. This truth is understood in Hatfield and the other new towns – with dramatic results. It is understood too in the Mother Church of the Diocese, the ancient Abbey of St. Alban, where in the narthex on Sunday morning I had the joy of counting thirty-seven perambulators. The whole parish family was present. One slightly crusty old gentleman remarked to me at the end of the celebration. "The wailing of these infants bothered me at first, but I would not do without it now. Merbecke and Willan were never more beautifully accompanied."

Another feature of the Church programme at Hatfield is renewed stress on Confirmation classes. A class meets one evening weekly for eighteen weeks. The members of the class, adults and children, are also pledged every Sunday to attend church, where a course of sermons is preached, explaining the whole rationale of worship. People who were confirmed many years ago are just as thankful for these instructions as are the intending confirmands.

Sunday worship by the whole family of God, instruction, and intensive pastoral visiting: by these means the Diocese of St. Albans has wrought a miracle that must surely be pleasing to England's proto-martyr.

A final word about the new town of St. Albans. In time, perhaps, each of the mission churches will become a parish in its own right, but there is much to be said for keeping them together at this stage as a family of churches. It may prove a system worth perpetuating to have the rector of the ancient parish church continue as senior priest, superintending with fatherly eye the work of his several curates, each of whom is in charge of one of the fledgling churches. Although each curate has a larger measure of autonomy than would have been given to a curate under the old plan, he is yet answerable to the rector. Once a week they assemble for a staff meeting to share their problems and their wisdom. These men operate almost like a Cathedral Chapter. It is a collegiate system of government in which the special talents of any one man are made available to all the churches involved. If, for example, one of the curates has a particular talent for youth work, he can be put in charge of youth work in the old parish church and in all the daughter churches. A curate extraordinarily gifted in pedagogy might be assigned to take over the adult Confirmation classes in all the churches.

How different from the nineteenth-century attempt of the Church to deal with the town created by the industrial revolution. The reaction then was to multiply parish churches in the same town, each parish having one priest-in-charge and each striving for "independence". Under that system, the rector of a parish had to be jack-of-all-trades, and all things to all men. How obviously wasteful! In the same town there would be duplicate parochial setups.

In the new towns today, however, a teamlike system appears that permits a measure of specialization. For example, the priest expert in marriage counselling or in helping alcoholics is available to all the people who need him. Each priest is set free to serve all the people in accordance with his special gift. There are, I think, great advantages in such a type of presbytery within a diocese. The Bishop of California has been experimenting similarly. Possibly we are on the verge of finding a new pattern, not applicable universally, but perhaps a Godsend for the towns.

What next? England has so much to offer that I am embarrassed by riches. What of her treasures old and new have I space enough to exhibit?

Of the exciting creative endeavours in Manchester, Leeds, and Sheffield I will write nothing. They have already been covered by others. I shall note activities less publicized.

I would mention, for example, the Missions to Seamen. England is a seafaring nation, and no English seafarer need ever be far from the English Church. Few are the major ports of the world in which he will not see fluttering over a dockside building a blue ensign on which is superimposed in white the familiar "Flying Angel". If he has the wisdom to head for that building he will be rewarded by finding there some of the most attractive specimens of his fellow countrymen. They will talk with him – small talk, if that is what he wants, serious talk, if that is what he seeks. Usually there is some of both. He can get mail, news from home, food, lodging, entertainment, a gymnasium for exercise, shore excursions, introductions to local families – English if he is homesick, foreign if he is adventurous enough to try to make friends with people of other nationalities. A chapel is there for quiet and worship, and a chaplain for counsel and confession. Let no landlocked citizen of the American Middle West think it a small-scale operation or an insignificant service. England lives by the sea, and therefore the Church has taken to the sea. Where its men go, it goes.

One of the highlights of my two years abroad was a day spent cruising up and down the Thames aboard the Missions to Seamen's M/V *John Ashley*. She is a proud little craft, with reason for pride. Her skipper, who is also a priest, incessantly plies the great river (see Pl. 33 and 34). Anchored midstream, waiting for berths, are tankers, freighters and colliers. The crews are bored stiff. They cannot go ashore, and sometimes wait as long as a week. It was a revelation to witness their joy when we pulled alongside – or else their consternation when for reasons of tide or wind we passed them by. Then they shook their fists at us. After tying up in the lee of a ship, the chaplain climbs aboard, gets clearance from the captain ("I've yet to meet one who didn't give the *John Ashley* a hearty welcome") then invites the crew to come aboard his own small craft. They head for the cabin, which is fitted as a library. Each book is an outright gift, on condition that when finished it be passed on to a buddy. People all over the British Isles keep the library well stocked, and publishers are generous in their gifts of complimentary copies. Newspaper publishers are helpful too. There is need, however, of more books, magazines, and papers from foreign publishing houses, for the *John Ashley* also serves ships of non-British registry. In the space of one rainy afternoon (filthy weather, characteristic of Old Father Thames) I myself boarded English, Irish, Scottish, German, Dutch, Norwegian, Swedish, and Danish vessels. Since I speak Danish, after a fashion, and can make myself understood in the other Scandinavian languages, I was invited to sign on as a member of the crew of the *John Ashley*. Ships are a hobby of mine, and I think I would enjoy being a member of "The World's Most Watery Parish". The 65-ton floating chapel which serves this fleet is 75 feet long, with an 18-foot beam. With the tide, she can make 14 knots, against it, 10. About two hundred ships a month are visited. About twenty-thousand seamen come aboard her every year.

As night descends, the *John Ashley* ties up alongside a ship. Crewmen, their day's work done, board her to see movies, one of which has a moral or religious theme on which the chaplain comments; then he offers prayer. Most of the men return to their ship after this to "hit the sack", but some hold back. They want to talk with the padre. And when they have had their turn, it is no uncommon experience for officers to come by night, like Nicodemus, for a word. Early next morning there will be a celebration of the Holy Communion. Some of the men will attend it. Then off sails the *John Ashley* for another day of ecclesiastical "piracy". It has taken captive many a ship. The whole operation – salaries, fuel, maintenance – costs only £3,500 per annum. Why, therefore, can we not have more such "pirates"? The *John Ashley* does good work ashore as well as afloat. I talked with one gruff piermaster who told me he and his entire household had been baptized after they had witnessed the accomplishments of this little ship.

I took particular pleasure in visiting several Flying Angel shore installations, but I single out for special mention one in the London dock area which caters to Chinese seamen. For the Chinese, who have a notorious difficulty with the English letter "l", it is the "Frying Angel"; this "name", however, does not lessen its popularity as a rendezvous. A Chinese priest from the Diocese of Singapore had been "seconded" to open the new venture. Providence alone could have prepared him for the strange complexity of his task. I have an inexact recollection of the actual order of events, but I know he was born in the Cantonese-speaking part of China and spent his youth in Shanghai, where he learned the speech of that region. As a refugee he went to Hong Kong, where he picked up new dialects, then moved to Singapore, where he mastered still other inflexions of the Chinese tongue, and also encountered and was mastered by Christ. I saw this man in an unattractive part of London. With his wife he had created a centre congenial to Chinese, whatever their dialect and whichever side of the Bamboo Curtain they came from. One evening I watched him go from table to table, shifting dialects as occasion required. He could speak seven of them. The food he and his wife prepared with the willing help of idle seamen was a delight to the Orientals – and to Occidentals too, if I am any judge.

Where, I thought, would these thirty-five or forty seamen have spent that night had it not been for the "Frying Angel"? I have never supposed that the Church's chief work is to keep people off the streets at night, but certainly this must be part of its mission. And the record is incontrovertible: More than one Chinese seaman who first met Christ in London sailed home to Singapore or Hong Kong or Shanghai or any other port, and by his testimony made Christians of his family. We should not be deterred by the fact that much seed is wasted. Much falls on fallow ground. Our sole concern should be to take good seed and sow it broadcast.

The Church of England's solicitude for men who go down to the sea in ships is one of her finest qualities. A related quality is her interest in the many Englishmen who emigrate. The Church of England has set up a Council for Commonwealth Settlements. In 1957, 1958, and 1959 it sponsored about five thousand families a year, advising them, commending the migrants to the Voyage Chaplain on board ship, and writing ahead about them to the priest in their intended new home parish. The Diocese of Toronto maintains an Anglican Information Office which offers advice to migrants from England whatever their religion. When I was "down under" I found Australians listening very sympathetically to a proposal set forth by the Bishop of Coventry. Every parish, if he could have his way, would buy or rent a house in which a migrant family could be accommodated temporarily on arrival.

I know not what may have become of this suggestion, but I am prompted to ask what my own American Episcopal Church does to commend to Canadian parishes the ten thousand American Episcopalians who migrate to Canada every year. Little, I suspect, for it is a well-known fact that few rectors of American parishes bestir themselves to the extent of writing letters to university chaplains referring to their care young parishioners who are going off to college. That the laity put up with the clergy and esteem them as they do is cause for wonderment. The English clergy are better about such referrals. That is the point I want to make. I hope it stings at least one conscience somewhere. The laity too deserve a scolding. Do they imagine the clergy to be clairvoyant? How is the priest to know that people are moving away if they do not tell him?

The Mothers' Union, with an international membership totalling more than six hundred thousand, deserves an individual chapter, but that would be entirely beyond me. Its primary purpose is to uphold the Christian standard of marriage, an aim it seeks to achieve by a far-reaching educational and devotional programme. When books or movies seem to be detrimental to public morals, they are often withdrawn by publishers and producers who have been the recipients of outraged maternal cries of extreme force. Even Parliament has been known to tremble and change its tactics when introducing new legislation to which the Mothers' Union was vociferously opposed.

The splendid evangelism of the Church Army and its fine social work with both the young and the old are known also in the United States and the Dominions. It was a heartening experience to stand in the crowds at Hyde Park Corner and find that amid all the rantings and railings of many speakers, Church Army officers were preaching the Gospel of Christ quietly, sanely, powerfully. The public meetings over, the officers, like the Pied Piper of Hamelin, led a goodly number of persons from the park to the Church Army headquarters, only a block away, where the preaching continued in the quiet of the chapel and where counselling with individuals was the next step.

The movement called "Christian Teamwork" deserves mention. Other parts of the Church, content to confine trained and talented laymen to the work of ushering, supervising financial drives, and serving on vestries, might well draw inspiration from the example set by Christian Teamwork. When parishioners have brought to their pastor problems so grave and complex that he feels inadequate to deal with them singlehandedly, he can turn to the members of "Christian Teamwork" for expert advice, for the team of proficient laymen includes lawyers, doctors, and psychiatrists.

A list of the Church of England's various voluntary guilds drawn at random from the 1961 Year Book is staggering even to a nation of "joiners" like America. Forty-two closely printed pages of the Year Book are required to give a thumbnail sketch of those that do not appear in the main sections. Even this list, say the editors, is "not exhaustive". Out of 496 I have picked twenty as representative of the range and variety of Anglican interests:

Actors' Church Union
Additional Curates Society
Ancient Society of College Youths
Anglican Group for the Ordination of Women to the Historic Ministry
    of the Church
Anglican Pacifist Fellowship
Association for Prayer on Behalf of the Condemned
Cambridge Fruiting Campaign
Cambridge Hopping Mission
Central Council of Church Bell-Ringers
Church Duty Money Movement
Church of England Temperance Society Mission to Hop-Pickers
Church's Fellowship for Psychical Study

The Friends of Friendless Churches
Guild of the Holy Spirit for Civil Servants
Imperial Alliance for the Defence of Sunday
Industrial Christian Fellowship
Operative Jewish Converts' Institution
Poor Clergy Relief Corporation
Soldiers' and Airmen's Scripture Readers' Association
Waifs and Strays Society

The supposedly archconservative Church of England is today in ferment. A second, or if you prefer, a third reformation is in full swing. The Canon Law is being revised and brought up to date. The creaking administrative machinery is being overhauled. All offices and ceremonies of the Prayer Book are being thought through with a view to revision, sometimes radical. The entire financial structure is being re-examined, and, under American influence, as we have seen in the case of the Diocese of St. Albans, church people are learning to know the meaning of stewardship and the benefits of planned giving. (See also Pl. 29-32.)

10

WALES: "The Old Mother"

MY TIMING WAS POOR. IF I HAD GONE TO WALES ONE WEEK EARLIER my visit would have coincided with the Eisteddfod. If I had gone a fortnight later it would have coincided with the visit of the Queen of England to attend the formal opening of the restored Cathedral of Llandaff.

The Cathedral, newly risen from the ravages of war, was shown to me and to my American friends, Betty and Henry Nichol, by the Bishop himself. Using the Cathedral as a visual aid, he was able to trace for us over a thousand years of Welsh ecclesiastical history, for each century has left a mark in the fabric. That there is in Wales today a Church that is part of the Anglican Communion must, I think, be attributed to a special dispensation of Providence. How else could it have survived a millennium of mistreatment?

Llandaff Cathedral is one of the most interesting buildings I have ever been in. One of its exciting features is the bold contemporary arch in the midst of the nave, an arch which supports Epstein's tremendous figure of "Christ in Majesty". It is a controversial work. While admiring the statue itself, the Nichols disliked it in that setting, feeling it had a jarring effect. I thought otherwise. I was glad, since so many periods of architecture are represented in the Cathedral, that an expression of Christian art from our own day is also included. Without question the Church in Wales is the oldest branch of the Anglican Communion, and to any impartial reader of history it can make good its claim to being, in terms of the historic past, *the* Catholic Church in Wales. The only remaining question is: Can it make good its claim to the retention of that historic title in the Wales of *today*? The presence of Epstein's colossal "Majestas" is a symbolic declaration of the Welsh Church's determination to prove its right to be and to become what historically it always was.

After touring the Cathedral I talked for a time with a jovial canon who reported on a conversation he had had the week before with two visiting Roman Catholic priests. After beholding the beautiful building, they shook their heads sadly and lamented, "To think! This once was ours!" To which quick-wittedly he replied, "When, may I ask, was it ever yours?" He then recited the facts of history. Wales can indeed claim to be the site of a Christianity which in its inception was quite independent of Rome. It is the oldest place of continuous worship in the British Isles. With a smile to his visitors from Rome he concluded, "The sooner the Church of Rome and the Church of England get out of Wales the better it will be for the Church in Wales."

The present position of the Welsh Church is quite unintelligible except against the background of its unfortunate past. The Church in Wales functioned independently until the twelfth century. Then, under protest, it submitted to the authority of Canterbury. Henceforth it became – to its own detriment – increasingly English; therefore, more foreign. The roots of the alienation of the Church from the people of the land had their beginnings long before the Reformation, but the great rift was reserved for post-Reformation days. The time was bound to come when the Welsh would have enough of bishops who could not speak their own language. The Welsh, many of whom were bilingual, might have tolerated bishops who could not speak Welsh, or else spoke it badly, but what they could not tolerate was bishops who never spoke at all. That is, a large number of English bishops appointed to Welsh sees never got as far west as Wales. They never set out, or, if they did, few troubled to learn the language, and they lived in hope of speedy translation to a plumper bishopric back home. While waiting for their deliverance, they occupied themselves chiefly in sipping tea or things stronger. Disaffection among the people grew apace. There were, of course, notable exceptions. Had it not been for certain great bishops from England, titanic in their self-giving, the new institution called the *Church of England* would surely have foundered. For a time it almost did. Its influence on Welsh national life in the nineteenth century was almost negligible.

The seeds of dissent had been sown. First efforts at reform were Anglican-inspired, having been nourished at Anglican altars, and were loyal to Church and Prayer Book. Yet ecclesiastical authority was less than enthusiastic about the enthusiasts, "the Methodists", even though their leaders were priests with no initial intention of breaking with the Church. Eventually, as in England and America, they were lost to the Church. The land became dotted with "chapels", and the Church, greatly enfeebled by the vast secession, was no longer the religious heart of the nation. It was stigmatized as being the champion of an alien ascendancy, the defender of a *status quo* inimical to the development of Welsh culture. Hierarchy and squirearchy, both English, were resented. The charges levelled against the Church were never fully justified – but that counts for little in a polemical situation, especially when religious zeal is fanned by the flames of nationalism. Non-conformity was in full swing, having carried a majority of the population with it. Agitation soon began for the disestablishment and disendowment of the Church of England in Wales.

For nearly four decades the controversy raged, Anglicans fighting stubbornly to retain the Establishment, Nonconformists fighting just as stubbornly to be rid of it, both sides growing progressively more bitter. In 1920 the Nonconformists won.

Very few people like to surrender money and a position of privilege. There were worthier reasons, as we shall see, for the Church's long resistance to disestablishment. But the severity of the financial blow is not to be underestimated. The Church had endowments amounting to £2,500,000. The present Archbishop of Wales suggested that I multiply the figure by four in order to understand the financial depreciation in contemporary terms. The Church disestablished had to begin the new chapter of her history with the loss of about seven-eighths of her former income.

Welsh Anglicans were understandably perturbed as they faced this prospect. Most of them, it must be emphasized, were just as patriotic, just as profoundly Welsh in sympathy, temperament, and culture, as any nationalistic Nonconformist. But they understood, better than is the wont of Nonconformity, that Christianity transcends nationality though it needs to express itself in various national cultures. And while the English connection had been resisted when first introduced in the twelfth century, the link with the English Church had come in time to be greatly treasured. It meant sharing in the life of a great Christian Communion. The fact that Welsh ordinands were often trained in English theological colleges and that English professors of theology came to Welsh institutions to teach had provided a measure of protection against the tendency of a small Church in a small land to become insular and ingrown. That safeguard against provincialism would, it was feared, be lost when severance from England was complete. How was a Church thus cut off to support herself?

Most people now realize that the dreaded disestablishment and disendowment worked to the advantage of the Church. Welsh Churchmen, rallying around her in this crisis, made the discovery that it is more blessed to give than it is to live off the bounty of remote forebears. They also found that fellowship with the Church of England and the entire Anglican Communion was as possible and as enriching as before. And most surprising of all – they found that disestablishment somehow drew the poison from the acrimonious debate with Nonconformity. Men who had hated one another became friends.

It would be wrong of me to convey the impression that these developments occurred overnight or that there is still not a long way to go. Financially, conditions are stringent to this very day, but so too even before disendowment. The Church in Wales has never known riches. It is now, however, self-supporting. Stipends for the clergy, though meagre, are better than they used to be; most parsonages are fit for human habitation which was not always true in the past; retirement, old age, and death have been robbed of a few of their terrors with the introduction of a compulsory Pensions Scheme; the Church in Wales requires most candidates for the Ministry to be Graduates in Arts with postgraduate training in theology. In short, the small and once discredited Church in Wales chalked up an impressive record during the forty-two years it has had to stand squarely on its own.

In an assessment of the Church in Wales today it must be borne in mind that despite the great antiquity of Christianity in that land, the Church as now organized is less than a half century old. Prior to 1920 it comprised but four dioceses lacking any kind of organic unity with one another. Each bishop held jurisdiction direct from Canterbury. There was no overarching regional organization. This Church needed time to build up an interior life of its own. The wonder is that everything has moved so fast. A well-knit province is in being, two new dioceses have been created, the canon law has been codified, a hymnal rich in the traditions of Welsh musical genius has been published, and a Prayer Book revision is under way. Church membership has increased. Meanwhile, Welsh Churchmen are mature enough – with some exceptions – not to gloat over the fact that Nonconformity is beginning to decline slightly. On the contrary, they regard this trend with alarm and sorrow, for they doubt that Anglicanism in Wales has the ability at present to do the job that Nonconformity did. It is a fact, however, that Nonconformity lost some of its strength and power to attract the moment *Yr Hên Fam* (The Old Mother) was disestablished. Another factor which is having a sad effect on Nonconformity is the indubitable, perhaps unfortunate but inevitable, decline of the Welsh language. Young Nonconformists in many areas are no longer Welsh-speaking.

Thus Nonconformity is no longer considered the shrine and guardian of a venerable tongue and culture. By a curious irony, there are many places in Wales where you will hear more of Welsh in the Church than in the Chapel. A churchman realizes anew the blessing of belonging to a Church with a set form of worship, a fixed liturgy. It matters less what language is spoken so long as the liturgy is discerningly the same.

In any event, Nonconformity, despite reverses, is still present in force on

Wales. And to the endless benefit of the ancient Church, it will be there for a long time. A big Church with a spiritually vigorous Chapel near by is kept on its toes – on its knees too. The challenge of Nonconformity will drive the Welsh Church to a rediscovery of itself. Meanwhile, although the Ecumenical Movement has had little effect in Wales, a start has been made. A Council of Churches has been formed, conversations are in progress. Brotherhood is yet to come, but at least the bitterness has gone. In the arena of secular politics, where fighting takes place with the gloves off, it is significant that nowadays, in contrast to the past, the vote is seldom determined any more by linguistic and denominational differences. This stems not from apathy but from a new level of mutual understanding and appreciation.

A new element in Welsh life is the growth of Rome. It is still small, probably less than 10 per cent of the population. Yet Rome alone, of all contenders, can claim an absolute increase in recent years. The claim must be granted, but to appraise statistics properly it must be remembered that the growth comes not so much from the winning of new converts as it does from the influx of Irish labourers into the industrial valleys and Polish farmers into the countryside. For all the strange tenacity with which Rome holds to Latin in public worship, she is wise: she compels the priests she sends (mostly from Ireland and England) to learn Welsh in order that preaching, teaching, and pastoral ministrations in the Welsh-speaking areas may proceed in the mother tongue. In this respect the modern Church of Rome is more reformed than the Reformed Church of England.

It takes no great powers of divination to predict that Rome – first, because of immigration; second, because of intermarriage; and third, because of Welsh-speaking zeal – may end by outstripping Anglicanism and Nonconformity both. Yet I am not so sure of myself as I sound. The present temper of the Anglican Christians in Wales, their readiness to adjust and to try new techniques, and above all their intelligence and their fervour, give me the tiny hope that "The Old Mother" will have many sons and daughters in the new Wales that is emerging today.

1. BRITISH WEST INDIES: The bow of a weathered fishing boat at Kingstown, in the Windward Islands, proclaims a strong and simple faith. Here is an older and simpler mode of life – hand-sewn nets, uncooped chickens, a child unashamed of his nakedness.

29, 30, 31, & 32. GREAT BRITAIN: The 99th Archbishop of Canterbury enters his Cathedral – the Mother Church of the Anglican Communion, *left*. Trinity College, Dublin, Eire, *below*, is considered a principal intellectual ornament of the Anglican Communion. But not everything is ancient in *Ecclesia Anglicana*, as we can see from the modern interior of a new parish church at Bishop's Hatfield, near London, *top right*, and the chapel of the theological college, *bottom right*, at Llandaff, Wales.

35. SOLOMON ISLANDS: Off the shores of Gela, an island under British Protection, one of the launches operated by the Diocese of Melanesia rides at anchor while girls of St. Hilda's School, Bunana, bend cheerfully to their work of unloading supplies. Such launches are vital lifelines for this South Pacific diocese.

33 & 34. GREAT BRITAIN: The *John Ashley* cruises on the Thames, a priest at its helm, offering the Church's ministry to dock workers and men of the sea, *top left*, while the three colliers, *bottom left*, are typical of the men the Church of England is reaching in answer to the charges that it has lost the working classes.

36. NEW ZEALAND: This Auckland church looks down on the Bay where New Zealand's first bishop, Augustus Selwyn, ended a perilous voyage from England in 1842 by wading ashore and kneeling down to kiss the sands. It was on the altar of this church that a constitution was signed which made the Province of New Zealand the first autonomous Church within the British Empire.

37. AUSTRALIA: These schoolgirls leaving an early service at Charleville are pupils at one of the many Anglican schools in the remote settlements of the vast 'Outback'.

38. MELANESIA: Animated gestures are part of a song of welcome to Canon Johnson by Anglican schoolgirls of Melanesia, which, though part of the Church of New Zealand, has had generous help in evangelization and education from the Church of Australia.

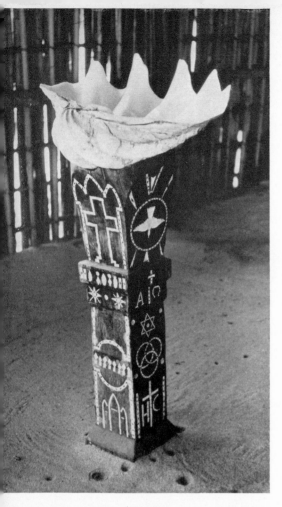

39 & 40. MELANESIA: The theological college at Siota boasts a baptismal font which utilizes perfectly local materials: for the base native wood inlaid with mother-of-pearl taken from shells gathered on the beach; for the bowl itself the shell of a giant clam. A superb example of indigenization. The Melanesian Brotherhood, a vigorous lay order, *below*, flourishes from its base at Guadalcanal, one of the famous battle-grounds of World War II. (See pp. 308 f.)

41. NEW GUINEA: Far from home base at Kelham in England, the Father Director of the Society of the Sacred Mission teaches the girls of the Anglican school at Dogura the game of ring-a-ring-o'-roses so that they will not pose too self-consciously for the camera.

42. SINGAPORE: The priest stands before the altar of a church that is an unmistakably Chinese departure from Victorian Gothic.

43. IRAN: The church of St. Simon the Zealot in Shiraz is regarded as a highly successful adaptation of Persian motifs for Christianity.

44. JAPAN: Newly-built Holy Trinity Church, Tokyo, raises a stark cross over a modern tower – typical of the contemporary styles preferred in Japan today.

45. PHILIPPINES: The new cathedral at Quezon City is an impressive part of the rebuilding and expansion in and around war-torn Manila.

46. BURMA: A gigantic golden Buddha dwarfs the figure of an Anglican priest – just as the religions of the East – Buddhism, Hinduism and Islam – overshadow Christianity in this area. The statue, at the summit of a holy mountain, stretches out a commanding arm towards Mandalay and the stupa-studded plain beyond.

47. BURMA: In Pa'an in Karen State, the Right Reverend Francis Ah Mya, an assistant of the Bishop of Rangoon, superintends construction of a new school.

48. HONG KONG: The clerical collar of this priest is only a part-time article of attire. During the business week he is a sanitation engineer in a soft collar and tie. The Diocese of Hong Kong is making a valiant effort to minister to the refugees who pour in from behind the Bamboo Curtain by ordaining men like him who will devote after-office hours and week-ends to the work of the Church.

49. BURMA: Children of an Anglican school in Pa'an.

50. KOREA: More children, this time from an Anglican school established in Korea to care for the generation growing up in the wake of the Korean War.

51. 52 & 53. KOREA: Women at prayer – the strength of the Church in "The Land of the Morning Calm". Eighteen hours after the serene picture, *above*, was taken revolutionary bullets whizzed across the Cathedral Close in Seoul. Yet the work of the Anglican Communion in the East goes on – whether in a confirmation ceremony in a Korean village, *top right*, or a West Pakistan parish, *bottom right*.

54. WEST PAKISTAN: Procession to the church for a Confirmation in a largely Anglican village called Bethlehem. Here, as also in India, the Church, although small, is on the march – 'With the Cross of Jesus going on before!'

4. SOUTHERN BRAZIL: This *Igreja Episcopal* is typical of the many Anglican churches built in recent years in the West Indies and in Central and South America. Rarely grand, they are nevertheless substantial, functional and attractive.

2 & 3. DOMINICAN REPUBLIC: Unhurried and frequently listless, children play while neighbours talk in a muddy street of Puerto Plata, *above left*. 'Whenever a crime is committed the police look first in this quarter,' said the Anglican priest. 'So here we build a church', (*gabled roof at right.*) Its rough-hewn altar and cross, *below*, draw parishioners away from the shrill cries of the crowded, depressed area.

5. PUERTO RICO, *top left*: In the city of Ponce is the Community of the Transfiguration, an Anglican sisterhood which has won high esteem for its work among underprivileged adolescents.   6. HAITI, *bottom left*: The victim of rickets, a four-year-old boy is comforted by a member of the Society of St. Margaret after being fitted with braces at St. Vincent's School for Handicapped Children at Port-au-Prince. Baptists help us with this work – as does the Haitian Air Force.   7. BRITISH GUIANA: Teaching children of different races and religions how to live together constructively is one of the objects of the Anglican sister, *above*, in a Georgetown school.   8. THE BAHAMAS: On All Hallows' Eve, a Canadian missionary, *below*, invites a girl pupil in a Nassau school to join in making masks from paper sacks.

9. MEXICO: The Bishop of Mexico is flanked by his chaplain and the Bishop of Puerto Rico, (left) at the dedication of a new church, the Mission de San Juan el Teólogo in Alejandro. The upcast eyes of the child, (right) contemplate the west window which the Bishop is consecrating to the glory of God.

10. BRAZIL: In Trinity Cathedral, Porto Alegre, a name is given, water is poured, and still another child is signed with the Sign of the Cross.

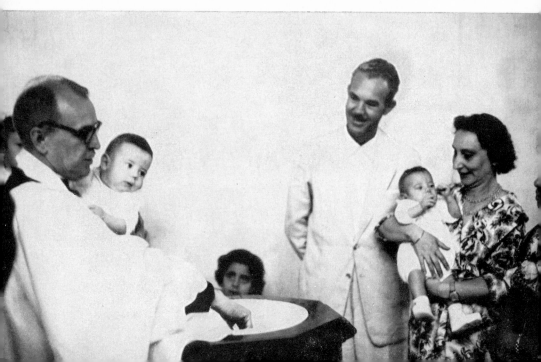

11. WEST AFRICA: A smile lights the face of a dignified seeker of honey as he pauses amid palms and brush before continuing his daily quest, see pp. 66 f.

12 & 13. AFRICA: The vastness, solitude, poverty and isolation of Zululand are suggested in this churchyard scene just before a dawn service. Most members of the congregation walked all night to receive Holy Communion. Other devout Anglicans, *below*, join in prayers within the fragile framework of their new church.

14 & 15. AFRICA: Church House, Nairobi, is headquarters for the Diocese of Mombasa. Africa is more than thatch and wattle and daub. It is also skyscrapers. The stunning new church, *below*, is in Southern Rhodesia, Diocese of Mashonaland.

16, 17, 18 & 19. AFRICA: Not far from the banks of the Nile in Uganda, a bishop, administers the rite of Confirmation. After the Benediction a joyous congregation broke into spontaneous dancing, *above right*. Elsewhere in Uganda students assemble for the groundbreaking of a new dormitory, *below right*, are making cement blocks to a new wing for their school. The students in Swaziland, *below left*.

20, 21 & 22. SOUTHERN RHODESIA: St. Patrick's Mission, Gwelo, Diocese of Matabeleland. The love of learning is apparent in the girl reciting in class, *left*. The future mothers of Africa learn sewing and child-care, *above*, while the processes of democracy are learned at a meeting of a parish council, *below*.

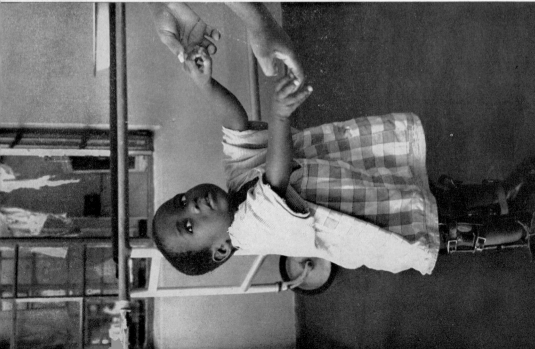

23, 24 & 25. AFRICA: A young patient, *left*, at Umlazi, Durban, South Africa, is treated for tuberculosis of the bone – a scourge of many parts of Africa. A line of small Anglicans, *above*, at Nqutu in Zululand, would have to travel 700 miles for medical care, were it not for the Church hospital. Christian concern shows in the countenance of this nurse, *below*, as she confronts human need in a hospital in Mpondas, Nyasaland.

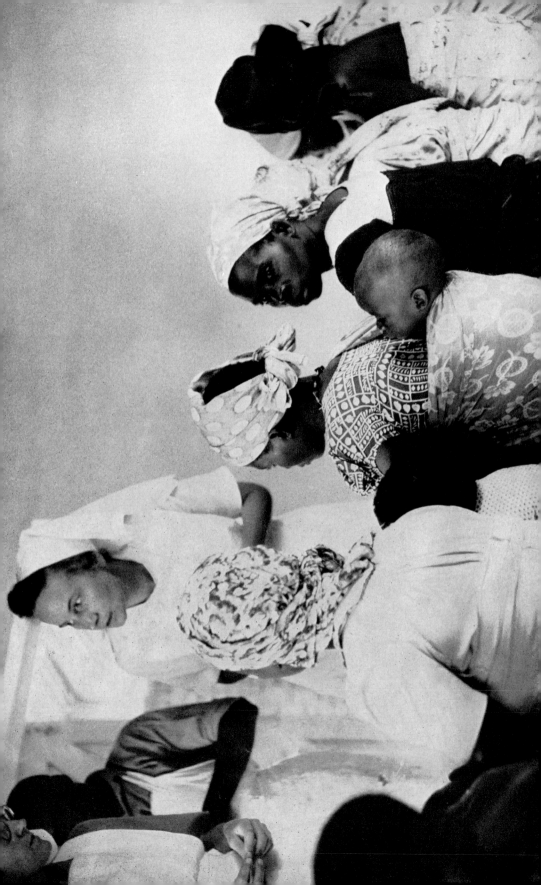

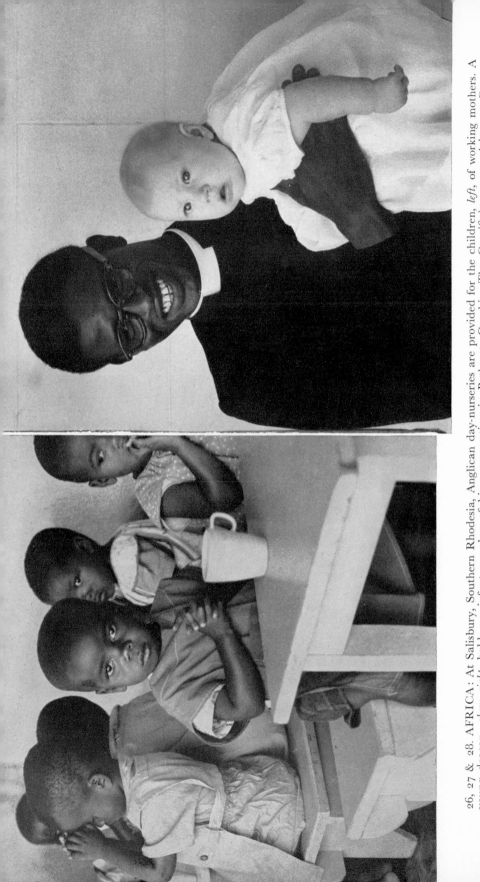

26, 27 & 28. AFRICA: At Salisbury, Southern Rhodesia, Anglican day-nurseries are provided for the children, *left*, of working mothers. A young deacon, *above right*, holds an infant member of his congregation in Bathurst, Gambia. The Crucifixion scene, *below*, at Cyrene, Southern Rhodesia, is an example of the Anglican Mission's revival of African arts to convey Christian themes. Many of the Mission's sculptors and painters are cripples who, in spite of withered limbs and gnarled hands, often produce works of surpassing beauty. The murals were badly smudged on October 13, 1962, when a fanatic threw two home-made bombs on to the thatched roof.

I I

IRELAND: Sanctity, Scholarship, and Shrinkage

IN MY EAGERNESS TO REACH THE EMERALD ISLE I QUITE OVERLOOKED that a Bank Holiday week-end had begun – a time when all dispersed sons and daughters of Erin are bent on returning home. No cabin or berth aboard the steamer from Fishguard to Cork was to be had at any price. I would have been glad if I could have reserved as much as a chair. I had to stand all night. The inside decks, the companionways, and the stairs were packed with people miserably trying to sleep. The gale that had forced all passengers to go below soon reduced over a third of them to *mal de mer*.

I myself weathered the storm without ill effect – proud descendant that I am of the Vikings. However, I thought it best not to speak too much of my remote ancestors in this crowded Irish environment, for I remembered the barbaric way in which the Men from the North had destroyed the brilliant Christian culture which Ireland had anciently achieved and liberally disseminated – all of which happened, though Irish Roman Catholics tend to forget it, long before the Church in Ireland came under the jurisdiction of Rome. From the Scandinavian depredations Ireland never recovered.

Nor could I deem it wise, on this stormy night, to mention the second source of the blood which flows in my veins: English. For the few things Irish which the Danes spared the English destroyed later. All in all, history has not been kind to the Irish.

Poor Ireland! Economically the country is so hard up that it enjoys a unique distinction: alone among the nations of the world it has a diminishing population. In order to earn a livelihood, masses of Irishmen have had to seek elsewhere. Since often the most enterprising emigrate, the mother country is not only depopulated but constantly drained of her best blood. The prospects are gloomy, for the end of this attrition is not yet in view.

By daybreak the storm had blown itself out, and the sailing into Cork was extremely beautiful. People were grey-faced after a sleepless night, but Holy Ground was in sight, and that brought a flush of expectancy. Even I, with no background of affection for Ireland, forgot my fatigue immediately on arrival because of the friendliness with which I was received by the Dean of Cork and his family. It was the first time I had seen the Irish in their own country. They promptly captured my heart.

The present Cork Cathedral is a late nineteenth-century building and a remarkable achievement when one considers how few Anglicans there were in this part of Ireland to build it and how poor many of them were. It was the first Irish church I had ever seen, and interestingly enough, although candlesticks are not permitted unless it can be proved that they are absolutely necessary in order to give light to read by, the Irish Anglicans have no fear of colour, stained glass, or statuary. The Churchmanship is Low, but not of the determined, deliberately dreary-and-drab school. Although the clergy at celebrations of the Lord's Supper may permit themselves no vestment more ornamental than surplice and black scarf, there are frontals and antependia in the whole spectrum of the traditional Latin colour scheme. There is, in other words, no cult of the ugly. Everything is beautiful – just so long as you see to it that no ensign of the Cross is on or above the Holy Table. A few Irish churches, I learned, have taken the bold step of putting candlesticks on the Holy Table, but of course their candles are never lighted – unless there is a power failure! Curious it is that "High Church" in one part of the world never seems so in another part. Every Irish parish, even the most fiercely Evangelical, chants the Psalms of David at Matins and Evensong. Hymns, after all, were meant to be sung. Yet in the United States to *sing* the Psalms is one of *the* badges of High Churchmanship. And so it goes. It would be easy to provide a score of examples. Actually, a little historical perspective is needed to preserve oneself from impatience, intolerance, fanaticism, or scornful laughter. "High Church" has been accurately defined as anything done in church to which one is unaccustomed.

In the Church of Ireland canon law forbids exhibition of the cross. Irish churchmen might do well to reflect that in Egypt, where Anglicanism has laboured under auspices equally Evangelical, it is a matter of principle and pride to *exhibit* the cross – all the more so because Muslims are bent on hiding it. We build an imposing cathedral on the banks of the Nile; the Muslims hasten to build a mosque on the opposite bank, the chief motivation being to outshine us and to lift their emblem higher than ours. A church goes up in Cairo – and suddenly it is hidden from view by hideous billboards two stories high in an attempt to conceal what we would show forth.

Take the example of the Church of Denmark. It can be just as foolish as we are in matters of externals. Although in theological terms the Danish

Reformation was far more radical than the English, it never took an icono-
clastic turn. There was in Denmark no toppling of altars, no smashing of
stained-glass windows, no decapitation of sculptured saints. Except for
incense, sacring bells, and the stole, everything was permitted to remain
as it was. Altars, candles, lace, statues, chasubles and albs were used as
before. Liturgically instructed Danish priests, however, have wanted to
restore the stole. Their chances of success are slim. Let a priest don a stole
and his congregation will throw up their hands in horror and cry, "Rome!"
But how strange! Surplice and stole are standard practice in most of
Anglicanism. *We* have to fight in many quarters for the restoration of the
chasuble, whereas no self-respecting Danish priest would be caught dead in
a surplice, that late and debased medieval invention.

Consider also our Anglican indecision as to whether Mass or Matins is
to be the principal service on the Lord's Day. In Anglican circles, for a long
time, Matins had the priority. Matins still rates as "*the* Morning Service"
in most of the Anglican world, but, as an option for people so inclined, a
late celebration is appended after most of the worshippers have gone, and,
for the exceptionally pious (and perhaps for those who cannot bear the
present calibre of Anglican preaching), there is an "early service", quiet and
devout, in which there is no pricking of conscience from the pulpit.

On Danish soils the battle is fought in different terms. To no member of
the Evangelical and Reformed Lutheran Church of Denmark would it
occur that anything but the Supper of the Lord was the most appropriate
act of worship on the first day of the week. The Church of Denmark has
never been in any doubt about the centrality of the Holy Communion. Yet
its certainty on that point has amounted almost to a fixation. So fixed is
the Danish Church that – except for occasional Offices like Baptism, Confirmation, Marriage, etc. – it has no non-eucharistic liturgical services.
Anything like Morning and Evening Prayer is totally unknown. But Danish
priests who have been to the United Kingdom return home with the perception that Danish Church life is impoverished by reason of its having no
common worship except in the context of the Eucharist. They agitate,
therefore, for the restoration of the Daily Offices. But they are shouted down.
"Don't give us any of that monkish, medieval mumbo jumbo! Just give us
the Gospel service of the Mass".

That is Danish talk, and it must sound strange to Irishmen. But the
Irish and all others of the Anglican persuasion might profit by bearing in
mind that most issues of churchmanship have little to do with theology.
They are, rather, merely allergic reactions to historical conditioning.
Knowing this background enables one to view ceremonial differences in
minor matters.

Many Irish churches never bother to enter in the register the number of persons present at divine service. Perhaps it would be discouraging to keep track of the steady dwindling. "It is the Americans who always demand statistics," one man said to me reproachfully. "This concern with the numerical is a disease with you people." I reminded him that there is a book in the canon of Holy Scripture called Numbers. I rather relished my rejoinder – and was pleased that he was not quick enough to retort, "Yes, but the man who took the census incurred divine displeasure."

The Anglican population of what is now the Republic has declined, since 1861, 61 per cent. According to the census of 1956, Eire had a population of 2,898,000. Of these 2,736,000 were Roman Catholics. The Church of Ireland reported 120,000; the Presbyterians, 22,000; the Methodists, 12,000. There is no other religious body of significant size.

We are the second largest church in the land but even so, we are small. The causes for this numerical weakness are complex, but the chief of them is the well-known weary and dreary one: The Church was too English from the days of Elizabeth I on, and the English bungled it. Although all but two of the Irish bishops accepted the Elizabethan Settlement, they made their great mistake by not hastening to get the Prayer Book translated into Gaelic. Having to worship in English did the Church little good. The language was more foreign to a majority of the Irish than Latin. By the time the Prayer Book in translation did appear (1608) the damage had already been done: in the public mind, it was an "English Church". Meanwhile, the great Tudor Queen, with her canny manœuvrings to keep Ireland out of the clutches of Spain, hardly endeared herself and the Church of which she claimed to be Supreme Governor to a people resentful of foreign rule, confiscation of property, and a steady influx of colonists from England.

The history of Irish-English relations is far too intricate a subject to admit of capsule treatment. But as an *aide de memoire* I submit by title three additional factors that, in one way or another, have radically affected the Church of Ireland. First, the "presence" in Ireland of too many absentee bishops – the special iniquity and curse of eighteenth-century English policy. Second, Mr. Gladstone's decision, in the hope of pacifying Ireland, to disestablish the Church; although this move was furiously resisted by churchmen at the time, it was carried out by the government in a fair and generous manner, and it is now conceded to have been a boon. Since 1870, a Church long deprived by the State of the power of self-government has slowly been learning again this lost art, and in the relearning of it has been gaining a new resoluteness, a new strength, a new consciousness of what the Church is. Also, disestablishment prepared the way for better relations between Anglicans and Roman Catholics. Third, the emergence in 1922, after dreadful strife, of the Irish Free State that is now the Irish Republic and not a member of the British Commonwealth of Nations.

In the light of this third development, one shudders to think what the fate of the Church would have been had it still been English and Established. To this day the Church, in the public mind, is too much the Church of the "English Connexion", the Church of "English loyalists", too little therefore the Church of the authentic Irish. Most Protestants were supporters of the Connexion and out of sympathy with the Republic. This has proved to be a handicap to the growth of the Church of Ireland. Prayers for the King of England continued to be offered in public worship long after the Republic had been declared. Nobody disputes the fact that the English Sovereign, like all others in authority, needs the prayers of the Faithful. Many a son of Eire might be inclined to think that that Sovereign *particularly* needs praying for. But for a minority Church, under the volatile circumstances of those times, not at once to accommodate her public prayers to the *de facto* political situation, betrays a stubbornness and a stupidity hard to forgive. Even a moment's hesitation was costly. Unfortunately, the Church hesitated.

There is, however, a bright side. Reason soon asserted itself in the Councils of the Church; and although hot-tempered individuals would have had it otherwise, the Church made it clear that she could not, without being false to herself, abandon her position as the historic Church of Ireland, which meant *all* of Ireland, the Republic in the South, the Six Counties in the North. Although pressure has been exerted many times, in the interests of efficiency and convenience, to shift the Church's administrative centre from Dublin in Eire to Belfast in Northern Ireland (where the Anglican numerical centre of gravity is), it has been successfully resisted. Inconvenience must not be allowed to dictate policy. Were headquarters transferred to Belfast, an essential would be lost. We would become, in effect, the Church of Ulster – with a small southern appendage. It would make us something less than the Church of *Ireland*, which basically we are but through bad inheritance and our own tomfoolery we are not.

The Church today encompasses two countries. The new political boundary cuts across four diocesan boundaries, yet wisely there has been no disposition to realign them. The Archbishop of Armagh must frequently pass in both directions the absurd political frontier which divides the island between north and south. He, his brother bishops, his clergy, and his laity pass that frontier and are equally at home on either side because they travel in the Name of Christ. A very considerable achievement of the Church of Ireland is the fact that it did not split along political lines. So far as the Church is concerned, the border does not exist. Not many institutions could transcend this tragic and bitter rift. That this branch of the Church has done so is a shining example of the Saviour's power to break down the "middle wall of partition".

Even so, for purposes of exposition let us consider the two parts of the island separately, for the complexion is a little different south of the border.

In Eire the Church of Rome has the allegiance of 94.3 per cent of the population. "Can you give me some notion of what it means in terms of the psychology of clergy and laity," I asked, "to be cast in the role of a minority church, one that apparently is destined in all foreseeable historical time to continue as a diminutive minority?"

To get my answer I chose an ecclesiastic well versed in Irish affairs, himself an Irishman, and thrust into his hands the microphone of the portable dictating machine I was carrying with me around the world. Here is a transcript of the answer he gave me – and I found no one who disagreed with him:

"I think it has two effects. One is good, in that when you are in a minority church you feel that each individual member is an advertisement for the Faith, and it keeps you on your toes. With a 94 or 95 per cent Roman majority around you, you feel that, to put it at the lowest level, you must pull your weight for your Church. The way the Holy Spirit works in this particular historical situation, though the motives of men are sometimes mixed, is to generate an intense loyalty which reflects itself in a high level of churchgoing and churchgiving.

"That is the good side of it. The other aspect of it is not good. Being in a minority makes you unnecessarily on the defensive, too self-conscious, too inclined to separate from the common life. Before the foundation of the Free State, as the present Republic was first called, a majority of Church of Ireland people had a strong British association, mentally at any rate if not actually, and the result was that when the Free State came into being, a very large number of Irish Church people seemed to take no part in politics. Half of the explanation is that they were not allowed in. The majority kept them out. The other half is that they stayed out from choice. It was a 'they' and 'we' complex, which was not good for the country as a whole and not good for the Church of Ireland in particular."

My informant was able to continue on a more cheerful note: "I think that's dying out now. My impression is that the younger generation of Irish Church people are tending more and more to play their part in the full life of the country. For instance, last year's Lord Mayor in Cork was a member of the Church of Ireland, the first for fifty years, and this year's Lord Mayor in Dublin is also a member of the Church of Ireland for the first time in sixty years. (I may not have the dates right, but it is more or less accurate.) And that in itself is significant, I think, because it means that they were elected by a very large Roman Catholic majority. Bit by bit it is becoming apparent to the thinking Roman Catholic that the average member of the Church of Ireland is just as good an Irishman as he."

My Irish acquaintance went on to speak of the active part taken by Church of Ireland members in the commercial and cultural affairs of the south, and he wanted me to understand that there was no discrimination: "There doesn't seem to be any kind of back kick from the 'others' for our being Protestants." He drove me through the countryside, pointing out one large farm after another and saying, "The owner is a member of our Church. Throughout the diocese we have a strong settled population of farmers who are what you might call a constant element. . . . They give vitality to each small country parish." Summing up the matter, he said, "You can quite fairly say that Church people in Eire are taking their part, by and large, in public affairs and they have a stake in the country. They're not retired people who just come here to live because the fishing and the shooting are good. They're people whose roots are here."

Disestablishment for the Church of Ireland did not involve disendowment, as was the case in Wales. Consequently, the Church's financial plight is less serious than its small size might indicate. With one priest to every 709 members, it is in a position to do better pastoral work than is possible in more understaffed parts of the Anglican Communion.

The Government of the Republic has dealt with the Church of Ireland in a manner consistently fair and courteous. It pays all but a small fraction of the cost of educating children in denominational schools, and religious instruction is encouraged by the secular authorities.

Small as we are, we are in Eire to stay. But our fate, alas, is probably to become smaller still – for reasons which have nothing to do with religion. This is Rome's fate too, for Ireland itself keeps shrinking. The population is just under three million. The natural increase is a skimpy twenty-five thousand annually, while every year it loses something like forty thousand through emigration. Part of this loss is due to the decrease in agriculture and to the movement, characteristic of all the world, towards industrial centres. Since the country itself is only beginning to be industrialized, the more ambitous young Irishmen book tickets for Liverpool, Coventry, or Birmingham or else for ports Welsh or American. And in those strange lands, unfortunately, quite a number of them – whether belonging to the Church of Ireland or to the Church of Rome – fall out of the habit of churchgoing. "When they come home on holiday," said one man I interviewed, "they spread their bad habits and sow seeds of discontent through their preaching of an 'evangel' about higher wages, bright lights, and the joys of television. But now," he continued, "we must gird ourselves for something far worse.

Since Ireland itself is beginning to be industrialized, many Irishmen will come home one of these days for something more than a holiday. They'll come home for good. But a lot of these returnees will be up to no good. Factory-ized and secularized Irish might change the complexion of Ireland very much, and not to its advantage."

In this declaration there are, I believe, overtones of a reactionary conservatism, a desire to keep Ireland frozen in the moulds of the past, which is not to be commended; yet there may also be here the accents of authentic prophecy. *All* the Churches in Ireland should start preparing for the day when the tides of emigration may turn and the flowing back may bring to its shores not only the benefits but also the disadvantages of a thoroughly contemporary world.

It should occasion no surprise, I suppose, that people who dwell on an island are sometimes insular. The Irish are not unique in this respect, although they rank high in the scale.

Except for those who have been privileged to travel widely, even the most enlightened of Irish Anglicans can think and speak of Roman Catholicism solely in terms of the Irish brand, which does not augur well for good interchurch relations. Conditioned as they are by their island situation, their outlook on Rome is narrow, the reaction bitter. There are serious failures in charity. Much of the youth work undertaken by the Irish Church has as its motivation a fear of mixed marriages. Admittedly, there is ground for this fear. Anglicans are lost to us at an alarming rate by intermarriage.* But the situation gives to our work a defensive quality which is not wholesome.

Some Dublin hosts of mine listened in open-mouthed astonishment to my report about a forum that we have held for eight years at the Cathedral Church in New York attended by psychologists, psychiatrists, and psychoanalysts, and by theologians, hospital chaplains, and parochial pastors. Together they wrestle earnestly with the question of the relationship between Christianity and psychiatry, without doubt one of the most urgent problems of our era. But psychiatry has yet to reach Ireland on any large scale, and the Church is far from having given any serious thought to it.

Irish attitudes towards the Church's use of radio and television also seemed to me to be behind the times. Although no Church in the Anglican Communion has much to boast of on this score, it must be recorded that the Church of England, in co-operation with the British Council of Churches

---

* Not with reference to Ireland especially but to the whole world, I would note that a book worthy of study is James A. Pike's *If You Marry Outside Your Faith.* It is fair, it sticks to the facts, it pulls no punches. But I found it has not been published in Great Britain – another example of our lamentable failure to share the wealth.

and the British Broadcasting Company, supports a school where selected clergy and laity receive training in the demanding, almost merciless, medium of television. Much thought remains to be given to the question of what materials, what types of approach lend themselves to the purposes of religious broadcasting. Hence the brand new school in England. America has nothing comparable.

Ireland, for the most part, still wonders if the Church has any business in television at all. In justice to the Diocese of Dublin and Glendalough and Kildare, it should be mentioned that it has a radio and television committee which explores the subject and uses such facilities as are available. In the midst of an overwhelmingly Roman Catholic population these facilities are less readily accessible to Anglicans than they are where the Church is established or at any rate proportionately larger. Nevertheless, the effort to use the newest mass media in order to introduce the Church to its neighbours should be pursued whatever the obstacles.

A new feature of the world landscape is forests of television antennae. Our Anglican Communion is not yet sufficiently alert to the fact that each and every mast is a standing invitation to enter, or at least the possibility of effecting an entry, into countless homes.

The Liturgical Movement has hardly dawned on the consciousness of Ireland. Suffering shock from the liturgical excesses of the brand of Romanism they are acquainted with, and painfully aware that the disestablishment of the Church of Ireland was one of the things that touched off the Tractarian Movement in England, the Irish Church is devoid of appetite for liturgical experimentation. After so many controversies, it wants no one to disturb the equilibrium which was achieved in the last century. "Better to leave things as they are than to stir up strife" is the attitude of virtually all the clergy, including those who because of their reading and travels would like to introduce change. No part of the Anglican Communion is more faithful to its Prayer Book, more scrupulous in obeying its rubrics, than the Church of Ireland. Obedience to constituted authority is one of the very Catholic marks of this, in some ways, very Protestant member of our Communion. Travel wherever you will throughout the length and breadth of the island, enter any church, and you can be certain of what you will find ritually and ceremonially.

But the point I wish to make is that those who desire change in the externals of worship are yearning for practices long out of date. Pleasure was expressed in my hearing over the fact that now, more and more, there are in Ireland "robed choirs". Don't they know that in England and America the whole desire is to get the choir into a gallery at the back of the church from which location it can do a far better job of "leading" the congregation and where, because it is out of view, there is no need of robes? And the Irish, having nothing else with which to adorn their Holy Tables, fight for the right to deck them with flowers, whereas in England and America the most advanced liturgical thought wants to clear the Table of flowers and put them, if present at all, in vases on the floor or on stands to one side.

An austere ritual can be quite compatible (as in the case of the early Tractarians) with Catholic theological insights, and the faith and doctrine of the Church of Ireland are by no means so exclusively and unbendingly Protestant as a casual observer of its liturgical usages might suppose.

Most of the preceding remarks apply to all of Ireland, but now it is necessary to point out a few characteristics peculiar to Northern Ireland. Unlike Eire, it is part of the British Commonwealth; it has more wealth, more industry, and a better chance of staging a comeback so far as population is concerned. While Rome is the largest Christian body even in the North (485,200), the non-Roman Churches outnumber it there. The Presbyterians claim some 410,000; the Church of Ireland, 354,000. Our Church in the North is big enough to make its voice heard and strong enough to attempt big things in a big way – all of which it is doing. Yet one suspects that in these Six Counties of Northern Ireland there is much "Political Protestantism": people espousing Protestantism, flocking to the churches, out of fear that an emancipated Northern Ireland would be dominated by the Roman Catholic majority. From apprehensive Protestants one hears the cry, "Home Rule is Rome Rule", a bad slogan – and a bad basis. It can be maintained, I think, that the Church of Ireland is less guilty of this attitude than are the Irish Presbyterians, although it is certainly not free from it.

Moreover, I had the impression that the farther north I travelled in Ireland, the more clearly Calvinism had tinged the life of Irish Anglicanism. This influence showed itself in such un-Anglican phenomena as Sabbatarianism, Puritanism, and bitter anti-Romanism. The historical causes are not far to seek. Ireland, especially the North, was an asylum for French Protestant refugees, and Scottish Presbyterian colonists in droves settled in the vicinity of Belfast. Belfast is one of the largest Presbyterian cities in the world. Thus cultural propinquity and intermarriage have left their mark on the Irish form of Anglicanism, and the two Churches have huddled together out of fear of a third Church, the big one. Ironically and inexplicably, relations between the two Churches are not especially cordial, since they feel themselves beleaguered. Culturally and theologically, they are much alike, but each is large enough to feel itself a competitor of the other. In

Eire, by contrast, both are so small (particularly Presbyterianism) and so overwhelmed numerically by Rome that they find it far easier to co-operate than do the two major non-Roman Churches of the North. How complicated, how involved are the affairs of one little island! I recount but the half, yet even that is enough to make one's head spin.

I confess here and now that at times on my journey, especially when travel fatigue had set in, I came near to despair about the present state of Christendom. How is it possible that the followers of Christ have managed to walk in so many different directions? How can disciples of the one Lord diverge and damage each other to such an extent? No wonder we Christians have difficulty converting the world when we so fail in love for one another.

12

SCOTLAND: Church and Kirk

SCOTTISH EPISCOPALIANS WOULD DOUBTLESS BE GRATEFUL IF, FOR a change, somebody would write a book about them without repeating Sir Walter Scott's celebrated remark that the Episcopal Church has been reduced to "but the shadow of a shade". Yet the phrase is apt.

"The Episcopal Church in Scotland": proud title, but what does it mean? It means a Church of some 108,000 members who constitute only 2 per cent of the total population. It is ringed by Presbyterians who are well on their way to having the allegiance of 50 per cent of the people. And Rome has far outstripped us. It can claim a solid 16 per cent.

I had my first direct experience of our smallness in Scotland when, after having arrived in Glasgow by steamer from Belfast, I asked three successive hall porters in the hotel where I could find the Episcopal Cathedral. Ordinarily hall porters are an extremely knowledgeable lot. Not one, however, could answer my question. I fared no better with a taxi driver. On hearing that I wanted to go to the Episcopal Cathedral, he said, "You mean the Protestant Cathedral?" I said, "No, I think not. The Protestant Cathedral must mean the Church of Scotland Cathedral. I want the one that belongs to the Episcopal Church." By way of amplification, since I saw I was not making myself understood, I added, "Anglican Cathedral – Church of England." That remark unleashed a lecture. "We're not English here," said he sourly, "we're Scots. And we've got two cathedrals, the Catholic one and the Protestant one. Now which do you want?" Although I had misgivings, I let him carry me off to the "Protestant Cathedral". As I had expected, it was *not* the building I was in search of, though I am glad, from a touristic point of view, to have seen it. Its Gothic magnificence caused me to sigh, "And to think that once this was 'ours'!" But unlike the two Roman priests at Llandaff, I had history on my side.

I asked a "cathedral" verger if he could tell me the way to the Episcopal

Cathedral. The friendly smile with which he had welcomed my approach vanished. "It's over on the other side of town," he sputtered, turning on his heel and striding away from me. There was no more to be got out of him. It may be that I was just unlucky in the guides I happened to meet.

I never did find the Cathedral, for I had to hustle to catch a one o'clock train to reach Edinburgh in time for the great ecumenical service in St. Giles' Cathedral – perhaps the only cathedral in all of Presbyterianism.

It was a good time for me to be in Scotland, first in Edinburgh for this service, and later in St. Andrews, where the committees toiled, for it gave me a chance to confer with Anglican leaders who had come from all over the world, many of whom I had not been able to visit in their native haunts. It also gave me a chance to form an opinion about the scope and depth of Anglican participation in the Ecumenical Movement.

The Primus was in town, having come in from Argyll and the Isles, his scattered, thinly populated Diocese of much rain, many mountains, and islands bleak and beautiful. Seeing the Primus again (I had once had the honour of showing him the sights of New York), I was reminded that much of the work of the Episcopal Church in Scotland is pastoral in character. I am using the word in its primary meaning. Big towns or even sizeable villages in much of the land are few and far between. The Church must attempt a ministry to isolated farmers and to roving shepherds. And in the Diocese of Aberdeen, for example, there are fisherfolk and crofters. Many have no electricity. They get newspapers and mail three times a week, weather permitting, as it seldom does. Some of the fiercest tides and currents in the world swirl around the Orkney Islands. The Danes gave these islands their name; it means "deserted" places. In 1946 I had an involuntary week-end off Kirkwall in the Pentland Firth when the freighter in which I was sailing burned out a bearing. We dragged our anchor and were nearly driven on to the rocks. It is a bleak region. "The *Wuthering Heights* kind of terrain" is the expression that came to my mind, and it would take the combined talents of all the Brontës to suggest in words how desolate and lonely, how wild and windswept, it is. Officials from the Admiralty would not let us land. "The current is too swift, too dangerous," they said. Marooned on the ship while repairs were being made to the engine, I scanned the Sunday landscape with my binoculars and enviously watched the citizens of Kirkwall file into their squat church with its ponderous roof of slate. Only the heaviest of stone would have a chance of withstanding the wind.

Small wonder that bishops have difficulty in finding ministers for such places! Life is lonely for a single man, and the wife of a married one might find it unbearable. The Orkneys on a map resemble the ink splotches of a

Rorschach test. Yet it is up to one priest to direct the spiritual life of two hundred Episcopalians who are widely scattered. The Shetland Islands present a similar picture, nor are conditions totally dissimilar in much of the Highlands. The Sutherland Clearances emptied the people from the Highlands. The populace has gone south to the cities or farther south still, across the border into England, or else to Nova Scotia or farther west in Canada. Not many people are left behind, and not many of those are Episcopalians.

"We are supposed to be the church of the better classes," one Scot at Inverness told me. "The laird belongs to us – the man in the big house. This is a bad condition. But we're beginning to make some headway." One of the means by which the Diocese of Moray, Ross and Caithness is trying to deal with the problems of depopulation and the radical decentralization of the shrunken remnant is by having two itinerant priests, each with a car and a portable altar, constantly on the go, holding services at fifteen different places. Episcopalians travel as much as forty miles to get to the monthly service. A laudable effort, but how many people does it reach? About four hundred. And there is the constant struggle, in the country districts, against poor roads, lack of transportation, and crippling weather. American tourists whose knowledge of Scotland is confined to the Edinburgh Festival do not realize how rugged and underdeveloped most of the country is. How, for example, do you run high-powered Sunday Schools of the American pattern under such conditions? You don't. For the most part you have Sunday School by post.

A triple-barrelled name like Moray, Ross and Caithness reminds one that a shrinking population has had to have as its corollary a contracting Church. Dioceses have had to be amalgamated to effect economy, just as within each diocese, parishes are always being amalgamated.

The Episcopal Church in Scotland is in a predicament. If it stresses its Scottishness, the English in Scotland – and they are many – are displeased. If it stresses its English connections, it offends the Scots. It seems we cannot win either way.

Ecumenical cordiality was much in evidence that summer at Edinburgh and St. Andrews, as delegates from all the world worked hard to prepare for New Delhi. Incongruous and jarring, therefore, were the reports I received about how difficult it is for the different denominations of Scottish Christians to get along with one another within their own land. It is true that conversations have been in progress between Anglicans and Presbyterians. They give some signs of hope, but when I was there they had bogged down temporarily. There are difficulties enough in trying to unite the various kinds of Presbyterians. The Established Church and the United Free Church have long struggled for unity. In many villages there are still two Presbyterian churches – with little fellowship. Not even to this day has the Church of Scotland been able to enfold within its structure all Presbyterian groups. Some Church of Scotland people, far more favourable to the Episcopal Church than the United Frees who did come into the Church of Scotland, none the less hold back in fear that dealings with the Episcopal Church will further alienate the scattered Free Churches which resist the embrace of the Kirk. "Still plenty of Wee Frees around, and we must bring them in first before we can talk more earnestly with you Episcopalians" is the explanation one Presbyterian gave me for the hesitation of his Church in pursuing further conversations with us. But if the Presbyterians hold back, the Anglicans do so even more.

When I visited the country, all Scotland was exercised by the fact that the Scottish bishops had announced, in terms courteous but uncompromising, that the Episcopal Church could take no part in the celebrations commemorating the four hundredth anniversary of the Scottish Reformation. I understand the reasoning, even have a certain sympathy with it. But what a blow! The Kirk felt insulted, and the announcement was heard with dismay by many loyal Episcopalians. The laity do not understand the issues. They long for intercommunion with the Presbyterians, partly because they are much intermarried with them. They have little aptitude and even less appetite for the theological niceties, abstruse and irrelevant to their way of thinking, that cause their own Episcopal Church to be so standoffish in its relations to the National Church. Those niceties are not nice at all. *They divide families.* There is substance in the suggestion that the clergy, generally High Church, have got too far ahead of the laity. They are no longer leading the laity but pushing them . . . and pushing them, all too frequently, out of the Church.

A tangled business. Motives are mixed. Pride is involved. On the one side there is the pride of the Presbyterians. The Church of Scotland is hungry for recognition. It wants to be acknowledged as being to Scotland what the Church of England is to England. It therefore desires that Anglican-Presbyterian conversations be conducted between the Church of England and the Church of Scotland as equals. It wants to talk, in other words, with the Archbishop of Canterbury, not with the Primus of Scotland. And this, in its turn, hurts the pride of the Scottish Episcopalians. To make matters worse, there are English Episcopalians in Scotland who quite agree with the Presbyterian Church of Scotland in this matter: the right person to talk to *is* the Archbishop of Canterbury. Thus, both for Scottish Calvinists and for English Episcopalians residing in Scotland, the Scottish Episcopal Church is felt to be a complication and an annoyance.

Not a healthy state of affairs.

I can see, however, how wrong it is – from the point of view of Scottish Episcopalians – that the Archbishop of Canterbury and the Moderator of the Church of Scotland should make a joint declaration on a civic or social issue. That is something they have done more than once. And each time it rankles among Scottish Episcopalians. The declaration should come from the Moderator and the *Primus*, not a foreign Archbishop. "Englishmen just don't understand such things," an aroused Scottish bishop roared at me, "and therefore they make all kinds of strategical blunders. For it to be Canterbury and not the Primus is tacitly to acknowledge the very point which the Church of Scotland claims – and the Episcopal Church exists to deny – namely, that the Church of Scotland is *the* Church of the land." But what is to be done about it all when the lovely Queen, in one part of her domain, worships in one Church; in another part, in another? And how difficult it is to enter into a history that is not one's own history!

When I grow impatient with the rather stiff nonecumenicalism of the Scottish Episcopal Church on the local level – our priests saying haughtily that they never go near the Ministers' Fraternal and that they will have no truck with union services of any kind, even on special occasions – I have to check myself with the reminder that the Presbyterians with whom the Scottish Episcopalians must deal are *not* the Presbyterians I know in America. They are, rather, a somewhat dour, fundamentalist, puritanical, Sabbath-keeping, arrogantly nationalistic kind of Presbyterian. (Dear Scottish Presbyterian friends of mine, forgive these harsh words! It is not of you as individuals that I am speaking. But I need not have voiced this apology, for it is more from you than from the Episcopalians that I have heard reports of how obstreperous "the Elect" can sometimes be.)

Yet difficult people on the one side tend to make their opponents difficult too. The laws of reciprocal relations are strange and inexorable. It is hard to fight the daemonic without becoming daemonic yourself. A vastly outnumbered Episcopal Church has grown edgy, testy, defensive. Why, for example, is the Provost of one Scottish cathedral determined to refer, in all that he writes or says, to the Mass as "the Mass"? In itself, "Mass" is an innocent word. There is nothing in its etymology to render it offensive. But a word is more than etymology. It is history, and in its history it has acquired connotations. It can become a red flag. That flag he waves. Does the Provost suppose that by such tactics he can commend Anglicanism to disaffected or indifferent Presbyterians? If disaffected, they will probably go to Rome. If indifferent, they will probably laugh.

It is calamitous that we allow our own position to be defined defensively, in frightened reaction to external forces, instead of calmly pursuing our own path and being what we are. If Ireland is a slightly hysterical Low Church reaction to Rome, Scotland is a slightly hysterical High Church reaction to Presbyterianism. Our alarm at being overwhelmingly outnumbered pushes us to extreme positions that we then must defend in shrill accents. A proud exclusiveness comes in as a psychological overcompensation for feelings of insecurity. But by this exclusivism we succeed only in cutting ourselves off from genuine participation in the life of the country.

I am referring now not only to Scotland but to many other places as well when I state that ill-considered ways of pressing our claim to be *the* Catholic Church of a land end up by turning us into a *sect* – arrogant, stiff, illiberal, irrelevant. Scotland and Ireland are not, in this respect, sinners above all other parts of the Anglican Communion. By no means. Yet we have little to offer in either country because in neither country are we sufficiently ourselves. We do not let the *via media* become visible because in both countries our aim is to make ourselves as *un*like the predominating religion as possible. This is the product of fear, not of faith.

Let it not be thought that the Episcopal Church in Scotland is "high and crazy". Actually, it is fairly conservative. On the other hand, it must not be imagined that by "bell, book and candle" we shall win many Presbyterians from among the Scots. Their own Church has a dignified, if somewhat austere, form of worship – one that by reason of its jabots and other frills shocks most Presbyterian visitors from America and secretly delights more than a few of them. Moreover, a kind of "Tractarian Movement" exists within the Church of Scotland. Among Calvinists there is now more use of liturgy. Communions are more frequent. Christmas and Easter have gained admittance to the calendar! Such developments within the Scottish Kirk mean that we get fewer conversions than we used to. We Episcopalians delude ourselves if we think we can make progress by liturgy alone. If *liturgics* is what a Scot is seeking, his own National Church is fast learning to supply his need. Or, if he wants something really fancy, Rome is on hand to take care of that. Why should he stop at the half-way house we run? For inevitably we appear to him as a pale imitation of the real thing. If Anglicanism is to be a redemptive power in the life of the Scots, it will have to outbid its "rivals" by outstripping them in the fields of pastoral care, social concern, scholarship, and relevant preaching.

I am not suggesting that our task in Scotland is to turn Presbyterians and Roman Catholics into Episcopalians. Not at all. There is plenty for everyone to do; in many respects Scotland is still a missionary district. Large areas are served by no Church or are served most inadequately. The Churches have no need to compete with each other. And in the great cities the number of people who have lapsed from Christianity or who have never effectively been touched by Christianity is legion. Of the five and a half million Scots it is reliably estimated that one and a half million are churchless, either through their having become disaffected or through our having neglected them. All of us – Presbyterian, Anglican, and Roman – should go after these "displaced" persons. Our work is cut out for us. The fact remains, however, that we Episcopalians have a special ministry to Calvinists who want Catholicism but without Rome, and to Romanists who want Reformation without Calvinism. Precisely *there* is a function we could perform. Precisely *there* we fail.

It would be misleading, however, to end on a pessimistic note. As one who tries to be an honest reporter, I felt I had to introduce a heavy element of gloom, but the same striving for reportorial honesty obliges me to point emphatically to a hopeful sign. The critique I have put on paper is not based on data I surreptitiously ferreted out. It rests, rather, on facts openly declared to me by leaders of the Scottish Episcopal Church. Thus, they are fully aware of the problems, and since to be forewarned is to be forearmed, there are good prospects that the picture may change.

But no American Episcopalian can fail to be moved by gratitude and reverence as he stands on the site of a certain house in Aberdeen. Here, in 1784, in secrecy and fear, three Nonjuring bishops conferred the Episcopate on the American Church. The site is marked by a plaque. Otherwise there is nothing to show for the great event that took place on that spot – unless you are generous enough to count the American Church as "something to show".

Too well known to merit repeating here is the story of how Seabury sought in vain for consecration in England. The English bishops were kindly disposed towards him, but they did not see how they could consecrate a man who, as a citizen of the new American Republic, could hardly be expected to take the required oath of allegiance to the British Crown. It would require an Act of Parliament first to make an exception in his case. Seabury waited for Parliament to act. It did not act. When he had run out of time, health, money, and patience, he went north to Scotland where the Nonjuring bishops agreed to consecrate him. These were the bishops who, believing in the right of the exiled House of Stuart, refused to accept the reigning king.

I believe I must be one of the few human beings now alive who has actually read the sermon which Bishop Kilgour, the Primus, preached on the occasion of the consecration of the first Bishop of Connecticut, who was also the first bishop of any kind whatsoever to set foot on American soil. In the course of the sermon, Kilgour wittily remarked that "the Scottish Bishops are more willing to follow the Acts of the Apostles than they are the Acts of the British Parliament, and therefore we proceed to the consecration of this godly man". This is a line I quoted several times in Scotland with great success. The Primus himself roared with laughter.

Where there is that kind of wit and that kind of spunk, we may yet have our day.

13

THE MEDITERRANEAN: Mission to the Military

LEUCHARS, LONDON, LYNEHAM, AND LIBYA COME NEXT. IF THAT sounds like a fortuitous grab-bag held together only by alliteration, I can give assurance that my visits to the four "L's" was not only a chronological fact but rested fair and square on a logical sequence.

While reading a ton of books in preparation for my Grand Tour I noticed that few books on Anglicanism call attention to the Church's ministry to people under arms. Usually this subject comes in for no attention at all, or, if mentioned, is accorded no significant discussion.

This seemed to me a defect. I discussed it with my Presiding Bishop, who then spoke to the Archbishop of Canterbury; and he, in turn, put the Bishop of Maidstone to work. The latter has pastoral oversight of all Anglican chaplains serving in the British Armed Forces. The machinery began to turn, and before long I received – by reason of my blameless conduct and my high sponsorship – clearance from all branches of Her Britannic Majesty's forces. After signing formidable documents in which I exonerated Her Majesty and all Her Majesty's Ministers from any responsibility for whatever untoward thing might befall me, I suddenly found myself being taken off to Navy bases, Army installations, Marine training stations, and Royal Air Force headquarters.

The British stand greatly on ceremony. For reasons of protocol, so that it might be known how I was to be treated, I had to be given a rank. For a fortnight I revelled in the fact that I was a Wing Commander! During this period I was ankle-deep in red carpet. I must admit that I enjoyed every minute of it.

At Leuchars in Fife, near St. Andrews, I abandoned the pacific endeavours of the delegates to the planning sessions of the World Council of Churches to watch for a day the more bellicose activities of the Royal Air Force.

From the Commanding Officer of this great base I learned a thing or two about the psychology of men under arms in the atomic age. They know that probably nothing of what they are learning and doing will be put to any use. No one speaks of it, but in a hidden way everybody understands that history could come to an end within a few hours of nuclear interchange, which means that none of this vast apparatus will ever be used. All too easily, but understandably, the enlisted men dub it "Operation Futility". In those circumstances, so unlike a time of war, it is hard to keep morale high. The wartime sense of lofty mission is lacking. "Never more difficult than now," said the Commanding Officer, "and never more important than now is the role of the chaplain."

The British chaplain is given opportunity to function *qua* chaplain. That is, he does not have to double as drama coach, athletic director, and welfare officer. If he has one or more of these talents and wishes to exercise them as a way of "getting close" to the men, well and good. That is his own business, his own decision about strategy. But he is never called upon to be what essentially he is not. In the British system other functionaries are on hand to do these necessary things. In this respect British chaplains are more favourably situated than their American counterparts. The chaplain does not have to be a "regular guy" or "one of the fellows". It is expected that he will be a *padre*.

One of the most notable features of the British chaplaincy system is to be found in the "Moral Leadership Schools" conducted in several areas in the world. I sampled four of them. I single out for special mention, because it is more or less typical of the others, the one at Bagshot Park in Surrey. This Training Centre and Depot is run by the Royal Army Chaplains' Department in a great country house once belonging to one of Queen Victoria's ducal offspring. The house, set in a beautiful park, is, in a way, like a first-class hotel, and each year about three thousand men in uniform resort to it. Some go at their own request. Others go because they were ordered to do so – like it or not.

The men arrive, about thirty at a time, from all over Britain to attend an intensive course that runs from Monday until Saturday morning. There is an ordered daily routine of devotions, lectures, discussion groups, and recreation. The personnel attending are not "Holy Joes". That type is rigorously debarred. Their presence would defeat the whole purpose of taking stalwart men, "regular chaps" of slightly superior ability and good character, even though some of them are rough-cut, and exposing them for one week to a reasoned exposition of Christianity in the context of a Christian household with its family prayers and its family fun. Some leave untouched by this encounter. Most, however, are profoundly affected. The Church of England will owe much in the future to the instructed laymen who were sparked into spiritual maturity at Bagshot Park and similar centres conducted by the Royal Army Chaplains. And here too are recruited many men for the ordained Ministry.

Bagshot Park holds conferences periodically for Ordination candidates who are serving in the Army. Released for a fortnight from regular duty, they go to the Centre for intensive training and for the "bull sessions" that are an indispensable part of any man's preparation for Ordination. In discussions of that sort he learns to put his thoughts into words – and he gets the rough edges knocked off. All to the good. Moreover, he establishes a permanent relationship with the chaplains in charge. They continue by mail to direct his reading while he is doing National Service, so that he will be ready at the end of his military stint to enter a theological college.

From Bagshot Park, one of the stately homes of England, to a rather run-down house at Kyrenia, a seaport town on the north coast of Cyprus, from which Turkey can be seen through the haze, is a long way. But there I spent the day watching the same type of programme in operation. Another school, still farther away, is maintained at Blanking Mati, an island in the spectacular harbour of Singapore.

I wish the American Episcopal Church could do as well. We are held back, of course, by the fact that we are not the Established Church. As a minority Church, and disestablished, we do not have the "pull" with the Armed Forces that the Church of England has, and proportionately we have fewer chaplains.

Until only a few years ago Episcopalians had to be "dog-tagged" as Protestants. Today, however, a distinctive marking can be had for the asking, but Episcopal chaplains are shocked and disappointed to discover that the majority of young church people of their denomination entering the services have little knowledge of the special ethos of Anglicanism and rarely claim for themselves the new privilege of having a distinctive label. Such persons content themselves with pan-Protestant worship or no worship at all.

Given Rome's numerical strength, there will almost always be a Roman chaplain on any sizeable American base, but unless an earnest Episcopalian is fortunate enough to be stationed at a base where the Protestant chaplain is an Anglican, he may be cut off for many months from the ministrations of his own Church. In consequence, more than one Episcopalian to whom the Liturgy and the Sacraments are of vital importance has gone over to Rome during his military service.

Even with the limitations of the American system we do far less than we could do and should do. It is a standing scandal that the American Episcopal

Church has yet to find chaplains enough to fill its quota. In America as in Britain, the number of chaplains allotted to the Armed Forces by the government is determined by the relative numerical strength of the various religious bodies. The English Church fills its quota which is far higher than ours. We do not. American churchmen seem not yet aware of the possibility of a significant Ministry – at a time, alas, when so many men and women are in military service.

Young people assuming their military obligations cannot be expected to remain faithful indefinitely to a Church that does not provide them with a priest and Sacraments. True, in time of war our clergy "flocked to the colours", but not many want to serve in peacetime, when the work of a chaplain is often more demanding. Most of the chaplains now in the American forces are either "old-timers", soon to be retired, or "short-timers", reservists serving short tours of duty. Because of the "quota system", any Church that does not supply chaplains to use up its apportionment of "pay-slots" is denied further chaplains in order to provide funds for those denominations that do. It is of vital concern that more young priests volunteer for at least one tour of active duty, in order to carry the Gospel to men "under authority". Otherwise, the Episcopal Church will be in grave danger of losing the few spaces it has.

At the Depot of Royal Marines at Deal in Kent I had a good day. All the men in training there, except Roman Catholics, Nonconformists, and Jews, attend a weekly class led by the chaplain and his assistant in religious instruction. More than a thousand men are involved. Impressive is the syllabus worked out for these English lads by the Welsh chaplain and his Irish assistant. That these two should be in charge caused me to think of the time-honoured English quip: Home Rule for England! In particular I applauded the inclusion in the course of material about the other religions of the world, for the enlightenment of the young Marines who will be sent out on duty to all parts of the globe where they will discover that Hinduism, Buddhism, and Mohammedanism are more than polysyllabic names. They are the living religions of living people.

The Chaplain Corps of the American Armed Forces might well take a leaf from the book of their British counterparts.

I boarded a train at London for Swindon. My destination was Lyneham, the great Royal Air Force base. In England all things must be done decently and in order. Pressed for time though we were (my train having been held up for an hour by a derailment on the line ahead of us), I was met with due solemnity by the Commanding Officer and the top brass for a welcoming drink. The libation poured, they retired. And, as if I had been the admiral of a fleet, I sat down to a solitary lunch, expertly waited upon by two corporals. Between courses I received visitors. First came the Movements Officer to examine my papers. Next came the Immigration and Customs man. Then came the Medical Officer intent on proving that I had been punctured with the proper inoculations. I went to nobody. Everybody came to me. It ministered dangerously to my ego, and I was forced to the conclusion that there is something to be said for an Established Church!

Lunch over, I was driven out to the ramp of a Comet, already filled except for my place. Salutes were exchanged. I boarded the plane, and the moment I was strapped in, off we went. Some of the young service men and women aboard were bound for Libya and other posts overseas. I was glad they would find their Church there, and most of them – being hurtled into the unknown – were glad too.

Landing at El Adem on the Libyan desert, I was met by the C.O. and the Anglican chaplain, a resourceful man who conducts Sunday Evensong on the beach, for that is where his people are on a Sunday afternoon. To my question, "Is this a hardship post?" he gave the answer, "No, more like a penal settlement." Many of us are too little conscious of, and too little grateful for, the enormous number of human beings who, in helping to maintain the peace of the world, are living in faraway and often uncomfortable places ranging from arctic cold to Libyan heat. These people, most of whom are in voluntary "exile", include military personnel and their dependents and also, as is commonly forgotten, civilian employees of their respective governments. The ministrations of the military chaplains are available to the civilians too. The exact number of all these persons military and civilian, is a state secret. Yet, at a conservative estimate, one and a half million United States citizens live and work abroad. What the figures are for the British Commonwealth I have no idea. But when we who are Anglo-Saxons count our blessings, we should remember to be thankful that the governments under which we live make provision for religious ministrations to the men who bear arms and to civilians in government employ. Thousands of Christians in the uniforms of certain other countries have no such advantage. The Church *would* follow them into the field but is not permitted to do so. In general, how insensitive English-speaking Anglicans are to the peculiar position in which most of our non-Anglo-Saxon fellow churchmen are placed! Often there is isolation in their being Christians at all, and even greater isolation in their being Anglican Christians. I refer not only to men under arms, but of them it is true especially.

The R.A.F. flew me to Malta, a parched island, where I took pride in our cathedral in the capital city, Valetta. It is a noble building in a photo-genic town. But our work has been confined to people of English speech, because (as noted before) it is a persistent part of British Church policy not to proselytize among people of a land already nominally Christian. It is this policy which commits our Church to being in perpetuity a tiny minority, a "foreign" enclave, where other reformed Churches do a necessary work. These others flourish while we remain a chaplaincy.

I began to grow tired of our being, in place after place, a separatist conventicle. If we have something to offer, why not offer it? Why hug it to ourselves? The thought, I know, is not to antagonize Rome in countries predominantly Catholic. Wherever Rome is alive, alert, progressive, and equal to the job, we should leave her in possession of the field. It is best that we stay out or, at most, confine ourselves to caring for our own. When Rome is less than this – which is often – there is work for us to do. Yet we hold back. It is a favourite device of ours to rationalize this hesitation. Our ecumenical horizons, we say, are so broad that we cannot be content with any kind of pan-Protestantism; Church Unity must include Rome, and it is for *this* reason we must not run competition with Rome. But what if, in some of the nations, Rome *needs* our competition and would benefit from it? I know as well as the next man that there can be no talk of Unity that does not include the great Church of Rome as well as the Orthodox Churches of the East. The idea is not to steal sheep but to save souls.

To the ecclesiastical despisers of television I would like to give one striking example of the unexpected results that this incredible modern invention can achieve. Television was still a recent arrival on the island of Malta when I touched there. The marriage of H.R.H. the Princess Margaret was one of the first events shown on television in Malta. The astonishment of the Maltese over the miracle of television was somewhat eclipsed by an even greater astonishment: the solemnization of Matrimony, with its celebration of the Holy Communion, in accordance with the rites and ceremonies of the Church of England, was unmistakably Christian! Our clergy on Malta told me that as a result of that single telecast, they had had more inquiries about our Church than in the whole history of Anglican work on that island.

From Malta the R.A.F. flew me to Cyprus. I arrived in time to watch the Church at work on an air force base on a typical Sunday morning.

A Sunday in Nicosia is proof that we do look after our own. Of that we have reason to be proud. Or, to state it differently, our own have a way of looking out for themselves, which should make us prouder still. That is to say, British airmen put up the funds and with their own hands built the chapel. Most chapels on British military bases are the product of what the British call "self-help". (How unlike the American system under which it is the government that builds the chapels!)

About thirty of us were present for the early celebration, after which the whole congregation was invited to a breakfast in the parish hall prepared by twelve airmen. "It's just the same menu we would have had in the mess," they said, "but it tastes better when we cook it ourselves after church and share it with others." They are profoundly right, of course. It is a secret not found in any cookery book, but food over which grace has been said *does* taste better.

These twelve men stayed on for Matins, to which came a great concourse of people, and when that was over and when six children had been baptized, the airmen served us all an ice-cold fruit punch. That social hour brought together officers, enlisted men, civilians, and children in friendly converse, not an easy achievement on an otherwise rank-conscious base. The twelve inductees originated the idea of having a social hour every Sunday. They "foot the bill" out of their own meagre pay. Our hosts were ordinary every-day fellows. Some of them had teeth missing. Some of them were tattooed. Most were burly. All seemed wholesome. The weekly gathering was their form of *diakonia*, their way of serving the Church. World-shaking? Perhaps not. But I find it touching, as we stand on the threshold of the Space Age, that air-minded men can still make room for Christian fellowship. That night – absolutely cloudless – I remembered their little act of service as I watched the new satellite Echo rise on schedule in the east, sail past our island at great speed, and sink in the black Mediterranean to the west.

Time fails me to tell of Limassol, Kyrenia, Episkopi, Curium, the Church's retreat house in the Troodos Mountains, and the huge R.A.F. base at Akrotiri on the southernmost tip of Cyprus where British soldiers with their wives and children from miles around had come to look upon the novelty of an American Anglican and to hear about the bigness of the Church to which they belong. But in every place I learned something worth knowing.

My debt to the Royal Air Force is immense. They gave me meals, care, planes, and comradeship. They permitted me to sit in the co-pilot's seat, helmet and earphones clamped to my head. Enough of the boy is left in me to be 100 per cent delighted by these adventures in flight. But most of all I was delighted by the fact that the Church is present wherever its people are.

14

THE MIDDLE EAST: Building on Old Foundations

JERUSALEM APPROACHED BY AIR FROM THE LEBANON IS A GREAT sight, although it bears scant resemblance to the city as it must have looked two thousand years ago. I am like Walter Lowrie. Religiously, I would prefer to visualize it through the eyes of St. Mark or St. John rather than to see the Arab city that was superimposed on the site many centuries later. And again, like Lowrie, I protest our habit of showing to Sunday School children pictures of our Lord and his Apostles dressed as if they were Bedouins. I boycott all Nativity pageants in which striped bathrobes are used for shepherds whose heads are swathed in Turkish towels. Such garb was not the fashion in "the days of his flesh".

One who has been brought up on detective stories expects the Middle East to be a land of intrigue, mystery, and complication, and in those expectations no visitor who knows where to look need be disappointed. I did not have time to look. The complications of Anglican Church life were sufficient for me.

To begin with, we have a sister who calls herself the Arab Evangelical Episcopal Church. She is a full-fledged member of the Anglican family. But she behaves strangely on occasion. She is, for example, evasive about giving out statistics, presumably because the numbers are so small that it would be humiliating to reveal them. Furthermore, some of her leaders – although I loved them as individuals – seemed to me to share every Arab illusion with respect to the political situation in the Middle East. "Soon we will drive them into the sea," they declared heatedly. "Them", of course, means the Israeli. But this is fanciful thinking and not without a taint of fanaticism. My hope was that Christian Arabs might have shown some power to transcend the hatreds of the moment. By and large, that was not true – any more, perhaps, than it is true of American Christians in the "cold war".

At long last the Arab Evangelical Episcopal Church has a bishop drawn from among her own sons. His Diocese, one of the five embraced by the Archbishopric, includes three countries: Jordan, Lebanon, and Syria. It is a pity that an Arab bishop was not consecrated years ago. We waited overlong – until 1958 – in our customary, costly way. We waited, that is, until the tides of nationalism were running so strong that we had no alternative but to do what should have been done a good deal sooner on spiritual grounds, unalloyed with any consideration of politics. The choice fell on a man as ideal as this imperfect world of ours is likely to offer, and under him we can hope for advance.

But some considerations give me pause. One is the draft I was shown of a proposed new Prayer Book. I believe I have several times made it clear that I am a staunch believer in liturgical adaptation. I favour such changes as will enable the Church to communicate the Gospel effectively in each locality. Yet it came as a surprise and a shock when I scanned what the Arabs intend to do. I noticed first that the one hundred and fifty Psalms of David had been reduced in number to one hundred. I have no quarrel with that *per se*. In public worship fifty of them might well go out. But my curiosity was instantly aroused. What was the principle of selection? By what criterion did some go out and some stay in? I was not long in discovering. Deleted was every Psalm mentioning Israel! Canticles also were eliminated if they were so impolitic as to make mention of the Chosen People. When next I met those responsible for the Arabic redaction of the Prayer Book, I maliciously initiated the conversation by saying, "Do you propose also to rule out every Psalm which mentions Jacob?" The answer was accompanied by a worldly-wise smile and a shrug of the shoulders: "The people do not realize that Jacob is Israel." I failed to make the obvious retort: "Why not let the Prayer Book read 'Jacob' wherever 'Israel' now stands?'

Marcion rides again! I thought the Church had settled the issue once and for all when in A.D. 144 it decided against the heretic Marcion by defending the unity of the two Testaments. But the Diocese of Jordan, Lebanon, and Syria has preferred to go along with the discredited Marcion. The Diocese of Egypt intends to follow suit. The Lectionary now advocated rests on untold hours of scholarship devoted to expurgating the Holy Scriptures of every favourable reference to the Jews. Have we no constitutional means within the Anglican Communion to put a stop to eccentricities of such proportions?*

* Precisely to defend herself against charges that might be levelled against her, the Arab Evangelical Episcopal Church has stated, in the Preface to the proposed Prayer Book, that doctrinally her position is enshrined in the Prayer Book of 1662. The declaration, the dogmatic guarantee, will, however, be printed in type so small that I shall need bifocals before I can see it and feel completely reassured.

.　　　.　　　.　　　.　　　.

That people of this temper of mind should be allowed to represent the totality of Anglicanism in Jerusalem was unthinkable. Therefore, by a master stroke of diplomatic genius, an Archbishopric was created in 1957. An Archbishop was placed in Jerusalem to oversee all Anglican work in the Middle East, while, to meet the legitimate aspirations and needs of Arab Anglicans, one of their own number was made Bishop for the newly created Diocese of Jordan, Lebanon, and Syria. Hence the whole area (it includes Israel, Jordan, Lebanon, Syria, Egypt, Libya, the Sudan, Cyprus, Iran, and Kuwait) becomes a quasi-province. "Quasi" because the Archbishop, although a Metropolitan, holds jurisdiction under the Archbishop of Canterbury, and because the five dioceses forming the Archbishopric are distant from one another and are not yet strong enough to shoulder all the burdens of provincial autonomy.

But the creation of the Jerusalem Archbishopric was, from many points of view, ecclesiastical statesmanship at its wisest. As I have indicated, the longings of the Arab Anglicans to have a bishop of their own were met. The Archbishopric also made possible a way of transcending the Arab-Israeli feud, since an Archbishop, not himself a Middle Easterner, could come and go freely between the two countries and be *persona gratissima* on both sides of the river of rubble tragically dividing Jerusalem and making of it a second Berlin. It provided episcopal oversight for Egypt, the number of whose Anglicans (since the skirmishes over Suez) has been so greatly reduced that it cannot afford a bishop in residence. Finally, it allowed us to be represented in the Holy City by someone of sufficient rank, scholarship, and breadth of outlook to command the respect, not only of all Christian leaders but also of leaders of the other two great monotheistic religions.

By all logic, the Bishop of Jordan, Lebanon, and Syria should place his *cathedra* in Amman, capital of Jordan. He has but to say a word and a cathedral will be built for him in the place where it should be. This word he has not said. So great is the *mystique* of Jerusalem that his people want him to be seated in the Holy City. Having rejected Amman, the Bishop puts up with the indignity of having no seat anywhere. Then, since Arab hopes are centred in Jerusalem, there was offered to him an already existing church within the walls of the ancient city where he could place his throne. It would make a fine pro-cathedral. But the Arab congregations would have none of it. And why? "It belongs to the Jews," they said to me, and that remark was supposed to close the discussion. "Nonsense," I replied. "The Jews don't own it. It is the property of an English society called The Church Missions to Jews, and since there are no longer any Jews left in Jordan, the society has no further use for it, and is willing to hand it over.

Why not take it? How splendid to have our Cathedral inside the city walls!"
To that argument the rather lame reply was that "the people don't like the
inscriptions in Hebrew over the Holy Table."*

The whole episode angered me, and I am not at pains to conceal it. Having
spoken in this unguarded way, I can never again hope to be received so
hospitably in Jordan.

The smallness of the Arab Evangelical Episcopal Church has to be
understood against its historical background. Anglicans did not go to
Jerusalem to create Arab congregations. We were concerned with two
things only: First, we wanted to be represented in Jerusalem, which is a
microcosm of the whole of Christendom. Rome is there in force, as are all
Eastern Churches, except the Assyrian. It was right, from an ecumenical
standpoint, that we should have representation too, and our presence there
has served and is serving the cause of "truth, unity, and concord". The
second reason for going was to do missionary work among the Jews. The
Arabs we largely ignored, though not by choice. There were laws to bar
our path. But even under the Ottoman Empire, which religiously was
repressive and kept the hands of Christians tied, missions to *Jews* were
permitted – on the somewhat puzzling theory that a conversion of Jews to
Christianity would bring them a step nearer Islam!

Our half-hearted efforts in the direction of Judaism have brought us a
few converts, some of them people of great stature, but the number of Hebrew
Christians in Israel today is small, and the present government, though it
makes much ado about religious liberty, manages somehow to impede our
progress. Gentiles can be Christians in Israel as much as they like. But a
Christian approach to the Jew is rendered extremely difficult. The reasons,
however, are more sociological than legal. Considerations of filial piety, for
example, make it very hard for a person to quit the Synagogue for the
Church. Whatever the reason, we have made hardly a dent in Palestinian
Judaism. The majority of Christians we once could claim in the Holy Land
were Arabs, and most of them, when the State of Israel was coming into being,
fled to the Lebanon, where today they constitute the backbone of our work.

St. Paul foresaw the time when the Jews would grow envious, would see
that the promises had been transferred to the Gentiles, and would sue to
come into the new Israel, the Church. There is little sign of this happening
now, partly because our missionary efforts are so deplorably feeble (in
spite of the zealous labours of the Church Missions to the Jews), and partly

* I thought with pride of the towering Menorah lights which adorn the sanctuary of the
Cathedral in New York. In dedicating these seven-branched candlesticks, an exact replica
of those which stood in the Temple built by Solomon, the tenth Bishop of New York said in
1930, "They will be to us a symbol of the relation between the Old and New Testaments,
and will portray the debt owed by Christianity to Judaism."

because the Arab Christianity with which Palestinian Jews have had most contact is hardly calculated to excite their envy.

Conversions from Judaism are few (I speak not of the world but of Palestine). Conversions from Islam are fewer. It is not chiefly of former followers of the Prophet that the Arab Evangelical Episcopal Church is made up but of Arabian Christians reacting negatively to Eastern Orthodoxy. They were orthodox enough to want valid bishops but also hostile enough to the ancient Churches of the East to want something radically reformed. This psychology gave to the early C.M.S. missionaries a first flush of success. Here was the possibility of a bishop for confirmations and ordinations but without faldstools and falderol. Episcopal they were intent upon being, but they had to be evangelical too. The C.M.S. fitted the situation perfectly. It could produce a bishop as occasion required, but in the meanwhile no episcopal hand rested heavily over the activities of enthusiastic evangelicals. Thus there came into being an Arab Evangelical Episcopal Church with primary accent on the word "evangelical". It had no strong consciousness of itself as belonging to a world-wide Anglican Communion.

Then when Arab nationalism flared at the spark of the new State of Israel, the accent shifted to the word "episcopal". As Arabs they *had* to have their own bishop, and they got him. But there are incongruities. An evangelical bishop, by reason of his upbringing, eschews the cope and mitre. For himself he wants nothing more than the "magpie" – rochet and chimere – and for his clergy, when they celebrate the Holy Communion, a black scarf instead of a stole. The people, as pupils of the last century's C.M.S., are accustomed to celebrations from the north end of the Holy Table. For many it is a matter of conviction, as if deep theological issues were involved in where the celebrant stands. The Bishop has been known to attempt to reconcile these conflicting stresses by celebrating from the north end – in cope and mitre! I am not poking fun. I am just enjoying the absurdities of Anglicanism. How strange that the north end position, a dubious characteristic of eighteenth-century English piety, has today become among Arab Anglicans a badge of nationalism!

If once the Anglicans stressed the word "evangelical" and later stressed the word "episcopal", now the word "Arab" is stressed. A better name, of course, and a name for which we formerly contended, was "The Palestinian Evangelical Episcopal Church". Such nomenclature would not have ruled out the Jews. But the tides of politics were too strong, and now that there are no Jews left in Jordan, the sting has been drawn from the word "Arab".

Regrettably, there is an apparent lack of concern on the part of the Arab Evangelical Episcopal Church for the evangelization of Islam. They regard

Islam as something with which peaceful co-existence is necessary, and in order to ensure it, they make no missionary advances. It proves far easier, more politic, less embarrassing, to leave the Muslims alone (and even to accept gifts from them to further their work – just as American Episcopalians do not say No when friendly Jews lend a helping hand).

The few Hebrew Christian congregations in Israel are no better. They early exhibited the same attitudes of particularism and exclusivism. The conversion of Islam was no concern of theirs. Yet this never became so apparent, partly because there were fewer Jewish than Arab Christians in the Holy Land and partly because the Jewish congregations remained small, their members often emigrating to Europe where Mohammed was only a name, not a neighbour.*

The Greek and Russian Churches in the Holy Land are not unacquainted with the same range of problems, for they too have converts among Arabs and among Jews. It is not, therefore, any sort of foreign "imperialism" that keeps people who are not of Middle Eastern origin in the top posts in all the great Churches. Foreigners must be retained in the hierarchy, since they can cross frontiers, not only the political frontier that cuts the city of Jerusalem in two but also the religious frontiers that separate Christianity from Judaism and from Islam. Arab Christians seem little disposed to address themselves to either frontier.

Is there a possibility that the new Anglican ordinands will transcend the old narrow outlook? Hopefully, I answer Yes. Yet the odds might seem to be against it. The men are being trained at a non-denominational seminary in Beirut under the auspices, principally, of Armenian Evangelicals and American Presbyterians. It is a good school, yet I am less than confident they will find there the grounding in Anglican ethos that will equip them with all the armour they need for the battles ahead. However, a brand-new venture – undertaken since the time of my visit – gives ground for more optimism. This is the formation of St. George's College in Jerusalem, a centre for theological study and research open to clergy and laity from all parts of the world. After their training in Beirut, some Middle Eastern postulants will have an opportunity to round out their training by spending a year at St. George's. Here they will receive the stimulus not only of life in the Holy City but of contact with scholars from the entire Anglican Communion – mature men, attracted to Jerusalem because it is an ideal setting

---

* Incidentally, I omitted a visit to Israel on my journey because I had been there before, in 1957, as a guest of the government, at which time I was shown everything from Dan to Beersheba. The Arab States still make such difficulties about anybody arriving at their borders from a country they claim to be non-existent that I resolved to simplify matters by skipping Israel. Yet let it be noted that there are Anglicans in Israel. Some are English and American, some are Arabians, some are Jewish.

for advanced research in the areas of Biblical archaeology, ecumenical relations, liturgics, and the comparative study of religions. The new college, already in existence but not yet in possession of buildings of its own, aspires to be, with modifications, a second St. Augustine's, Canterbury. If it is to be that, however, the whole of our Communion must go to its aid.

In Syria, at the time of my brief passage through the Middle East, Anglicans had no work. That may have changed by now. In Iraq there was nothing. In Lebanon we were dealing chiefly with Arab Christian refugees from Israel, many of whom – because we are not well equipped to meet their needs – will probably be absorbed into the Presbyterian Church. The same absorption may happen in Egypt. In Jordan, however, there is little likelihood of the same thing happening, largely because *we* are the Evangelical Church of Jordan – and there is not much of anything else for dissident evangelicals to be absorbed into.

Egypt deserves separate mention. Of Egypt's twenty-three million people, only three million are Christians. Most of these belong to the Coptic Church. The Presbyterians, claiming one hundred thousand adherents (most of them proselytes from the Coptic Church), are in second place. Rome is third. Some twenty-five sects divide the rest among them, leaving Anglicans a grand total of less than two thousand.

All honour to the four or five Egyptian priests and to the handful of the Faithful who carried on during the difficult days of the Suez crisis. As a church we were suspect. We smacked of hated Britain. Yet Egyptian Anglicans stood fast when it was not easy.

It still is not easy. The possibility of Anglican growth is slight. Conversions from Islam are exceedingly rare, for terrible social ostracism is the result of a Muslim's becoming a Christian. We labour under a double handicap in that we are not only Christian but, a thousand times worse, English – English and, allegedly, pro-Israel! In pre-war days whole Coptic congregations wanted to come in. We might have grown by leaps and bounds. But true to our principles, we refused to permit it. In an ecumenical interest, our only thought, beyond ministering to British personnel residing in Egypt, was to do unobtrusively what we could to assist the Coptic Church in its own desire to reform and revitalize itself. Yet many Coptic Christians joined our ranks of their own accord. Now that the Coptic Church has to some extent awakened and amended its ways, few Copts have any desire to leave it. In fact, the traffic today is in the opposite direction: Egyptian Anglicans, finding that their former Church is reformed, go back to it.

The Copts, I must record, ill repay the benefits we have conferred upon them. In most instances, they insist on rebaptism. This is heresy. In ecumenical negotiations I am often astonished at the patience and forbearance we show towards various members of the Eastern Orthodox family of Churches when, far more often, we are short-tempered with classical Protestants. Anglican concern with *Order* often outweighs concern with *Faith*. Let a man's orders be valid, we do not care so much about what he believes or teaches. But can that be right? In such a controversy it is I who am the orthodox one. Let me be sure a man has continued steadfastly in the Apostles' doctrine, and I am less concerned to scrutinize minutely the several parchments, neatly framed and affixed with seals, that hang on his office walls to prove he stands in the Succession. Apostolicity in order, important as it is, for the fullness of the Church, must surely be conjoined with apostolicity of doctrine.

To my regret, although I made every effort to reach the Sudan, red tape in connection with getting a visa made this impossible. I should have liked to visit Bishop Gwynne College, the only Anglican theological school in the Jerusalem Archbishopric before the creation of St. George's. Ordinands in the area have been encouraged to supplement at Bishop Gwynne in Mundri the training they receive at the Union Seminary in Beirut, but expense and various government travel restrictions often make it difficult.

The independent Muslim Government of the Sudan has closed all church schools except for Bishop Gwynne College itself. It does, however, permit religious instruction in the government schools of the Southern Provinces, to which Christian missionary work is limited, since the North is solidly and intransigently Muslim.

In spite of the obstacles besetting the Diocese, it is largely self-supporting and reports a baptized membership of ninety thousand. It suffers, as do so many other parts of the Anglican Communion, from a staff shortage, but since foreign missionaries are unwelcome, the chief reliance must be on indigenous clergy.

The sleek airport of Teheran was in such contrast to that of Cairo that I did not object to having to pay a substantial tax for the privilege of using it. And during my first full day in the land of the Shah of Shahs, long walks through the streets of Isfahan were a pleasure, not merely for the unexcelled splendour of the mosques, but also because one could proceed unmolested by beggars. Nor was one plagued by flies, whereas in Cairo it would be hard to say which are the more pestiferous and the more difficult to elude: flies or beggars.

Iran is a big country, and in it the Christian forces are small. Over 95 per cent of its twenty million inhabitants are Muslims. It takes all varieties of Christians to amass a total of three hundred thousand. Most of them are not Persians but Armenians and Syrians who gratefully found refuge here when driven out of their own lands. On the score of religious toleration, Iran has a good record. The State recognizes four religions: Islam, Judaism, Zoroastrianism, and Christianity. Each religious group enjoys freedom, subject to one strict prohibition: Thou shalt not proselytize from any of the other groups. This is the official attitude, but in fact converts – in one direction or another – are made every day.

The Presbyterians have gathered quite a following, mostly from Armenians and Syrians. There are perhaps ten thousand of them. Anglicans pursued a different policy. So far as our limited finances – and Armenian-Syrian uncertainty about us – permitted, we tried to work *with* the ancient Churches, not in competition against them. Chiefly for this reason our own numbers are small. At a generous estimate, we have not many more than fifteen hundred. Most of them, be it noted, are not proselytes from other Christian bodies but converts from Islam, Judaism, and Zoroastrianism.

Two things can be said in our favour: first, we have been reluctant to address ourselves to persons already Christian; second, we have been more courageous than other Christian bodies in presenting Christ to non-Christians. At least four hundred of our fellow churchmen in Iran are of Muslim antecedents, and at least three hundred of them have as their background either Judaism or the dualism of Zoroaster. One moment I especially remember from my stay in Isfahan, where Anglican work is centred: a celebration of the Holy Communion in which the celebrant had been a Muslim, the gospeller a Jew, and the epistler a Zoroastrian. That was not staged for my benefit. It is the order of the day.

It has been suggested to me that one reason there are more conversions to Christianity in Iran than in other Middle Eastern countries is that Persians are not Arabs. Accordingly, there is no connection in the Iranian mind between the religion of Mohammed and nationalistic aspiration. The fact that the services of the mosque are in Arabic means that many Persians have no idea what is going on. If and when they are exposed to Christian worship, they are often startled and deeply moved to hear Scripture, prayers, and hymns in their own language. Not because we pursue them but because of our simple practice of having the liturgy in a language they can understand, they come to us.

On the other hand, it is hard to win converts. In Iran, as in other non-Christian cultures, the sense of filial piety is strong. How can one base one's eternal blessedness on something in which one's kinfolk cannot share? And if one is ambitious to hold public office or to make a mark in the world, the profession of Christianity is a distinct disadvantage. Finally, there is the hold of Islamic fatalism: "If God had wanted me to be a Christian, he would have made me one."

But it is precisely in Iran that our Anglican schools have made such a difference. When the recently retired Bishop went to Persia nearly a half-century
ago, there was not a single real school in the whole country. To be found,
at best, were small establishments where the reading and writing of Persian
were taught, along with prayers in Arabic to be learned by rote. The Church
had an open field, opposed only, and at most sporadically, by the mullahs.

There was at that time no central government to oppose the Church.
The situation was completely feudal. A few families of enormous wealth
lorded it over serfs whose rights were few and for whom nothing was being
done. The Church brought hospitals and schools, and we tend to forget
how recent an occurrence that was. The first hospital to be built in Persia
was the achievement of the father-in-law of Bishop Thompson. It is still in
use in Isfahan, and to this day is chosen by the citizens in preference to the
better equipped government hospitals. The need of an increased staff is so
pressing, however, that unless it can be met, the future of the hospitals in
both Isfahan and Shiraz is in doubt. More important than maintaining the
hospitals might be the provision of mobile units and clinics for use in villages
and rural regions.

Our schools were beloved by all. Muslim, Jewish, and Zoroastrian parents
sent their children to us. They were willing to put up with our religion for
the sake of our language, English! I say that the schools *were* beloved because,
alas, in the time of troubles over Iranian oil the government forced the
Church to close its schools. Only gradually, and very diffidently, are we
getting them open again. But they are coming back – and on a more secure
foundation. They are no longer "mission schools" but institutions of the
Episcopal Church of Iran. Fortunately for us, the now grown-up children
of the Anglican missionary pioneers were born in Iran and are citizens.
For the most part our schools today are staffed by them and by Irani,
graduates of our earlier educational effort. If ever the government should
turn hostile again, they could not so easily be expelled as were the English
missionaries in the last crisis.

Periodic attempts have been made to crack down on our schools, at least
to the extent of making us limit our enrolment to Christian pupils. Interestingly enough, it is the Muslim parents who have gone to the government
and insisted that their own children be allowed to attend.

An unsolicited testimony to the worth of the schools administered by the
recently retired Bishop came from the Muslim manager of a bank where
I had gone to cash a cheque. When he asked me for a local reference, I gave
him the Bishop's name. "Ah!" he said, "most of the honest men in Isfahan
are 'old boys' of Bishop Thompson." He hastened, of course, to assure me
that he too was an "old boy". And I received my money.

In the case of Christian and Muslim parents alike whose children have reached the sixth grade (which at present is as far as we go in the newly reopened schools), there is frantic questioning: "But what is to become of our children now?" Good question! Currently the government seems willing enough that we should expand. Hence, the question is addressed, not to Persian politicians, but to the Churches abroad. Are *they* willing? For without their help, what can this valiant but tiny Episcopal Church of Iran do?

Hostels for girls and boys are operated by the Church in Isfahan, where there is also a Christian bookshop. All the World Christian Books, edited by Bishop Stephen Neill, are being translated into Persian, and one of them is by the new Bishop of Iran himself, describing his conversion from Islam. At Teheran, the capital city, a new church centre has been opened, where a chaplain, working in co-operation with The Church Missions to Jews, will try to make a spiritual home for both Hebrew and Muslim converts, helping at the same time to meet the needs of the growing English-speaking community.

A School of Nursing was within two weeks of opening when I was in Isfahan. Few and far between are such schools in Iran. Permission to open had been granted by the secular authorities, and the school – even in advance of its opening – was declared to be "accredited".

Proof of the favour in which we are held is to be found in the circumstance that financial support for our Blind School pours in from Christians, Muslims, Jews, Zoroastrians, and British and Americans residing in Iran, not to mention societies for the blind in several countries. An Iranian royal princess is one of its most ardent supporters. The Episcopal Church in Iran literally stumbled into the work. The Blind School was originally an activity of the German Mission. But in World War II the Germans were expelled from the country because a German pastor was accused, whether rightly or wrongly, of harbouring Nazi parachutists. The pupils were abandoned. Something had to be done. The Bishop and his wife stepped in and saw that these sightless ones were fed and bathed and loved. But the Thompsons had had no training in the science of teaching the blind. Almost the first act of the Bishop, after his return from exile, was to import from England Gwendolyn Gaster, specialist in ministering to the blind, a vibrant Christian who accomplishes wonders, not by restoring vision in a literal sense, but by equipping the blind for more than the weaving of rush mats and the fashioning of brooms, important as those avenues of service are. Her more gifted pupils, with some of whom I talked, are telephone operators, radio announcers, translators, teachers. "Blind leaders of the blind" need not be, in every circumstance, an odious phrase.

There is not time in this brief account to describe the hospital in Shiraz, with its great record of service, physical and spiritual, and of the dedicated nurses and doctors who are there on stipends so small that at least they will not have the worry, in any country, of having to pay income tax. Nor is there time to tell of the Church of St. Simon the Zealot in Shiraz (see Pl. 43), a church whose architecture gives perfect expression, in terms Persians understand, to the placeless but irreplaceable verities of the Gospel. It is Israel for Iran, the eternal for now, the universal for here. That remarkable building – would that there were more of them – should be studied by all persons who are concerned about "indigenization" – concerned, that is, that Christ should speak not as a foreigner but as the eternal Son of God who also for *this* place was born, suffered, died, rose, and ascended into heaven.

Our Church in Persia has been exemplary in the matter of indigenization. It has, for example, wisely taken it upon itself to insert into the Nicene Creed the words "and died" after "he suffered". This is the Church's way of ruling out the contention of some Muslims that Christ merely swooned in the tomb, since so good a man could not possibly have died. In the Persian Prayer Book a most attractive example of liturgical adaptation to local conditions is provided by a supplementary collect for the Feast of the Epiphany:

O merciful Lord, who when you didst send thy Son into the world gavest to certain of the Magi the honour of admittance to his Presence, grant that we, Persians of the present century, may enter into the inheritance of our forefathers, and worship him, who with thee and the Holy Ghost liveth and reigneth, One God, world without end.

From such exalted considerations it may seem a descent into bathos to speak of oil, but oil – so needful to man – was placed under the seemingly unfruitful soil of the Middle East for the use of human beings, and it took Anglo-American ingenuity (and acquisitiveness) to bring it to the surface. I had hoped to go to one of the oil-producing areas in order to see what sort of response the Church was making to the sudden presence of hordes of people from Britain and the States. I chose for the purpose Kuwait, a sheikdom at the head of the Persian Gulf. Unfortunately, however, the Kuwait authorities sent my visa to London instead of to Jerusalem. No amount of frantic telegraphing between the British Embassy in Jerusalem and the authorities in Kuwait availed to produce an entry permit in time. In the end, I had to skip that small principality.

It can be reported, however, that Anglican chaplains are at work in virtually every important oil field, refinery, and shipping centre, though few of these spheres of action have clergymen in permanent residence. Yet it is a pity the ministry is confined largely to foreigners, especially as the recent arrivals are rich by Irani standards, and are getting richer by the day on their diet of Iranian oil. Understandably, they are, in certain quarters, resented; and it is not wise that the Church should seem to be identified exclusively with them. Moreover, it is precisely in the oil fields that we find a concentration of many of the best educated and most highly qualified Iranians. For them we need a full-time Persian priest.

The consecration in the summer of 1961 of the first Persian bishop is a token of the degree to which, despite its smallness, the Church in Iran is coming of age.

15

INDIA, PAKISTAN, BURMA AND CEYLON:
A "Peculiar Vineyard"

ONCE I HAD LEFT THE JERUSALEM ARCHBISHOPRIC, HEADING EAST-ward, everything was new territory to me until I reached familiar Japan – but that was a good eight months away. Ahead of me, although I little realized it, was the most difficult, fascinating, and exhausting phase of my exploration of the Anglican Communion.

Africa had presented obstacles to me as a traveller. Asia nearly did me in.

On departure from Iran I entered into a complex segment of the Church which, by fortuities of history far too intricate to be traced here, is an autonomous province embracing such unlikely partners as Pakistan, India, Ceylon, and Burma. In spite of national jealousies, linguistic differences, and ethnic enmities, a united Anglican Church has been forged – and it works.

The bishops of India and Pakistan, whenever they can get permission from their respective governments, cross the frontier to meet in easy converse to take counsel for the well-being of the Church. Although Burma is no longer a part of the British Commonwealth of Nations, the Anglicans of Burma have no difficulty in getting along with fellow Churchmen in the Commonwealth countries which make up the rest of the province. A Sinhalese bishop was elected Metropolitan of India in 1962. This I account a noteworthy instance of the Church's capacity to put the qualifications of a man above all thought of his nationality. He lives now in Calcutta and from there presides over the destinies of the Indian Church as well as the whole of his four-nation province. The province was "Made in Britain", one might say, but today it maintains itself. Also it grows. This is on the credit side.

On the other side of the ledger we must enter the distressing fact that the

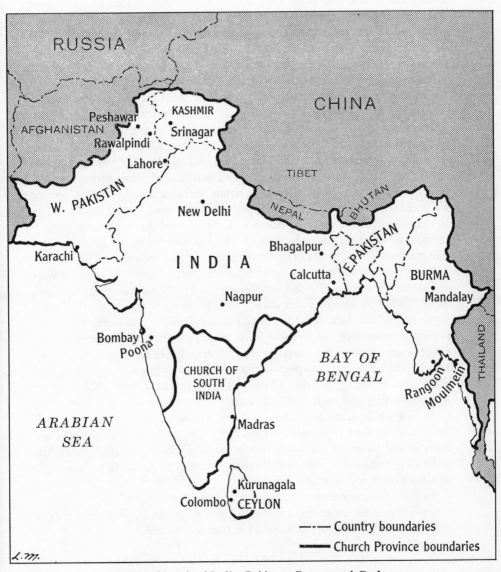

RUSSIA

CHINA

AFGHANISTAN

Peshawar

KASHMIR

Srinagar

Rawalpindi

Lahore

TIBET

W. PAKISTAN

NEPAL

BHUTAN

New Delhi

Karachi

I N D I A

Bhagalpur

E. PAKISTAN

Calcutta

BURMA

Mandalay

Nagpur

Bombay

Poona

CHURCH OF
SOUTH
INDIA

BAY OF
BENGAL

Rangoon

Moulmein

THAILAND

ARABIAN
SEA

Madras

Kurunagala

Colombo

CEYLON

--- Country boundaries

——— Church Province boundaries

3. The Church of India, Pakistan, Burma and Ceylon

growth is small in comparison with the population increase. Moreover, in the race to win men's souls, Christianity here faces the stiff competition of Islam, Hinduism, and Buddhism, and is a slow starter (see Pl. 46). Take Pakistan, concisely described by *Life* Magazine as "a raw young country put together as a nation in 1947 out of two vast and widely separated chunks of British India". In 1962 it had an estimated population of 86,823,000 of whom but 416,253 stood up to be counted as Christians, and only 102,000 of these called themselves Anglicans. A number in excess of 100,000 is not unimpressive, but our claims would have less bombast and greater realism were we to remind ourselves that probably no more than 25,000 are adults, confirmed and active. In Pakistan, Roman Catholics and Presbyterians are tied for first place, each of these Communions listing about 200,000 members. In terms of numbers, Anglicanism comes next, and trailing behind us are the 40,000 Methodists and some 30,000 Christians of other denominations. The non-Christian world in West Pakistan is almost wholly Muslim, except for fewer than 200,000 Hindus or Scheduled Caste people. The most succinct description of Anglicanism's situation in this part of the world was given to me in two short sentences by a man who knows whereof he speaks: "Our Church grows – by excess of births over deaths. Converts are only a few."

Many people have no taste for statistics and would find it tedious if I were to list them for India, Ceylon, and Burma as I have for Pakistan. After all, those who crave specifics can always look them up in almanacs of various sorts, one of the best of which is the *World Christian Handbook*. Here it is sufficient to observe that what I have reported of the one country is, in a general way, true of the other three. Christian forces are small. That is no novelty. But the tragic aspect is that Christians are too largely engaged solely in ministering to other Christians. In a properly responsible way we are cultivating our own gardens, which is a necessary and praiseworthy task; but we do not excel when it comes to the breaking of new ground. Seldom do we lay the plough to virgin soil. This I call blameworthy. Christianity in the Orient is much too much "enclave religion" – piety inside the walls of a compound, tongue-tied when it comes to speaking with persons of other religions . . . or of none.

To this statement there are, however, shining exceptions.

I offer you no more than *vignettes*, brief glimpses of four countries. I present them in the order in which I encountered them.

PAKISTAN

Pandit Nehru and I chose the same week to arrive in Karachi.

My own plane beat his by a few hours, which enabled me to mill among the crowds to watch him ride by with the president of the largest Muslim state in the world. (The second largest Muslim state is Turkey; the third, Egypt.) It was an epochal moment, the first meeting of the two heads of state since the partition of India and Pakistan in 1947.

Scarlet-coated soldiers in turbans, bearing lances from which fluttered regimental banners, sat astride magnificent black steeds. This cavalcade prepared the way for the two statesmen whose business it was to discuss the waters of the Punjab and the ticklish question of the Kashmir.

Our Church in Pakistan and India, little as it is, is not unaffected by these grave matters of state.

Political partition had the incidental effect of cutting the Anglican Mission in half. All without warning, our leading institutions – so far as Pakistan is concerned – were on the wrong side of the border. The Diocese of Lahore, coextensive with the whole of West Pakistan, was summarily called upon to make a go of it alone. That is not easy when there are only seventy thousand baptized members, of whom but seventeen thousand are confirmed, and the vast majority desperately poor.

It should not surprise us that a diocese this small and this much cut off from accustomed means of support and supply should look with friendly eye upon other Christian bodies in the area. Economics has its own – perhaps God-given – way of making a contribution to ecumenics! Encouraged by the example of the Church of South India, Christians in Pakistan and in North India are deep in discussions which may lead to the formation of two autocephalous Churches, one for North India and one for Pakistan. If they do come into being, they will not be parts of the Anglican Communion. Most Indian and Pakistani Anglicans, however, are concerned not to rush into a Church newly organized until they can be assured that such a Church, although independent, will be in full intercommunion with the whole family of Anglican Churches. A similar sense of loyalty causes Methodists, Presbyterians, and the other negotiating bodies to desire to preserve ties with *their* respective spiritual progenitors. This is understandable, commendable – and a source of endless difficulty. Not to be overlooked is the fact that the North India Plan is somewhat more audacious than was the pioneer venture of the South Indians. It would embrace within its fold elements more diverse. For example, Baptists have participated in the North Indian discussion.

When I was in Pakistan, some of the Baptists were threatening withdrawal. Although the draft formularies made provision both for Infant Baptism *and* for Believer's Baptism, and would have allowed parents who were conscientiously committed to Adult or Believer's Baptism to defer Baptism of their children until they should reach the age of discretion, certain Baptists panicked. They demanded that a person who had been baptized in infancy should have the right, if he so desired, to be baptized again when, as an adult, he had had the conscious experience of conversion. On this jagged point the whole scheme was doomed, apparently, to founder – at least so far as the Baptists were concerned. "I believe in one baptism for the remission of sins", says the Nicene Creed.

One day in Peshawar my scheduled excursion to the Khyber Pass had to be cancelled because there had been a border incident between the Pakistani and the Afghans. The Pass, bristling with guns, was closed. I used the unexpected free afternoon to motor many miles in the opposite direction to ask a Danish-American Lutheran bishop why his flock displayed no interest in the North India Plan. "We simply do not understand you Anglicans," he said. "Why are you perennially flirting with Presbyterians and even Baptists, while you overlook your most natural allies, the Lutherans? You are interested always in *Order* – and too little concerned about *Faith*." To this candid utterance I had mixed reactions at the time, and still do. In part, he is right. Anglicans do tolerate all manner of doctrinal vagary, provided that everything is in order with respect to Orders. But our Lutheran friend must be wrong in his insistence upon having every article of faith exhaustively defined and assented to unquestioningly before there can be any thought of uniting. Here I am in waters too deep for me. Perhaps stronger swimmers will know to which shore we should head. It is, I suppose, Anglicanism's sure perception that *both* shores matter which makes life so hard for us – and makes it doubly important that we never absent ourselves from ecumenical consultations.

I do not intend to say much more about the North India Plan or the Ceylon Scheme. My reasons for reticence are twofold. For one thing, much has already been written on the subject.* Second, events are moving so fast that anything I say now will be obsolete (and therefore misleading, perhaps) by the time this book appears.

But to Anglicans in the rest of the world who are chary about the various Indian and Sinhalese Christian experiments in our day I would like to issue a reminder in the form of a query. What chance do you think Christianity will have of succeeding in countries like India, Pakistan, and Ceylon, where it is not only, humanly speaking, hopelessly outnumbered, but where also its few adherents are inhumanly divided into competitive sects?

The question might have more point – and more poignancy – if we consider the case of two Indian brothers. Early in life they were separated, though always maintaining close contact by mail. One of the brothers, after

---

* Cf. the book Bishop Bayne has edited, *Ceylon, North India, Pakistan – A Study in Ecumenical Decision* (London: S.P.C.K., 1960) and the convenient summary given by Bishop Rawlinson in *The Anglican Communion in Christendom* (London: S.P.C.K., 1960).

a long, agonizing intellectual struggle, fought his way through to faith in Christ. This happened to him in a section of India which, because of the comity of missions, had been assigned to the Methodists. He was radiant in his new faith. Meanwhile, his brother, who had gone to seek his fortunes in that portion of the land which had been assigned to Anglicans, had also fought "the long dialectical wars of faith" and had finally found victory and liberation when his mind was taken captive by Christ. After many years of separation, there was to be a family reunion. The brothers, transformed in character and transported by joy, met. The date was 24th December. They saluted each other with a holy kiss. Brothers they now were not only after the flesh but also after the Spirit. But they were informed by the local Anglican priest that they could not communicate together at the same altar on the eve of that wondrous night on which the Saviour was born. One was a Methodist. One was an Anglican. Supposedly, this was sufficient ground for dividing them.

I met these brothers. I had to hang my head in shame before them as, stammeringly, I tried to explain the reasons for the hideous irrationality of our keeping them apart.

Because of a time change between Teheran and Karachi, it was after two o'clock before I got to bed in West Pakistan's great coastal city. It was, moreover, a hot night. Deep sleep was impossible, and I was not particularly happy when church bells summoned me to consciousness before daybreak. There was a service, well conducted, commemorating the Battle of Britain. The British were in attendance in full regalia. We basked for an hour and a half in parade, panoply, and panegyric. That was fine. I agree that the Battle of Britain is definitely worth commemorating. And since many British live in Karachi, I was glad they were in church. At the same time, this service demonstrated clearly one of our chief problems: the Church is so closely identified with Britain that it constitutes a permanent handicap in becoming the Church of the people, the Church of the land. Throughout Pakistan and India, as I was to find, the walls of cathedrals and churches are disfigured by plaques in memory of brave and gallant Britons who were "foully ambushed" in one or another nasty Indian uprising. I do not suggest that these memorial tablets, glittering in brass, should come down. History cannot be obliterated. Nor do I recommend a coat of whitewash for the walls. But these reminders of a vanished empire might well distract a "native" trying to be devout.

Later on during the same Karachi Sunday there was a service in Urdu, attended by only a handful of worshippers. Still later, at Evensong in English, we numbered exactly eighteen people. Perhaps the congregation would have been larger on a normal Sunday when all energies had not been expended on the "State Shinto" in connection with the Battle of Britain.

The following day my interest in Pakistan picked up decidedly. Chandu Ray, the Assistant Bishop of Lahore, took me in tow, and my eyes were opened. After showing me an orphanage, a school, and a church, he walked me for hours through the slum quarters of Karachi. Here was privation and misery on a scale exceeding my powers of description. I did not know until then that people could maintain their humanity under conditions so destructive of human dignity. When India was granted self-government in 1947, four million Hindus and Sikhs fled from Pakistan to India, and an even greater number of Muslims came running to Pakistan. It has been called "the greatest interchange of population in history". Many of those who came from India still have nowhere to sleep save the sidewalks of Karachi. "Many" means about five hundred thousand persons. Unfortunately, the Anglican Church has not the knack of sidewalk or street-corner preaching.

Chandu Ray, first of his nation to be a bishop, drove me out to Korangi, a new large-scale development for refugees being built by the government. Officials of state have begged the Bishop to open twenty schools in this crowded area. What an opportunity! An officially Muslim government says to the Christian Church, "We need your help, we need your schools; we will give you all the assistance we can. Please go to it!" But even with the offer of government subsidy, Bishop Chandu Ray can produce neither the manpower nor the money. As a venture of faith he was in process of creating six or seven schools, although this was straining his resources to the uttermost and involved his firm decision to cancel plans the Diocese had for building him a decent house. Anglicans are rarely able to strike when the iron is hot, because we never have funds in reserve. It is chronic with us that we live from hand to mouth.

This official friendliness of a Muslim government does not always find an echo in person-to-person relationships. A son who embraces Christianity will, in most cases, find himself disowned and disinherited. Usually he loses his job as well, and it will be hard for him to find a new one.* The costliness of discipleship, especially in a country like Pakistan, explains the importance of Selwyn House in Karachi, a place to which inquirers come. If eventually they are converted from Islam, it serves as a hostel where they may live, strengthened by the fellowship of the Church, until such time as they have made the difficult transition. It helps them to live in a Christian household

* Girls, of course, don't matter so much! But if they are flighty enough to become Christians, it will not be easy for them to find husbands, and they cannot expect much of a welcome at home.

where they meet not only convinced Christians who have trod the painful path before them but also other young men who, like themselves, stand only at the beginning of their pilgrimage. This takes away a little of the loneliness. There must be more places like Selwyn House – *many* more.

First in Karachi, later in Lahore, and elsewhere in Pakistan, I encountered a type of Anglicanism that was new to my experience. It was an evangelical-ism marred, as it seemed to me, by Biblical Fundamentalism, Puritanism, and Pietism. In my vocabulary, these are *not* complimentary words! I can best define my terms by describing an average Sunday. A New Zealand missionary, his wife, their children, and I, their guest, had been to Holy Communion at seven and Matins at nine – a long service with a very long sermon. There was to be Sunday School in the middle of the afternoon and Evening Prayer still later in the day. One might have thought that was "religion" enough for one day, especially for young children; but immedi-ately after lunch, while still sitting at table, we had a long Scripture reading, followed by commentary and family prayers. Then we studied the Ten Commandments with the help of a tract in which, for example, the Com-mandment, "Thou shalt not take the Name of the Lord thy God in vain", was interpreted simply as a prohibition against profanity. While the use of profanity is unlovely and unchristian, its prohibition is not precisely the point of the Commandment! And the second Commandment was inter-preted as a divine veto against stained-glass windows and statues in Christian churches! My New Zealand host, a priest of the Church, then folded his napkin and his hands – and we had more prayers. I do not say this pious man is fully representative of all the missionaries at work in this country, but enough resemble him to enable me to comprehend at least some of the reasons why Church Unity is full of trials.

I would beg the reader not to misunderstand me. I am happy that a man of this persuasion can find a place within the Anglican fold. The more all-inclusive we are the better – so long as we do not fall into self-contradiction. I greatly prefer having the "chapel" *inside* the Church, as it were, instead of outside, as a "rival" outfit. I favour the whole movement for Church Union in Pakistan and India. But is it not curious – and a worthy subject for meditation – that such a low churchman as my host at lunch and a man as "high" as the Bishop of Bombay (who was a principal architect of the North India Plan) can both be Anglicans and can both endorse the same scheme? The difference between them, however, is this: the Bishop (Dr. Lash, who has since retired) knows what Anglicanism is, knows what Anglicanism has to give to a united Church, knows to what extent Anglicanism can learn and gain from such a union; whereas the other man is theologically too naïve to see that much is at issue in the negotiations between the Churches. Perhaps both types of men are necessary: the theologian to see to it that the formularies are correct and that no principle of importance is compromised, the untutored man of goodwill who can swing enough votes to ensure that a bold step is taken.

Fifty-three priests to minister to seventy thousand members – that was the situation in the Diocese of Lahore (West Pakistan) in 1962. Inevitably, a thoroughgoing pastoral ministry is impossible. Many of the clergy have twenty scattered congregations. Few own cars. Villages predominantly Anglican are often remote from rail and bus lines. The padre has to use the camel, the horse-drawn tonga, and the bullock cart.

Recruiting for the Ministry is not simple. A priest receives only one-fourth of what a schoolteacher gets. Most graduates gravitate to teaching, law, medicine, or government. A sacerdotal stipend exacts too severe a sacrifice.

"Even in the cities," I was told, "most of the clergy know very little English." I did not at once grasp the import of this remark. My informant must have seen this in my face, for he at once explained: "To have no English is to have no reading, no theological reading. These men can be wonderfully faithful, good pastors, effective in villages; but in cities they cannot reach the generation that is growing up." How strangely, therefore, the words of an alarmingly pious foreign missionary fell on my ears when he bemoaned the fact that the United Theological Seminary at Gujranwala (where our postulants are trained) is "putting too much emphasis on the intellectual side".

Also strange to my ears – but for another reason – were the snorts of disapprobation issuing from a New York Churchman who said, "I simply cannot abide these union theological seminaries. To place our students in these Protestant institutions is to threaten the purity of the Catholic Faith." This gentleman was blissfully unaware that the Partition of India left that part of the Church which is now the Diocese of Lahore without a single seminary – and with no chance of building one and with little or no possibility of sending men across the border. If he is so concerned about the purity of the Faith, let him build for Lahore a seminary purely Anglican, and let him endow it heavily. He has the money to do both.

Somebody with less money, but with greater liberality towards the principle of a union seminary, might well provide funds for the purchase of a few rat traps. When the Anglican member of the Gujranwala faculty took me into the library we found one dead rat (I think he must have died of indigestion after having gnawed his way through the first three volumes of

Hooker's *Laws of Ecclesiastical Polity*), and with a broom we chased out a live one.

Money is always a problem. The principal cities of Pakistan and India can boast of handsome churches. In the days of the Empire they were garrison churches. Now that the British have gone, most of these edifices are much too elaborate for the Christians of these countries to maintain. The cost of upkeep puts too great a strain on the local purse.

It was sad in India to see, here and there, great cantonment churches boarded up, decaying, or even in total ruin. Squatters have moved into the churchyard. There they have put up their shacks. Attempts to dislodge them have proved unavailing. Litigation goes on endlessly. The courts will not act. "The dockets are too full" is the reason alleged for maddening postponements – sometimes five years and more. One suspects that in certain instances the Church can get no action because of its unwillingness to resort to bribery.

The rural areas of Pakistan present problems of a different order. Floods are the enemy of the people and of their church in scores of villages. For the last decade the rains have been unusually heavy. In district after district the water level is only three or four feet below the surface, and the mud houses of the people frequently collapse because of the saltpetre. Since the rain falls on the just as well as on the unjust, the local House of God is not spared and is often a pathetic spectacle. The saltpetre which is ruining the soil makes poor farmers even poorer and consequently it is all the more difficult for the Christians among them to give substantial sums of money for the support of the Church. Gradually the Diocese is building new churches of brick. They are rather unfinished in appearance, though more likely to remain firm than their predecessors built of mud bricks. The new buildings will be better able to withstand the inordinate appetite of the white ant. However, it was never easy to make bricks without straw – yet this is what some of us seem to expect of the Diocese of Lahore.*

One is grateful that the Church cares for the poor. Without this, she would not be following in the footsteps of her Master. The Church in Pakistan and in India must be credited with great fidelity. She has walked in this way. Yet too little has she seen that sometimes the steps of the Master were directed towards the houses of the well-to-do and the well-educated. Neither the rich nor the learned doctors intimidated him. I had the

* Warm friendships throughout the Anglican Communion are the greatest personal dividends of my prolonged odyssey. Returning the questionnaire I had sent out, the Bishop of Lahore wrote good-humouredly, "Dear Canon Sahib . . . The Infliction upon Bishops (by these questionnaires) is nothing compared with the infliction on yourself! . . . Yours sincerely, Laurence Lahore."

impression, however, that the Church in the Indian subcontinent has accepted a kind of silent defeat in approaching people of wealth and education. There are exceptions, of course, but most of the missionaries turned only to the sweepers (the ex-Scheduled Classes) and identified themselves with them – also emotionally. As a result, the missionaries and the indigenous Ministry raised up by their labours seem to share the Christian lower-classes' distrust and disdain for the Muslims or the Hindus. There is virtually no contact between Christians and those of other religions, especially with persons highly placed either educationally or economically.

Why is it that it occurred to no bishop (except for the then Bishop of Kurunagala) to arrange for me to meet with leaders of non-Christian religions? This struck me as odd, because all of the bishops had been told well in advance that the particular focus of my interest was to try to understand the Church's situation in its given milieu. I said explicitly that my task was to "tune in" on the dialogue between the Church and its environing culture. That our Reverend Fathers in God failed me in this matter – failed to set up appointments with responsible people who could have told me how Christianity looks to non-Christian eyes – was the signal, the dead giveaway, that our own leaders are not themselves engaged in dialogue. To repeat phrases used earlier in this book, we are too much an "enclave religion". We suffer from "compound mentality". We are constantly enlarging the mission compound and the number of its dwellers, but we are still fenced in.

To tell of the violent dust storm which rudely overturned the charming and imaginative exhibits prepared by our schoolchildren in an all-Anglican village called Bethlehem for the delectation of the Bishop and me; to tell of the gritty picnic lunch that followed in the wake of the storm; to tell of the triumphal procession to the church for the Confirmation of a large class (see Pl. 53 and 54) (the village has only four streets, none paved, and we executed all manner of flanking manoeuvres in order to prolong the joy of the procession); to tell of the Bishop's sitting out-of-doors in the village's only chair, talking first with the women who by their sewing are the chief support of the church, and then with the village elders, a colourful-looking lot, who had grave matters to discuss with their shepherd: to tell of all this, I say, would require more space than I am allotted. Yet this kind of village, waterlogged, dust tormented, saltpetre ruined, its people largely illiterate and impoverished, is the heart of the Church in Pakistan. Parsonages are often unsafe for human habitation. Church buildings crumble. But the work of the Church is of good quality.

.   .   .   .   .

In cities such as Lahore, Rawalpindi, and Peshawar we can be proud of schools, colleges, and hospitals. These institutions are almost never ours alone. They are, rather, joint ventures in which Anglicans co-operate happily with other Christian bodies. What separate denominations are too poor to do single-handedly we can usually manage if all of us join forces. One of the reasons Indian and Pakistani Christians have been able to engage constructively in the creation of united Churches is that they have long been occupied with united works of mercy. People of different denominations who are old hands at combating together illiteracy and disease have come to know, trust, and love one another – and there is, on their part, a sudden fierce impatience with the prohibition against their worshipping side by side. Denominationalism is an opulent and obsolete luxury which only the rich countries of the West can afford. Do we live, as many are suggesting nowadays, in a post-Christian era? Perhaps. But if Christians are again becoming a minority group, there may yet be hope for us. For minorities have a way of learning to reconcile petty differences and of finding the means to pull together powerfully.

A notable feature of Anglican work in Pakistan is the great hospital at Quetta in Baluchistan. Sir Henry Holland, the surgeon-missionary who built it up, is now retired, after fifty years of service, but his son has come to take his father's place. This is a region particularly afflicted by diseases of the eye. An octogenarian Sir Henry humbly remarked that the source of his deepest gratitude was the fact that he and his Christian staff had been the human instrumentality in restoring the sight of more than seventy thousand persons.

"Lord, that I might have my sight." This is the cry of the blind. It might well be the cry and the prayer of every sighted person who, like the priest and the Levite in the parable, looked at a stricken man but passed by on the other side. The sins most commonly confessed to the priests of the Church have to do with the lust of the eye. But these sins, unattractive and unprofitable as they are, are as *nothing* compared to looking at the blind without really seeing them.

INDIA

In India I got off to a poor start.

As we arrived from Lahore along towards sundown, I could see from the air that every park, athletic field, and race track in the city of New Delhi was teeming with people. The crowds were intent upon great papier-mâché effigies, thirty or forty feet high.

Once Customs were cleared, I deposited my dusty luggage with a group of English missionaries – the Cambridge Brotherhood – and was promptly clapped into nothing less than a monastery. I had but one minute to slap some cold water on my face before a bell summoned us to chapel. During the recitation of psalms innumerable my mind strayed. I could not help but wonder as we chanted what all the commotion was about outside. The air reverberated with the sound of fireworks. It was not possible, however, to raise questions, for the supper which followed the Office was in silence, except for the droning of a lector who read to us improving literature, first of a serious kind, then of a supposedly more diverting nature. When finally the silence was lifted, I inquired, "What was all that excitement about?"

They replied with a shrug: "Oh, that was in connection with Dusserah, the major Hindu feast of the year."

"Couldn't we go out to have a look?' I pleaded.

"No, it's all over now."

To say I was annoyed would be putting it mildly. I can read Evening Prayer anytime between noon and midnight. Here I was in India, for the first time in my life, and I was confined to a monastic establishment, involved in Vespers, while ceremonially costumed Hindus – shooting flaming arrows to set the effigies on fire – were having their principal celebration.

I might have forgiven these holy men had I not learned, belatedly, that the next morning was the ninetieth anniversary of the birth of Mahatma Gandhi, an event commemorated by mass demonstrations of weaving while I sat mumbling Matins and Mass with the monks.

My anger was not directed against the monks. They are fine men. They do a wonderful work. It was only that nobody in authority had told them the purpose of my visit, which was to try to understand the Church's situation in a particular locale.

Even so, anger is rarely productive, and I think now that I might have learned much of value if I had not, in high dudgeon, packed my bags and hurried away.

At least, the place from which I fled was an excellent starting point from which to see Delhi and the sprawling twentieth-century city called New Delhi. In marked contrast to crowded conditions of ancient Delhi, the new city is spaciously laid out. Its British planners were obviously inspired by the examples of Paris and Washington. From the fortress-like Ashoka Hotel, I saw spread out before me the sparkling new American Embassy, the walled compound housing the British diplomatic families, and the Roman Catholic chancery flying a yellow-and-white papal flag. I admired the grand boulevards that led to the red sandstone cupolas and buildings which once housed the Viceroys and now are the centre of governmental activities. And at last I came to the Cathedral of the Redemption, a magnificently landscaped, lofty-domed structure that is a handsome reminder of the positive contributions which the British made during their years in India.

My hasty and ill-tempered departure from Delhi was proof, no doubt, that I was by this time in need of the brief holiday I had planned for myself in the Kashmir. Thus I arrived in Srinagar two days early. Here I was to take my rest.

There are in the world mountains more imposing, lakes more splendid, villages more picturesque than those to be seen in the vicinity of Srinagar. But the *tout ensemble* has no equal anywhere. It must be the never-ending play of light and shadow which works its enchantment. Not twice in an hour does the Kashmir look the same.

Here, as I have said, after twelve months of continuous travel, I had scheduled a halt. The time had come to rest and reflect on what I had learned so far.

It was unfortunate for me, as you will see, that as a Churchman I felt the need of obeying the dominical precept about worshipping God every Sunday in his Church. Having looked up the local Anglican priest as soon as I arrived, I gladly accepted his invitation to accompany him and his wife on a Sunday visit to a mission hospital high in the Himalayas. The road which climbs to Anantnag offers views of ineffable beauty, but life in these parts is not always beautiful – especially for the women. Their health, their safe delivery in childbirth, is of little concern. Only the Church seems to care about saving them from the absolutely barbaric and hopelessly unscientific, insanitary methods of Indian midwifery. I was thankful to find in this little village our hospital with its thirty beds for women.

Our hospital tour was interrupted by the mission bell calling us to the chapel. A nurse thoughtfully handed me a blanket to cover my feet (the Indians remain barefoot in church). As I rounded a corner to enter by the front door, I stopped in my tracks when I saw an Indian orderly suddenly rip the sari off an Indian woman and start beating her over the head with it. There flashed through my mind the thought "What goes on here? Is this a form of sportiveness between the sexes on a Sunday morning in the Kashmir? Or a damsel in distress whom I must try to rescue?" But in the same moment I saw the real situation. The unlucky woman was being attacked by a swarm of hornets. The orderly was attempting to drive them away and had seized upon the sari as the only available weapon. He was being savagely bitten in the process. In the same split second, the hornets – knowing, as I did not, that their nest was on the chapel wall directly above my head – made straight for me. At first I stood stock still, in the vain belief that immobility would be my best defence. After repeated stings about the face and ears I could stand it no longer. I dropped my costly camera equipment and started running, beating at the hornets with the blanket.

When I finally eluded the hornets and came back to the hospital, I found that the woman had gone into hysterics and needed to be put under sedation. Within an hour the orderly had broken out in a fearsome rash from head to toe. In my case, the after-effects took a different turn: swelling, fever, and excruciating pain. For the first five hours I was not sure I could take it. The head nurse said, "It is a good thing that this happened at a hospital. Without prompt medication, this might have been fatal to all three of you." If I hadn't believed unconditionally in mission hospitals before, I believed in them then!

To distract my mind from my misery, I carefully worked out the wording of a memorial plaque to be affixed to a wall of the Cathedral Church of New York:

IN MEMORIAM
The Reverend Howard A. Johnson, D.D.
Canon Theologian of this Cathedral Church
1954–1960
Martyred by hornets in the Kashmir
"O death, where is thy sting?"

Hornets were not the whole of my misfortunes in India. I do not hold it against India that there I was pickpocketed. That could have happened anywhere, just as it happens many times a day in my own city of New York, perhaps particularly nearby or even *inside* the Cathedral.

Fortunately, the light-fingered thief at Ranchi did not empty the pocket containing the passport and my tickets. Even so, I lost things like the prescription for my glasses, an X-ray of my teeth, my driver's licence, my social security card, my voting registration and – most serious of all – a notebook in which were hundreds of entries such as "Mrs. Thus and Thus of Bimini wishes to be remembered to the Bishop of Borneo who confirmed her", "Mr. Cooper of Liverpool says that the man who can give you the information you're seeking in Colombo is Mr. Eks." Hundreds of personal reminders, useless to the thief but of great value to me, were lost, presumably thrown into a canal somewhere.

Lost also was a card on which I had set great store. It had been given to me by a gentleman seated next to me on a plane flying from Porto Alegre to São Paulo in Brazil. It was a long flight, and eventually we fell into conversation. Names were exchanged. When he had learned the nature of my errand, he disclosed the fact that he was an Anglican and an Australian. Producing a calling card which showed him to be a high official in a large Australian firm, he strictly charged me, "When you get to Australia, the very first thing you must do is get in touch with me, for we can fly you in the company plane to places difficult of access." I tell this story here because it is the sole remaining chance I have of letting that Churchman know why it is he never heard from me again. Although I ransacked my memory, I could not recall his name or that of his firm.

The Kashmir is only slightly smaller than the whole of Great Britain, yet there is but one Anglican priest for the whole of it. "Kashmir," said he, surveying the marvellous view from the terrace of my hotel, "is my parish." Had I arrived in Srinagar but a few days later I would have missed this Englishman and his Canadian wife. For they, who serve under the Canadian Board of Missions, were even then packing for a year's furlough. This, by the way, is not the same as a year's holiday. Much of a missionary's furlough has to be spent in deputation work, i.e., travelling around in the country which sent him, going from parish to parish making speeches designed to whip up enthusiasm for the mission. A certain amount of this is right and proper. Indeed, imperative. But my general impression is that the Church as a whole overworks its missionaries. We tend to exhaust them in the field. And then, when they return to their home country for a rest and for study, we overload them by making circuit riders and barnstormers out of them.

But that is only part of the problem. Who is to replace the man on furlough? In that particular instance which prompts these general reflections, the problem was to be dealt with by importing a succession of priests for a month or two at a time. Doubtless this is as good a solution as can be hit upon, but it is "good night" to the principle of continuity in pastoral ministration.

Anglicans have had work in the Kashmir for one hundred years. It is no reflection on the heroic men and women who have worked so hard in this territory that we have so little to show for it. It reflects, rather, on a Church unwilling or unable to send a sufficient task force; it reflects on a Church whose passion for extension was not matched by a zeal for intension. And thus we have condemned to insignificance the total outpouring of self of the few pioneers who were sent in.

I hope I make myself clear. This is a serious accusation of much of past Anglican strategy. We have wasted good men and women because we did not surround them with colleagues.

From the Kashmir I pressed southward to Bombay, city of more than three million people, a commercial and cultural centre which rightly calls itself "The Gateway of India". It has the air of a great city. To be truthful, it is the only one of the Indian cities I visited where I could settle down to live and work without feeling that in so doing I had made a heroic sacrifice.

The Diocese of Bombay, shaped like a butterfly, spreads over an area of more than 104,000 square miles. The See City is a cosmopolitan community, built on seven islands, with glistening buildings ringing its crescent-shaped harbour. The bishop is assisted in the diocese by twenty-one Indians, three Anglo-Indians, and eleven European priests. They have to distribute themselves very thinly, indeed, to make any mark at all in a diocese of nineteen thousand persons.*

The Bishop of Bombay showed me the impressive Cathedral of St. Thomas as well as churches, schools, and diocesan welfare agencies, then put me on a train for Poona which can be reached only by surmounting the bluish slopes of the majestic Western Ghats.

Our work at Poona is a vivid example of what can be done for the multitudes of India. More than a score of sisters of the Community of St. Mary the Virgin, coming out to India from their motherhouse at Wantage in the Diocese of Oxford, have established a primary school, two hostels, and an institute for ecclesiastical needlework embroidery and altar breads. Five monks of the Society of St. John the Evangelist operate a boys' school, an orphanage, and two hostels. Both of these religious orders work with a Scottish Mission of the C.M.S. in operating two high schools serving six hundred students. Poona can also boast a church-run medical school with an enrolment of four hundred, a welfare home, and the exceedingly beautiful seventy-seven-year-old Church of the Holy Name. All of these activities are conducted in an area that is overwhelmingly Hindu with a smattering of Muslims and some Parsees and Jews. The Cowley Fathers (S.S.J.E.) could tell me nothing of statistics, population, sociological factors. They were too busy with the needs of their people to study the over-all picture. Also, they were preoccupied with the possibility of having to forsake their flocks because their Constitution forbids their working with any church not in communion with all other Anglicans.

"We Christians are always talking about 'the Christian religion'," said Murray Rogers, a priest of the Diocese of Lucknow, whom I encountered on the train from Poona. "We are always making it one of several religions: the Hindu religion, the Muslim religion, the Christian religion, and so on.

---

* Somewhere I read (and the phrase has stuck in my mind) that "with the subsequent rise to power of the Dutch and the British, Roman Catholicism in India *faded away* with Portugal's decline". When I mentioned this to the Bishop of Bombay he replied with a smile, "Perhaps you've noted how much Roman Catholicism has 'faded away'. The place is *stiff* with Roman Catholics." He was entirely correct and their achievements, particularly by the religious orders, are impressive: for example, in Bombay, the Society of Jesus runs seven of the eight Roman Catholic high schools, and in all of India the Jesuits can count eleven provinces with twenty-five colleges, one hundred and twenty high schools, and ten thousand primary schools.

But surely Christianity is *above* all religions. We act as if it were up to us to make Christ the Lord of India. But he *is* the Lord of India!"

The train jounced along as Rogers continued to speak in a paradoxical manner Anglicans have difficulty in understanding though he is right: "We don't trust the Indians to be free: free to be Christians or non-Christians, free to be orthodox or heretics, free to obey or disobey. We think that the Catholic Faith has no future unless the forms of that Faith are dictated by us. We won't let the Indians who are Christians really care for us. If missionaries fall ill, it is the C.M.S. hospital, with money, doctors, and nurses from 'home' who care for us; if we need a holiday we go to the hills because an office thousands of miles away decides for us that we shall go to the hills for six weeks, never asking whether *native* clergy can go to the hills for six weeks when they need a holiday. It is not the Indian Christians who say, 'You are in need of a rest.' It is decided, like everything else, at Salisbury Square in London."

Besides the Indian Christians of whom Murray spoke, I had also learned more of another group set aside as Anglo-Indians. The Archdeacon of Bombay told me there were wealthy members of this group who emigrated in large numbers, usually to the United Kingdom, leaving behind their economically less-favoured and generally less-talented brothers. Those who remain continue to be a self-contained group, not often marrying Indians or Europeans. The Anglo-Indians are constantly diminishing in number and are an increasingly impoverished group. The British had given them many concessions and so did the new Indian government, but the latter feels it cannot continue to treat them as privileged citizens. The plight of the Anglo-Indian comes to rest with the Anglican Church, of which most of them are members, and the Church must deal with the finance of Anglo-Indian schools and many other specialized problems.

The Anglo-Indian problem is only part of a crown of thorns that has come to rest on our Church in India, a painful burden for a small Church. As a whole, Anglican India is so poor that it becomes a major problem, particularly in villages, to buy sacramental wine. A low-quality bottle of portlike wine costs twenty-seven rupees – more than half of the fifty rupees which are the total diocesan assessment for many village parishes.

Looking out at the Bishop of Bombay's garden, I asked, "Why not plant grapes and make your own wine?" The answer came back, "There are so many regulations about the transport of wine that we gave up the idea as impracticable."

The mention of governmental restrictions reminded me of India's laws against liquor. "How is prohibition going?" I asked this witty and perceptible bishop.

"Prohibition?" he repeated. "Oh, it has created the largest cottage industry in India."

Indian Airways flew me to Nagpur. In my pocket diary I wrote:

To Nagpur I went. My purpose was to see its Indian bishop, John Sadiq, renowned as a scholar and an intellectual. Bishop Sadiq I did not see because he was away for an engagement of long standing. But if of long standing, he had had a long time to let me know so that I could come at a different time. His secretary says that in his modesty it never occurred to him that I was coming here solely or even primarily to see *him*. A flight from Bombay got me here at 2:00 A.M. It took an interminable time to get my baggage because Nagpur, at almost the centre of India, is a great airline junction and therefore is a congested place. Four planes (from Delhi, Bombay, Calcutta, and Madras) all arrive within a few minutes of each other in the middle of the night, and there is a great reshuffling of the passengers as they transfer from one plane to another. Not until 3:30 A.M. did I reach the inelegant Mount Hotel, not until 4 did I climb under the mosquito netting, and not until 4:30 did I doze off. No bedspread or sheet was provided, and by five o'clock I could no longer deny that I was cold. The coolness was refreshing after Bombay's stickiness, but I did not particularly welcome the necessity of getting out of bed to fetch my raincoat for covering. At six o'clock, though I had specifically left instructions that I wanted no morning tea, it none the less arrived with a loud knock and a great clatter of cracked china. I growled out a "No, take it away" and thereupon fell into a sleep so deep that I didn't hear the 7:15 alarm which should have wakened me in time to assist at an 8 A.M. sung Eucharist.

The Archdeacon, G. B. Wells, who is priest-in-charge of All Saints' Cathedral, was to have come to the hotel at 10:30 but arrived at 11, having had to go to the police station because of the theft of a brass vase from the Cathedral. The Archdeacon had sent me a cordial note and he made good on his promise of a tour of the town. But he could not tell me its population nor the numerical strength of the various religious groups.

The Reverend Richard Fenn, an American priest, had arrived with his wife the day before, on loan to the Diocese of Nagpur from the National Council in New York. Since Nagpur is a diocese which is the special concern of the Scottish Episcopal Church, there is a nice pattern of co-operation: the American Episcopal Church lends a man to the Scottish Episcopal Church for work in an Indian Diocese.

Ill fortune continued to dog my steps in India. For five stifling days I sat cooped up in a Madras hotel waiting for an unseasonable monsoon to blow itself out. Roads in much of South India were impassable. Transportation had ground to a standstill. Finally I could tarry no longer. Soon I would be overdue in Calcutta. But thus I was obliged to cancel the short circle tour I had counted on for sampling the life and work of the Church of South India. This Church is not part of the Anglican Communion. Yet it would be impossible to assess Anglicanism's accomplishments in India if one were to ignore the fact that in 1947 four large dioceses – with a half million Anglicans – went into the making of that adventurous new Church and have been a powerful factor in setting its tone. It was, after all, in the southern part of the country that the Church of England had had her greatest successes, and when she became part of the United Church of South India she went in in force – not only force of numbers but also force of scholarship. It is for this reason that many Anglicans throughout the world have looked more favourably on the Church of South India than on the proposed new Church of North India and Pakistan. By some it is felt that the Anglican ingredient in the North is too weak to maintain the proper "tone" and that Anglicanism's specific contribution to a united Church in the North might, unlike the situation in the South, be engulfed in the strong currents of other traditions. Personally I feel that these fears are groundless. I could be wrong. I often am. But if bishops in Apostolic Succession (and if the other principles we Anglicans stand for) are as good and as necessary as we think they are, can we not trust that they will have the power to validate themselves in the experience of Christians who previously have not been exposed to them?

From the whole ecumenical discussion two facts stand out with supreme clarity. Anglicans are guilty of arrogance and myopia in their persistent notion that we are on the giving end only. Anglicans would do well to reflect that other Christian bodies are far more eager to concede our points than we are to listen to their testimony. For the peace of the Church, for the sake of "The Coming Great Church", Christians hitherto committed to presbyterial or congregational forms of church government are more than willing to embrace episcopacy – not merely in a pragmatic interest but because prompted by theological insight and – more important still – by love of the brethren. Why, then, do some of our numbers demand of these negotiating bodies assent to a particular *doctrine* of episcopacy whereas Anglicans allow themselves a wide latitude on this very point? If only bishops will behave like bishops, they will prove their worth. This is what happened in South India.

These were some of the thoughts – none new, none very profound – I had while waiting in Madras for a monsoon to subside. Meanwhile, I was not entirely idle. Although excursions to Bangalore and other strongholds of the Church of South India were ruled out by "those immoderate rains, wherewith thou hast afflicted us", I talked with leaders who have their headquarters at Madras.* I came away – in a storm-tossed plane – with the greatest optimism about Christianity's future in South India. Those areas of the Church of South India which formerly were predominantly Anglican are still predominantly Anglican in ethos and expression of their worship. Ditto for those areas which previously had as their centre of gravity the traditions of Methodism or Congregationalism. Yet, little by little the new South Indian liturgy – and there is none finer in the world – wins its way. One generation more and there will be a Church, Catholic and Reformed, which will be known in history as a place where the Holy Spirit had his way in a significant breaking of the ecumenical log jam.

Calcutta and I were a case of hatred at first sight. It is the most hideous city in the world. Bombay, as I have said, has the air of a great city; Calcutta, the air of a great slum. Nehru himself has called Calcutta "the nightmare city of India" – a haunting description. The foreign visitor cannot walk for two minutes without gathering to himself a retinue of beggars, most of them horribly maimed. Neither by entreaties nor by imprecations can one be quit of them. The unhappiest part is the realization that most of these beggars were purposely maimed in infancy in order that their supplications might be touching. To this very day kidnapping is one of India's most prevalent crimes. Steal a child, maim him, set him to begging: this is the pattern. Cows, razor thin, sacred but uncared for, roam the streets. In front of the ultramodern skyscraper which houses the First National City Bank of New York, where I had gone to cash a cheque, one cow keeled over and died at my feet.

The Metropolitan of India, a wise and gifted man, now retired, summoned his clergy to meet me at lunch. At that table I disgraced myself. I am not proud of what follows, but it will do me good to make a confession. Intelligent questions were put to me by the clergy of Calcutta. One question was: "As a result of your travels, what general impression have you formed of Anglicanism?" "I can answer that question in one word," said I. "Ineptitude." This was flip and irresponsible. Moreover, it was the wrong thing to say to people who already have reason enough to feel depressed and discouraged. Publicly I recant and repent myself of this outburst. I do not mean to deny that we have been, and still are, inept in much of our doings. But to have blurted out this word as my general impression of Anglicanism

* "Have you ever heard of the Chinese American Dutch Reformed Church?" asked the Bishop of Madras. His diocese abounds in such titles. On one short stretch of road in the See City I noted the following: a Y.M.C.A., two English Methodist bungalows, a Seventh Day Adventist Church and School, the Salvation Army Headquarters, an American Methodist nursery school, the American Methodist Episcopal Tamil Church, the Jehova Shamah (a dissident sect), a Y.W.C.A., and a high school run by the Church of South India.

is proof only of my own ineptitude. Imagine the use of such a word when present at the table were faculty members from Bishop's College, Calcutta, some of the ablest theologians in the entire Anglican Communion! Students come there from as far away as Iran and Singapore. Within its spacious grounds they receive as fine a training as can be had any place in Britain or America.

There were happier moments in India. Many of them. They occurred, for the most part, in villages, the heart of India. Here the people, although poor, were friendly and clean, and there was no need to hold tight to one's wallet.

In the Diocese of Bhagalpur, presided over by an Indian bishop whom boastingly I claim as a pupil because he patiently sat out a course of lectures I once gave at St. Augustine's, Canterbury, I walked for several miles in blistering heat through rice fields to reach a village to which no road gives access. The entire village, numbering about two hundred and fifty, was present at the "city limits" to greet me. When they had decked me with garlands of flowers, they burst into hymnody and escorted me to the house of the principal layman. In the shade of the porch of his tiny and immaculate dwelling I sat enthroned and embarrassed while each man, woman, and child of the village passed by to do me homage. The depth of bow and the form of obeisance was prescribed by the strictest protocol. Thoughtfully, the surgeon who heads our Anglican hospital five miles away had briefed me on how to behave. "Just do what they do," was his counsel. "If they shake your hand, shake theirs – and in precisely the same way. If they bow, bow – and to the same degree. If they dance a little dance in front of you, try to duplicate it." I obeyed as best I could. But a severe test was yet ahead of me. The initial ceremony completed, a demure young woman appeared with a beautiful copper bowl, and in the presence of the whole village she washed my feet and anointed them with oil. A little hard to take it was, except for the realization that this was their way of bidding a brother welcome. Not many minutes later, food arrived. My portion was borne in a beautiful copper bowl. I am mortally certain that it was the same copper bowl in which my feet had been washed! Yet never before had I been so grateful for a meal shared in Fellowship.

On the return trip to Calcutta I stopped to see the House of Mercy, one of the finest activities in the Diocese of Barrackpore. The hospital was known to me as the place where, in 1947, a doctor and two nursing sisters were shot to death by a male nurse. Standing by their graves, I reflected on the bravery that was required of two women doctors, an Indian and a New

Zealander, who arrived to re-establish the work. The staff at the time of my visit included a New Zealand nursing sister and two women physicians, one Anglo-Burmese, the other Irish. It struck me as a marvellous example of inter-Anglican co-operation.

After visiting the hospital I went to see a jute mill. It employed five thousand workers, few among them Christian and hardly any Anglicans. Sadly, Christianity has not taken hold of the sprawling industrial development along the banks of the Hooghly, a tributary of the Ganges that is the boundary line between the Diocese of Calcutta and the Diocese of Barrackpore.

In area, Barrackpore is a compact diocese that was carved out of Calcutta. Smallness of size makes it possible to bring in all its clergy once a month for two days of Bible study and theological discussion. The clergy go home after such conferences to hold similar meetings for catechists and other lay readers. Here the spoken word comes into its own because there is virtually no theological literature in the whole area. "We can't even read the *Church Times*," one priest told me.

As my stay in India lengthened, I became increasingly aware of certain historical facts that tell a great deal about the Church as it exists there. The Anglican bishops, foreseeing the advent of Indian independence, achieved their own ecclesiastical independence from the Church of England in 1930 and consequently had seventeen years to get ready to serve an India that stood completely free of Britain. The ninth Bishop of Bombay, the Right Reverend William Quinlan Lash, was consecrated only five days before India was given her independence on 15th August, 1947. One of his first acts was to preside over a farewell luncheon for government chaplains. While their departure symbolized the new independence, it also meant the loss of grants and, gradually, the support of the missionary societies which now came under diocesan jurisdiction.

Where once the Bishop of Bombay had been the third man in the state, ranking after the governor and the chief justice, he now must take his place with the Cardinal Archbishop of Bombay and other ecclesiastics. But it is a rank gladly relinquished because in letting go they were relieved of the stigma of being known as "the Church of the British Raj".

In Bombay and much of India, as in Pakistan, there has long been the problem called "compound mentality" – Christians huddling together around the mission station, always receiving, permanently dependent, never really re-entering the community.

But do the diocesan pastoral boards still ponder such broad sociological problems? Perhaps they do, but on the day that I sat in on a meeting I heard only such mundane discussions as whether a priest could receive his holiday allowance even though the scarcity of priests obliged him to remain on the job. (Eventual answer: No). The board also took up a priest's request for a thousand rupees (to be repaid *out of his own stipend* at the rate of fifty rupees per month) to buy a motorcycle to make the rounds of many mission stations in a large area. (The "yeas" won by a slight margin!) In spite of having to deal with such "elemental" problems, the board handled every-thing, I felt, with far more maturity and dispatch (and democracy) than would have been the case in most areas of Africa and other parts of the board-minded Anglican Communion.

The reading of Indian newspapers was instructive. Alongside reports of Mr. Nehru's prominent role in the United Nations were such headlines as these:

FAMILY SUICIDE PACT: EIGHT BODIES FOUND IN A WELL

SHOULD BULLS BE CASTRATED?

3000 DIE IN EAST PAKISTAN CYCLONE AND TIDAL WAVE

HOUSES COLLAPSE BECAUSE OF FLOODS

MAN CUTS OUT HIS TONGUE AND OFFERS IT TO GODDESS

And the matrimonial columns among the classified advertisements! They give more than a clue to the role played by caste and one wonders how far Christianity has been able to transcend caste. A man in search of a bride, or parents on the lookout for a suitable mate for their daughter, state clearly what caste is involved, and many of the advertisements call for a horoscope as well. It perhaps suggests of better days that some of these advertisements carry the line, "caste no object".

India is a land of mystical beauty. It is also a land of great cruelty and misery. Thousands cook their meals, take their baths, and deliver their babies in the railway station or on the streets. There is never enough of anything – except people. In Calcutta some six million Indians scramble for their daily existence; of this number, at least six hundred thousand have no shelter and must literally hunt for their food. All of this came flooding back to me when months later I heard the American news commentator, Chet Huntley, say of this metropolis, "Calcutta may drown to death in its own sea of humanity."

Finally, there lingers in my mind the wording of a memorial tablet in St. Mary's Church, Fort St. George, Madras, a parish church consecrated in 1680 – an astoundingly long time ago. "Sacred to the memory of the

Reverend Christian William Gericke," it reads, "destined to labour in a peculiar vineyard." It suggests only too tellingly how the East India Company looked upon India and its people. But it well describes the India of centuries gone by and the India of today – *a peculiar vineyard!*

CEYLON

"*Where every prospect pleases, and only man is vile. . . .*" This line, made familiar by a hymn, is the sum total of most Americans' knowledge of Ceylon.

The first part of this description is unquestionably right; the second, unjustifiably rude. The people of Ceylon (they are called Sinhalese and their country, Lanka), although sinners like the rest of us, are as beautiful and winning as the tear-shaped, tea-producing island they inhabit. Seeing Ceylon, I was reminded of a quotation of which I do not know the source but would like to share with you:

> When Adam and Eve were cast out of heaven, they had a choice, according to Moslem tradition, of all the world's loveliest places for their earthly Garden of Eden. They chose the Island of Ceylon. In the central hills of Ceylon rises Adam's Peak, the holiest mountain in the world. It is revered by millions of different faiths, because of the footlike impression in the rock at the summit. Moslems say it is Adam's footprint; Buddhists claim the print was made by Buddha on his third and last visit to Ceylon; Hindus regard it as that of Siva; and Eastern Christians claim it as the footprint of St. Thomas the Doubter, the Apostle of India.

These legends attest both the splendour of the landscape and the religious diversity of the peoples of Lanka (to call the country by its ancient name). Anglicanism in Ceylon is concerned with four different groups: The urban Sinhalese, the rural Sinhalese (chiefly in the interior), the Jaffna Tamils who came from South India, and the South Indian Tamils who work on tea estates. Most of the general population is Buddhist. In 1956 the relative numerical strength of the various religious traditions was reported as follows: 5,217,143 Buddhists; 1,614,000 Hindus; 714,874 Christians; 541,812 Muslims; and 10,804 persons of other religions. The population has increased, but the proportions remain.

Of the Christians, the Roman Catholics constitute the vast majority – a legacy, probably, of Portuguese rule in the sixteenth and early seventeenth centuries, as well as of the religious freedom granted by the British when they took over from the repressive Dutch in 1796.

The Anglicans are in second place with about 42,000. The only other group with a membership in five figures is Wesleyan (*ca.* 24,000). Not a single other denomination exceeds five thousand. Taken as a whole, Christian forces are numerically small. Their impact, however, is not negligible, for they have been the *educators*. The gift of rhetoric, the incredible eloquence of every Sinhalese I ever met, must lie innate in the national character; but the capacity to exercise this gift in flawless and compelling English* is indubitably the contribution of mission schools – which schools, alas, are more and more being taken away from the Churches. The day of government grants is over. Unless a Christian institution of learning can fully pay its own way, it must retire from the field. On this basis, the Anglicans have lost most of their schools, as have the other Christians. Political exigency has put Buddhism and Hinduism in a favoured place. In modern Ceylon, Christianity, though tolerated, must shift for itself.

There is in this a sad irony. Parents whose children have unreasonably rebelled against them will know what I mean. Youngsters, restless for independence, sometimes employ – in their struggle to be free – the very weapons whose use was taught to them by their elders in the hope that they might *become* free. But headlong youth often turn these weapons *against* their elders – and thereby incur the guilt of ingratitude. Nurtured in Christian parishes and taught in Christian schools, many Sinhalese learned the principles that helped Ceylon to become independent as a nation. A free Ceylon today disavows this inheritance. In time this adolescent phase may pass. Indeed, many Sinhalese – even when they are not Christian – know full well what they and their country owe to Christianity. They are vocal in acknowledging this debt. The weight of their testimony gives us still a breathing spell, a toehold, an opportunity. But delay will spell our doom. And by "delay" I mean the tardiness of the rest of Christendom to lend a hand in Ceylon.

The fact that the Anglican Church in this delectable land can count among its members many persons of wealth and political influence does not exempt the rest of us from the obligation to report for duty. I myself draw the opposite inference. Precisely *because* there is wealth there and intelligence and a strong willingness to work we have all the more reason for reposing confidence in this Church and for rendering assistance.

Where but in Ceylon have the Oriental Churches of the Anglican Communion made conspicuous headway with the "upper classes" and the moneyed? The poor are not neglected – but neither are the rich! Why penalize this Church because it has distinguished itself in this way? It is

* In addition to English, two other languages are spoken – Tamil (from South India) and Sinhalese. Language groups get along all right in joint worship but prefer their own churches for regular services. While I well understood the necessity for translation of sermons, I was shocked that some priests after many years had not learned to celebrate the Holy Communion in one of the other tongues.

unique in most of Asia in that it was never established, never heavily subsidized from abroad. From the start, it knew that it would have to make its own way. Largely it has. But especially in this case I would like to see substantial verification of the principle that "to him who hath shall be given."

We move in for a close-up.

There are two Dioceses, Colombo* and Kurunagala. The former once covered the entire island. Kurunagala is a recent creation dating from 1950. It is – without disrespect – the hole in the doughnut. The older diocese surrounds it entirely. To Colombo belong all of the coastal areas. The mountainous centre, encircled by Colombo, is Kurunagala.

The larger Diocese, Colombo, centres its activities in Christ Church Cathedral. But it was All Saints', Pettah, which I was to know best because the fiftieth anniversary of its consecration was observed at the time of my visit. It is situated in the heart of Pettah, close by the market and the bus stand, the noisiest, busiest, dirtiest, and most crowded part of Colombo. From outside the church came a sound of horns tooting, brakes screeching, bicycle bells tinkling, carts and lorries rumbling, and the cries of street vendors mingling with the voices of the moving crowd. Inside I noted among the crowds of handsome worshippers many women who wore rubies, diamonds, or other precious stones on a side of the nose as well as in their pierced ear lobes. The whole service was tremendously colourful, marred only by the inclusion of too many hymns – an even dozen, all sung noisily and slowly.

My introduction to the interior diocese was abrupt, unexpected, and unorthodox. The very first evening I was at dinner in Ceylon, the Bishop of Colombo's other guest at dinner was the manager of a tea estate. I eagerly seized the opportunity to accompany him the next morning to the estate to see how tea is grown and processed. This excursion, heartily endorsed by the Lord Bishop of Colombo, carried me into regions shepherded by his brother Bishop of Kurunagala. Tea is big business and its cultivation a complicated process. English planters brought their Church with them to Ceylon. The mountain slopes where tea flourishes – slopes of singular beauty – are therefore dotted with churches such as you would find in Surrey or Sussex. There was something incongruous about these transplants from Victorian England when, nearby, elephants were at work and lizards five

* The Diocese of Colombo gained an unusual distinction in the Anglican Communion in July, 1962, when its Archdeacon, the Venerable Harold de Soysa, was one of three priests appointed by the Archbishop of Canterbury as official observers at the Second Vatican Council. The others: the Bishop of Ripon, the Right Reverend John Moorman, and a retired seminary dean and professor, Dr. Frederick C. Grant of the American Church, a scholar who is an Honcrary Canon of the Cathedral Church of St. John the Divine.

feet long scurried harmlessly across the path leading from lich gate to narthex. However, these churches, which were created out of loyalty to the Church of England by people who also suffered from homesickness and expressed their nostalgia in their architecture, proved effective. That understanding of God which in these churches was proclaimed from pulpit, font, and altar attracted large congregations of Sinhalese and Tamil labourers. The next cup of tea you drink may well be served you, so to speak, across thousands of miles, by Anglican hands in Ceylon.

My managerial host, after taking me through a tea-tasting tour of his factory (I sampled ten brands), drove me to one of these churches. It was high on a mountain, scenic but remote, a bit of England wrenched out of context. Entering the churchyard, we saw eighteen people standing around an open grave. Prayer Books in hand, they were about to read the Order for the Burial of the Dead over the body of the woman who to some of them had been mother, to others mother-in-law, and to the younger mourners grandmother. She had died, this Sinhalese woman, full of years and full of faith. Although bereaved, the family were not weeping. They understood full well that the old lady's time had come and that the day of her death was also her birthday in eternity. But since there was no resident priest, they knew that it was up to them to provide Christian burial.

My appearance on the scene had been unscheduled and was totally unexpected. The eighteen looked up as the English planter and I came through the gate. A man in a clerical collar! Surprise was the first reaction registered on their bronze countenances, then amazement, and at once thereafter, gratitude. Would I please officiate? Fleetingly it crossed my mind that I had no licence to officiate in the Diocese of Kurunagala. But reason instructed me to sin boldly. Licence or no, this was no time to hesitate. There are occasions when rules and rubrics must be broken. Accordingly, I proceeded to read the Burial Office, never doubting that I was doing right – and confident that the Bishop of Kurunagala would have objected only if I had failed these people in their need.

I will not conceal that this experience had emotional overtones for me. These Sinhalese Christians made firmly the response to every versicle. The psalms we read antiphonally. The music of two hymns, echoing across the valley, had for bellows naught but the lungs of twenty Anglicans – one English, one American, and eighteen citizens of Ceylon.

The funeral over, I was introduced and my errand explained. That a priest should have appeared out of nowhere at precisely this moment was a source of wonderment to these people. It gave them a glimpse of that strange and wonderful mystery which is the Church. But anything I may have been prospered to do for them was nothing compared to what they did for me. By the side of a grave in the mountains of Ceylon something of the life and reality of our Communion became clear to me.

As in India, so also in Ceylon. The desire for Church Unity is intense. Among its most ardent proponents are men who are "Catholic Churchmen".

To a High Church dignitary in Ceylon – a man whose great ambition is to help bring into being a united Church of Lanka – I put this question: "Now that you have asked the other Provinces of our Church to render judgement on the proposed Scheme for reunion and to tell you whether or not the envisaged Church of Lanka could be in full communion with the Anglican Communion, what would you Sinhalese Anglicans do if some or even all of the Provinces turned you down, gave you a No?"

"In that event," he replied, "we would have to withdraw from the negotiations, for we are determined to be faithful to the principles of Anglicanism. *But*," he added, his dark eyes flashing, "I would say to the Methodists, Presbyterians, and Congregationalists of Ceylon: 'If, after seeing how stupidly bishops can act, you still believe in the historic Episcopate and want it for the Church of Lanka, then (in God's Name) go get your Orders from the Church of South India. Later, when sanity reasserts itself among the Reverend Fathers in God of the Anglican Communion, we will be prospered to join you."

Strong language. I applaud it.

The Cathedral Church of Christ the King in Kurunagala is thrilling. It is situated at the foot of a gigantic monolith which resembles an elephant and thereby gives to the city its name, for elephant is what Kurunagala means. This great rock towers above it but does not succeed in dwarfing it. The new cathedral, strong in line, stands out. The mountain has come to the cathedral, and the cathedral to the mountain. The two enhance each other, complement each other, minister to each other. In short, the cathedral *belongs*. Upswept eves, Sinhalese motifs in its adornment, mark it as authentically a part of Ceylon – yet, in its massiveness and arrangement, it bespeaks a Ceylon claimed by the finality and universality of Christ. Kurunagala's first bishop, now Metropolitan of India, was its founder. He built the cathedral as he did in conscious protest. He knew that in Christ there is no east nor west, but a king worthy of acknowledgement by all nations – and this is what his eclectic cathedral declares. Christ is neither Gothic nor Georgian, neither Romanesque nor Byzantine. He is all of these – and more. He is, for example, Sinhalese as well. But the bishop did not fall into the opposite trap, which would be to make Christ a native of Ceylon. I know of no church in the world which more perfectly expresses both the universality and particularity of Christ. I rather gloried, too, in the unfinished appearance of this cathedral. It points to the full and perfect sacrifice of Christ, yet reminds us that we still must make up in our own bodies that which is lacking. The cymbals and gongs which at the Words of Institution tell us that "It is finished" also summon us to the realization that we stand only at the beginning. The *fact* is not yet completely acknowledged in actuality. Lakdasa de Mel, the bishop, prime architect of this cathedral, said to me something like this: "Christianity was not really planted in the soil of Ceylon. Rather, it was brought here in flower pots – its blooms pleasant to the eye and the nose – but without possibility of taking root because the treasure remained within its earthen vessels."

BURMA

Kipling must have failed geography in school or else, hard-pressed for a rhyme, have strained poetic licence to its uttermost. I myself have stood "by the old Moulmein Pagoda" and know that there is no possibility, from that vantage point, of "lookin' eastward to the sea". Nor could the dawn have come up "like thunder outer China, 'crost the Bay!" At Moulmein there is no bay, only a broad bend in the river. The sea is to the west. China lies to the east, seven hundred miles away.

> On the road to Mandalay,
> Where the flyin'-fishes play. . .

That must have been exhausting for them, for Mandalay is a city far inland, a good three hundred and fifty miles from the coast.

The Bishop of Rangoon needs to know his Burmese geography more exactly, since his diocese is coextensive with the whole of the country – a big country, over five times the size of England. The Church's work being scattered and the cart roads poor, a geographically disoriented bishop might easily go astray and never be heard from again.

A bishop in these parts must also possess a measure of the wisdom of Solomon. In his wisdom, the present Bishop of Rangoon, a robust and civilized English monk, forbade me to accompany him on a Confirmation Visitation to a part of Burma where trouble was brewing between the government and insurgent forces. He sent me instead to calm and lovely Mandalay to look at our hospital and schools and the fabulous Buddhist temples, while he himself – ignoring his own safety – carried out his Visitation to five places on schedule. Happily, no ill befell him. The threatened rebellion came to naught. This made me all the more sorry that he had not permitted me to go along with him, for his wary decision deprived me of a chance to see the work which is being carried on by the Bible Churchmen's Missionary Society, in Upper Burma.

At an inland airport the Bishop and I rejoined forces, he coming from the north and I from Mandalay. The passengers who were about to board the plane were in an uproar. An enormous king cobra, destined for the Rangoon Zoo and held captive in a flimsy cardboard box, was to fly with us. To this companionable arrangement the human members of the cargo took violent exception. Yet the pilot had been given definite instructions: the cobra must be taken aboard. Voluble arguments between passengers and pilot ensued. Finally the pilot turned to the Bishop, "My Lord, what should we do?" Solomon might well have been proud of the Bishop's reply: "By all means we take the cobra with us, provided it stays up in the cockpit with you." Everybody laughed, the pilot included. The cobra did *not* come with us.

Burma has had more than its share of trials and tribulations in modern times. Even so, its citizens looked healthier and happier than the people I had left behind in India. The towns were cleaner. And although Rangoon is only one of several Eastern cities claiming the title "Pearl of the Orient", I am disposed to think that Rangoon has more right than any other to this appellative. I liked the place and its people. I find, now that I am home, that – without being conscious of what I was doing – I took more photographs in Burma than in any other country.

The Bishop occupies the oldest and most historic of the great houses built by the British. It was spared the ravages of the last war because the Japanese conquerors requisitioned this mansion to store within its walls urns containing the ashes of their war dead. The bedroom I occupied had been reserved for the ashes of only the highest-ranking officers.

His cathedral also was spared, for it seemed to the invaders the most desirable building in the city to serve as a brewery. The edifice was big enough to meet their thirst and central enough to be of convenient access. The floors of the sanctuary, chancel, and nave are stained with rings, interlocking circles, where once great vats had stood in which rice by fermentation was converted into *saki*. They left their mark, giving the Cathedral an unprecedented number of symbols of the Holy and Undivided Trinity —

There must be ten thousand such sacred signs in Rangoon Cathedral. Perhaps this is part of what the Psalmist meant when he said that God makes even the wrath of men to praise him.

Only slowly is the Church in Burma recovering from the havoc of war. Many of our churches and institutions did suffer damage. More than a few of our faithful people, both clerical and lay, after bearing their witness, had to take to the hills and were hunted from pillar to post. Not all of them were lucky enough to make their escape. Of those who were caught, not all were permitted to die quickly.

Rangoon has one of the finest theological colleges in the whole of the Orient. The teaching staff, although small, inspired confidence; and the penetrating questions put to me by thirteen skirted postulants gave reason for hope that a Church fully indigenous is in the making. This is something to be desired in any case, but it is all the more important here because the government – officially Buddhist – is not keen to have an influx of missionaries from the outside. The policy has been to admit a new foreign missionary only if he is coming as a replacement for an outgoing one. Except for this restriction, however, the present government has been friendly towards the Churches. Although Buddhism in Burma has a strongly nationalistic flavour, Buddhist political leaders give every indication of recognizing that Burmese Christians are allies in the country's struggle against materialism and Communism.

Anglicanism in Rangoon is distinguished for its schools. There are two high schools, one for boys and one for girls, both of them enormous and excellent. Smaller but even more remarkable are a school for the blind and a school for the deaf and dumb. The latter, which is run by the Bible Churchmen's Missionary Society, is the only school for such children in the whole of Burma. Until the Church came, nobody cared for these soundless, worldless ones who, because they went untaught, were thought to be imbecile as well as dumb. Some deaf children do indeed have mental defects which make them uneducable, but it is estimated that two hundred deaf children are born every year in the Union of Burma. If we reduce this number by 20 per cent and reckon on a child's school life as lasting ten years, it means that there should be approximately sixteen hundred deaf children in Burma at any given time. Our school, wonderful as it is, accommodates only one hundred. It strains our imagination beyond its capacity to try to conceive what it is like for a human being to be condemned his whole life long to complete lack of language. "He who has ears to hear, let him hear." Maybe some reader of this book, in gratitude for the Gospel he has *heard*, will be moved to do something for the deaf.

Forty years ago, when these schools were started, most people saw no point in trying to do anything for the blind and the deaf. They were written off as an almost total loss. Moreover, in the early days the schools had to contend against every sort of perverse misunderstanding. It took the blind school many years to live down the vicious rumour that every Sunday morning these foreigners called Christians slew one of the pupils in order to eat his flesh and drink his blood. Things are different today. A Deputy Prime Minister, although a Buddhist, is proud to dedicate a new building for the school. Government and community lend a helping hand. Burmese physicians and dentists serve in an honorary capacity. Help is given too by sources from the outside, such as UNICEF and the World Council of Churches. Anglicans sometimes need to be reminded how much they owe to non-Anglicans.

It is commonly forgotten that not all the citizens of the Union of Burma are Burmese. Nor are all of them Buddhists. The Karens, for example, were originally Animists. Many of them still are, although some have been won over either to Buddhism or to Christianity. While the Karens come basically of the same Mongolian stock as do the Burmese, they are conscious of themselves as a separate group. They constitute a substantial minority – perhaps 2,000,000 out of a nation whose total population is 20,662,000. For them a special Karen State was formed in 1955. I went there to have a look.

The first part of the flight from Rangoon to Pa'an, the newly created capital of the Karen State, took me over fairly dull, flat territory and after that a stretch of sea. But suddenly, as I sighted the Karen coast, nature put on a show. If ever there was a Dali-esque landscape, this was it. From flat, fertile plains there emerged, without preparation of foothills, mountains so abrupt, so jagged, that only a child or a great surrealistic painter could have drawn them. This was not a *range* of mountains. Rather, each peak was free-standing, slender, and grotesquely tall. I was so excited looking at them that I forgot to photograph them.

To meet me at Pa'an Airport was Bishop Francis Ah Mya (see Pl. 48), himself a Karen, and Suffragan to the Bishop of Rangoon. He was a man of mettle if ever I met one. He and his charming wife had come to live here in May, 1957. At that time Pa'an was hardly more than an insignificant village, but it was slated to be the capital of the new state, and the Bishop understood the importance of the Church's being there from the beginning.

Perhaps the best way to suggest something of what he managed to carve out during the first two years of his being in residence is to read into the record here certain excerpts I wrote in my diary at the time:

Bishop Ah Mya is short of stature, sturdily built, full of sanctity and spunk. From the airport he drove me to St. Peter's Church which he has just built with his own hands and the help of a few schoolboys. The north transept of the church had been screened off to form a sacristy and a bedroom for me. Then in his own house, a tidy but modest structure (also built by him), his wife gave me a mouth-watering breakfast of ingredients I would be hard-pressed to identify. They made the American breakfast seem an idea-forsaken repast. But I was not permitted to tarry at table. Down we went on foot to near-by St. Peter's School to attend assembly and to inspect every class. That done, a holiday was declared. This makes the foreign visitor a popular figure, but it killed my chances of making an extensive photographic study of these beautiful, skirted children. At one moment three hundred and ten of them stood before me, beaming and bowing. Ten minutes later they had all vanished without a trace. An enrolment of more than three hundred at the end of the first two years is not a bad showing for a Christian school which began with almost no resources in a non-Christian milieu not fully awake to the necessity for education. If all who have applied for admission could be accepted, next year would see the school twice its present size. But where to put the pupils? And where to find the teachers? (see Pl. 49).

The school is the product of the Bishop's own hands and ingenuity. To begin with, he secured the land, ten acres in the very centre of the capital city. The Bishop bought one acre; the government, although officially Buddhist, gave him the other nine. The marsh which is at the foot of the slight rise of ground on which church and school stand (a marsh which at present breeds mosquitoes of rapacious appetite) is to be drained; a beautiful lake will take its place, and around its shores, mirrored on its surface, are to be the principal government buildings. I am glad that these waters will also catch the reflection of a church spire.

With the help of books, the Bishop then taught himself how to make concrete blocks and roofing tiles, how to dig wells and wire buildings for electricity. The electricity is yet to come. But it will. And when it does, his buildings are ready to receive it.

The uses of books – as of bishops – are many. Francis Ah Mya, autodidact of the first order, also taught himself how to raise poultry and grow jute. He has great schemes for founding a co-operative movement – collective farming with co-operative marketing and a collective credit association.

The weekend I was with him (25th to 27th November, 1960), he invited men in from all over his archdeaconry – many of them not Christians – to try to fire their imagination with his ideas for raising the tone of life and the standard of living for the whole area. I had the fun of watching him overcome their age-old conservatism. Before the weekend was over he had captured these cautious men in the web of his logic and enthusiasm. Few things could make me happier than the opportunity to go back to this region five or ten years from now to see what these people may have been able to accomplish under the leadership of a bishop who knows that Christianity is more than a Sunday *divertissement*. Bishop Ah Mya has the vision of reaching *all* of the people – and the *total* man in the case of each individual. A merely intellectual approach through preaching will not suffice. This he has seen quite independently of the great example of Denmark's Bishop Grundtvig.

Proof of the esteem in which Bishop Ah Mya is held – proof of the impact he has made on the local culture – arrived the next morning in tangible form. It came in the form of a jeep and a truck. These hardy vehicles put in their appearance at the order of the Secretary of State, himself a Buddhist. The jeep was his own property which he put at my disposal in order that I might be transported to parts of the Karen State which at that time were still dangerous because of insurgent snipers.

The District Executive of Police provided the truck with an armed guard, ten burly men with rifles and mounted bayonets. Going before us, the truck set up such clouds of dust that there was a perfect smokescreen. Enveloped in dust, I nearly choked to death, but no insurgent bullet could find me. Thus, with the help of Buddhists, bullets, and bayonets, the Bishop and I completed our journey to certain outstations without harm. I will not forget the Secretary of State's parting words as we set forth on our dusty excursion: "You are a foreigner. I feel a responsibility for your safety. But the Bishop, when he goes, I give him no guard. For all the bad people know the Bishop and would never do him any harm." Could any bishop desire a better encomium? That a bishop should be known and loved by "all the bad people" and yet be *persona grata* with all the, shall we say, good people: who could ask for a higher tribute than that? A bishop free to cross safely between the political lines which divide men and make them bitter foes; a bishop who, without any compromise of his own principles, talks freely with Baptists and Buddhists, Christians and Communists; a bishop given to scholarship but willing to roll up his sleeves and dig a well; a bishop who traded in his elephant for a tractor: such a bishop is Francis Ah Mya.

16

SINGAPORE AND MALAYA: The Hodgepodge Absolute

I CANNOT IMAGINE GREATER COMPLICATIONS THAN THOSE WHICH face the Bishop of Singapore and Malaya.

In terms of Church-State relations he has to deal with the nine states and two settlements which in 1948 banded together to form the Federation of Malaya, a federation which became independent in 1957 – the British Commonwealth's tenth Dominion. Although it is one country now, and in the course of time will become increasingly unified, each of the constituent Malay States has retained a large measure of autonomy. The Chief Minister of the Church is therefore obliged to confer with the Prime Ministers of many different Sultanates. Singapore is, again, something else: a self-governing state. That adds the twelfth element to be dealt with.

Nor is this an end to the political involutions. The man whose *cathedra* is at Singapore is charged also with responsibility for the Church's work in Thailand, Indonesia, Cambodia, Laos, and Vietnam. It must be said that our labours in the lands outside the Federation and Singapore are distressingly small, amounting to little more than chaplaincies for British and Americans who find themselves in those parts, but none the less it means five more governments for the Bishop to cope with, not to mention the expense and exertion of endless travel.

Intricate also are the linguistic and racial problems confronting this diocese. Of the seven million people who live within the Federation proper, only half are Malaysians of Malay or Indonesian origin. Two and a half million are Chinese, who brought with them six different dialects. Three-quarters of a million came to Malaya from India, Pakistan, and Ceylon, thereby introducing Tamil and Malayalam. Some sixteen thousand Europeans and Americans add their accents to this variegated pattern of sound.

It is not without reason that a recent writer has said that "a sojourn in Singapore is actually a journey through nearly every country in the Pacific area. For in this teeming metropolis you see all the peoples of the East, their way of life and habits, their hopes and traditions, rolled into a national confluence, which is known in Singapore as the effort to create a Malayan culture".

The sky above Singapore is punctured by skyscrapers, high-rise low-cost housing developments, minarets, pagodas, and steeples. Many nations are here, many races, many religions. The thrills of the roller coaster in the amusement park are advertised by neon signs in four languages. Buddhism, Confucianism, Hinduism, and Christianity are all present in force, not to mention Communism, which only lately, after the letting of much blood, was driven back.

Such is the Diocese of Singapore and Malaya, this pear-shaped peninsula depending from Thailand on the north and stretching southwards to within one degree of the Equator. Here is the dividing line between India and China, the centre of South-east Asia, a country the size of England, and it is the hodgepodge absolute. (See Pl. 42).

My first exposure to this polyglot diocese occurred when I landed in Bangkok. In that exotic city the sight of many worshippers prostrate before resplendent Buddhist temples moves a Christian to reflect upon the relationship of his faith to other religions. The Anglican form of Christianity has made little impact on Thailand. Except for occasional ministrations to tin-miners on the west coast, our work is limited to one fine Bangkok Church. A few Thais find their way to it, as do a few Chinese, but it is mostly a chapel for foreigners from Britain and America.

The two schools we once had, built by S.P.G., foundered during the storms of the two World Wars. Missionary work is carried on valiantly by the Presbyterians, but Thailand is a country so big that we could enter without incurring the guilt of wasteful competition. The Assistant Bishop of Singapore and Malaya, himself a Chinese, longs to expand our mission to Thailand – not least for the reason that Chinese innumerable are living there. Because of the linguistic and cultural factors, these members of the Chinese dispersion could best be approached by missionaries of their own speech and background. What impedes this development is the old story: men and money are lacking.

Penang was my next port of call. A more beautiful island would be hard to find. No wonder so many cruise ships were moored to the wharves of its principal city, George Town. At the disposal of these lucky tourists are tree-clad mountains, fine bays and beaches, thatched houses set on stilts amid orderly rows of coco-nut palm forests. In the up-to-date city itself they will find smart shops, handsome houses with luxurious gardens, many-storied Chinese temples, and a great, slightly gaudy complex of Buddhist buildings, headquarters of a "reformed" Buddhism all tied up with re-surgent nationalism and presided over, I regret to say, by an American.

This reformed Buddhism shows Christian influence all the way – from its revised rules for mourning customs at funerals to an awakened social consciousness and a zeal for missions. Old-line, conservative Buddhism exists side by side with this newer version of an ancient faith, and it occurs to me to say here – as often I said to Orientals who complained to me of the denominational splits in Christendom – that our divisions are as nothing compared with the sectarian variations within Buddhism and Hinduism. It is unreasonable of people to expect Christianity to speak always with a single voice. On matters of such ultimate importance as those raised by Christianity there will *of course* be different interpretations, variant versions, rival schools of thought. What impresses me, after touring the world, is not so much what separates Christians as what unites them. Distressing as our denominational differences are, I submit that Christians come closer to speaking with a concordant voice than any other major religious body in the world.

In the riot of scenic beauty and "local colour" which is Penang I was glad to find Anglicanism well represented. On the afternoon of my first day there, a Sunday, I made my way to St. Paul's Church, where I was impressed by the sight of seventy Chinese teenagers, not all of them Anglicans or Christians, pummelling the Chinese priest with questions in an honest free-for-all. With wisdom and bright flashes of wit he addressed himself to each and every question, never flinching or ducking a blow. Questions and answers, translated into English, were whispered into my ear by a friend. "Are Christianity and science opposed?" "Why are there so many sects?" "Why do you use only the Bible and not the writings of Confucius and Buddha?" "What is the difference between Protestant Churches and the Roman Catholic Church?" "What is the difference between Christian religion and Buddhist religion – and do the differences matter very much if you live a good life?" "Can one be a Christian without being baptized?" "If parents don't want their child to be baptized," asked one youth with a ducktail haircut and with, I thought, a wistful note in his voice, "is it un-filial to go ahead and be baptized?" As a sample of the pastor's sagacity I record his answer to the last question: "When the people at home see that you really are a transformed person, then perhaps their opposition to baptism will be less."

The setting in which this colloquy occurred could not have been more "foreign". It was a church of Chinese design in a predominantly Muslim country called Malaya on which I had set foot only an hour before. But the questions asked were so typical, universal, and perennial – identical, in fact, with those a student group would ask in New York – that I was struck in Penang by the fact that humanity is *one* – one in its quest, and ultimately, I dare say, one in its response . . . though the oneness can never be perfectly achieved in historical time.

The oneness of humankind was demonstrated in yet another way when, at Evensong that same day, in a perfectly proportioned Georgian church, I joined an enormous congregation made up – in about equal parts – of English, American, Australian, New Zealand, Chinese, and Indian elements. In need, identical; in praise, united. But alas, no Malays! Most Malayans are Muslims. There are probably fewer than a dozen Malayan Christians in the whole land. Propagation of Christianity among Muslims is much hemmed in by legal restrictions. In fairness to the Government of the Federation it must be said that this is nothing new. These restrictions do no more than follow a pattern inherited from the British. For the sake of political expediency the British did not allow direct evangelism among the Malays either. The present policy is simply an old one perpetuated.

The Church in Malaya is, in fact, an immigrant Church. Had it not been for the Chinese and the Indians there would be no Church in this land except for a few chapels for the Europeans. While the new government is amicably disposed towards the Church, its immigration policies have not made life easier. Certain of the Chinese clergy and lay workers are not eligible for naturalization as citizens of either Singapore or Malaya and have been under the necessity of returning to Hong Kong once every three years in order to obtain a renewal of their Professional Visit Passes. This puts the Diocese to heavy expense.

I began to be introduced to this and other vexing problems when, after a bumpy flight from Penang, I landed in Kuala Lumpur in the midst of the most violent electrical storm I have ever witnessed.

How musical is the name *Kuala Lumpur*! It came as a little shock to learn that it means "muddy river mouth". Three-quarters of a century ago it was hardly more than a huddle of Malay huts and Chinese "shop-houses" encircled by tapioca plantations. But then came rubber and tin and a boom that brought into existence a delightful, prosperous, cosmopolitan city, the seat of the federal government today. It is also the city in which the Assistant Bishop, a Chinese, resides.

Four things about Kuala Lumpur stand out in my memory.

The first is a celebration of the Holy Communion in St. Mary's Church, a beautiful edifice situated in the very heart of town, not more than a stone's throw from the chief governmental buildings. We are definitely on the map here. Indeed, we are at the centre of it. I mention this particular service only because of the composition of its congregation. All of us were in Holy Orders, at one in our faith in spite of the multifarious character of our natural origins. We were Chinese, Indian, English, Irish, Australian, New Zealander, and American. This was not any kind of special convocation. Such meetings are a weekly occurrence. Once a week the Assistant Bishop brings together the clergy of the city and its vicinity. After communicating together, they break-fast together – and they talk over problems which never could have occurred to me had I stayed at home.

I see no indelicacy in citing a concrete example. During a breakfast of indefinable but delicious components, the clergy considered what steps could be taken to train the women of the diocese that they need not absent themselves from the Holy Communion during their monthly period. This led on to a discussion of the iniquity of the Service of the Churching of Women. Radical revisions are required if it is to be brought up to date and made consonant with Christianity's best and clearest thinking on the subject. I was asked how the problem was solved in America. I had to answer, lamely, that we solve the problem by the simple but incorrect expedient of ignoring altogether the Service of the Churching of Women. American women are no less thankful than the rest of the women in the world for the birth of a child, but they have little inclination to express their gratitude in the form of Thanksgiving their Prayer Book provides. We are thinking too much, still, of "purification" when in fact there has been no impurity at all.

I remark, merely *en passant*, that it is a dubious circumstance that the Church's canon law respecting marriage and divorce, as well as its Service of Churching, was drawn up, for the most part, by celibates. Why should the father have no part in this moment of public thanksgiving? And why should an exultant mother be required, at this point, as the Prayer Book of 1662 does require of her, to say, "All men are liars"? Our "incomparable" Anglican liturgy is often incomparably tasteless.

What next impressed me about Kuala Lumpur is that the citizens wear shoes. I mean this quite seriously. The people are shod – and they are not shoddy, nor do they walk about the streets in pyjamas or other varying states of undress. The variety of attire is immense, but the people here are well clothed – which was in marked contrast to many of the places I had been since my arrival in the East. A few beggars approach the tourist, but it is nothing like the onslaught of the indigent in Egypt or India. And nobody is asleep on the sidewalks. Here, both because they have a home in which to sleep and because they have adequate food to ward off perpetual sleepiness, people are on their feet – alert and going somewhere. It helps to have tin and rubber! The world's largest tin dredge operates at Petaling, six miles from Kuala Lumpur, and it is claimed that the largest man-made hole in the world is to be found at the Open Cast Tin Mine at Sungei Besi, nine miles from town. The other most notable feature of the landscape is the miles and miles of symmetrical rubber trees. The relative prosperity of Malaya has enabled a small church to do more than the fewness of its members would have led one to expect of it. But there may be problems ahead. Anglicanism in Malaya, like so much of English church work, has been largely dependent on the largess, the substantial annual contribution, of big business corporations. In former years the tin and rubber estates were in English hands, and these hands were open to the Church. But ownership is now in process of passing over into the hands of hard-working, hard-thinking Chinese, most of whom are non-Christian. There is little reason to expect that the Chinese-controlled tin and rubber estates of the future will be quite so generous towards the Church as were the British proprietors of a day fast vanishing.

Beyond that, there is the fact – from which no prosperous country is exempt – of mounting income taxes. Individuals and corporations will simply not have, in years to come, the means to be as charitable as they were in previous years. Their surplus will go to a new and vigorous government. Gone are the "good old days". The Church – benefiting by it in the long run – will have to create its own good days through the teaching of stewardship. Even so, our Church in Malaya, with no more than twenty thousand baptized members at present, only seven thousand of whom are confirmed, can hardly be expected to extend work on any large scale within the Federation – let alone boldly launching new ventures in the neighbouring countries. Without gigantic support from abroad, work in Thailand, Indonesia, and the others cannot become much more than what it is: a chaplaincy for foreigners from the West.*

The third thing to impress me was the new University in the suburbs of Kuala Lumpur. The paint was hardly dry when Bishop Koh took me to see it, but it was already in operation with seven hundred students – on a seven-hundred-acre campus! The ultramodernistic buildings utilize dramatically the contours of the hilly ground on which they are built. An enrolment of 5,000 is being prepared for – and for one of the few times in the Church's life she herself is prepared to receive them. Presbyterians, Methodists, and Anglicans banded together to build a fine student centre immediately

* Anglicans have allies in Malaya, but we are altogether a small company: Roman Catholics, 124,000; Methodists, some 20,000; Presbyterians, 3,000; Brethren, 3,000, plus their children whom they do not suffer to count as Christians.

adjacent to the campus. The resident pastor, at the time of my visit, was an American Methodist, but the special needs of Anglican students are attended to by the near-by parish priest who gives part of his time and all of his heart to the centre.

The fourth thing in Kuala Lumpur to leave its mark on a memory which, after so many months of travel, was beginning to bog down, was the quickness of our Church's uptake when it came to seeing the need and the opportunity presented by the government's creation of the "artificial villages". Here we need the reminder that Malaya was occupied by the Japanese from 1942 to 1945. Guerrilla troops, mostly Chinese immigrants, bravely withstood the invaders. Some of them, however, at the end of the war continued operations but now with the intent, Communist-inspired, of seizing control of the territory. Their hostility was quickly countered by British and Malayan forces. In 1948 a state of emergency was declared which dragged on, lamentably and enervatingly, for twelve long years. In 1950 a drastic step was taken. Half a million people – some of whom sympathized with the terrorists and gave them aid, and some of whom, *being* terrorized, unwillingly gave aid – were moved bag and baggage into more than six hundred artificially created new villages. At first the city limits were clearly demarced by barbed-wire fences – and picnic excursions into the countryside were pointedly discouraged by force of arms. Yet the term "new village" is not a euphemism for "concentration camp". Although people were sometimes concentrated in these villages forcibly, it was only a matter of protective custody. They were not criminals rounded up to restrain them from illegal activity. Quite the reverse, they were citizens who had been living on isolated farms who now were compelled to live in community for defence against Communist terrorism. The Church, to its credit, lost little time in addressing itself to this "captive" audience. The Anglican approach to these new villages was through hospitals, clinics, dispensaries, schools, churches. I visited several such villages. They are now open townships. I saw what the Church was doing, and rejoiced that not always are we irrelevant.

So then south I went to Singapore, a city that bulges with humanity, and is almost as romantic and intrigue-ridden as a thousand money-making scenarios have portrayed it to be. My own experiences there, however, provide no grist for the Hollywood mill.

My excitements were of a sort more staid – as befits a man of the cloth, especially when both cloth and man are about worn out from too much travel. Despite my decrepitude, I took pleasure in being present for the ceremony of the capping of nurses at St. Andrew's Mission Hospital, an

Anglican institution so large and well run that no amount of pride in it could be accounted inordinate. The new young nurses were so pretty in their Chinese way that I do not see how any of them could be expected to get a true reading of the pulse of male patients, but their beauty will give them therapeutic power quite apart from the practise of medicine.

There was comfort to be derived from the size, equipment, and leadership of Trinity College, the seminary maintained jointly by the Presbyterian, Methodist, and Anglican Churches. We have our own residence hall, St. Peter's, so that the Christians of our persuasion can have a common devotional life, and also training in specifically Anglican disciplines, but otherwise they participate fully and with great benefit in the broader fellowship of the whole college.

Of churches and schools in Singapore I saw aplenty – some Chinese, some Indian – most of them admirable and held in high esteem by the public but kept separate by reason of ethnic and linguistic differences. Even the Chinese community is divided because there is no common dialect, and the clannishness characterizing all aspects of Chinese life has carried over into the Church itself. A Chinese Christian of one clan cannot be sure always of a hearty welcome in a church whose members are of another clan. If I weren't a clergyman I would be free to say that this is a damn shame. But precisely because I am a clergyman, having therefore some training in divinity, I can face these facts about the Church without becoming cynical. Baptism helps to curb our pride, and in principle – in powerful beginning – Pentecost reverses Babel. But it does not automatically make of us good conversationalists, at home in foreign tongues and at ease in foreign cultures.

It should be enough for us that we are occasionally given a foretaste (*arrabon*, a first instalment) of the grand unity that is to be.

Such an earnest or foretaste of the future that has begun to be I was vouchsafed in Singapore's large Cathedral when I attended an ordination. The ordinand was an Indian; the bishop who ordered him deacon, a Chinese. The people who fulfilled the other liturgical roles, such as Preacher, Precentor, and Litanist, were a New Zealander, an Englishman, a Norwegian. Five different species of man were in the chancel that day, and we who were in the jam-packed nave would have increased to ten the number of languages in which was being outpoured prayers of thanksgiving.

The Church has already attained, on a small scale, the very thing for which Malaya yearns: unity. It makes for a thought-provoking promenade to go from such an ordination into crowded and crooked streets (I mean "crooked" in both senses of the word) and to observe not only how divided Singapore is but also how *young* it is. Most of the people you pass (52.2 per cent) are less than twenty years old and they are prolific in generation.

Who is to claim the allegiance of them and their offspring? Who is to define goals, values, morals? Buddha, Mohammed, Marx?

In such a contest is Christ out of the running?

It is perhaps worth remembering that "they who run in a race run all, but *one* obtaineth the prize".

All the Anglican parts of South-east Asia buzz with the questions, "What of the formation of a new Anglican Province for South-east Asia? Is it feasible? And if feasible, is it possible? And if possible how and when is it to be accomplished?" These are questions which divide men.

Those who propose the formation of a new province take the view that it is time to grant the Church in South-east Asia a greater measure of self-direction. Canterbury, though benevolently concerned, is too far away, they argue, too out of touch with the local scene, to exercise metropolitical jurisdiction with complete understanding.

But the situation is complicated.

How much territory should the new province take in? Some say that it should include all the dioceses originating from the Church of England (Singapore and Malaya, Borneo, Korea, Rangoon, and Hong Kong), plus the American-born Diocese of the Philippines. Others, more ambitious still, would like to see the inclusion of Taiwan, which, though not yet a diocese, is now shepherded by a bishop who is a Suffragan to the Bishop of Honolulu. Still others contend that even the Church in Japan should be embraced in this one great province.

The problems are manifold.

Distance is one of them. How, for example, are delegates from Burma and Korea to get together for synod? The expense would be prohibitive.

Moreover, the jurisdictional problems would require protracted efforts at law. The properties and endowments of Singapore, Borneo, and Korea are all tied up with the Church of England. Then there is Rangoon which is part of the Church of India, Pakistan, Burma and Ceylon. It is, however, looking more to the East in these days than it is to the "West" – i.e. India. Racially and culturally, Burma has greater affinities with South-east Asia than with the Indo-Pakistan subcontinent. Moreover, the Diocese of Rangoon has never been included in the North India Reunion Plan. Should that Plan go through, the Church in Burma would find itself isolated. Its recourse would be to join a South-east province, if it exists by that time, or else to return under the metropolitical jurisdiction of Canterbury – a dubious course, for it might arouse again all Burmese suspicions that the Church of Burma is only a dependent part of the Church of England.

Hong Kong, though it has reverted for the time being to the metropolitical jurisdiction of the Archbishop of Canterbury, is in intention still part of the Church of China and will rejoin it as soon as political conditions permit. The Philippines and Taiwan are American in orientation and organization. They might hesitate before signing up with a province which would be essentially English in inception and inspiration. Moreover, as I shall explain in due course, there is a possibility that the Church in the Philippines might one day be strong enough to form a province of its own. One also has to take into account the unhappy fact that at this juncture in history there is little love between Hong Kong and Taiwan. Hong Kong seems to fear that entering into a province which included Taiwan (Free China) might jeopardize its own future relationship with the Church on the Chinese mainland. As for the Japanese Church, it is, like the Church in China, a fully constituted and self-governing province within the Anglican Communion. It is doubtful whether the Church in Japan would welcome the idea of surrendering part of its autonomy through membership in a Southeast Asia province.

Could ever a new province be fashioned out of such diverse elements?

One of the arguments put forward against the creation of a province is that any movement in that direction might throw a wet blanket over negotiations for Church Union in Malaya. The formation of a province, so runs the argument, would look like the marshalling of a mighty Anglican force bent on standing apart from the rest of reformed Christianity in Malaya. Among the opponents of a province are some – but not all – of the "old China hands", missionaries of the former China Inland Mission who now are at work in Malaya under the new name of the Oversea Missionary Fellowship. I share the earnest desire of these dedicated people for the union of the Churches. But I regard this argument as preposterous. I cannot understand their apparent blindness to what is distinctive about historic Anglicanism. Nor can I easily condone their readiness to sacrifice it for an effortless amalgamation with Protestants instead of guarding it zealously as an element destined to enrich eventually a profounder kind of union in which Anglicanism could happily and rightly be absorbed.

Objection to a province has sometimes found expression in a fear of "being dominated by other dioceses". This veiled language can mean only one thing: Low Church missionaries who transferred their labours to Malaya when they were forced out of China are apprehensive about High Church Borneo, High Church Korea, and High Church Burma. I wish I could whisper reassuringly into the ears of these fearful folk that not one of these dioceses is as "high" as it is reputed to be and as I myself had feared before visiting them. "High" they are by the standards of Malaya, South India, and Hong Kong but they are staunch adherents of the Book of Common

Prayer. Fundamentals do not divide us, only frills. If workers in South-east Asia could know one another as persons and be mutually inspired by the evidences of one another's devotion to the essential task, suspicion and distrust would fall away. It is possible to frown at a biretta, though without falling into despair or schism, if one esteems as a brother the man on whose head this outrageous piece of millinery is perched.

There are, however, weighty reasons for questioning the advisability of forming a province at the present moment. The basic one is that there is neither a community of interests nor a common cultural background. Urban Hong Kong, to take but one example, can be forgiven for feeling that it has little to learn from primitive Borneo. This does not mean that Hong Kong takes no interest in Borneo. It has given of its own sons to minister to the Chinese in that land. But it doubts the benefits to be had from the banding together of elements so diverse. The Church scattered throughout South-east Asia has indeed *some* problems in common, but the several cultural settings in which the Church is at work are so dissimilar – linguistically, racially, religiously, nationally – that, when coupled with the deterrent factor of the expense of travel, the provi..ce as envisaged seems impracticable. Someday it may come about. Or there might emerge several provinces, each smaller, more manageable, than the single grand province.

Meanwhile, nobody sits idly by. Two steps, of an interim nature, have been taken. When Dr. Sansbury, formerly Warden of St. Augustine's College, Canterbury, was appointed Bishop of Singapore and Malaya, the Archbishop of Canterbury made clear to all Oriental dioceses holding mission from the See of Canterbury that he was also appointing Dr. Sansbury to assist him in an advisory capacity in the special responsibilities which he bears as Metropolitan for the Dioceses under his jurisdiction in South-east Asia and Korea. This means, in short, that Singapore's new bishop – whose enthronement on 1st March, 1961, was accompanied by the sound of trumpets, bells, and firecrackers – has a somewhat ill-defined but important responsibility for exploring, with fellow bishops of the area, the form the future should take. Everybody can agree on one thing: a grand, concerted strategy for evangelization of the Pacific is needed.

Perhaps it is not a province or provinces that will answer to the needs of this area. Some are now asking if organizing the Church into tidy provinces is not predominantly an *English* preoccupation, something for which the English seem to have a special predilection and for which not all the rest of the world may yet be ready. In so saying I have asked a question which I cannot answer. I confess that I too have a predilection for provinces, but, to be honest, I must add that there is something attractive to me in the provisional arrangements now existing. A Council of the Church in

Southeast Asia has been formed and has met several times. This might be a stepping-stone towards an eventual province. Yet it could prove to be a sufficient organ of intra-Anglican communication and co-operation in this century. The Bishops meet from time to time for consultation. I regret the absence of a sufficiently strong representation on the presbyteral and lay levels, but one must be realistic: the travel that is an education in itself is also a killing drain on the exchequer. Decisions of this Council are without the force of law, but nobody affected by its deliberations turns a deaf ear with impunity. Anglican procedures, of which this is an example, are the despair of efficiency experts, yet their despair is confounded and compounded by amazement when they discover how much can be accomplished by Anglicans who have been persuaded rather than commanded.

Even if we must forego for the time being the design for a far-ranging province, the moment may be upon us for creating one that will be coterminous with the emerging new political entity of Greater Malaysia. The Church, which began to think of the formation of such a province a long while back, anticipated in this area, as it did in parts of Africa and in the West Indies, the developments within the political realm. The Bishop of Singapore and Malaya writes that "the prospect of a Greater Malaysia, embracing the Federation, Singapore and the Borneo territories, has passed from the world of dreams and is now an agreed policy".

If the secular world is attempting strategic unification, why should the Church drag its feet? Traditionalists hesitate and would retard this movement by issuing the reminder that Anglicanism has never gone in for provinces unless there were at least four dioceses to unite. That is a time-honoured custom, but it is not law. But rather than oppose custom, I would recommend the subdivision of the existing dioceses. Even without my recommendation (!) it is likely that Borneo will soon be two dioceses. Why kill off prematurely the existing admirable Bishop by holding him to an area impossibly large and incredibly difficult of access when there is already in existence an admirable suffragan whose competence to administer a diocese of his own is beyond question? And then, the present-day Diocese of Singapore and Malaya is certainly capable of subdivision. The Assistant Bishop is a man of stature. Why not make him a Diocesan? Give him the Federation or most of it. People who fight me on this point have, as their chief objection, the contention that Singapore by itself is not big enough to engage fully the tremendous talents of the incumbent. I disagree. This is another man I would not like to see killed prematurely by overwork. In view of our aspirations for extending work in Thailand, Indonesia, and other neighbouring lands, which would be his responsibility, Singapore would not be too little for him. Its size, on the contrary, would be just right.

Moreover, this man needs to be spared some time for scholarly pursuits, for research and for writing. He has something to teach us all. We cannot afford *not* to give him the requisite leisure without which scholarship is quenched.

In this way – things being simpler on paper than in practice – I have produced for you the four dioceses necessary, by the decree of custom, to the formation of a Greater Malaysia province.

Before taking leave of this subject, I would put in a plea for the lonesome Diocese of Rangoon. Admit it, I beg of the appropriate authorities, to your fellowship. It was only by fortuity, never by logic, that it was conjoined to the Church of India. If the Plan for Church Union in North India and Pakistan should go through, it will be left an orphan. In such case, a foster parent will be a prime desideratum for so vivacious a youngster.

17

BORNEO: Miracles out of Mud

WHEN I ALIGHTED FROM THE PLANE AT KUCHING, CAPITAL OF Sarawak, the Bishop of Borneo and his Lady were on hand to bid me a cordial welcome.* A minute later the Bishop turned to his wife and said, "All right, my dear, it will be Plan B." I looked a little puzzled. The Bishop's wife came to my aid. "We thought," she explained, "that a canon theologian might be a doddering old man, so we prepared a somewhat sedentary programme which we called Plan A. But, just in case, we also worked out a rather more athletic Plan B."

Plan B proved almost too athletic for me. It involved, first of all, a trip by motor boat down the Sarawak River, a watercourse that twists and turns until finally it meets an ocean too angry at many seasons for a craft as small as ours. The missionaries put out to sea, as often as they dare, to reach other rivers. Sailing up between slimy, densely forested banks, they come to villages of the people called Sea Dayaks.

Each one of the villages is one great longhouse, raised above the ground on posts, and divided into living quarters for the different families. To reach the Sea Dayaks by a journey overland is impossible. There are practically no roads, no trails. The whole of the coastal region is a bog. It is not ideal for walking. Only by going down one tortuous river, by risking the open ocean, and by sailing up another river, can you hope to get anywhere.

Midstream, our motor broke down. Neither by prayers nor by oaths could we get it going again. We attempted to row, but the tide was against us. Just when I thought the time had come for the Provost and me to take

* Because the Diocese of Borneo was big and geographically unmanageable, it has lately been subdivided into the Diocese of Kuching and the Diocese of Jesselton, the latter shepherded by a Chinese.

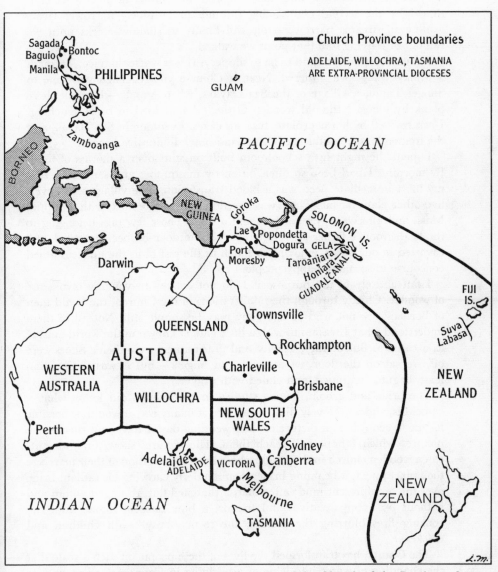

Church Province boundaries

ADELAIDE, WILLOCHRA, TASMANIA
ARE EXTRA-PROVINCIAL DIOCESES

PHILIPPINES

Sagada
Baguio Bontoc
Manila

GUAM

Zamboanga

BORNEO

PACIFIC OCEAN

NEW GUINEA

Goroka
Lae Popondetta
Dogura GELA
Port Taroaniara
Moresby Honiara
GUADALCANAL

SOLOMON IS.

FIJI IS.

Suva
Labasa

Darwin

QUEENSLAND

Townsville

Rockhampton

AUSTRALIA

Charleville

Brisbane

NEW ZEALAND

WESTERN AUSTRALIA

WILLOCHRA

NEW SOUTH WALES

Perth

Adelaide
ADELAIDE

VICTORIA

Sydney
Canberra

Melbourne

INDIAN OCEAN

TASMANIA

NEW ZEALAND

L.m.

4. The Church of England in Australia, parts of the Church of the Province of
New Zealand and the missionary district of the Philippines

turns in saying the Last Rites over each other, another motor boat came into view and took us in tow. We found a place where we could tie up our boat for the night; then, after haggling and the transfer of silver – we continued by the second craft, going through progressively narrower rivers leading to streams narrower still, and finally to shallow creeks until we ran out of water. From that point we walked.

I have never known mud to be so slippery. It was worse than ice. Through a Malay village we slithered. Next, a Chinese village. Then we came to Sungei Tanju, a village of the Sea Dayaks, where stands – brought there plank by plank – the old wooden Cathedral that used to be at Kuching. I was revived by hot chocolate, luscious cakes, Evensong in Sea Dayak, and the tremendous friendliness of these handsome, diminutive people.

I spent the night in a schoolroom built on stilts over a morass of mud. By morning I had been so often bitten by mosquitoes and sand fleas that my most immediate need was a blood transfusion. The villagers, however, had other plans for me. There was a wedding to be attended, with a nuptial Mass, and afterwards firecrackers and a feast. Those few pigs belonging to the bridegroom's father *not* selected for the outdoor barbecue snorted and cavorted in our midst, enjoying as much as the rest of us the unaccustomed concourse of so many happy people.

I fail entirely of my purpose if I do not convey to you my own sense of wonder. Chiefly through the ministrations of the Church, the "wild men of Borneo" are not wild at all. They may be simple still. Not all of them understood what I was up to with a little gadget known in the world outside as a camera. But dignity, gravity and graciousness were theirs. Shoes were off, we sat on the floor, we ate with our fingers – but it was a Christian feast, begun, continued, and ended with prayer.

The bride and groom, having studied in our school, did know what a camera is, and with lovely diffidence asked if in any way it would be possible for me to send them a picture of their wedding day. I have sent them some pictures which I hope will reach them. The pictures show, first, an ant-eaten wooden church in the jungle where the solemnization of their marriage took place; next, a beaming bridegroom tenderly carrying his radiant bride over the omnipresent mud; after that, a thatched hut, thronged within and without by happy relatives and friends, a blue haze of smoke from the cooking fires blurring the picture, the scene "busy" with children and chickens.

The Church has transformed the lives of these people on such a scale that the changing of water into wine at a wedding in Cana of Galilee was, as St. John says, but the "beginning of miracles". Not so long ago they were head-hunters and earned their living by piracy. The religion from which they have been delivered was mainly one of fear, a constant, apprehensive placating of evil spirits.

The next excursion took us up into the mountains to meet the Land Dayaks. We drove in a car as far as we could. Then we climbed on foot. It was hard work, for the soil of Sarawak is of two kinds: the kind on which you slide and the kind which sucks the shoes right off your feet. All that afternoon, during which the rain never ceased, I was engaged either in losing my footing or in losing my footgear. How sensible of the Land Dayaks to go barefoot!

But most terrifying were the bridges – mere logs thrown across narrow gullies, with at best a single bamboo pole rigged up to serve as a handrail. We must have crossed fifty such bridges. To increase my terror, many of them were pitched at a steep angle, one bank of the ravine being higher than the other. And since the Land Dayaks are short of stature, the handrail is placed so low that for me to reach it I had to bend nearly double, which forced me to look at the boulders and rushing mountain streams below. To bolster my courage, the Bishop of Borneo, as we came to each new bridge, recited appropriate and comforting verses from the Psalms until we were safely over. I was chagrined that the Land Dayaks accompanying us should see me for what I am, a clumsy person and a coward. They scampered across the bridges with the agility of tightrope walkers. "But think," said the Bishop, "of the mortal terror they would be in if they had to cross Times Square."

Occasionally there would be no bridge at all. Then we had to ford the streams. Sometimes we were in water up to the waist, I balancing my camera kit on top of my head. It is a tribute to the fine construction of Leica cameras, by the way, that they could withstand, with no signs of deterioration, the brutal treatment my journey inflicted upon them.

Just before nightfall we forded our last stream and, sopping wet, arrived at a village. I had no dry garment to put on; but that does not matter when the weather is warm. It is supposed to be a sign of civilization to wear clothes, but I see now how wise it is of those who live in places permanently hot, perennially rainy, to wear little or nothing.

The supper the Land Dayaks set before us was delicious, but my lids grew heavy before I could finish the last course. I was tired enough that night to sleep well in spite of the fact that I lay on a bare wood floor with nothing under or over me.

The next morning, a Sunday, the bamboo rafters of the church rang to the singing of several hundred persons, among them the simply but smartly uniformed boys and girls of the schools we have in this mountain plateau.

Confirmed in the Faith that day were some sixty well-prepared persons. It did something to confirm my own faith too – but not quite enough to deliver me from all anxiety about those bridges to be negotiated again on the return journey. Yes, Plan B turned out to be a bit too athletic! It greatly shortened the life of the shoes I was wearing. At times – when a log was slanted crazily and the rocks below looked like hungry teeth – I thought it might not only shorten my life but even terminate it. Yet I could have died happily right there, for I had seen things worth seeing, and there would be Christians in that green and slimy mountain fastness to bury my body and pray for my soul.

My own adventures are of no consequence. I cite them solely to picture the conditions under which the Bishop and his clergy must labour. I was in Sarawak for a few days only. They are there for years on end. It is nothing to put up with isolation and mud and rain and a sizzling, soggy, stifling, enervating climate for half a week. But to put up with it for half a lifetime (a lifetime likely to be shortened because of these conditions) and to continue to work hard when, physically, it is an effort to cross a room or write a letter, *that* is what I call devotion. As for me, I would probably become a beachcomber before the end of the first year. But I begin to see now the wisdom of certain procedures about which the British are often teased. Their dressing for dinner in the jungles has been the subject of many jokes and cartoons, a standing invitation to caricaturists. The dress parade, the heavy uniforms, the stiff standing on ceremony have all helped people to keep a tight rein on themselves when the easiest thing in the world would have been to sink to the animal level. Also beneficial has been the English Church's insistence on reciting the Daily Offices. When a man knows that there are definite things that definitely *must* be done each and every day, it adds dignity to life. It is a discipline that affords a measure of protection against dry rot and degeneracy.

In his novel *Arrival and Departure*, Arthur Koestler causes one of his characters to say, "Statistics don't bleed. Do you know what counts? The detail. Only the detail counts." Although in this book I have not been averse to setting forth statistics occasionally, I hope it is apparent that I have a preference for the detail. To spend one week with the Bishop of Borneo, sailing his rivers, scaling his mountains, supping with his people, meant more to me, gave me more "feeling" for his diocese than any amount of time spent mulling over tabulated statistics in a Year Book.

But writing now in a more conventional way, it should be said that Anglicanism has as yet tackled no more than one-third of the huge island. Sarawak, where we are strongest, is the size of England; Brunei, a Malay

State governed by a Malay Sultan, with whose non-Muslim people we are able to work, is the size of Wales; North Borneo, a British colony, is the size of Scotland. Indonesian Borneo is still untouched by us, and the lack of a strong Church of any kind in Indonesian Borneo means that weird sects flourish there.

To serve the island we have a total of thirty-six priests. "To bring the twelve priests from North Borneo to Kuching for a conference costs £480. Impossible!" said the Bishop. It makes for great isolation and loneliness of the clergy and other workers, and it does nothing to speed the development of a constitutional or synodical form of diocesan life. Perforce, the Bishop must rule almost singlehanded.

The financial problems of the Church in Borneo were greatly complicated by World War II. Buildings had suffered extensive damage from Japanese occupation and Allied bombing. Yet the Christians of the island came through the ordeal with deepened faith, and, with strong support from England and Australia, were able to repair the destruction. In spite of this fine achievement, Borneo remains poor and understaffed.

"Leave" or furlough is a constant headache. It is essential that workers from abroad get home once in a while to refresh themselves in the bracing air of a better climate, to stimulate their minds by immersion in the intellectual mainstreams of the Church at large, and to do the inevitable deputation work – i.e. try to raise money. Yet the Bishop of Borneo has not a single person in reserve. The furlough of one means double duty for somebody else already overburdened – or, worse still, letting work lie dormant for a while. If the problem were Borneo's alone, I would not take the space to mention it. Alas, it is a problem afflicting bishops everywhere.

It would alleviate the difficulty, no doubt, if each Province or general area of the Church could have a reserve corps, even if it consisted of only one, two, or three "freewheelers", persons willing to rotate, to step in as substitutes whenever somebody fell ill or was away on leave. This is a luxury we cannot afford – although it might pay for itself in the long run. My "reserve corps" idea founders, in any case, on the hard rocks of the language problem. In a diocese like Borneo we are having to minister in eight different languages. What one reservist is sufficient for that? The Dayaks comprise five races, not one, and they speak five different languages. To meet the need of the Chinese Anglicans in Borneo three dialects are required. In all of these tongues, except Mandarin, we are hard up for Christian literature, and there is neither staff enough nor money enough to get on with the work of translation. As for the Dayaks, few of them are sufficiently educated to lend a hand. It is seldom, therefore, that one will hear an Old Testament lection. Only a few of its stories and high points have been translated.

And there are dietetic problems! What British or American schoolmaster has to plan separate menus and see to it that meals are cooked in separate kitchens and served in separate refectories in order not to offend the religious scruples of the various groups composing his student body? This is a requisite in Borneo if we are to have schools at all. I met the same problem in India and a hundred other places as well. "Destroy not him with thy meat, for whom Christ died" (Rom. 14:15), and "For meat destroy not the work of God" (Rom. 14:20) is the teaching of the Apostle Paul. We try to obey his injunctions. All of which does not simplify life for the principal of any one of our fine schools in Sarawak.

The *Sarawak Gazette* in setting forthcoming events for the month, gives the dates in accordance with three calendars: Western, Chinese, and Muslim. This is one illustration of the complex nature of the Church's task.

The same periodical, in an issue I read one afternoon when it was too hot to take a siesta, published the main findings of the 1960 census and made some trenchant comments:

These innocent groups of digits carry grave implications which pose far-reaching problems. The elemental fact is that the total population of Sarawak has grown from 546,385 in 1947 to 744,391 in 1960, which represents an increase of 36.23 per cent over thirteen years, or an annual increase of 2.4 per cent. Put more baldly, the population of Sarawak has gone up by one-third over thirteen years, and so, precluding any extraneous factors such as immigration, epidemics or cataclysms, it will continue to do so for each subsequent period of thirteen years; thus there emerges the following pattern:

1947	–	546,385
1960	–	744,391
1973	–	1,024,513
1986	–	1,424,699
1999	–	2,002,457

By the end of the century there will be nearly three times as many persons in Sarawak as there are today.

My reaction was: How on earth are so many to be fed? I was thinking equally of physical and spiritual food. It is true that a degree of industrialization has come to Borneo, which possesses the largest oil field in the British Commonwealth, and in Sarawak and Brunei approximately thirty-five thousand people depend upon the Shell Oil Company for their living. On the whole, however, the inhabitants of Borneo live by agriculture, raising a variety of products on a small scale, but relying chiefly on rubber, pepper, coconut, timber, and rice. In a country where transportation is so difficult and rainfall so heavy, the economy is precarious and great suffering can result from failure of crops, especially of rice.

I asked an agricultural expert whom I met at Rotary in Kuching if, by the use of scientific method, there was anything new Borneo could produce to improve its financial position. "Nothing I can think of," was his reply.

Nevertheless, as a fine example of inter-Anglican co-operation, I am glad to report that the Missionary District of the Philippines has sent an Igorot priest to help open up new work in North Borneo, and incidentally to give advice and aid in scientific methods of rice-growing, a side line in which he is an expert.

Although I was unable myself to visit the Community Development Scheme in Padawan, I heard from the Bishop of the promising effort, financed by the government but manned by the Church, to improve the health and living conditions of about four thousand Land Dayaks in fifteen villages. In this mountainous area adults are being taught to read and write and are receiving training in agriculture and trades. Another Development Scheme was opened in 1961 among the Sea Dayaks far up the Lupar River.

Such efforts are admirable but inadequate. A difficult future lies in store. The probabilities are that within forty years Sarawak will have to support a population of 2,404,000 – the size of the present population of New Zealand. Is the whole area to become "a festering rural slum"?

Many Americans have never even heard of Sarawak, and few American Episcopalians have felt any impulse to send our Church there as much as a dime. One reason is that they have not been offered the opportunity, and the other is because of demands of similar urgency arising all over the world. Quite a few enlightened people speak learnedly and even worriedly of "the population explosion", but as long as they do so in terms of bloodless statistics and from spacious air-conditioned apartments, they are talking through their Sunday hats. Walk through the shockingly congested streets of Kuching, however, and visit families who live in cubicles the size of a butler's pantry, and the problem comes alive – as a matter of life and death.

The Chinese, who were brought to Borneo as labourers and cheap help to assist in opening up the land, have, by their own industry, virtually taken command of the commerce of the country. By reason of the economic prosperity they have won by honest toil, they can afford to be and are the most fruitful in reproducing their kind. Even before the end of the century they will have been numerically what already they are economically: the predominant ethnic group. And yet the Church is still thinking primarily in terms, first, of a mission to Sea and Land Dayaks and, second, of a mission to British businessmen. British and Dayaks are in no wise to be neglected, but the accent should now shift to the Chinese, for by 1999 they will have constituted, it appears, about half of the total population.

The Diocese knows all these facts. An Assistant Bishop who is Chinese, James Chang-Ling Wong, has been consecrated. Before long – probably before this book is published – a new Diocese for North Borneo will have been created, and he will be the Diocesan. Excellent! But it will still mean that provision for ministering to the Chinese in other parts of the island is inadequate. Where are the men to be found? And when found, where trained? Until the Church on the mainland of China is once again free to come and go as a free citizen in the world, we must look to the Chinese dispersion: principally Singapore, Hong Kong, Taiwan, and the Philippines. Yet each of these places is itself so hard up for men!

Great is the need of Borneo. An acute shortage of priests results in infrequent administration of the sacraments and sporadic instruction of the faithful. "This," said the Bishop, "could bring the whole structure down in ruins. More priests we must have and more teachers. Radio, outboard motors, and rubber are introducing even this primitive and isolated land to modern civilization and breaking down many of the old religious sanctions. The people are seeking a religion and must have it quickly. Given staff, Christianity could sweep the board."

18

AUSTRALIA: Growing Pains Down Under

AT SEVEN O'CLOCK ON THE MORNING OF CHRISTMAS DAY, 1960, the thermometer registered one hundred and four degrees. As I stood before the altar of the church in Darwin, I had to flick sweat from my eyes in order to see the hymnal and continue singing, "In the bleak midwinter".

The plane that had brought me from Singapore to Darwin in the dead of the previous night paused briefly to refuel before hurrying on to the great Australian cities of the east, over two thousand miles away. The man who cleared me through Customs was efficient, polite, and official. But when the formalities were over, he broke into a broad smile, extended his hand, and announced that he was to be my host for Christmas dinner. He told me that planes land regularly at Darwin to be serviced, but that only about five hundred passengers a year alight there. "I congratulate you," he said, "on your decision to enter Australia by what is sometimes called the 'back door'. Most visitors from abroad know only our cities in the southeast, but you will come to know something about pioneer Australia, our north and our west. And some of the first people you will be seeing tomorrow are the *first* Australians, the aborigines."

My introduction to Australia was but an earnest of the friendliness I was to meet everywhere. It does not take long to get acquainted with Australians, and to perceive their love for the Church. But the visitor also quickly senses their loneliness and isolation.

The Christmas service was broadcast. The radio is important in Australia. For thousands of the people in the "Outback" it is their sole possibility, for years on end, of going to church. Later in my Australian sojourn I was to witness still other ways in which the radio is, in the strictest sense, a godsend. In remote Charleville, for example, I watched the "Flying Doctors" at work. With earphones clamped to my head, I listened to such exchanges by radio as the following:

"Mrs. Thompson at such-and-such a ranch had a restless night; her cough is worse; and this morning she complains of a swelling and throbbing behind the left ear. Her temperature is up two degrees over the last report." The static-distorted voice was that of a sheep rancher who was also a "ham" operator calling in a report about the wife of one of his ranch hands.

The "Flying Doctor" studied Mrs. Thompson's chart, considered the new symptoms, then prescribed treatment. "Try this," he said by radio, going carefully into detail so that the troubled rancher and the anxious husband of the ailing woman, neither of whom had had medical training, would make no mistake. "Call me back in four hours. If she has not responded to treatment, we'll try one other thing, and if that doesn't work, I'll hop in the plane and fly out." Mrs. Thompson lived eight hundred miles away. There might be no connecting road, or at best a poor one, or a flooded one.

All Australia is dotted with centres that makes possible diagnosis by air – and, when necessary, a house visit by aeroplane. This remarkable service – originally the inspiration and achievement of the Presbyterian Church – has become a concern shared by several denominations, the Anglicans among them. It involves doctors and nurses, underpaid, who know not only medicine but also how to use the radio and how to fly. In addition, the "Flying Doctors" broadcast the news, abet the police in their search for missing persons or for fugitives from justice, and help the meteorologists predict the weather.

Anglicanism's contribution to the enterprise is smaller than it should be, a fact I am relating not in order to scold the Anglicans but to suggest the vastness of the continent "Down Under" and the difficulties of existence in a chapped and underpopulated land.

The Northern Territory, arid and torrid, is over three times as large as California and roughly ten times the size of England. To inhabit the vast domain, however, there were, at the time of my visit, but 20,354 people. Darwin, the capital city, is a pleasant community, but after you have reached the city limits, where is there to go? Even with the help of aeroplanes, it takes six full days for the Bishop, who has his seat on Thursday Island, to reach his people in Darwin.

Darwin, my introduction to Australia, was also an introduction to one of the most distinctive and constructive features of Australian church life: the Bush Brotherhoods. I was to meet members of several such brotherhoods – some high church, some low church. One brother I remember in particular, not only for his excellence but because, as Providence would have it, his name was Brother Hood. From him, stationed at Charleville, a frontier town, I learned that the brotherhoods are companies of priests who share a common life and are bound together by semi-monastic rules.

With a community house as headquarters, they move out separately – by horse, car, or aeroplane – to minister to detached and lonely people in the "Outback". (See Pl. 37).

A panorama from the air reveals best the emptiness of the land from Darwin to Perth in the south-west corner of the continent. We made four intermediate stops that interminable day, and at each halting point all there was to greet us was an airstrip, a police station, and a pub. These remote outstations provide for sheep ranchers and miners their sole contact with the outside world. It is Utah, Nevada, New Mexico, Colorado, Wyoming, and Arizona all rolled into one – without Salt Lake City or Reno or Albuquerque or Denver or Cheyenne or Phoenix to break the monotony. What towns there are could be readied in a quarter of an hour by any Hollywood director for the filming of a "western". Except for the car, the radio, and the aeroplane, there are no conspicuous indications that the twentieth century has arrived.

The Bishop of North-West Australia, over whose diocese I flew that day (though without paying him the courtesy of a visit, since he had gone far into the interior for a Confirmation), long ago gave up counting the number of flights he had made in seeking out his dispersed sheep. When he had run up the staggering total of two thousand visitations by air, the airline that is most active in servicing his area presented the Bishop with a Gold Pass.

After ten hours aloft, I came to Perth. Californians will understand me when I say that this capital of Western Australia is a miniature San Francisco, with overtones of Long Beach and San Bernardino.

It resembles San Francisco because, when viewed from the heights of King's Park, there may be seen steep hills, bay, harbour, bridges, white skyscrapers, neon signs, superhighways, "clover leaves". It is hard to believe that in attractive Perth, less than a century ago, the British – having asked for trouble in more ways than one – had to fend off the spears of furious aborigines.

Perth resembles California's Long Beach with its fine swimming facilities, four-family flats, palm trees, pleasant bungalows with gardens, and huge new housing developments. Perth, even more than Long Beach, finds it hard to draw people to church. "This climate," said one of my hosts, conscious that he was exaggerating, "produces magnificent bodies without brains." They are suntanned specimens luxuriating on a beach.

Perth is reminiscent of San Bernardino because, in old frame and adobe buildings still standing with their red-painted, corrugated-iron roofs, well suited to catching the rain water, there are signs that the pioneer days are not far removed. Also the flora suggests that a desert lies not far from the city limits.

"Perth," I was told, "actually *has* the climate which California claims to have." I could happily settle down in this highly favoured region when I retire – if only Perth were not so far from any other place in Australia, and if only Australia itself were not so distant from the rest of the world.

With pride the Archbishop of Perth, Metropolitan of the Province of West Australia, showed me the newly constructed Theological College. At present there are but one full-time faculty member and a few postulants. I asked the Archbishop why he felt the need of building still another theological college. Australia does not lack for them! He replied that for him to send a candidate to an eastern theological college would be like the Bishop of London sending a man as far east as Moscow! The distance is exactly the same. But I am not wholly convinced. With dependable aeroplane service available today, I imagine that to keep seminarians shuttling back and forth by air for many years would still represent a saving over the cost of building and maintaining a separate college in the west. That, however, is not my present point. I am only trying to suggest what Australian distances are.

Many people stepped forward in Perth to help me. From them I rapidly learned of their problems and potentialities. Problem No. 1 – which confronts not Perth alone but every other Australian city – is the sudden arrival of immigrants. Their appearance on the scene by the thousands is, I am convinced, the Australian Church's greatest opportunity; but the fact that in the eyes of the average Australian churchman these immigrants loom larger as a problem than as an opportunity defines precisely the depth of the problem. Our Church is ill prepared to receive them.

Let me explain.

In 1961 Australia had a population of just over ten million. That is not exactly a plethora for a land area almost as big as the continental United States. At the conclusion of World War II, Australians suddenly developed a conscience, or at least a concern, about how to justify the retention of so much land by so few people.

Immediately to the north is Indonesia, groaning under the burden of a population of ninety-three million, and crowded into an area only one-fourth the size of Australia. Still farther north, confined to its islands, is Japan with a population as big as Indonesia's.

Great stretches of the Australian continent are not arable, it must be admitted, although much of it can be reclaimed by irrigation as soon as an economical way of converting salt water into fresh water has been found. But even allowing for this, there is so much land here, with so many resources, that overcrowded neighbours are bound to look upon it with envious eyes.

The Australian answer, dictated by humanitarian concern as well as by self-interest, has been to encourage immigration. The immigrants, however, have to be white, and at least 50 per cent of them must be from the United Kingdom.

From October, 1945, to December, 1960, Australia welcomed 1,644,000 immigrants. Hence when you walk down the street of an Australian city, at least one in every ten persons you pass is a recent arrival. He has come within the last fifteen years. In my diary I find this note: "While window shopping in Adelaide, I heard in the course of a half-hour's stroll on a summer evening (January!) snatches of conversation in Dutch, German, Greek, and Italian, plus some other languages I could not identify. This city – until recently so staid, so British – now teems with espresso bars, cafés called *Sorrento* or *Luigi's*, and shops displaying signs in Greek.

The "New Australians", as the immigrants are called, are rapidly changing the "feel" of every city. Eating patterns are different. So also are entertainment patterns. The "fair dinkum Aussies", whose prewar cookery had been an unimaginative reproduction of England's own idea-forsaken culinary effort, are now to be seen consuming with continental gusto all manner of gourmet food. And the "Continental Sunday", so different from a Sabbath circumscribed by blue laws, is rapidly finding favour. Australians are learning that man cannot live by beef, Yorkshire pudding, boiled potatoes, and Brussels sprouts alone. Of course he can live – but not well. Under influence of the immigrants, old Australians are beginning to question an ancient law, hitherto sacrosanct, that requires liquor stores (bottle shops) and public houses to shut down at 6 P.M. The immigrants have introduced the new idea that in more sophisticated countries people are urged to refrain from imbibing alcoholic beverages until *after* sundown.

Australians have been in the habit of stampeding from office to pub at the close of day for their "sundowner", with the one idea of fortifying themselves as quickly as possible against a long, dry night. On an empty stomach these "sundowners" have sent many an Australian reeling home.

What have such things to do with the Church? Much in every way. Old Australians find little guidance from their Church about how one is to adjust to the new patterns of life. New Australians arriving from Europe cannot be assured that there is a place for them in the Australian Church.

"The Church of England in Australia and Tasmania" does not even suspect that its name is unwieldy and uninviting. Could a Slav, a Scandinavian, a Dutchman, a German, an Italian, or a Greek be expected to think that a Church so named was possibly a spiritual home for *him*? Yet when I asked Australian Anglicans whether they felt the name had a forbidding and deterrent aspect, they looked at me blankly. Except for a few imaginative ones, the question had never entered their minds. They have yet to think of *Ecclesia Anglicana* as an option for anybody not of British descent.

Melbourne, a progressive Australian diocese, has gone so far as to print for distribution a placard which sets forth, in ten different languages, what this Church is and that it welcomes all. Yet the placards, if they have been put up at all, are usually posted *inside* the churches, in the narthex, not outside where a passer-by could be expected to see them. How typical of us! Once the stranger comes in on his own initiative we find a pew for him. But we ourselves do not go out into the highways and byways to "compel" people to come in . . . Still who am I to complain of the Australians? In New York I have been voted down in Chapter. To this day we have no sign to indicate to the public what the Cathedral Church of St. John the Divine is. Apparently it would be vulgar to put up a sign. My interest, however, is in the *Plebs Dei*. Canterbury Cathedral may not need a sign. New York Cathedral does. We are not *the* Church. Only part of it.

The Australian Church might wake up more quickly to the challenges and opportunities presented by the new arrivals if the latter were not confined, for the most part, to the cities. It is rural Australia, where foreigners are still a matter of hearsay, that is dragging its feet, and the rural Church that lags behind.

How many cities does Australia have? Two major ones: Sydney and Melbourne. In them dwell 40 per cent of the total population. Add Brisbane and Adelaide, and we have accounted for 60 per cent of the population. This leaves but four million people to be strewn over the rest of the continent. We shall never understand Australia unless we take into account the loneliness of the "Outback"; of Scots, Irish, and English living in a kind of "exile", nostalgic for a Great Britain remembered from childhood or from what they learned at their father's knee – a Great Britain vastly changed now. These "exiles" fight ecclesiastical battles that Britain herself fought and resolved decades ago.

Comparisons can be invidious, but sometimes they are instructive. Suppose we compare and contrast Australia and the United States. In terms of square miles, they are about the same. Australia claims three million Anglicans; we in America claim the same. Yet to minister to three million souls the Australians have only twenty-five diocesan bishops; we have seventy-eight. Of priests to tend the flocks, the Australian Church has about fifteen hundred; the American Church over eighty-nine hundred. I am not boasting about American size but am commiserating with the Australian clergy. In these circumstances, how *can* they be expected to do an adequate pastoral job – to say nothing of undertaking some new and creative evangelical work? The Australian clergy are not at fault. They are hard workers, hard-pressed – and hopelessly outnumbered.

Australia does not lack for Eastern Orthodox Churches. As always, we try to link people with the Church from which they sprang. But what of the expanses of Australia where the Orthodox Churches have not yet gone and where we are already in operation? Some of the orphaned Orthodox have turned to Rome or to the Presbyterians and found a home there. But the majority have turned away from us in disappointment because we have repelled them by our lack of cordiality. Our iciness drives them off.

Dutch immigrants have reacted in a simiiar manner. Those among them who are Reformed seek out the Presbyterians, and some remain to pray, but many do not. This is not the Church they knew at home! Roman Catholics from the Netherlands meet, for the first time, an Irish hierarchy little to the liking of most of them. The new-comers from Italy fare no better. The Italian migrant and the Irish priest are not immediately attracted to each other. One evening when I was dining alone at an Italian restaurant in an Australian city, the Neapolitan proprietor and his wife, having at the moment few other guests to serve, exerted themselves to give me a good meal, their attentions heightened by their discovery that despite my clerical collar I was neither Irish nor a Roman Catholic. "The Irish," they said, "are our worst enemies here. We like much better the Protestants as people, though when we try their churches, all they do is talk. There is no action. Nothing happens." Neapolitans are a notoriously volatile people, vehement in expression. The reaction of these gastronomic giants may not have been typical – yet I wonder. In a magazine I read the amusing remark that most Italian migrants would be "enthusiastic supporters of the Kon O'Tiki project suggested by [native born] Australian priests: that all the Irish clergy here should drift on a raft across the Pacific".

Such people as the restaurateur and his wife are anticlerical but not anti-Christ or even anti-church. What they are seeking is a Church resembling in its appearance the Church at home but devoid of the authoritarianism only too reminiscent of the political régimes from which they have escaped. Anglicanism is the obvious answer – obvious, that is, to all but the Anglicans. The immigrants – most of them – are D.P.'s, persons displaced religiously as well as culturally. They have taken the bold step of seeking a new home and a new life in a faraway place. More than a few of them are seeking a new Church as well – for what are home and life without the Church? Most forms of Protestantism cannot quite fill the bill. This could be Anglicanism's moment in Australia. We are letting it slip through our fingers. "Anglicans are born and bred, not acquired by conversion" was the mournful and bitterly ironic way in which one enlightened but discouraged Australian churchman commented on the somnolence of his Church to people not of Anglo-Saxon origin.

New Australians streaming in from the United Kingdom present problems of a different order. The Anglicans among them carry over into their adopted homeland a common English misunderstanding. They think the Church receives its money from the state, and hence they, as taxpayers, should not be expected to contribute additional sums for the maintenance of the local parish church. And strangely enough, although these people are willing to accept pioneer conditions in all other respects, they feel it is not quite seemly to worship in rented store buildings, private houses, parish halls, and other temporary quarters. "We'll come when there is a proper church" is the excuse commonly given for their abstention. In the United States, where a revolutionary war made clear and sharp the break between Church and state, people understood from the start that if they wanted a church they would have to roll up their sleeves and build it for themselves. In an Australia predominantly English, however, people simply expect the Church to be *there*, a useful and hereditary part of the landscape to which resort may be had when occasion requires – which is not often, for one is born and dies but once, and generally extra-ecclesiastical arrangements must be sought for a second or third marriage.

If I seem here to contradict my earlier remark about the love of Australians for their "C. of E.", it is because I refer now only to *new* Australians. The old Australians do indeed love it, though often in a curiously old-fashioned way. That is, they do not welcome change.

Conservatism is putting the Church out of step with a continent where change is the order of the day. Unless the Church alters its tactics – and perhaps even if it does – it will find itself, in the near future, no longer the majority Church. Sociologists, whatever their religion or lack of it, predict that Orwell's year of 1984 will see Australia a predominantly Roman Catholic country. Anglicans will be in second place.

Despite the defections from Rome, most Roman Catholic immigrants continue loyal to their Church. So many have arrived that Rome already has 25 per cent of the population, and there are hopeful signs that the migrants, by the weight of their numbers, will bring about a liberalization within the Australian-Roman system. If such liberalization occurs, it will mean fewer defections in the future, which in turn will increase the size of the Roman flock even more. I wish them all prosperity. Anglicanism has no desire to grow at the expense of Roman Catholicism – provided the latter is doing its job. It is beginning to do so.

Here is an example of how our friends of the "Italian Mission" get down to work. Although Rome has 25 per cent of the population, it has only 5 per cent in university circles. One of its first steps, therefore, is to place chaplains of ability on or near university campuses. There is a conscious Roman Catholic intellectual revival. Roman scholars are issuing learned journals which, for writing and perspicacity, excel anything being done by Anglicans or Protestants. This revival will have tremendous repercussions in the next generation.

When the great National Research University was built in Canberra, the newly created Federal Capital, Rome quickly sent a priest to serve full time as chaplain to students in that strategic centre. We had not yet managed to take a similar step when I was there in January, 1961. In some Australian universities there are, of course, Anglican Colleges, but for the most part they are designed for Anglicans alone. Our whole endeavour is too inbred. I failed to find much evidence of there being anyone with vision enough to contemplate a ministry to an entire university community. Yet such a ministry could be accomplished by a clergyman with apologetic gifts and who himself was the intellectual peer of the brightest professor on campus. Australia needs something comparable to America's "Church Society for College Work", which was formed to "strengthen the work of the Protestant Episcopal Church in college and university centres".

More than once I was told that superior young men, after being attracted to our Ministry, shy away, discouraged, when they see how mediocre much of our work is. One professor, devout as an Anglican and distinguished as an academician, told me that his own son was a case in point. It is a sad fact that only one-fifth of the Australian clergy have themselves attended university. His latest concern is that one of his daughters may become a Roman Catholic because a Dominican was able to answer her questions when her own clergy apparently could not. "I have come painfully to the conclusion," he said, "that the influence of the Church of England in Australia and Tasmania will decline, and that it will become a minority church in the land – but perhaps she will recover herself by becoming so."

If immigrants constitute the Australian Church's Number One "Problem", as I have suggested, I now submit that the Number Two Problem (and here I use no quotation marks) is that Church's lack of centralized organization.

Australia is not only an immense island (call it a subcontinent or a continent, if you prefer) but a whole series of "islands", regional areas that until lately have lived mostly to themselves, their attention concentrated upon local concerns. It is easy to understand why this had to be. Pioneer settlers have their hands full "digging in" and establishing a place for themselves.

And when one group of settlers is separated by a thousand roadless miles or more from the next settlement, there is little opportunity to drop in on each other for a companionable cup of tea.

Life, therefore, came to be organized provincially rather than nationally. After all, Australia became a nation as recently as 1901. And to this day, so fierce is pride in one's own province that within two minutes of your being introduced to an Australian he will let you know that he is not just any kind of Australian but rather a West Australian or a South Australian or that he comes from Tasmania or New South Wales. (Bostonians, Virginians, and Texans often comport themselves in similar manner!) Both politically and ecclesiastically, the first loyalty has been to a state or province, not to the Nation or the National Church. Only slowly is Australia learning to pull together.

To me this lack of cohesion is symbolized by the fact that in order to cross Australia by rail, one must change trains four times. Why? There are four different kinds of gauges! Each state built its own railway, apparently with no thought of eventually connecting up with anybody else. It should not surprise us, therefore, that the Church is still disjointed.

Unlike the Church of geographically compact New Zealand, which early sued for – and promptly received – its independence, the Australian Church is still, in a strict legal sense, the Church of England, its powers of self-government sorely restricted. Even after fifty years of trying to formulate a constitution of its own, the Church in Australia had not yet achieved it at the time of my Australian "walk-about". The failure to attain ecclesiastical autonomy was caused not so much by any desire on the part of England to bind Australia tyrannically to itself as it was to the inability of Australian Churchmen to agree among themselves. Blame must be laid to the charge of the "rugged individualism" of the four Provinces. But more than that: blame attaches to people, priests, and prelates of one school of churchmanship deeply suspicious of people, priests, and prelates of any other school of churchmanship. Nowhere in my entire tour of Anglicanism did I encounter questions of churchmanship so divisive, so much a source of distrust and rancour. Here again, the pattern of Australia's historical development has left its mark on the present day. Provinces that grew up in isolation from each other tended to be "monochrome". The Highs were in the saddle in one region, uncontested by the Lows – and vice versa. And now the people are having to learn to live with each other. What that most excellent gift of charity had difficulty in achieving, the aeroplane is demanding. Australians – churchmen included – are at last being forced by history to think, act, and work together.

In the meantime the stresses and strains are many.

The preparation of Sunday School materials, for example, causes endless agony. Some dioceses flatly refuse to use a student handbook if the word "altar" appears in it and will ban absolutely a filmstrip if it shows candles upon the Holy Table. A diocese so minded proceeds thereupon to produce educational materials of its own – an expense the Australian Church can ill afford. A unified system of lessons, acceptable to the whole Church, has hitherto been impossible. To produce one is the despair of those who lately have been charged with this responsibility.

Australian churchmen squabble interminably over issues which most of the rest of the Communion settled decades ago. Hence the perpetuation of redundant theological colleges. In the day of the horse and buggy, these many seminaries were a necessity. Today, however, regional pride is involved: it would be humiliating to surrender a single one of them. But the plain fact is: Australia does not have enough authentic doctors of divinity to staff so many colleges adequately. Yet on they go, small as they are, understaffed as they are, with libraries so tiny and obsolete that they made me weep. The obvious solution, it seems to me, is for many of these colleges to join forces. By amalgamating teaching staff and libraries it would be possible to produce a few strong seminaries instead of a raft of feeble ones. But High Church bishops are, apparently, loath to let their candidates come into contact with Low Church ones, and Low Church bishops seem apprehensive about exposing their own candidates to the discipline of matching wits with people of another persuasion. Only by keeping each school of thought hermetically sealed off from other schools of thought, it would seem, can we hope to preserve purity of doctrine.

"'Theology' in Sydney," said an informed layman sardonically, "means being able to explain the Thirty-nine Articles. Tillich, of course, isn't theology!" Now, to be able to explain the Articles of Religion is no mean feat in divinity. I have often championed the Articles against those who would have us be quit of them. I go along with "black Protestant" Sydney in its insistence upon the importance of the Articles. On the other hand, it is a poor conception of theology that feels no need to come to grips with a thinker like Tillich – if only to do him battle. Curiously enough, a Tillich fares no better at the hands of Australian High Churchmen. I found not a single volume of his on the library shelves of one of Australia's most "advanced" seminaries. When I commented to the Warden on the absence from the collection not only of Tillich but also of Niebuhr, Barth, Brunner, and Kierkegaard, he said, "Well, really, we have nothing to learn from these people." Anglicans, High or Low, seem to think we already have it all.

I am reminded of an angry outburst of Walter Lowrie's. In 1932 he returned to the United States after having served for twenty-three years as Rector of the American Episcopal Church in Rome. When he discovered that hardly anybody in America had even heard of Kierkegaard and the others, he exclaimed, "But for what reason have we so many universities? Is it to ensure that studious youth shall be shielded from all contacts with contemporary thought?" If he could say that of America in the 1930's, how much more of Australia in the 1960's!

In the not so distant past Australian churchmen were greatly exercised by the celebrated Red Book Case (The Diocese of Sydney *v.* the Bishop of Bathurst). It concerned the *jus liturgicum*, the right of a bishop to authorize certain permissive rites and ceremonies for use in his own diocese. All parties to the litigation were dismayed when the court ruled that the Church of England in Australia and Tasmania must be regarded in law as if it were the Church of England in England, i.e. bound by all legislation appertaining to the Church of England. When it was pointed out to the learned judges that the time is long past when the Church of England takes literally all of the legislation by which it is legally bound, the judges replied in effect, "It is just too bad that the Church of England is a lawless body; here in Australia we are law-abiding."

The Evangelical diehards were as frightened by this ruling as were the High Churchmen – for it convicted all Anglicans in Australia of being lawbreakers. Evangelicals coveted for themselves freedom from certain canons and rubrics not to their taste, and they saw that they could hardly claim for themselves freedom unless they were willing to grant a like freedom, albeit in an opposite direction, to those of a different cast of mind. Everybody, of every school of thought, suddenly saw the danger. The door was open to every litigious-minded person or party. Whatever their stamp, they could perennially involve the Church in court battles – unless the Church clarified its own legal position. In that roundabout, backhanded manner came the impetus for a constitution, national in scope and roomy enough to include all shades of churchmanship.

After numerous abortive attempts, and nearly fifty years of squabbling, Australian churchmen at last have a constitution. Their Church is becoming a united one, with central organs of government enabling it to speak with one voice and to act in a concerted manner. Enactment of a constitution cannot accomplish changes overnight, but a start has been made. A national church is coming into being. The learned Bishop of Armidale, writing in the Whitsun number of *Anglican World*, compares and contrasts the new and the old constitutions succinctly as follows: "The former constitution provided for a voluntary association of the twenty-five autonomous dioceses within the Australian Commonwealth by means of a consensual compact. The determinations of the General Synod were subject to acceptance or rejection by any or all of the constituent dioceses. The new Constitution, which has been brought into legal being within the six states of the Commonwealth by Act of Parliament in each state, gives to the Australian Church self-determination and self-government by severing the legal nexus between England and Australia in ecclesiastical matters. The Australian Church may now legally revise the Book of Common Prayer, make statements concerning the faith of the Church, and take united action, but it still leaves to the constituent dioceses much of their former autonomy in making it possible for a diocese to refuse to accept a Canon of the General Synod which affects the order and good government of the diocese concerned. The new Constitution therefore establishes a federation of Australian Dioceses rather than a united Church governed by a central representative body."

It is a pity that not enough Australian churchmen share Ernest Henry Burgmann's vision of the role Australia and the Australian Church might play in relation to Africa and Asia, by speaking to their peoples in words intelligible to them. Dr. Burgmann had not yet retired as Bishop of Canberra and Goulburn when he received me in his office at St. Mark's National Memorial Library in the Federal Capital City. It is tragic, too, that not many will speak out as courageously as did S. Barton Babbage, who until recently was Dean of Melbourne, when he denounced the government's "white Australia" immigration policy as a "standing affront to the national susceptibilities of non-European countries because of its flagrantly discriminatory character".

Isolated Australia is fast ceasing to be a continent detached from the rest of the world. The Indian Ocean and the Pacific Ocean have both shrunk. Africa is no longer so far away, and Asia is a next-door neighbour. We need more Burgmanns and Babbages who realize that Australia's synthesizing within itself elements British, European, and also American, could have as its future the role of a bridge-builder between East and West.

I cheered when I read that the citizens of Perth had turned on all their lights in the middle of the night in order to salute Colonel John Glenn as he soared past them in orbital flight. This heart-warming gesture of sympathy and participation was in marked contrast to what I myself experienced in Perth on 31st December, 1960. I sat on a terrace with some Australian friends, enjoying the cool of the evening. I remember my remark – and how flat it fell.

"Just to think!" I exclaimed as I gazed up into a star-studded sky. "This New Year's Eve we stand at the threshold of the year in which a member of the human race is going to go into space!" My hosts were singularly unimpressed. The prospect and its repercussions were remote in their thinking. But a Russian brother did go into space in 1961 and he was followed in 1962 by an American. When the latter passed over Perth, the lights went on. To me it was a symbol that Australia now knows it fully belongs to the world.

19

NEW ZEALAND: England Transplanted

WHEN AN AIRBORNE PASSENGER FROM SYDNEY, AFTER A FLIGHT OF thirteen hundred miles, approaches Christchurch on the South Island of New Zealand he has three immediate impressions: One, how beautiful the island is; two, how sparsely it is populated; three, how few the roads are and how antiquated are the few cars moving on the roads. The overall effect is of an England depopulated. Not one of those impressions is dispelled by closer acquaintance.

All of life, including church life, follows closely the English pattern. There is therefore little for me to tell about the Church in New Zealand, save that it is doing a good and responsible job, ministering to folk of British antecedents in a British sort of way – the *best* British way. It operates quietly, efficiently, conservatively, and often imaginatively.

Christchurch Cathedral, named after Canterbury Cathedral, is a noble Gothic building that stands in the exact geographical and commercial centre of the city. All important arteries converge on the Cathedral, and traffic swirls around it ceaselessly, day and night – symbolical of the centrality of the Church in New Zealand. Each of the thoroughfares bears the name of an English diocese. Many of the squares in the city commemorate martyrs in the history of the Church of England, such as Latimer, Cranmer, and Ridley. The College is called Canterbury.

It was clear that I had arrived in "the most English of all English colonies". Of course it lost colonial status years ago, but it has lost little of its English-ness. Nor does it have the great influx of European immigrants that makes neighbouring Australia less and less English. English it is, and English it seems determined to remain. Unemployment is virtually unknown in New Zealand, a compact and smoothly-functioning welfare state, and the authorities have no wish to threaten a delicate economic balance by allowing foreigners to come in numbers as settlers. But this policy, when coupled with the extreme loneliness of New Zealand's geographical situation, has resulted in a kind of cultural isolationism. New Zealand intellectuals are an impressive lot, but they are the first to confess their need of fresh stimulus by wider contacts with the world at large.

Narrowing our attention to the Church of the Province of New Zealand, which celebrated its centenary in 1950, we find that it is composed of nine dioceses, seven of them within New Zealand proper and two of them – Melanesia and Polynesia – at a great distance, far removed from the home-land, on tropical and sometimes terrible islands which, in spite of their being part of the South Pacific, bear little resemblance to "Bali Ha'i". As we shall presently be visiting these island dioceses, we confine our attention here to New Zealand proper.

It is refreshing to be able to report *once in a while* that Anglicans are in the majority. New Zealand provides us with this opportunity. Official government statistics show that in 1956 the Anglicans numbered 780,999, the Presbyterians following with 483,884, and the Roman Catholics third with 310,723. The only other denomination of considerable size is Methodist; its rolls show a membership of 161,823. After these "Big Four" there is a tremendous drop, clear down to 33,910 before we come to the next group. These are the Baptists. Next come the Plymouth Brethren with 22,444. Of the remaining plethora of religious bodies, only two – the Mormons and the Church of Christ – have more than 10,000 members.

Caution must be used in interpreting statistics, lest we glory without a sufficient foundation in fact. It should be remembered that when an Ameri-can is asked to state his "religious preference", he usually falls back on the vague designation "Protestant" unless he happens to be a convinced member of a particular denomination. So too within the British Common-wealth of Nations people not actively committed to one or another Christian tradition tend to settle, for purposes of a census, on the designation "C. of E." If one is not a "conscientious objector" to all religion, or if one is not by tradition or conviction affiliated with a denomination or a sect, what else is there to be if not "C. of E."? Therefore, a much better index to the strength and vitality of Anglicanism in a Commonwealth country like New Zealand is the number of Easter Communions. In the Diocese of Auckland, for example, 206,000 people may be registered as Anglicans, but only 17,903 of them cared enough to make their Communion within the Easter Octave. Similarly, the Church population of the Diocese of Christchurch stands at 126,000, but in 1960 only 15,460 communicated at Eastertide. Naturally, there are many children involved who have not yet been confirmed and who, according to Anglican practice, are yet to receive the Holy Communion. For this reason the situation is not so depressing as it appears, but neither is it so encouraging as it sounds, if, uncritically, we take at face value the quite true assertion that in the Diocese of Christchurch, for instance, Anglicans constitute 40 per cent of the population.

And so it goes, diocese after diocese, not only in New Zealand but in half the Anglican world. Like a boy whistling in the dark as he passes a cemetery, we marshal statistics that will give us a sense of security. But we delude ourselves.

On the basis of conversations I had with a number of perceptive Anglicans in New Zealand, I have reason to believe that the General Secretary of the Board of Missions is not wide of the mark when he says that "every Anglican must be utterly ashamed of the missionary giving of his Church. No large Church in the world gives less in proportion to its numbers. The average Anglican in this rich land [of New Zealand] gave last year 1s 10d. [ca. twenty-four cents, American] – less than ½d. a week [half a cent] – to the extension of Christ's Kingdom overseas. Three million Presbyterians in the U.S.A. gave to missions four times what three million Anglicans there gave and about twice as much as *all* the forty million Anglicans in the world! One large (non-Anglican) congregation in the City of Toronto gave in 1959 to overseas missions twice as much as the two and one-half million Anglicans in Canada gave! And twice as much as the Provincial Quota for New Zealand this year! The Plymouth Brethren in New Zealand have twice as many missionaries overseas as we have, and they number only about 18,000 adult members compared with our 300,000 adults."

Sobering considerations!

Yet let us give credit where credit is due. The New Zealand missionary record is not altogether unimpressive. Although both Australia and England lend a hand, Polynesia and Melanesia are the brilliant achievements of the New Zealand Church. Beyond that, New Zealand has fourteen missionaries in Tanganyika, fourteen in Pakistan, and a sprinkling of others in nine additional countries.

In New Zealand, as in all other places I visited, I had my heart set on getting outside the main cities. It is important to see the countryside and the hinterland. Of those the "Britain of the South" has plenty, which creates special difficulties for the Church.

With the Provincial Secretary as companion, guide, and chauffeur, I headed south from Christchurch. On a fast tar-sealed highway we traversed the low-lying Canterbury Plains. Twenty-two miles out of town we crossed the Selwyn River Bridge. Not every bishop has a river and a bridge named for him, but Selwyn – the Apostle of New Zealand and of Melanesia – was no run-of-the-mill bishop. A bit farther on we came to the Takaia River Bridge, one mile in length, the longest in all of New Zealand. New Zealanders take great pride in it. The fact that the bridge seems so stupendous to them is indicative of the small scale on which everything is done there. It is only two lanes wide and does not rise more than twenty feet above the river-bed. Before the day was over I came to understand the reason for pride in the coastal highway and its bridges, for we soon ran out of tar-sealed roads and had to negotiate dozens of one-way rickety wooden bridges. The good road, however, was with us until we reached Timaru, a bustling seaport of twenty-five thousand inhabitants. On the way to Timaru we passed many small country towns like Burnham, Dunsandel, Orari, Winchester, and Temuka, whose names were a pleasant mixture of the Scottish, English and Maori. The towns are so small that the Diocese cannot afford to erect a church and maintain a resident priest in each. Yet the difficulties here are as nothing compared to those presented by the "back blocks" I was to see that afternoon and the following day.

After lunching in Timaru with the Archdeacon, a man with an educated heart, and after being shown his fine, well-appointed church (a *direct* English transplant), the Provincial Secretary and I left the flatness of the Canterbury Plains behind, and passing through undulating countryside, reached Fairlie. The purpose of my visit was to see a typical country parish. Alas, the Vicarage was empty – a most typical characteristic! Keeping the country churches staffed is a continuing episcopal problem. Too many of the clergy want to move to town. It is, moreover, almost impossible to build up and train a settled congregation anywhere. For although the landowners stay on for ever, the "hands" they employ are recruited from town, return after a year or two to the towns whose bright lights prove too strong a lure.

Fairlie is the county town of the Mackenzie country, the centre of a district renowned for hunting. If more priests cared for shooting goats, deer, pigs, wild cattle, swan, geese, hare, rabbits, and wild duck, the bishops would have an easier time of it! There is good fishing, too – not only of fish but also of men, because people who live on lonely farms and sheep stations and who operate remote sawmills have a special hunger for the Church and for the culture of which it is a bearer. It is a fact of New Zealand Church life that people in the country districts give more to the support of the Ministry than do their cousins in the cities. But a price is paid. Because parsons must spend so much of their time on the roads, seeking out dispersed flocks and holding services in farmhouses, "the literacy of the clergy", as one of them has expressed it, is adversely affected.

It is not unusual for a man to have to minister to an area ten thousand miles square in which may dwell not more than two to five thousand persons. Nearly half of the people are not Anglicans at all, though in many instances the Anglican priest finds he is the only "minister of religion" in the whole region. He has the care of non-Anglicans as well as Anglicans. The principle of "economy" is wisely invoked. If a person is a communicant member in good standing of any Church recognized by the World Council of Churches, but is cut off geographically from the ministration of his own Church, he is welcome to communicate at Anglican altars. While such an arrangement implies no mutual recognition of "denominations", it must be applauded as the only charitable and Christian way of proceeding. It meets human need. It minimizes the dread nisus towards sectarianism and splintering. It helps prepare the way for the unity we seek. I should like to remark that I found Anglicans acting on this principle of "economy" throughout most of the world. Let nobody think that churchmanship is involved here. Dioceses representing the highest of high churchmanship are, with few exceptions, acting in accordance with this principle; and among the lowest of low churchmen, few there are who, motivated by opposite considerations, attempt to "fence the Table".

The country parson in New Zealand finds a strong ally in the Church Mail Bag School. We have met its counterpart before in Africa, Europe, and Australia. It is a plan whereby Sunday School lessons are sent out by post to children living in isolated areas. Though it might seem to be a small operation, actually it is a complicated one. It calls for the voluntary co-operation of a great many city-based laymen, each one of whom takes on from ten to fifteen pupils. Most of the tutors and pupils will never meet, except by mail. Lessons are mailed out on time, the answers come back to be graded, and monthly letters are exchanged. Tutor and pupil become "pen pals" on a level often sublime.

If I had thought Fairlie and its vicinity a region somewhat remote from the rest of the world, it was because I had not yet pressed on, in the direction of Mt. Cook, through the barren-looking sheep lands of the Mackenzie country. When we had climbed from sea level to an altitude of 2,321 feet, riding on gravelled roads where skidding was easy and where turns were dangerously deceptive, we came to the shores of Lake Tekapo where we stopped to take photographs of the picturesquely situated Church of the Good Shepherd. The church's name was appropriate, for we were in the heart of sheep-raising country.

Finally we came to the Hermitage at the foot of Mt. Cook, which thrusting its head 12,349 feet into the air, is called by the Maoris "The Cloud Breaker". There are in the area five peaks whose summits exceed 10,000 feet. The Tasman Glacier, twice the size of the largest to be found in Switzerland, tumbles down the mountains almost to the door of the Hermitage. It kept me awake half the night with its explosive sounds of ice cracking off and of avalanches roaring down from the peaks above.

In certain respects New Zealand, a land otherwise so trim, tame, and British, is wild and woolly. The Church is doing, on the whole, a good job reaching out to lonely homesteaders. This is all the more impressive when it is remembered that enormous pressure is exerted upon the bishops to bring men in from the thinly settled "back blocks" to fortify the work in the newly crowded cities. The Church, however, while not neglecting the cities, is resolved not to retreat from the hinterland.

From the craggy magnificence of the South Island Alps, and the Nevada-like emptiness of its tussock-covered grazing lands, it is a long step to Auckland on North Island, but the Church takes it in its stride and so did I – with the help of an aeroplane.

How different was my arrival in New Zealand's largest urban and industrial centre from that of George Augustus Selwyn! I arrived by Electra, without having had time to read my newspaper. He arrived in 1842, after a voyage full of hardship, peril, and delay – the delay he had used to advantage, for he had taught himself the language of the Maoris and was able on his arrival to preach to them in their own tongue. On my own tongue-tied arrival I promptly made my way to the stretch of beach where Selwyn, wading ashore, knelt down and kissed the sand. I climbed from the beach to the little hill above, where that first Bishop of New Zealand built his church (of wood, as were all the others he built, in the hope that it would withstand the New Zealand earthquakes; see Pl. 36). In the charming wooden edifice is the Holy Table on which the Constitution for the Church in New Zealand was signed. The document, of which Selwyn was the chief architect, had the Constitution of the American Church as its model. It has required but little modification in the years since its signing. Thus, the Church of New Zealand was the first of the daughters of the Church of England within the British Empire or Commonwealth to come of age. It is not without interest that the most "English" member of the Anglican Communion was nevertheless the first to make herself constitutionally independent of the English Church.

Shortly after establishing the Church in Auckland, Bishop Selwyn set out for Nelson and Wellington. Then he undertook to visit all the mission stations, although they were separated from each other by hundreds of miles of roadless terrain. By the simple expedient of going on foot he answered Governor Hobson's question, "What is the use of a Bishop in a country where there are no roads for his Lordship's carriage to drive on?" After six itinerant months in exploration of his new diocese, Selwyn made this entry in his diary:

Tuesday, Jan. 3 [1842]: My last pair of thick shoes being worn out, and my feet much blistered with walking the day before on the stumps, which I was obliged to tie to my insteps with pieces of native flax, I borrowed a horse from the native teacher, and started at 4 A.M. to go 12 miles to Mr. Hamlin's mission station, where I arrived at 7 A.M. After breakfast I sailed in his boat 10 miles across Manukau Harbour. A beautiful run of 2 hours brought us to Onehunga by noon. I landed there with my faithful Maori, Rota (Lot), who had steadily accompanied me from Kapiti, carrying my bag with gown and cassock, the only remaining articles in my possession of the least value. The suit which I wore was kept sufficiently decent, by much care, to enable me to enter Auckland by daylight; and my last remaining pair of shoes (thin ones) were strong enough for the light and sandy walk of six miles from Manukau to Auckland. At 2 P.M. I reached the Judge's house, by a path avoiding the town, passing over land which I have bought for the site of the cathedral; a spot which I hope may be hereafter traversed by the feet of many bishops, better shod and far less ragged than myself.

The plot of ground of which the Bishop wrote is the site on which a cathedral of noble proportions is being erected – only one of three cathedrals in process of construction in New Zealand today.

Auckland itself is a city of about 415,000 people, with a provincial total rapidly approaching one million. This figure represents more than 40 per cent of the entire population of New Zealand. What happens in the city, therefore, is of primary importance for Nation and Church. The Church is doing its best to keep up with new large-scale housing developments. It is not afraid of contemporary architecture in the building of new churches. It is willing to experiment with radio and television. And, in a welfare state whose prosperity has largely done away with the need for old-fashioned types of eleemosynary institutions, it is seeking new ways to put to the best use endowment funds it holds for the alleviation of those human needs that somehow persist in even the best regulated of welfare states.

Although we have been talking about "a very English country", the account would be incomplete if no mention is made of the Maoris. It was to them that the Church first went to minister, long before there was any thought of British colonization.

Warlike but intelligent, this sturdy and handsome race was quickly won for Christ – but Christians from Britain fast undid the victories. The original site of Auckland, to take but a single example, was purchased from the Maoris in 1860 for £66 in cash and £215 worth of trade goods. (It was almost as good a bargain as the Dutch received when they bought Manhattan from the American Indians.) From then on the New Zealand pattern followed all too closely the American. Colonization brought Christianity as its blessing; war, disease, expropriation, and exploitation as its bane. A vigorous race, once two hundred thousand strong, it dwindled until, by 1896, there were but forty-two thousand Maoris left. "A feeling of race despair" gripped the whole nation. It was everywhere assumed that the Maori would disappear altogether.

One of the surprising anthropological facts of the twentieth century is the sudden resurgence of the Maoris. Of full-blooded Maoris there are now more than twice the number that there were in 1896; and because many of them have intermarried with Europeans, one out of every ten New Zealanders can boast of having Maori blood in his veins. The Hunn Report, a recent scientific study commissioned by the government, predicts that by the year 2000, if the present trend continues, one out of every four persons you will have passed on Queen's Street in Auckland will be Maori – and two out of the four will be part Maori.

Such predictions provide additional ground for rejoicing that race relations in New Zealand on the whole, and especially within the Church, are good; but they also give reason for concern. The Church of England has never fully recovered from the loss of prestige it suffered in Maori estimation when English settlers, for a season, behaved so badly. To which must be added another factor. The initial evangelization of the Maoris, which is one of the most glorious chapters in the history of the Church Missionary Society, had the defect of its own virtue. Its teaching was more "Bible-centred" than "Church-centred". I put these phrases in quotation marks because we know that any proper exegesis of the Holy Scriptures leads straight on to Holy Church. But in history there has been a kind of Biblicism sometimes divorced from its proper setting in an ecclesiastical and sacramental context. A good illustration of this is the accusation, unjust though it is, brought against Luther himself that he discovered the Epistle to the Romans but did not discover the Epistle to the Ephesians. The Church Missionary Society has not always been guiltless in this respect. New Zealand is a case in point. So great is a Maori's veneration for the Bible and so scant is his instruction in the teachings of the Church that he is easily persuaded by any teacher who comes along with a Bible in his hand, able to quote without effort chapter and verse to bolster any doctrine whatsoever. For this reason the Mormon missionaries have been successful in New Zealand, I was told by one of the greatest champions of the Maoris. A man who knows his Bible, who can quote it from memory, and who has no trouble in opening it to find his proof-text, however much it may be wrenched from the context, at once wins recognition as a Christian teacher.

The plain but unpalatable truth is that we are fast losing our Anglican Maoris to Mormons, Seventh Day Adventists, and Jehovah's Witnesses. This is a judgement on us because, as one bishop expressed it, "we have taken too little trouble to come alongside our Maori brethren – and because we do not know our Bibles well enough".

Septuagesima 1961 found me worshipping with a small but enthusiastic group of Maori families in an Auckland suburb. I emphasize the word "families", for everything the Maoris do is done as a family. They are present in church from sightless grandmothers to toothless babies. These people are Maoris first, Christians second, Anglicans third. Whenever a bishop or priest of their own race arrives in a Maori village, all the citizens turn out to greet him, whatever their religious denomination, *because* he is a Maori and is recognized as an "elder" worthy of esteem.

My diary for that day contains the following notation: "Such hearty responses, done extempore in the form of a semi-chant! With spontaneity the congregation singing without accompaniment, fell into four-part harmony. The congregation has come from all over the greater Auckland area, many on foot from long distances and by bus (for few have cars) because, although most of them know English and are entirely welcome in parish churches, they prefer to worship in their own tongue. Time is no object. Only with difficulty did we begin as promptly as fifteen minutes late. The sermon – a good one – was preached first in Maori and then repeated in fluent English for the sake of the young people and children who are fast forgetting Maori. The Eucharist over, we all stayed on for the Baptism of three children. Then we repaired to the Parish Hall for tea – a kind of pot-luck supper – the main object of which was to fortify us for the many speeches, the shower-bath of oratory, which lay before us. Deeply beloved by the Maori is the meeting-house, the place where people get up and declare themselves. The Maori Christians have wisely incorporated this feature of village life into their system. Any slightest occasion is sufficient to provide the theme for elaborate addresses. Today the theme was me. Even though I was a total stranger to these folk (having descended upon them without warning), I set their tongues wagging for two full hours of speeches of welcome, both in Maori and in English. Principally they were glad to see me because I was the first American Anglican they had ever met. There was lusty audience participation in the speeches in the form of frequent exclamations of the Maori equivalent of '*i Olé!*' What chiefly delighted me was the fact that each speaker would interrupt his discourse from time to time and go into a *haka*, a combined song and dance, an improvisation based on old folk tunes and traditional steps combined with impromptu features born of the inspiration of the moment. The intervals in the music were new to my ears and I had never before known human feet to be capable of such astonishing percussive effects. The man who danced most gracefully of all was the retired priest, a patriarch of eighty-four."

My other contact with the Maoris was at Rotorua, a thermal region south-east of Auckland. The meeting-houses, splendid in a manner all their own, exhibit the artistic power of this race. Rotorua's large church built in the same style shows how Christianity – when it has the sense to do it– can baptize culture and bring it into the service of Christ's Kingdom. But we are far from consistent. Even though no Maori speech, Christian or otherwise, fails to eulogize the departed, there are still white Anglicans of evangelical persuasion in New Zealand who bitterly and vocally oppose prayers for the dead! Mormons with their genealogical studies and baptisms for the dead make sense to Maoris who wonder that Anglicans are so little mindful that it is a work of love to remember the dead.

The Church of the Province of New Zealand still claims the allegiance of 36 per cent of the Maori population. A major task of Anglicanism now is not to lose them. They are needed for the future of the country, and it is not fanciful to suppose that from their ranks could come a generation of missionaries to colour-conscious South-east Asia.

20

POLYNESIA: A Cinderella Story

FOUR HUNDRED OF US – ANGLICANS ALL – SAT DOWN TO LUNCH IN Nuku'alofa, the royal residential city of the Kingdom of Tonga.

The food was brought to us on litters – stretchers made of bamboo and attractively covered with ti leaves. The Bishop in Polynesia and I were placed with ten other persons at what I suppose must be called the "head litter". For the twelve of us seated in the place of honour on the grass there were, by actual count, twelve roasted suckling pigs entire, eighteen boiled lobsters, and twenty barbecued chickens. To ensure a balanced diet, there were also yams, assorted greens, and a cornucopia of fruit. The other guests fared just as richly.

For forks we used fingers. The function normally assigned to napkins was taken over by garlands of flowers around our necks and by beautiful cinctures of frangipani tied about our waists.

For hours we feasted, being entertained all the while by songs and dances. Hands gesturing expressively in accompaniment to song conveyed their story in spite of the language barrier. The bodies of dancers, bending in grace and in fury, quickly recapitulated the history, frustrations, fears, and hopes of an island people of whom, until recently, the outside world has taken little cognizance.

When the banquet was ended, the leftovers were borne in state to the Royal Palace as a gift to the court of Her Majesty Queen Salote Tubou. Truly, the leftovers, as well as the meal itself, were fit for a Queen.

Everybody remembers with affection how Queen Salote quite unintentionally nearly stole the show from Elizabeth of England at the latter's coronation. The London weather on that day was up to its old tricks. For every visiting head of state there had been provided both an open carriage and a closed limousine. Since rain was falling all other visitors elected the limousine. But not the Queen of Tonga! She rode to the Abbey in the rain, dispelling by her smile every trace of nature's gloom and winning by her gracious manner millions of friends for her island kingdom in the South Pacific. Although this royal Lady is herself a Methodist, she has been a great friend of ours. Under her protection, Anglican work is growing silently, slowly, but surely.

After sundown on the day of the feast I have described I remember exchanging a few pointed words with a young Mormon missionary whom I met at a reception given for the Bishop by the Premier, the princely brother of the Queen. Only lately have the Mormons begun work in the Kingdom of Tonga, but they have lost no time. "Riding in from the airport this morning," I said by way of making conversation, "I passed three brand-new churches, all of them good-looking, all of them belonging to the Latter Day Saints, one of them flanked by a splendid school building and another flanked by a Mission House resembling a superior American motel. For saints who arrived so late in the day," I added, guilty simultaneously of a bad pun and a breach of etiquette, "you have lost little time! Our own one church and school look pretty shabby by comparison."

"I don't understand you Episcopalians," he replied. "Don't you believe in the truth of what you stand for?"

I am not willing to do serious battle at a social function when I am a guest in somebody else's house – and in this case a royal house. Yet I permitted myself this much by way of rejoinder: "Yes, we believe in the truth entrusted to us, but we have never imagined ourselves to have a monopoly on it. And whereas we have not fallen into the relativistic idea that one Church is as good as any other, we realize that the field of the unevangelized is so large that it is strategically of paramount importance to accept the principle of the comity of missions. In other words, let us agree on a division of labour. Above all, let us refrain from sheep-stealing."

"You are an Episcopalian, right enough," said he, "and that is why your Church is doomed to remain a little one."

There was no anger in the interchange. It was just that two worlds of thought met – without meeting – on a tiny speck of land that for a few short miles is bold enough to raise its head above a great engulfing ocean.

In this oblique way I have been introducing you to the Diocese of Polynesia. Part of the Church of the Province of New Zealand, eleven hundred miles away, it may reasonably claim to be the biggest diocese in the world. There are some eleven million square miles of it, though most of it is water. Numerically, it is one of the smallest of the dioceses. The baptized membership totals no more than ten thousand persons.

Its Bishop must minister to people living under five different flags. Fiji, the real headquarters, is British (and geographically part of Melanesia, not Polynesia). Tonga is an independent kingdom under British protection. Tahiti is French. Eastern Samoa belongs to the United States.* The Cook Islands and Western Samoa fly the flag of New Zealand. Where but in Lambeth Palace could such a diocese have been dreamed up? Ever since its inception in 1908 it has remained a Cinderella diocese without even a Prince Charming to pay it an occasional visit. Unlike the Bishop of New Guinea with his aeroplane and the Bishop of Melanesia with his launch, the Bishop of this part of Oceania has no regular means of transportation. Sometimes he travels by commercial aircraft, although he can ill afford it. Occasionally he is carried gratis by the Royal New Zealand Air Force, and at other times, when the fleet is holding manœuvres in the area, the Bishop is welcome aboard a ship of the Royal New Zealand Navy. But how difficult to sit in Suva and plan one's work when most of the transportation factors are unknown quantities!

Because of the five flags, the Diocesan's title is Bishop *in* Polynesia rather than Bishop *of* Polynesia. Most of his flock are not Polynesians at all, but Melanesians and East Indians. And when a glorious grab-bag of Chinese, English, Americans, Australians, New Zealanders, Maoris, and French is added, it will be realized what a joy it is to see them kneeling side by side in the Cathedral at Suva.

To understand how it happens that this Polynesian diocese is chiefly Melanesian and East Indian we must take a quick glance at certain unsavoury facts of history.

Unscrupulous white men in the last century took their sailing ships into the bays and inlets of Melanesia – the Solomon and New Hebrides groups – and there, by fair talk, accomplished a foul deed. They "blackbirded" (i.e. kidnapped) labourers for the cotton and sugar cane fields of Fiji. That bad beginning had an even worse sequel. The Solomon Islander, having been brought to the islands under false pretences, could not adapt himself to his new surroundings and soon found himself "emancipated" but unemployed. The place intended for him was taken by indentured labour brought in from India. What, then, were the Solomon Islanders to do? They were not welcome any more in Fiji, but most of them – totally ignorant of geography – had no idea where they had come from. They would not have known how to find their home, even if they had had a means of getting there. They became, in the words of the Archdeacon of Fiji, "an unwanted remnant, landless, homeless, workless, and poverty-stricken".

* For the time being, Anglicans in American Samoa are under the ecclesiastical jurisdiction of the Bishop of Honolulu.

It must be remembered that in the Victorian era the Fiji Islanders were all Christian, thanks largely to the missionary efforts of the Methodists. No Anglican had yet appeared. But a committee that had been formed in Melbourne, Australia, sent to Fiji in 1870 the Reverend William Floyd to serve as a chaplain to British settlers at Levuka, then the capital of Fiji. On seeing the plight of the dispossessed imported labourers from the Solomon and New Hebrides island groups, he was not content to confine his ministry to the Europeans. And so he turned to the involuntary exiles, most of whom were not Christians, and laboured among them until his death in 1909.

The point I am making is that here as elsewhere Anglicanism did not proselytize from any orthodox Christian body. For this reason few native Fijians and Polynesians are Anglicans. Our ranks were recruited first from among the "blackbirded" ones, later from among the Indians. That in Polynesia we have won some Polynesian converts has been only a by-product, welcome but not calculated, of our "Melanesian Mission carried on within the Diocese of Polynesia".

I was taken to two of the Diocese's four settlements for these homeless and landless people. One of them, named for the martyred Bishop Patteson, is at Wailoku, seven miles from Suva. Here, on a 250-acre tract of land, the Church has built several villages. It operates a farm, runs a school, maintains a hospital.

The second settlement I visited was near Levuka on the island of Ovalau. To get to Levuka you can go by air if you are lucky enough to find a plane willing to fly and able to fly on the day you want to travel. Otherwise you take the bus from Suva and after a long ride transfer to a launch. In my case, it had to be the bus-launch combination because that day the aeroplane was ailing.

At the end of the line the Archdeacon and I tumbled out of the bus and toted our luggage out onto the jetty. Eyes more practised than mine scanned the sea to discern some sign of the launch. It was an hour before it hove into sight and another hour before it was alongside. The big launch that should have come for us much earlier was out of commission. A smaller, much slower craft had had to be pressed into service in its stead.

I wonder if people sitting at home in urban and industrial centres have any idea how much of an overseas missionary's time is consumed by waiting for planes that cannot fly, for buses that break down, for ships that have sprung a leak, and for punctured tyres that need patching. The transportation problems, the delays, the false starts, the mechanical failures, make planning your day the most tentative of all ventures. "Subject to change without notice" is the chief rubric under which missionaries must proceed.

By actual count, I was held up by thirty-nine punctures or blowouts in the course of my getting around the world. I changed five of the tyres myself when I was motoring with bishops who by reason of age or heart condition ought not to bend down to such tasks. For some time I have been trying to screw up my courage to address a personal letter to one manufacturer of automobile tyres, an Episcopalian of great wealth, to suggest to him that if he wishes to abet the Christian enterprise he can do it by sending out several carloads of tyres to missionaries. He is a literate man, and so would understand if I expatiated playfully on the connection between *pneuma* (even Holy *Pneuma*) and *pneumatiques*.

Landed at Levuka, I slithered up a mountain to be received tumultuously by a village of Melanesian Anglicans who staged for me marvellous dancing and singing. Yet "staged" is hardly the right word. This was nothing "put on" for tourists. No tourists ever come there. The stomping of bare feet on the ground, the snorting, the mock violence of preparing for war, the re-enactment of the tender rituals of courtship, were only their way of entertaining a visitor. Could I but bring a troupe of these dancers to New York, the Rockettes would have to look to their laurels.

When the sun immersed itself in the Pacific, there was a sudden mood of devotion. Evensong was sung in the open air by people who saw no necessity for making any quick change from grass skirts to Mother Hubbards. The beads, feathers, and flowers the women had on their heads and around their necks, wrists, and ankles stayed there, as did the red-and-black smudges simulating war paint on the bodies of the men.

With the coming of nightfall I half fell, half slid down the mountainside, where I had had one of the great afternoons of my life, and repaired to the rectory to spruce up a bit for dinner. By the time I emerged, the screened-in porch was full of guests. And this company of politely spoken, conservatively clad people was the same group that I had seen only an hour before. Gone were the grass skirts, the garlands of flowers, and the necklaces of sharks' teeth. Instead were simple evening frocks of European design for women, the sack suit for men. The extraordinary thing was that these people were as much at home in the one world as in the other. They took equal pride in both, and with equal gravity and sagacity they discussed with me Melanesian folklore and the coming Every Member Canvass. They mingled with unconscious grace and poise among the Europeans who had also come to dinner. They did not ape Europeans. They were themselves. Nor did the Europeans act condescendingly. White, black, Indian, or mixed they all simply were having a good time together.

These are the islanders whom I joined the next morning just at daybreak for a celebration of the Holy Communion. Throughout the service one fact was uppermost in my mind. We were the first Anglican congregation in the whole world to offer on that day the Holy Eucharist. Levuka lies only slightly west of the International Date Line. From the altar of the church at Levuka rises, day after day, that day's first outpouring of Thanksgiving. Long before we had finished, other congregations to the west of us had taken up our paean of praise and grateful remembrance, and so it would go on, hour after hour, without ceasing until day was done . . . to be accomplished again the next day, but always a day that begins, by human reckoning, in the Diocese of Polynesia.

There is now no hymn that I sing with more feeling than the one which begins, "The day thou gavest, Lord, is ended."

Some evening, if you find yourself in Labasa on the island of Vanua Levu and have nothing better to do, hop into the Land Rover with the local priest, as I did, and drive out to a little village north of town whose inhabitants are Indians, many of them unemployed because the factories where sugar cane is refined have had to curtail production and in some cases are shut down completely. Most of the older people are either Hindus or Muslims. The immigration of Indian indentured labour began in 1879. Today the non-Christian Indians outnumber the Fijians, who are all Christians. Of one hundred and fifty thousand Indians, only about five thousand are Anglicans.

The younger Indians born in Fiji, knowing no other land and yet not loved in this one, are not quite sure *what* they are. The evening I was at the village above Labasa, they came by the hundreds from miles around to look at the movies the priest was going to show. I helped him get the projector out and set up the generator. It balked. Three times during the evening it broke down, for it was old. The film broke, too, and had to be spliced. But the people patiently waited. They had nothing else to do, and they did not seem to mind delay. He showed films about health and hygiene and the care of infants. He showed a film depicting an episode from the Life of our Lord and a dramatization of one of his parables. He flashed on the screen a sequence taken during the Lambeth Conference: the bishops were seen entering St. Paul's. When I exhibited colour slides of New York Cathedral, "ohs" and "ahs" of astonished admiration came from the audience. "We did not *know* that Christians have temples such as these!"

What is the meaning of such a scene? Is it just the white man trying to bedazzle a gullible and uneducated son of an indentured labourer brought from India, who does not know where he is going or what he is getting into? Cynics may answer Yes. But what if the white man who prods the balky generator, silently cursing, and threads the film is a highly intelligent, highly educated New Zealander, whose face might have been his fortune if he had applied to J. Arthur Rank; a man who worked like a slave to master Hindi precisely for the purpose of sailing out to this remote and apparently insignificant island; a man worried about the fact that his children are reaching an age at which they must be sent away to school – because they soon will have outgrown our Indian schools at Labasa. But where? New Zealand and Australia are too far. Hawaii – 2,776 miles to the north – is also too far. Even Suva is too far in view of the paltry stipend he receives from a diocese willing to pay, but chronically on the verge of bankruptcy. A ministry like his has the quality of sacrifice: a fact the cynic would do well to take into consideration, even if the cynic were still to regard it as a case of misplaced zeal.

This points to one of the chief problems of a diocese like Polynesia. How, when a bishop is habitually short of funds, is he going to be able to staff the outer islands?

In the afternoon before our evening excursion to show films to Muslims and Hindus just north of Labasa I had been taken south of Labasa to a village called Batanikama whose citizens are Indian Anglicans. We had Evening Prayer in Hindi, not far from a sugar-cane refinery that was shut down for a season. We worshipped in a rude hut, a *bure* made of lime and clay and cow dung with a thatched roof, dark, without electricity or windows, yet scrupulously clean. We sat on reed m'ats on the floor. The congregation of about forty was devout and eager to participate, but not too well instructed. Only a few knew the Psalms and Canticles by heart, and there were not enough Prayer Books in Hindi to go around even to those who could read. And who *could* read in this darkness? Many were recent converts – often at considerable cost to themselves, for it seems that Indians, though long separated from Mother India, have yet carried with them their Mother's abhorrence of people who embrace Christianity.

After service I was interested in a list the Indian evangelist possesses of the ships that arrived from India bearing indentured labourers. This list is helpful in establishing the approximate age of the older Indians who often do not know how old they are, except that they remember they arrived as children on such and such a ship. Tea was served in the same building where we had worshipped. That seemed to me singularly appropriate – a genuine *agapé*.

With grave dignity, a young girl, representing the congregation, came forward and placed a garland of flowers around my neck. Then I was asked many questions about the Cathedral in New York. "What is your church like?" they wanted to know. I told of its dimensions – not to boast but to let this small simple isolated congregation, which knows of the fabulous Hindu temples and Muslim mosques, realize that Christianity also has outward magnificence. Fortunately, I had pictures of the Cathedral. As they were passed about, the gasps of amazement and delight were loudly audible. The length and height staggered them. But the proportions were too gigantic for their imaginations to grasp. What they really appreciated, interestingly enough, was a picture of a stained-glass window which I told them was forty feet high. "Why, that," they exclaimed delightedly, "is exactly the height of the tower we hope to build on the new church in Labasa!" Here was something within their ken. Later that evening, when the Indian evangelist came to dinner, he said to me, "I went straight home from Evening Prayer and told my wife that the window in St. John the Divine is as tall as our tower is going to be." "The window" were his very words. It could not occur to him that the Cathedral has sixteen such windows. I did not tell him. There is no point in overdoing it, no point in straining people's credulity.

What I liked best was that there was not a trace of envy. There was only joy in realizing that Christianity too has its worthy monuments – and a proper pride in the fact that the Christians of near-by Labasa were going to have a tower – not a tower so high that it would reach into the heavens (for that, we know, would be *hubris*), but one that would be as high as the window of the Cathedral Church of St. John the Divine. These people are part of the Anglican Family; they too lift up their hearts – and just as highly. Let anyone smile who will. I myself found it beautiful and humbling.

If you can sit on a cow-dung floor and be unemployed and uncertain of your next meal, yet want to erect for the glory of God a tower that shall be forty feet high, and to that end are willing to fast, work, and pray – well, I leave it to the reader to complete this sentence, remarking only that before the sentence can be declared complete, it should contain some meed of praise for those who harbour such aspirations – and perhaps also a word of exhortation to others who, being possessed of such windows, seem not to care that certain of their brothers not only have no tower for their church – their church is windowless.

2 1

NEW GUINEA: Martyrs and Missions

AN OVERNIGHT FLIGHT FROM AUSTRALIA BROUGHT ME EARLY ONE
February morning in 1961 to Port Moresby, capital of the Territory of
Papua and New Guinea. After a brief visit to the Franciscan Priory and
after taking breakfast with the parish priest, I was put aboard a spic-and-
span Cessna 188, the name of which was "St. Gabriel" – with "Alfa Bravo
Mike" as its call sign, A.B.M. to stand for the Australian Board of Missions.
Papua and New Guinea are the special responsibility of the Australian
Church. "St. Gabriel," it might be noted, was a gift of the American
Church.

Father Hume, Director of the Society of the Sacred Mission, was my
fellow passenger. Off we flew, piloted expertly by a young man splendidly
named Henri Jules Monod de Froideville. He made things easier for us:
"Call me Hans," he said.

We had flown for an hour or so when the radio barked out an order to
the pilot: "Go to such and such a plantation. Pick up a Papuan who's
been bitten by a black snake. Take him to hospital in Moresby." Hans
found the plantation and landed in a small clearing. Some forty or fifty
Papuans, wrapped in grief and not much else, were wailing hysterically.
They knew the black snake and the deadliness of its bite. They feared they
were saying good-bye for ever to their stricken friend. Father Hume and
I, bag and baggage, were pitched out of the plane. The Papuan, more
frightened perhaps by the plane than by his wound, was put aboard. Saying
that he'd be back for us "sometime", Hans revved his engine and flew
away.

Treading our way carefully so as not to step on a black snake ourselves,
the monk and I walked over to a tractor-pulled cart that conveyed us to
the plantation house. The English owner and his two Australian overseers,
though deeply sorry about the reason for our presence, were none the less

overjoyed to have visitors. Outsiders do not come calling every day in Papua. Their hunger for news of the world at large gave me a clue to the isolation and loneliness of this area.

Hours later "St. Gabriel" buzzed us from above, and by the time the plane had landed we were already tractorborne back to the tiny clearing.

The mountains of New Guinea constitute a formidable barrier, and a Cessna 188 is really no match for them. But we surmounted them and came at last to Dogura, on the north coast of New Guinea, where the Cathedral is located. A splendid sight that edifice is from the air! A building of noble proportions and perfectly suited to the terrain and the climate, it crowns a promontory jutting out into a lonely sea. Never in my life, I think, have I felt so cut off from the rest of the world. Dogura enjoys little else but isolation.

That first impression, however, was an airborne mistake promptly corrected as soon as we were on the ground. To meet us were a bishop, a dean, schoolteachers and schoolchildren – Episcopalians all, waving and friendly, and as attractive a group of human beings as I had ever seen. The welcome they gave us was tumultuous, and Evening Prayer in the great Cathedral Church was exactly like one I would have experienced in Canterbury, New York, or Melbourne, except that the singing was heartier and the congregation somewhat on the naked side. Strangely enough, in such a setting near-nudity did not seem conspicuous. Apart from my noticing it on first arrival, it was promptly forgotten. The grass skirts worn by women and girls shone like cloth of gold and complemented perfectly the fine texture of their very dark skin. Acolytes at the altar, clad only in a wraparound, knee-length white skirt, moved with the dignity of Egyptian princes. Had either men or women worn more, they would have seemed overdressed.

Dinner ended, we discharged the sacred obligation of listening to the news. Even in so isolated a place as Dogura one must take world events into account – for how else might a Christian's prayers be *informed*? I have heard the Bishop of California remark that for a Christian "the Eleventh Commandment is: 'Thou *shalt* read the daily papers'." In Dogura there are, of course, no newspapers. The wireless is the thing. How many, many nights during my junket I sat with mission folk as they clustered around the one radio, straining their ears to catch the news that was often scarcely audible above the splutter of static. One gets a sense of the size and reality of the British Commonwealth of Nations when one has seen, in hundreds of lonely outposts, the fidelity with which the B.B.C. newscast is listened to. "This is London calling" are comfortable words, almost mystical in their power to bind together a people dispersed throughout the world.

The plan had been for a mission launch to carry Father Hume and me the next morning to the village where Bishop Ambo makes his headquarters. George Ambo is a Papuan, the first of his nation to be elevated to high office in the Church. He is one of two bishops who assist the Diocesan. Our journey proved impossible because the launch had had to be commandeered to take a person stricken with appendicitis to the hospital at Samarai. Since we could not go to him, it was agreed that Bishop Ambo would come to us in his small boat. He was to arrive at ten o'clock in the morning.

While waiting for him, we used the time to visit the mission schools. As buildings they would win no prize, but it is phenomenal what the teachers – Australians and Papuans – are able to accomplish with equipment of the meanest sort. Of "teaching aids" there is hardly anything. The word "school" suggests to British and Americans such obvious requisites as books, paper, pencil, maps, blackboards, and chalk. But teaching aids of this sort are in short supply, not only in New Guinea but throughout much of the Anglican world. I marvel that teachers can "make do" with so little. No praise is too high for their ingenuity in concocting educational tools that nobody has provided for them. It comes closer to *creatio ex nihilo* than anything I have ever beheld.

The schoolchildren at Dogura have been brought there from all over the Territory. It is the busy work of mission launches to sail around and pick them up and to take them home again once a year for vacation. The eager young pupils do not come by train or bus for the simple but all sufficient reason that there are none. "But why, then, was the central mission station built in such a remote and inaccessible place?" was the question asked of me by a New York lady. The answer was that in New Guinea *every* place is equally remote from every other place. New Guinea is a wilderness of savage green. As someone has said, "This place is good for despair. Nature must have been in a foul mood when she fashioned New Guinea." It was only with difficulty, however, that I convinced this lady that the purchase of gasoline has something to do with the propagation of the Gospel. No gas, no Gospel. No launch, no liberation. It is as elementary and as evangelical as that.

The schools at Dogura carry children through the eighth grade. Then, if they show signs of promise, they are sent on to secondary schools located elsewhere in the Diocese. On reaching manhood some of them come back to Dogura to enrol either in the excellent school where catechists are trained or else in the theological college where an Australian, single-handed, and in a tumbledown house, does a remarkable job of preparing them for Ordination. Girls grown to womanhood sometimes come back to test their vocation for the religious life at Dogura's convent. Others come back to teach or to nurse. (see Pl. 41).

Our inspection of the elementary schools, the catechetical school, the theological college, and the convent was repeatedly interrupted by side trips to the edge of the promontory to scan the sea for some sign of Bishop Ambo. Where could he be? As the day wore on I could feel Bishop Strong's anxiety mount. By suppertime he was almost ill, though he did his best to conceal it. He tried to be a good host. My questions were courteously answered. But every few minutes the Bishop, not realizing that his sighs were audible, muttered, "But where is he?" For one of the rare times in his missionary career, the Bishop absented himself from the nightly ritual of listening to the B.B.C. Nobody commented, but we knew he had gone in all stillness to the Cathedral to pray. For few are the men who know better than the Bishop of New Guinea the treachery of those seas.

The silence of an uneasy night was broken at ten-thirty when the youth who had been posted at the headland to watch cried out, "A light, a light!" And then he arrived. Tall, handsome in face, magnificent in build: a bishop bone-tired. His engine had failed him, and he had been swept out to sea. That, he explained in apology, was the reason for his being twelve and a half hours late. In spite of fatigue, he was more than willing to let me ply him with questions until after midnight, for he knew that I had to press on early the next morning.

Now this was the man who nearly gave his life to help me with my Grand Tour of Anglicanism. After Mass on the morrow, I asked to photograph him. He consented, but requested time that he might go first and array himself in purple cassock. He understood enough about the outside world to know that cassock and pectoral cross would be expected of him. One must look the part. The attire became him superbly. But in my eyes he never looked more a bishop than when I first saw him by the feeble ray of my flashlight, climbing ashore, dripping wet in shorts and drooping with fatigue. Seldom in my life have I seen a face as strong as his or as gentle. There were mystic depths in his eyes and infectious gaiety in his smile – wisdom, too, in what he had to tell me.

Because his motor was so far gone that it could not be repaired until the engineer of the big launch returned, Bishop Ambo decided to go back to his village on foot. And so this dignified but unassuming man, as if he had done a mere *nothing* for me, set off to tackle the twenty-five miles of mountain and swamp between Dogura and his village. It is not often that I weep, but as I watched him go, his broad black shoulders hidden finally by the bush, I wept. There went a Prince of the Church, whose father had been a headhunter and a cannibal.

"St. Gabriel's" wings were soon heard in the skies over Dogura, and before long we were airborne, *en route* to visit, in rapid succession, several mission stations, including an Anglican sanatorium for victims of tuberculosis. But once again careful plans miscarried. After about thirty-five minutes, the plane's radio conked out. "This is serious," said Hans, "for if they do not hear from us every half-hour they send out a search plane." While debating what to do Hans spotted a mission launch riding at anchor in a bay. He set the plane down at a mission station called Wanigela, only about three miles distant from the launch.

Luck was with us. An English planter by the name of Imlay was passing just at that moment, and in his jeep we rode to the shore. There we pressed into service an outrigger canoe and paddled out to the mission launch. Nobody was aboard. We used its radio and called and called: Port Moresby, Samarai, Lae. No answer. Presently we heard the drone of a motor. There was the search plane out looking for us. It spotted the grounded "St. Gabriel" and was waiting for us when we returned. The pilot used its radio to tell the Aeronautical Authorities in Port Moresby why we were on silence. Instructions totally unambiguous were shot back. "You can't fly with passengers aboard when your radio is on the blink. Ditch them, fly to Moresby, get the radio repaired, then go back and retrieve them."

The search plane, not powerful enough to carry two men and their baggage, took to the skies. So for a second time Father Hume and I were pitched out into the awful greenery that is New Guinea. Meanwhile, ominous clouds had rolled up to blacken and obscure the mountains. I could read apprehension in the young pilot's face. "Hans," I said, "don't you go to Moresby out of any mistaken loyalty to Father Hume and me, in an effort to salvage our schedule. That's knocked into a cocked hat anyway. The main thing is your safety and also the safety of this plane." "No," he said, "I think I must go." So, feeling more than a little abandoned, we watched him disappear, a tiny speck moving up to affront that wall of mountains. What happened we learned only later. Hans forced the Cessna to 16,000 feet in an attempt to get over the mountains and the storm. Its ceiling is 10,000 feet. Realizing that he could not make it across, Hans turned back to the nearest mission station, landed his plane, alighted, and fell to the ground in a dead faint from cold, lack of oxygen, and sheer anxiety.

Thus it came about that Father Hume and I had an impromptu weekend at Wanigela. A finer week-end I have never spent. More comfortable ones, yes. But it was a joy to see a bit of village life at close range and to begin to understand what a difference it has made that the Church is there.

Hans came back for us two days later. By-passing intermediate stops called for by the original itinerary, he took us to the great station at Popondetta. Here I found schools in profusion, here I said good-bye to Father Hume, and here I made contact with a burly bull-necked bishop by the name of

Hand, the senior of Bishop Strong's two assistants. Only later did I learn that he is a cousin of my own Bishop of New York.

By this time I felt a great bond with Hans, and it saddened me when this manly pilot confessed to me that the following week he was resigning. "I'm sorry," he said, "but these mountains give me the creeps. A two-engine plane would be all right, but a one-engine job just isn't up to it." What a pity it is that the Diocese of New Guinea knew so little about aviation that it did not ask the American Church for a twin-engine plane from the start. Americans would gladly have given it in the beginning but would be less generously inclined today, for they are impatient of technical incompetence. And in addition to that, the whole American act of generosity in having presented a plane to New Guinea must be called into question. Great-hearted was the gift. So like my fellow countrymen. But why was the American Church not wise enough first to inquire about the geography of New Guinea and the type of plane that would be most useful? And who made further inquiry into the capacity of the Diocese to maintain this plane?

In point of fact, "St. Gabriel" has had to be grounded much of the time because of the financial inability of the Diocese to keep it in operation. And Hans was not the first pilot to be frightened away by sabre-toothed mountains for which the Cessna was never designed. His predecessor, who now flies two-engine planes for a commercial airline and who several times let me join him in the cockpit as we soared over fierce terrain, told me the whole story. It is folly, he said, to attempt a twelve- to fifteen-thousand-foot mountain range with only one engine. The Aeronautical Authorities require that the pilot have at least five hundred hours of previous experience in the air and that he be able to repair his own plane. Mechanic he must be as well as pilot. And the Diocese, in its turn, must require that the pilot risk his neck day after day for a salary barely equal to the cost of simple board and room for a single man. Not that the Diocese is niggardly. It merely is hard up. These are the facts that have kept the Diocese of New Guinea from using for many months its beautiful, American-given "St. Gabriel". It has had to be rented out to a commercial firm – the rates have been useful – and the Diocese occasionally charters it back when it has to entertain "visiting firemen" like Father Hume and me.

Americans should think twice before they give. Sometimes by their very generosity they succeed only in embarrassing and impoverishing people. Since coming home from my Grand Tour I spoke to a wealthy American businessman about one wonderful diocese that is hampered by the fact that it owns not a single automobile. Typically American, he reached down into his pocket and was ready to hand me the price of an automobile on the spot. But that would avail nothing! Of what use would an automobile be to that diocese so long as it had not the wherewithal to buy the gasoline to keep it going? The wealth of even the poorest of Americans prevents them from understanding the rest of the world.

My host at Popondetta was suffering from hepatitis, a disease that seems to have a particular fondness for missionaries, or else missionaries have a special vulnerability to it. Leaving him to languish in the shade, I surveyed his church and his schools. A feature of Popondetta is its technical school where Papuans and citizens of New Guinea are introduced to such puzzling contraptions as motors and generators – a strange new world. The speed with which young men master these intricacies quickly teaches the outsider a necessary lesson I have learned many times over, though these people may be primitive, they are not stupid.

I was taken upcountry over an unbelievable stretch of road to see the Martyrs' School and, across the river, a mission compound. The school was in turmoil. One of the students had just died. Death struck with unexpected swiftness, and, although most deaths are irrationally premature, this one was especially sinister. The Church had been trying for years to coax a shy mountain tribe to come down from the heights and avail itself of the education we offer. At length the chief, dubious still, had sent six young men to the Martyrs' School, his own son one of them. He was the lad who, unaccountably, sickened and died in the space of one afternoon, the fifth day of term. The death might easily have been prevented if only our school had been equipped with an infirmary. But now our work there may be put back for who knows how many years because the first time a chief entrusted his son to us, there was death.

My host, Australian-born and New York-trained, came from the autopsy and drove me out to a village where elders, gravely squatting in a square listened to my credentials as set forth by their pastor and nodded in quiet acknowledgement when I thanked them for the way in which New Guinea had received and helped American servicemen during World War II. Then their gift to me arrived. On a stout bamboo pole borne on the shoulders of Herculean men came a pig, trussed up by its feet, very much alive and very vocal in protest. I explained to my benefactors that airlines are firm in their prohibition against taking animals aboard. The villagers seemed not displeased by my suggestion that the pig be given to the students at the Martyrs' School for a feast.

The martyrs for whom this fine secondary school is named were Christians slaughtered by the Japanese in World War II. They were in my mind as I fell asleep that night, and also in my consciousness before slumber overtook me was the awareness that I made my bed on the slopes of Mount Lamington which, erupting violently in 1951, had smothered, with sovereign indifference, pagan and Christian alike. The volcano all but extinguished the Church. It snuffed out the lives of fourteen missionaries, and of the four thousand persons killed, a great many were followers of the Way.

The next day I took a farewell look at the pig – and almost resolved to become a vegetarian. I pressed on to a remotely situated Franciscan priory. The monks are accustomed to eat in silence, but being given to hospitality, they broke the rule in order to talk with me. My stay, however, was cut short because one novice had been taken ill just before I arrived. Polio- myelitis was feared, and it proved to be so. We got him as quickly as we could to a hospital; and then, when I wanted most of all to bathe and rest, having been exposed to both hepatitis and poliomyelitis, I found that Bishop Hand had other plans for me. We were off for Gona.

Gona was famous in World War II because it was there that the Japanese invaders behaved so cruelly. Church buildings were turned into barracks, and churchmen valiant enough to defend the buildings were promptly beheaded. Later, in pitched battle involving a quarter of a million men, American forces drove out the foe and took over. It is today, however, a quiet place. Only spiritual warfare is being waged – but that is of an intensive sort, with a central station, schools, and outstations.

To get to Gona you drive down to the coast from Popondetta, park the Jeep, borrow a flimsy raft, and punt your way across a broad and shallow lagoon. Then you have a walk of several miles along the beach and in the shade of palm trees. Villagers you pass look up from their labours and give you a friendly wave. That night, when we retraced our steps with only flashlights to point out the path, it was raining ferociously. When we reached the lagoon, the raft was nowhere to be found. We had to decide whether to follow the shoreline all the way around, which would have meant a trek of many miles, or else plunge into the lagoon and wade across. We chose the latter course. Being wet to the skin already, it mattered little that we should get in deeper. So the Bishop, his houseboy Aidan, and I spent the next hour, not unpleasantly, sloshing through water that most of the time was only knee-deep, though occasionally it liked to surprise us by taking us in up to our waists, and once for sheer caprice – to keep us from monotony – it took the bottom out from under us altogether.

I enjoyed that midnight walk. But enough is enough, and therefore I thought it was one hardship too many that the jeep, when we returned to it, would not start. It did not respond to treatment, though the Bishop tinkered with it diligently. The three of us were unable to push it fast enough through the sand to get it going again. So the Bishop went and woke up the near-by village. Men and boys came most willingly, although it was by now two o'clock in the morning. Nothing was too much or too good for their Shepherd. By their united strength we were soon bouncing merrily along the road back to Popondetta.

On entering the missionary's darkened house, I nearly tripped over a human figure lying prone on the floor. That afternoon the dormitory of the girls' school, perched on stilts, had gently subsided to the ground and then collapsed altogether. Thus the missionary's wife had on her hands not only a sick husband and their small children but also a bishop and his servant and a visiting canon and a missionary couple in transit *and* twenty-seven adolescent girls asleep on the floor. Quite a household – and in such an inadequate house! She had neither electricity nor running water to help her. But she took it all with total calm. I thought to myself: The day of the pioneer woman is not over.

And so came to an end a day which perhaps I have described in greater detail than it deserves, yet I know of no better way to convey an impression of what life is like in some of the mission fields. These are the conditions under which the Church labours in New Guinea, and there are other places just as rugged. Not that a girls' dormitory collapses every day or that a missionary comes down with hepatitis. But if it is not that, it is always something else. Or, as we say in French, *Il y a quelque damn chose tout le temps!*

There was an eighteen-year-old boy at the Martyrs' School, Gideon, who had especially distinguished himself in his studies. As a reward, and in the hope that it would prove an incentive to the boy to continue his education, the Bishop wanted him to see something of the world outside. To me was accorded the privilege of superintending that lad's introduction to the world. I was to take him with me by air from Popondetta to Port Moresby. Until that day, Gideon's world had been an area twenty miles square, all of it alike, a uniform tangle of green. The aeroplane did not excite him as much as I had thought it would. He was not afraid of it, but neither did he show any special elation. Thinking back on this, I believe the reason for his almost phlegmatic indifference to the flight and the stunning aerial views was that it was too much for him, more than he could fully take in.

The fun for him and for me began, however, the moment we landed at Moresby. Gideon's first act was to stamp the pavement with his foot – and then stamp it again. He was intrigued by the hard surface. I realized then that he had never seen a paved road before. The next novelty to absorb his interest was the sedan in which the rector of Port Moresby had come to fetch us. Gideon's eyes lighted up, and shaking his head slowly from left to right, an admiring smile on his face, he paid his tribute to the sedan: "*Nice* truck!" he said, and for emphasis he said it again, "*Nice* truck!" Prior to this moment he had seen nothing more elegant than a Land Rover or jeep. When he was about to get into the car, his eye fell on the ceiling light which had automatically gone on by the opening of the door. Gideon paused, still standing outside the car. Then gently he shut the door and saw that the light had gone out. Cautiously he opened the door – and behold! there was light. Whereupon, in a kind of ecstasy, he shut it, opened it, shut it, opened it. It was as if he could not get his fill of this culminating miracle.

Bishop Hand was concerned that Gideon should go down to the docks and board a freighter. For the first time in his life he saw white men doing manual labour. That was important. He had not known that whites, except for missionaries, ever worked. We obliged him to watch as barrels and crates were hoisted out of the hold. We made him read how they were marked: "Made in Britain", "Made in U.S.A.", "Made in Japan", etc. This was more important still, for New Guinea, like many parts of the South Pacific, is in the grip of a strong delusion called the "Cargo Cult". Where this delusion originated and how it got around is unknown, but thousands of these people are honestly convinced that their ancient gods have beneficently sent shipload after shipload of wonderful presents to them but that wicked white men, pirates, have hijacked the cargoes at sea and appropriated the whole loot to their own selfish use. The "Cargo Cult" is the dominant religion here today. It was no waste, therefore, of a bishop's time to see to it that a promising young man like Gideon, potential leader of his people, should talk with stevedores and merchant seamen. When people in Britain or America or Canada, stimulated by a missionary sermon and a rousing hymn, "fork out" half a crown or half a dollar, do they give half a care as to how their money is used? Would they, I wonder, give less or more if they knew that some of their money might go to letting a Gideon see for himself?

We handed Gideon over to the good Franciscan Fathers for safekeeping. Bishop Hand and I flew on into the interior. Ruined for ever were the plans for my hiking to several stations in the mountains, but the Bishop was unwilling that I should leave the Diocese without having a taste at least of the Highlands. This part of New Guinea was virtually unknown to the white man prior to 1933, and much of it remains to be explored. The Highlands are far more densely populated than the coastal areas. The climate is better; the soil, superior. The voracious white ant, curse of the Lowlands, cannot stand these heights. There is almost no malaria nor tuberculosis. People, having more to eat, are better built and more energetic. Here it is possible to do a day's work. "The future," declared Bishop Hand, "belongs to the Highlands."

On our way we touched down at a mining centre named Wau, which has a short, slanting airstrip, and is hemmed in by steep mountains on all sides. The gradient on the runway is one in twelve! Wau and places like it, all of them new, not only bring Europeans on to the scene, who need the ministrations of the Church, but also serve as a magnet drawing from the mountains shy folk who until now have lived beyond the perimeter of the rest of the human race. Everything develops so rapidly that the Diocese, though straining every nerve, cannot keep abreast.

Somehow or other our DC-3 with bucket seats got in and out of Wau, and on we flew to Goroka, a mile-high city created by coffee. Ten years ago there was nothing on this site save a government patrol post and one trader. Today it bustles. But it is a town built by air. Absolutely everything which went into its making was flown in. Even now the town is totally dependent on air transport, for the existing roads are of little use. Although obviously destined to become a big city, it is still the pioneer town of general stores and unpaved muddy streets. But the homes of the Europeans are big and sumptuous, the beauty of their lawns enhanced by massive banks of poinsettias . . . and defaced by large ugly signs that display, in red paint, the forbiddingly upraised palm of a man's hand, under which is printed the uninviting word TAMPU, taboo.

Most of the owners of these homes, if they go to church at all, go to the Anglican church. Most of the Papuans are Seventh Day Adventists, Roman Catholics, and Lutherans. Our church *looks* the more flourishing i.e. there are more cars parked in front of it on a Sunday morning; but there will be more people inside the other churches – Papuans who come on foot. I am not criticizing the work we are doing among the Europeans – necessary and splendid as it is. They too have souls! And it is by their industry that Papuans are being brought to a level of culture, health, and financial security undreamed of before. But not enough of these Papuans are in church *with* us. It is significant that the Roman Catholics have a complete Mass in Pidgin, a language which philologists call Neo-Melanesian, while we in the towns continue to minister in Elizabethan English. But all of this will change in due course under the leadership of Bishop Hand and the Melanesian Brothers who have come from the Solomon Islands to help him. Of this Brotherhood more will be said in the next chapter, when we thrust out into the incredible far reaches of the South Pacific.

Bishop Hand loves these towns, but I surmise that his heart is even higher in the Highlands, up among peoples who have never been evangelized by anybody. Civilization has passed them by. As for the calendar, it could be *any* century. Not far removed is the time when a Highlander's prowess was reckoned in terms of the number of heads he had shrunk – and not all love for this sport has been eradicated yet. The picture is gradually changing, thanks to the combined efforts of Church and State. The optimistic report contained in government surveys is that "the natives" are now – nice euphemism – "pacified". But most of them do not yet know the peace of Christ.

"One of the deepest factors in New Guinean life," the Bishop told me as we waited for the overdue aeroplane that was to return me to the coast, "is fear – fear of sorcery, fear of evil spirits. And now there are the new fears engendered by the sudden eruption of modernity – the baffling presence of bulldozers and banks and the even more baffling people, the pale ones, who run them."

This hiker-bishop and his mountain-climbing Melanesian associates already see proof, in village after village, that Christ is more than a match for the ancient fear-inspiring *tampus*. Yet it remains to be seen whether or not Christ can conquer in the towns so long as his progress is impeded by rich European settlers who plant their gardens with signs reading TAMPU. Divine omnicompetence I do not mean to question. But European stubbornness must never be underestimated.

It is only fair to add that numerous Europeans are benefactors of the Bishop's work and rally around him as his staunchest allies.

The population of Papua and New Guinea is estimated to be 2,000,000. Rome has 500,000 of these on her rolls; the Lutherans, 200,000 (this was formerly German territory); the London Missionary Society (chiefly Congregationalist), over 100,000; the Methodists, probably 80,000; ourselves, about 50,000, although, if we add catechumens, our numbers would be much higher. But here again, as so often is the case, we are low down in the scale. My judgement on the *quality* of the work carried on here by Australian Anglicans can best be conveyed if I relate the following story.

At the end of my journey around the world – a journey I have called a "long, lovely, laborious lark" – I had the honour of addressing the House of Deputies of the General Convention of the Protestant Episcopal Church of the U.S.A. assembled in Detroit. Afterwards a layman came up to me in the corridor and handed me two checks, saying, "I wish these could be larger. But will you not send them to the two places you found in your travels where you felt the need is greatest and some money might do the most good." Without hesitation I said, "I can tell you right now that your money will go to New Guinea and Melanesia."

And to Melanesia the reader is now invited to go. I volunteer my services as guide. For after New Guinea I myself took flight for those distant isles which our Maker, for reasons obscure to me, chose to place in the middle of nowhere.

22

MELANESIA: The "Do-it-yourself" Diocese

IT TOOK ELEVEN HOURS OF ERRATIC FLIGHT TO GO FROM LAE, ON THE north coast of New Guinea, to Honiara, capital of the British Solomon Islands. Here the Bishop has his seat but not his palace. His palace is a ship, and he himself holds papers as a Master Mariner.

People who do not know the name Honiara will more quickly get their bearings if I say that we have arrived now at Guadalcanal, an island which cost many lives in World War II. The route there involved stops at New Britain, Bougainville, New Georgia, and the Russell Islands: exact line of advance of the Japanese invasion.

I was glad I had not missed my early morning flight. A late-comer would have been obliged to wait in Lae a fortnight. Service in this part of the world is not frequent. But we were storm-tossed all the way, and since it was not possible to get above the storm, we tried to fly under it. For hours on end we skimmed along at an elevation of no more than six hundred feet, and I had the feeling that at any moment waves would wash the belly of the plane.

I landed at Honiara, a town which did not exist until the great Pacific War brought it into being. It was just time for Evensong. The pro-Cathedral of this extraterritorial New Zealand Diocese consists of two Quonset huts thrown together. Six hundred persons were present – quite a congregation when you take into account that the total population of the capital of this protectorate is less than three thousand. Impressed by what I saw, I asked, "Is today something special?" "No," was the reply, "we average about six hundred on ordinary weekdays. On Holy Days, of course, the number is greater." I do not want to be guilty of romanticizing and therefore I must add that part of the reason for this phenomenon is that in Honiara there is simply nothing else to do. Churchgoing provides a break in the monotony. Yet the Church in these islands *is* the centre of life.

In my naïveté I requested a half-hour's freedom the next morning to get a haircut. "We have no barber in town," I was told, "but Luke, our Polynesian skipper, will take care of you as we sail today to Nggela, the island the Spaniards called Florida. He keeps us all in trim." Honiara, capital city though it is, has neither a barber nor a jeweller. Nor does it have either a lawyer or doctor in private practice.

On the 7th March, 1961, the twenty-first anniversary of my Ordination to the Priesthood, I received a Polynesian tonsure. The barbershop was the forward deck of a fifty-two-foot launch, the *Fauabu Twomey*, which rolled alarmingly in a choppy sea. Throughout the day I observed my fellow passengers with interest. Some were children being transferred from one mission school to another. Others were convalescents being brought home from hospital. We put them ashore at appropriate places. And some, whether Anglicans or not, and on what errands I did not know, the Church was accommodating as a public service in a part of the world where transportation is a major problem. By carrying freight in its ships the Diocese helps to pay its own way.

We trolled as we sailed. Once or twice a day someone would cry out "Fish!" Then there was merry excitement trying to bring it aboard. Sometimes the fish got away. But when we landed one – often five to six feet long and of a species new to me – all hands rejoiced, for passengers and crew alike would feast that night and we would be able to share our bounty with the residents of the mission station where we anchored.

For nine unforgettable days the veteran and Venerable Archdeacon Reynolds was my host, and the *Fauabu Twomey* was my home. We slept on deck. It was too hot in the cramped quarters below. We pitched and rolled from island to island, village to village, mission station to mission station. But each day's projected itinerary was subject to revision moment by moment. The Archdeacon and the Polynesian captain would test the wind, listen to the ship's radio, confer, and then alter course. We either could or could not go to the intended island. For the weather in the Solomons is variable, the tides are tricky, the reefs razor-sharp.

A few years back the Diocese had lost its principal ship, the *Southern Cross*. One night, when nobody was on board, a freak storm put her on a reef, relatively unhurt but so high and dry that not even the ingenuity of a Japanese salvage firm availed to set her afloat again. In that same storm the salvage people lost one of their own vessels. The insurance companies, after exhaustive investigation of the wreck of the *Southern Cross*, satisfied themselves that there was no question of negligence and paid in full. Since this was not the first of the mission ships to founder, New Zealanders, Australians, and Britishers who had given the money for them and were asked to supply funds for a new *Southern Cross* had some doubt about the navigational skill of the Melanesian Mission. These doubts, however, were dispelled by the unambiguous testimony of the Japanese salvage experts and the unprotesting willingness of the insurers to honour the policies held by the Diocese. Additional reassurance came in tragic form. In the same year the British High Commission suffered a loss. Its principal ship, of 241 gross tons and carrying sixty-four persons, vanished without a trace. Of the twenty-eight vessels that searched intensively but in vain for survivors, one of them, a sixty-foot medical vessel, ran on the reef and became a complete wreck.

Anglicanism has not only a Church Army but also a sizeable "Navy". It would be instructive if someone would list all the places in which the Church goes down to the sea in ships. I propose the formation of a new society: *The Fellowship of Anglican Mariners*. And since one good society deserves another, I will tuck in here the recommendation that there be established a *Confraternity of Anglican "Hams"*, i.e. an association of those expert amateurs, the radio operators both clerical and lay, who in many countries carry on as a holy hobby their incessant conversations with all the world. In Melanesia I found them, in Australia, Alaska, and Honduras, too. They are forever sending information vital to the Mission, the meteorologists, the police, and the medicos. No one will ever be able to estimate the number of friends won and the good work done by these "hams".

But to return to ships. The Melanesian "Navy" once again has a flagship, the proud new *Southern Cross*, built in Australia, 100 gross tons, eighty-five feet long. Her twin-screw Diesel engines give her a cruising speed of ten knots, which is none too fast for a bishop charged with overseeing the most watery diocese in the world. He has the care of the islands of the New Hebrides, Banks, Torres, Santa Cruz, and the Solomons, islands which swing for fifteen hundred miles in a vast and irregular curve parallel to the north-east coast of Australia. The new flagship, like its predecessors, is not only the Bishop's palace but a symbol of Christian unity, affectionately hailed by all islanders as "Our Ship". The fleet it heads is composed of old standbys, the *Fauabu Twomey* (52 feet), the *Baddeley* (45 feet), the *Mavis* (30 feet), and a couple of small open launches. A hope – far from realization – is that every one of the eight rural deans will one day have his own twenty-foot launch. Meanwhile, the deans hitch a ride when they can from a passing motor-powered craft or else risk their lives (and waste their time) by paddling their own canoes.

Not even the Duke of Edinburgh received a more wonderful welcome than I did at St. Hilda's School, Bunana, on the island of Gela. The girls curtsied to him, as befitted his rank, but otherwise they sang for me the

same songs and danced the same dances. They were also attired in the
same school uniform: turkey-red calico skirts that set off to advantage the
blackness of their skin (natural) and the blondeness of their hair (unnatural).
Few pictures are so vivid in my mind as the one I saw while approaching
the shore by dinghy. Between the foreground of aquamarine water and the
background of palm-fronded tropical green is a beach of whitest sand, and
on it stood in single line one hundred and nine Melanesian maidens dressed
in red. And the girls were singing, first in English, then in Motu, "For he's
a jolly good fellow." Actually I *felt* jolly when, borne ashore on the shoulders
of barefoot crew members who did not mind the sharp-toothed coral that
would have cut my shoes to ribbons, I was deposited on the beach and
presented to the headmistress (see also Pl. 35).

Where did these girls come from? From all over the islands. What will
they become? Nurses, schoolteachers, or enlightened wives able to instruct
whole villages by the example of maintaining a Christian home and by
imparting the salutary science of mothercraft. What would they have
become except for this school and others like it? Frightened mothers of
frightened children, easily victimized by sorcerers, and with little knowledge of how best to feed their families and help ward off malaria, tuberculosis, leprosy, hookworm, and yaws.

I asked why it was that nearly everybody had at least one bandage. The
answer I myself could have supplied within a day or two. A mosquito bite
scratched in one's sleep or else the slightest bruise – like the one I got on
an ankle when I was clambering over the side of the launch to a dinghy
that suddenly was not where I had last seen it – is sufficient to produce an
ulcer unless you know what to do for it. Melanesia is not a place in which it
is easy to keep well. Thank Heaven we have hospitals there!

How fortunate the girls at St. Hilda's are! Most of them know they are
and show it (see Pl. 38). In the British Solomon Islands where (at least when
I was present) there was not a single secondary school for girls, only 3,270
girls were in any kind of school at all, and 451 of them were in Anglican
Schools. On this level, only the Roman Catholics and the Methodists have
exceeded us. The Romans had 705; the Methodists, 1,766.

We do better by the boys. At the last count available to me, 2,068 of
them were in Anglican Schools. The Methodist Mission had 2,290; the
Roman Catholic Mission, 1,024.

One wise and friendly critic of what I am writing exclaimed impatiently,
"But what do all of these statistics you have been gathering matter? Don't
you realize that the children of these children will all be Communists?"
He may, of course, be right. Almost certainly he is right—unless we organize
for action. He was not speaking with particular reference to Melanesia, for

not even trade unionism has announced itself in this little-developed area. He was speaking of the world.

To feel the devastating force of his observation you need to know that it is a profound and radiant Christian who spoke to me in these despairing accents, a man who never could be accused of the alarmist chauvinism that today champions Christianity as our "best defence against the Communist menace". No; on the contrary, this man, one of Anglicanism's best theologians, has himself – by a curious irony – been suspect, in the writings of dullard hyperpatriots, of being "pink". The fact is, few people understand better than he the havoc and the harm that may come if Christianity loses out to Communism. It is not, however, for *that* reason that he contends with Communism. He fights *for* Christianity – in the conviction that it is right, the salvation of the human race. But he wonders – and rightly – if the flaccid Christians of today can be a match for the tough-minded, superbly disciplined foes they face.

I hope he is wrong – I hope so for many reasons, but not least for the sake of the girls at St. Hilda's who presented me with the farewell gift of a palm-woven basket filled with shells designed to excite the envy of every museum of natural history. Some day I shall hand this collection over to a museum, but I am sentimental enough, in the meantime, to retain it. On a winter's evening in New York when a blizzard rages I am wont to hold a shell to my ear so that I may listen to the roar of the South Pacific and be reminded of what Christ can accomplish.

The idea that the South Pacific is a paradise is balderdash, as any G.I. or Japanese soldier can tell you. Missionaries on most of the islands spend much of their time fighting with their axes the encroachments of a jungle intent upon reasserting itself. Try to go beyond the mission clearing and either you meet impenetrable jungle (where perhaps you may see, in the crotch of a tree, the skeleton of a Japanese sniper) or else you find swamps alive with noxious terrors. Walking is out. So also is swimming, for the sea abounds in sharks and man-eating clams. The missionaries count themselves lucky if they get mail once in five weeks. For this reason the arrival of a mission launch occasions fiesta.

From St. Hilda's we sailed over a rough stretch of sea which American servicemen in World War II nicknamed "Iron Bottom Bay". The area was the scene of invasion and counter-invasion, the graveyard of many ships and of many men. Taroniara, where we put ashore, is a beauty spot. Here the jungle has been tamed. It is the working centre of the Diocese. But like St. Hilda's School, its Mission buildings were captured and used by the Japanese, then wrested from the Japanese by the Americans and used by them. The Mission workshop served as a fleet post office. Another building became an Officers' Club. The coconut trees outside the Archdeacon's house still show the marks where bullets ripped into them. A flight of concrete stairs leading to nowhere once led to the Bishop's House which the enemy, in a night of careless revelry, burned to the ground and which the Diocese has not been able to rebuild for lack of funds.

The Melanesians look upon the Americans as their liberators. American prestige was so high in the Solomons immediately after the war (and is even now), that the Mission's distinguished scholar, the lively octogenarian Canon C. E. Fox, is of the opinion that it would have worked wonders for the whole Melanesian Mission if the American Church had sent in a few priests after the war. It still would be "a mighty smart move", the Canon insists. And I think he must be right.

At Taroniara I saw that this is strictly a "Do-it-yourself" Diocese, for there is nobody else to do it for you. Whatever you may want in the way of construction, electricity, plumbing, machinery, printing, etc., is all up to you. Every one of the five hundred or so churches in the Diocese has been built by the people themselves. The Mission has set itself up in the boat-building business. In addition to the smaller boats it makes and repairs for its own use, it does the same on a commercial basis for others. The advantages are twofold: economic and educational. The Mission helps to support itself, and under the direction of white lay missionaries, now seventeen in number, Melanesians are taught skills which will help to raise the standard of living for them and their families. On islands where economic opportunities and prospects are severely limited, such skills are very important.

With great resourcefulness the Mission is also making books, not only Bibles, Prayer Books, and hymnals, but also textbooks for use in its own schools and those of the government. A battery of translators is at work, for there are in the Diocese about one hundred different languages. Yes, *languages*, not dialects; cognate languages, to be sure, but yet so different from each other that a single language will not take you far. Obviously no Diocese could afford to buy commercially Prayer Books and hymnals in a great variety of tongues, especially when the market is small. Therefore the Diocese must produce its own. It does its own translating (into thirty languages so far), typesetting, printing, folding, sewing, binding, distributing. Each vessel in its fleet is a floating bookshop.

This remarkable enterprise is made possible solely by sacrifice. I take my hat off to the laymen – these translators, these printers of books, these mechanics, electricians, and builders of boats – who have come here from Australia, New Zealand, and Great Britain to live in a debilitating climate, cut off from all they know as culture, and content with a yearly stipend so

small that no American would believe it if I told him. With nowhere to
walk and nothing to do, they do the two things that absolutely need to be
done. They work and they pray. I have never known men to work so hard,
and nowhere else in the world have I felt prayer to be more authentic.
A life of prayer, unmarred by religious fanaticism or sticky pietism, displays
its curative power by its capacity to hold together in charity and in concord
people who see too much of one another because geography makes it impossible for them to escape. Personality clashes do occur from time to time,
and occasionally a member of the Mission can no longer take it – but not
often.

And while I have my hat raised in salute, I want especially to mention
the wives and children. Theirs is often the greater sacrifice. I want also to
mention the Polynesian skipper of the *Fauabu Twomey*, a stalwart, sharp-
sighted man who puts into the service of God his inbuilt radar system by
means of which he guides the Mission launch safely through the reefs.
Were it not for the constraint of divine love, he would be making four or
five times his present salary piloting a commercial vessel, or as a government clerk or policeman. Nor do I forget the well-trained nurse who has
ventured from the familiarity of her native Polynesia to help bring up to
date the standards and techniques of our Melanesian hospitals. Though
the word "missionary" still denotes to most people a white man going to
minister to persons of colour, it has a much broader meaning today when you
have Polynesian missionaries in Melanesia and Melanesian missionaries in
New Guinea. In the Diocese of Melanesia itself there are one hundred and
one native Melanesian to only ten European clergy.

Which brings me to the subject of *Retatasiu*, the Melanesian Brotherhood.
We met the Brothers briefly in the last chapter, but now we encounter
them in their home islands (see Pl. 40). In 1925, Ini Kopuria, a dark,
strongly-built police-sergeant, trained as a boy in our schools, went to his
Bishop and told him of his resolve to found a Brotherhood. This man, whose
job had been to hunt for criminals in the name of the Law, was intent
upon seeking out sinners in the Name of Christ. He knew he must have
associates, and so he purposed to gather about him for training young
men who would promise, for at least a year at a time, not to marry, not to
receive pay, and not to disobey the spiritual direction of the Bishop. At
the end of each year they could renew their vows for another year; or,
without disgrace, a man could leave the Brotherhood to take a job and to
take a wife. It was to be a semimonastic community of laymen, living
together for prayer and study but also for cultivating the community garden
so that they might feed themselves and be no charge upon the Church.

Kopuria's vision – now amply fulfilled – included the day when the

Brotherhood would be numerous enough, well-versed enough, to subdivide into Households of eight. A team of eight men would move out to a new village, unevangelized before, or press on to an island still heathen, and there, by the concerted efforts of their Christian Household, preach Christ. As soon as a congregation was gathered and duly prepared, a priest would come in to baptize the converts and settle among them, and the Brothers themselves would feel free to move on to the next place.

And so it is today. They are claiming island after island for Christ. If the Anglican Communion has aught to boast of, it may boast of this! These Christian "Commandos", fun-loving and adventurous, receive for their labours rude housing, simple clothing, good food, medical care when needed, and not a penny they can call their own. Many of them remain in the Brotherhood for several years; some of them, all their lives. Smart in their uniform – a white *lava lava* or wraparound skirt, with a broad blue cincture and a narrow black belt, and an oval medal hanging by a chain from the neck – they are to Melanesian boys what astronauts are to boys in the outside world: heroes.

There were seventy-four of them when I was in the Solomon Islands, and many more of them were in training to become Brothers the day I laboured up a slippery path to reach Tabalia, the central station. Already two Households of eight each had gone to help Bishop Hand open up the Highlands of New Guinea. Another Household was poised for flight, when I was there, waiting for their visas to come through so that they might pioneer work in New Britain. Is it not extraordinary that this missionary Diocese of Melanesia, operating on a shoestring, has – in proportion to its numerical strength – more "foreign" missionaries than has the entire Episcopal Church in the United States of America? The Melanesian Brothers, with a zeal devoid of fanaticism, will tell you that they have been called by God to go to West New Guinea and eventually to Indonesia itself. And that, by God, is where they will go.

23

THE PHILIPPINES: A Great Day Ahead

IT WOULD BE WRONG FOR ME TO MAKE PUBLIC THE NAME OF AN IGOROT father who wrote to me about the death of his daughter. Yet I am quoting parts of his letter so that the depth of his faith may serve to strengthen the faith of others, as it has strengthened my own.

It is a layman who writes, a schoolmaster. He had entertained me in his home high in the mountains on the happy occasion of the graduation of a son from St. Mary's School in Sagada. The letter reads:

It is with great sorrow that we inform you of the death of one of our dear little ones, Helena, aged 5 years, 10 months exactly to the day she died. . . . She got briefly ill Dec. 7th and died Dec. 10th. I took care of her since she got ill at home and in the Hospital [the Episcopal Hospital at Sagada]. The doctor diagnosed her case as "necrotic pharyngitis with gastric complications." It was quite sudden and this added more to our grief. . . In the late afternoon of Dec. 10th she got down fast and expired 8:15 P.M. that night. Our Christian faith braces us up. We know and are assured that she being sinless and innocent child, she was completely and immediately received by God when she died and is in His Kingdom among His angels serving and loving Him eternally – which reasons God has created man – to serve and love Him. Also she is there constantly praying for us. It is we the family left behind who need the prayers of friends that God's Holy Spirit comfort and uplift us up soon. Our Helena surely would not want us to grieve in excess. This child was different from all our other children who are generally shy. Helena was talkative, talked with anybody, go with anybody, go with any of our neighbours' children and eat in their houses, and so oftentimes we had to send for her especially at noon time. These characteristics of hers made those of our neighbours who knew her grieve so much with us. . . . Our consolation, as the Canon may confirm, is that although her life on earth is so short, yet we give thanks to Almighty God for the favour and privilege He has given us in having had

Helena and having raised her. Surely it is a gift from God to have had such a beautiful child. And so please pray for us that God may also bless all of us in everything that is good – in our lives and in our work or vocation.

I cannot, in reason, expect this letter to have for you quite the emotional impact it has for me, for to you did not fall, as it did to me, the good fortune of visiting this man and his family in their own home. To get to it I had the most uncomfortable bus ride in all my life – six hours, right over the rear wheels, with my knees almost touching my chin because of the bulge in the floor required to accommodate the wheels. It was a fearful road, so narrow that an error of six inches on the driver's part would a hundred times have plunged us two or three thousand feet straight down into an abyss. The bus was overloaded with scantily clad fellow passengers. Half of them were carsick. The other half, red of mouth, were chewing betel nut and washing it down with swigs of raw gin. Whenever we got behind another bus or truck there was no way of overtaking it for many miles, and so we were nearly smothered in clouds of chalky dust. By the time we reached Sagada, my black suit had turned white, and I had hair to match.

It was Easter Even, 1961. And there at Sagada, a small town of surpassing beauty, I was privileged to celebrate the Paschal Feast. The Episcopal Church has done a fine piece of work in this Mountain Province. As I witnessed the baptism of some thirty persons, both children and adults, and beheld the kindling of the New Fire and the lighting of the Paschal Candle, I found myself wondering what this region must have been like as recently as 1904 when the Church, bringing schools and convents and a hospital, first came here to light a light and set people on fire. It must have been grim. Headhunting was not a sport in those days but a religion. Against diseases there was no defence except in herbs stumbled upon by folk wisdom and in incantations darkly devised. How different now, since by the finger of God Christ has cast out demons! All the city thronged to the church on Easter Day – people devout, well and clean. And from Sagada as a headquarters, the Church's work has fanned out to a score of villages, one of which I visited that afternoon where I could no more resist the sweet and sombre children who put on an Easter pageant than I could the elders who with gongs and measured grace danced in honour of the Risen King.

On Easter Monday, at St. Mary's High School in Sagada,* I had the

* The high school is one of several undertakings of the Community of St. Mary (mother-house: Mount St. Gabriel, Peekskill, N.Y.) which will celebrate in 1965 its hundredth anniversary – the American Church's oldest order for women. Continuously at work in the Philippines since 1917, it was instrumental in the founding of the native Sisterhood of St. Mary the Virgin which consequently maintained the work at Sagada during World War II when the American nuns were imprisoned.

joy of handing out diplomas to the eighty or so members of the graduating class: Igorots no longer ignorant, no longer tyrannized over by the evil spirits that once dwelt in their mountains; Igorots who with considerable dignity could meet the public and deliver addresses salutatory and vale-dictory. The valedictorian, I remember, exhorted his classmates to carry over into life, into whatever vocation they might choose, the Christian principles learned at St. Mary's. He brought a smile to my lips when he said, "And if you are lucky enough to become a politician, remember to stand firm on essentials but be flexible enough to compromise strategically on non-essentials." The mature wisdom of a St. Augustine of Hippo in the mouth of a sixteen-year-old Igorot boy!

The graduation ceremonies completed, I went by rented Jeep over seven or eight hair-raising miles to the town where lives the writer of the letter with which I began this chapter. To his eldest son I had that morning handed a diploma, and now I was invited to join in a graduation party.

The town in which he lives is without streets save for the unpaved two-rut road which, exhausted from the effort of crossing the mountains, gives up and dies the moment it deposits you in front of the new city hall. To get beyond that point you must walk, either steeply up or steeply down, usually something of both. The paths are irregular. At times they taper to the width of a foot or less. On your left will be a water-drenched rice paddy; on your right, only inches away, is a drop of several yards to the rice paddy below. You are crossing along the uneven top of one of the stone dikes – when built, nobody knows – by which whole mountains have been converted into arable terraces. They rise row on row. Sometimes there are as many as forty-five tiers of them. They deserve to rank among the Wonders of the World. It was an engineering achievement of the first order to have contrived this colossal system of irrigation working solely by gravity. Were the Igorots once great enough to have discovered it for themselves, or was it something imported from China? Nobody could tell me. Nobody seemed even to have asked the question.

Treading my way carefully – for I am not good at heights – I nodded to pigs and goats as we passed through tiny farms, and we stopped to talk with the farmers. Nothing would do in each place but that we enter the house to receive some refreshment to fortify us for the climb. You get into an Igorot house by bending double. It is minutes before your eyes adjust to the dark, for there are no windows. But you are safe on the floor or else on a short-legged stool, and eyes sharper than yours have seen clearly enough to pour out a libation and press the cup into your hands. In friendly ritual, the cup is passed around. It makes you feel accepted among these fellow Anglicans whose language you cannot speak. It does not contribute, however, to your sureness of foot as you attempt to negotiate the next flight of terraces! At the end of our trek we came to a church, a school and the schoolmaster who wrote the letter which I have quoted. This is where he lives in cleanliness and dignity, a pillar of Church and city, devoid of pretentiousness, given to good works, full of the Holy Ghost. The Christian head of a household, he said Grace before meat, and after the meal we had family prayers. Then in came twenty laymen. For once *I* had no desire to speak. I wanted *them* to talk. I longed to hear from them their story, how they had become Christians and how the Church affected the life of this Mountain Province. But they were equally intent on hearing from me about the great world-wide Church of which they are members. As a conversational battle it defied the usual pattern. Nobody was struggling for mastery. Rather, everybody was intent upon shifting the burden of conversation to the other side because all parties were eager to learn. Early next morning I met these men again to drink with them in church from the great Common Cup, the means of our unity, of which the cup I had shared in their blackened farmhouses was type and shadow.

It was not easy to take leave of these new friends. It will be a long wait before I see them again. And I had to face a return journey as dust-choked and as cliff-hanging as the outward journey had been. My travel companions, as before, were persons red-mouthed from the betel nut or raucous with gin or else afflicted with the nausea to which people unaccustomed to the automobile are easily subject.

But as we careened along, in perils equal to those of Pauline at every turn, I had long thoughts. If the Episcopal Church had accomplished nothing more in the Philippines than to build an altar in that remote mountain fastness, to have gathered about it a family in God and to have produced the kind of human being who could compose such a letter as the one I have shared with you, it would have proved its worth.

But it has, in fact, accomplished very much more.

In addition to work among the Igorots in the north, we have several churches, schools, and a hospital in the far south, chiefly at Upi and at Cotabato and at a place with the gorgeous name of Zamboanga. I flew south to Mindanao to have a look. The Moros who dwell there are chiefly Muslims, which means that the work is slow going. Yet a good many Muslims are willing to entrust their children to us for education and so far have made no objection to chapel services and religious instruction. The instruction, however, is what I call "low-pitched". Perhaps considerations of strategy dictate this policy. Maybe we would forfeit all contact with Muslims if we tried to be more explicitly Christian in our teaching. One

Muslim parent said to me, "We prefer your Episcopal Schools to those of any other Church because your Anglican education is not 'conversion-oriented'." I am not sure whether that is a compliment or not! Our indirect approach is a slow way, but in the long run it may be the only way.

Certainly we have made friends among the Muslims in and around Zamboanga, a city of about sixty-five thousand inhabitants (with outskirts included, it would be more like one hundred thousand). Friends we make, but not many Episcopalians! At least, not yet. With Holy Trinity Church and Brent Hospital in the centre of town and with two smaller churches in the outlying districts, we can claim a membership of only about three hundred and eighty-two. Yet the mission has some eighty persons on its payroll, everybody included. The return seems hardly proportionate.

At the present time the fifty-bed hospital, where I spent the night (but not as a patient), rarely has more than twenty beds occupied. Once we had a school here, but it was demolished by American bombs during the liberation and has never been rebuilt. It is true that church, hospital, and school did in prewar times create a favourable climate of opinion for the Church, but as I say, it did not make many Episcopalians – if that is at least part of what we are after.

It is a good thing that people wiser than I will have to make the decision whether, with results so small, we should continue the work patiently or else admit defeat, pull out, and put our resources to work where the soil seems more fertile.

We tried hard in Zamboanga. Much devotion was lavished there. But we look poor in comparison with, for example, the Evangelical Missionary Alliance. This body has been at work on Mindanao for a much shorter time than we, yet already it has six American couples leading a Bible School with one hundred and fifty laymen in training to be preachers. It has a string of missions all the way from Zamboanga to Cotabato. It is far nearer self-government and self-support than we have ever thought of being.

I have seen this happen in so many places all over the world that I can no longer evade the question: What *is* it about us that commits us, time after time, to smallness of numbers? I am unsure of the answer.

The third area in which the Church in the Philippines has concentrated its work is Manila. Here persons of many nationalities must be served. They are the Anglo-Americans, the Filipinos themselves, and the Chinese. Not until I reached Manila did I realize what a cosmopolitan city it is. The Chinese colony is tremendous, and we have churches and schools for the Chinese of which we can be proud. But Manila is an ugly city which seems to have hit an unlucky sort of jackpot. Its streets choked in traffic, this sprawling, strangely disorganized town is an untidy *mélange* of ingredients Spanish, Oriental, and American. In many ways it perpetuates the *worst* aspects of the three cultures that went into its heritage. And it bears to this day the scars of the horrible mangling it received in World War II.

The war left its mark on the Church too. We lost our cathedral and several other buildings. Before the war Manila was a comfortable small city of half a million. Now, with Greater Manila counted, it is pressing two million. It grows and grows. There is no sign of let-up. People keep streaming in from the Provinces in search of a city of gold. Those who were Episcopalians in the mountain and rural districts are often lost to us in the moving, for we are unprepared in Manila to receive them. Our unreadiness today is the result of a decision taken years ago, at the very inception of our mission, to leave the nominally Roman Catholic cities alone, to enter into no competition and to take ourselves, instead, to unevangelized hinterlands. Undoubtedly a wise and Christian decision at the time, it now leaves us with few facilities for following the migration to the cities. On coming to town, too many of our flock become Roman Catholics or Protestants or else forget the Church altogether. Our churches in town were too much in the nature of Yankee outposts to assimilate the new-comers.

It is to combat this problem that under the present leadership we are concentrating on Manila. A majestic new cathedral of striking design has recently gone up in Quezon City, a satellite of Manila (see Pl. 45). Next door is a five-story hospital, with three hundred beds, high-speed elevators, and tons of chromium and stainless steel. Next door to that we have built a first-class School of Nursing. And at the door beyond is St. Andrew's Theological Seminary, for which I have unqualified praise, for reasons soon to be set forth. This cluster of buildings on Cathedral Heights is an imposing pile. Before turning the first spadeful of earth, the Diocesan authorities ascertained, in consultation with city planners, that the city will in time grow out in this direction. At present, it must be confessed, our great Episcopal centre is eccentric, not in the centre of things at all. It occupies a curious limbo between town and country. It fronts on an ill-paved arterial highway that is defaced by a straggly shoestring of vacant lots, used-car lots, drive-in restaurants, and liquor stores. The scene is American: unattractive and intractable. At any rate, it took faith to settle out there. I hope the faith will not have been unfounded.

I have given an inadequate account of what is, after all, the largest overseas missionary district of the Protestant Episcopal Church in the United States of America. But it has to be admitted that our largest is not, after all, very large! Forty-five thousand baptized members, of whom about twenty-five thousand are communicants, would be a generous estimate. There are three hospitals, one with its school of nursing; five high schools; fifteen elementary schools; and that about winds it up. The ravages of World War II took their toll, it must be allowed. Muslims in the south, like Muslims everywhere, show a singular capacity for being impervious to the claims of Christ – at least to the way we present those claims. In subtle ways Rome also adds to our difficulties. The newspapers, heavily influenced by the Roman Church, rarely deign to take notice of the existence of other Christian bodies. During Holy Week, for example, there was column after column listing Roman Catholic services. I sought in vain for one single reference to services in non-Roman churches. Then finally, on Maundy Thursday, the first reference to any non-Roman form of Christianity appeared. It was a long article, prominently displayed. It told of an Anglican vicar in England who had been deposed for misconduct with a member of his choir.

There are times, however, when I do not blame Rome for resenting us. And that is in those instances when we copy her exactly.

I am at a church, one of ours, on Maundy Thursday. It is as garishly Franciscan as you will find anywhere. Before its Italianate altar of repose, with banks of candles and paper flowers, is a congregation that will watch all the night until the Mass of the Presanctified on the morrow. My clerical host is away at an outstation carrying out a similar all-night vigil when he might better, in my opinion, be home preparing something to say from the pulpit tomorrow, Good Friday. Certainly he said nothing today – except Masses. When the last of several Maundy Thursday celebrations was over, he went into silence. I am quite sure that all these devotions are pleasing to the Lord. But they do not please me! This man had much he might teach me, but I hit him on the wrong day of the year. I really wonder what business the Protestant Episcopal Church in the United States of America has supporting, totally underwriting, the budget of this "dead ringer" for Rome. If we were clearly different from our Roman brethren in the externals of worship, they would probably oppose us and preach against us. But as it is, we are bound to strike them as doubly pernicious. For wherever we *look* exactly like them it must seem to them that we lead the faithful astray by deceit.

The Republic of the Philippines is a nominally Christian country (the only one in Asia) and is almost entirely under the Roman discipline. Unless we Episcopalians have an authentic Christian alternative to offer, then let us keep out.

Yet I vacillate! The fuzzy, bungling Low Churchmanship that I witnessed in another part of the Philippines is not the answer: the clergyman's casual leaning on the lectern; his confidential manner of reading the Lessons; his failure to have the General Confession at Morning Prayer on a Fast Day (though the rubric strictly enjoins it unless the Litany or Holy Communion is immediately to follow); his putting a *Gloria Patri* at the end of the *Te Deum* – and his having the *Te Deum* and *Jubilate* in Holy Week when all tradition is against it: these things gave me the fidgits.

Happily, there are signs that a reform is now under way and that the Liturgical Movement is beginning to moderate the excesses of both parties.

My spirits were lifted when at the gold mines above Baguio I met Episcopalians of deep devotion, unostentatious piety, and simple goodness. The form of service there was highly ornamental, but all at once I realized that external forms – be they elaborate, be they austere – are nothing to get excited about, one way or the other, *provided* that they are consonant with sound theology and good pedagogy and *provided*, further, that they are forms familiar to the congregation, forms which make it possible for the people to participate. Participation is the chief requisite. Not until a congregation has been carefully prepared for an alteration in the accustomed mode of public worship should there be ceremonial addition or subtraction. Rectors bent on liturgical changes within their parishes would do well to go slow, lest by an innovation too radical and introduced too abruptly they reduce their people to stunned silence. Better an inferior liturgy than a mute congregation.

When I reached the Philippines, it was the first time in fifteen months I had been within the American sphere of influence. Manila is perhaps the most Western city in the Orient, and Anglican work in the Republic (as already noted) is under the auspices of the American Episcopal Church. Five minutes after arriving on Cathedral Heights I knew that I had again entered the American orbit. This flotilla of shiny new cars! These ultramodern buildings! This battery of typewriters! Commodious homes for missionaries! How efficient! How welcome! How American!

Yet to go in one day from New Guinea to the Philippines is to suffer shock. American opulence is overwhelming even to an American when he comes back to it after fifteen months of exposure to British frugality. At this juncture in history, America is an affluent society. American churches share in that affluence.

Consider two contrasting pictures. At a single mission station high in the mountains of Luzon I had eight American typewriters to choose from when I wanted to write a letter; better still, there was an intelligent secretary on hand to take dictation and do my typing for me. The second picture is that of an English missionary archbishop up late at night, working by the light of an oil lamp, laboriously doing his letters by hand. More than one diocese in the Anglican Communion must make shift without the help of a single typewriter. Apostolic Poverty, I know, is accounted a virtue. I have never seen the point of it. If you have money, make the most of it. But I cannot see that we Americans are getting proportionate returns for our dollars. The most urgent task before the American Episcopal Church is to learn from the British how it is that they manage to accomplish so much with so little. The mite under their management is a mighty thing. The dollar with us is a drop in the bucket.

It may seem that I am praising our work in the Philippines with faint damn. Nothing could be further from my intention or further from the truth. Over and above our own indubitable achievements in spite of many obstacles is the giant-sized fact of what we have been able to do for the Philippine Independent Church.

Iglesia Filipina Independiente is acknowledged by two contemporary Jesuit scholars to have been "an exceedingly significant movement that carried away almost one-fourth of the Catholic population".*

The quarrel was more with Spain than it was with Rome, but the struggle for political independence was necessarily coupled, in those days, with a struggle against Spanish Catholicism. Given the relationship then obtaining in the Philippines between Church and state, it was impossible to combat the one without combating the other, for they were hand in glove. The break came in 1898.

Once separated from fellowship with any major tradition in the mainstream of classical Christianity, the Philippine Independent Church (or some sections of it) began to exhibit symptoms of eccentricity. In this way it provided yet another historic instance of the validity of the point made by St. Augustine against Donatists and other splinter groups. The wise Bishop of Hippo did not disown them or disallow their right to be called Christians; he merely pointed out an inexorable fact: Only within the fellowship of the entire Christian Church can the grace conveyed by Word

---

* Pedro S. de Achútegui, S. J., and Miguel A. Bernad, S. J., in *Religious Revolution in the Philippines* (Manila: Ateneo de Manila, 1960), Vol. I (1860–1940), p. 227. Although the conclusions drawn by these authors are sometimes in need of correction, I believe they have been scrupulously fair in tracing the history. The authors rightly point out that the movement, in its beginning and subsequent development, had ambiguous elements, its leaders being somewhat confused theologically. One wonders whether it was principally considerations of religion or patriotism that drove them. Actually, in my opinion, it was a mixture of both. The Episcopal Church is treated kindly by these Jesuit authors. We are complimented for our consistent refusal to proselytize among Roman Catholics. But this is all in Volume I, which I read from cover to cover. That volume carries the story only down to 1940. Volume II, not yet published when I was in the Philippines, and which I have not been able to procure, will probably take a less friendly line towards us, for in the last years our relations with the Independent Church have changed dramatically.

and Sacrament achieve its maximum effect. Apart from *koinonia*, participation in the life of the whole Church, the sanctifying power of the Gospel is not – cannot be – fully operative. Christianity is not isolation but community. Hermits and recluses tend to become odd. Rome itself, it must be said, is not exempt from this inexorable logic. It too, having withdrawn from the rest of us, has become a little strange. Indeed, by reason of our estrangement from each other, *all* Christian bodies become a little strange. In our need of each other lies the necessity and the promise of the new irenic spirit and ecumenical temperament of these latter days.

There is no failure in charity when I state the plain fact: sections of the Philippine Independent Church got off the track. Many reverted to Rome. Many more, without loss of their love for lavish ceremonial, became shaky in their Christology. They became, as it were, High Church Unitarians. A core, however, remained sound and sane. They entreated us and the Old Catholics to regularize their orders. Unfortunately, we delayed. We wanted too many dogmatic guarantees first. Even so ecumenical-minded a man as Bishop Brent held back. Maybe his orthodox caution will one day be seen, in historical retrospect, to have had a sobering and salutary effect on the independent Church. In any event, it was a man no less orthodox, Bishop Binsted, who determined upon a venture of faith. Let us confer upon them the valid orders they plead for, he reasoned, and receive them into fellowship, in trust that their incorporation into the main body will eventually engender that wholeness of the Faith which they seek. It was a great moment, attended by risk and incurring displeasure in many Anglican quarters, when in 1948 three American bishops bestowed the historic Episcopate upon four members of the Philippine Independent Church.

Binsted – what a man he was! Transferred to the Philippines, rather against his will, from Japan, where he had been Bishop of Sendai, he arrived just in time to see his new Diocese go up in smoke. War struck. For him and for many of his clergy it meant internment and the suffering of indignities. Yet, by the mysterious ways in which God moves, it meant also that we had in those islands at that moment of history a bishop who could speak Japanese. His ability to communicate with his captors did an incalculable service – as Christians of all denominations in the Philippines today will tell you – in reducing the amount of destruction to church property and in limiting the number of martyrdoms. He survived it all, in the Providence of God, for there was yet before him the venturesome task of ordaining and consecrating bishops for the *Iglesia Filipina Independiente*.

Under necessity of making a good story, journalists in search of copy occasionally exaggerate. Even in responsible Church periodicals I have sometimes read that this is a Church of two or even three million people.

No, that is an overstatement. But why exaggerate when the actual story is good enough in itself? The figures are these:

1,500,000 baptized members (*más o menos*, but mostly *menos*)
500 priests
44 bishops (some a bit aged)
50 men in training for Ordination

The men preparing for Ordination receive their training at our own St. Andrew's Theological Seminary in Manila. They live, study, worship, and play side by side with our own candidates. But there is no effort to make Anglicans out of them. Our intention is not to absorb this Church but to rehabilitate it. If some day it should feel moved by the Holy Spirit to become part of the Anglican Communion, the right hand of fellowship would not be denied it. Or – who can say? – the time might come when the Episcopal Church in the Philippines might feel called upon to enter into organic union with the Independent Church and thus cease to exist as a separate entity. One great new Province of the Church – Catholic and Reformed, indigenous to the islands and independent of outside control – might result. If so, it would certainly be in intercommunion with the Anglicans, like the Old Catholics of Holland, though perhaps not actually a part of the Anglican structure.

Peering even farther ahead, there is just the possibility of a great Oriental Church embracing many parts of South-east Asia. It would be rather Anglican in outlook, yet an indigenous Church on its own. All of this is conjecture. A point about Anglicanism I like is its not trying to force the future. Let these developments come about in their own time, under the guidance of the Spirit. We must be given credit, I think, for the fact that there is not in our make-up or manner of procedure one shred of ecclesiastical imperialism. Orders were bestowed, ordinands are trained, not to buy allegiance or to make people over in our own image. It was and is done in the simple desire to set brothers on their feet.

I asked the *Obispo Maximo*, a heroic and humble man who has led the Philippine Independent Church into orthodoxy, to recommend where I should worship. "Do not send me," I begged, "to a parish which, under a priest trained by us, has become, as it were, partially Anglicanized. Don't send me either to a parish which is a pocket of resistance, where the new trends have been stubbornly refused. May I not, instead, be sent to a parish really typical of the stage now reached?"

It was to precisely such a place that the Supreme Bishop sent me. I am glad I went. And if anybody thinks that the description of the service I am about to give is meant derisively, it would be a perverse misreading of my words. The judgement I now make is aesthetic, not religious. Religiously, the service was above criticism, for the people participated with total devotion. Aesthetically, however, what I saw was Hispanic liturgical taste at the nadir. The sizeable church suggested a waxworks of bleeding saints. The colour scheme had got completely out of control. In a building so stuffed with statues, side altars, banners, chintz, plaster of Paris, and other religious paraphernalia, it was difficult at first to focus on anything; but when my eyes did finally come to rest on the high altar, I saw, first of all, a proscenium arch outlined by Christmas-tree lights flashing on and off. Then I sighted the wedding-cake altar, under which, in a glass casket suffused with lavender light, were the mouldering remains of some holy person long dead. The sanctuary walls were lined with hideous lithographs, hagiographically displayed, of patriots from the old days of the struggle against Spanish oppression. An organ loft was in a gallery at the back (which Anglicans might learn is the right place for it).

Throughout the service the organist, assisted by a choir and small string orchestra, played music in the style of what I call "Poor Man's Puccini". That is, it was music in the manner of Puccini but without his talent. The *sotto voce* mumblings of the celebrant were seldom audible above this torrent of sound. I am assured on high authority that in many of the churches, though it did not happen here, at the Words of Institution the band plays the National Anthem!

What fascinated me most was the "rubricator". It was like the "teleprompter" or "idiot card" so indispensable to the television industry, an electronic device that the celebrant at the altar can operate by flicking switches. The rubricator, shaped and placed like a hymn board, flashes out instructions to the congregation at appropriate moments. "Sit." "Stand." "Kneel." "Say Amen." Really, it seemed to me a sensible invention. Might not congregational participation be a little more hearty, more self-assured, in many a Protestant Episcopal Church if the congregation were given this kind of assistance?

So that was my exposure to a typical, middle-of-the-road parish of the *Iglesia Filipina Independiente*. The pastor assured me that "things have been very much toned down in the last few years".

When people ask me if the Anglican Communion has a special vocation, some particular reason for being, I answer with an emphatic *Yes*. Take, for example, the phenomenon of the Philippine Independent Church. Can you imagine any Church in Christendom, other than our own, with the patience and particular faculty for dealing with it, for taking it up and nurturing it and gently leading it into paths of sanity and orthodoxy? By its very nature, Rome is prevented from doing it. Lutherans, keen always to have orthodoxy precisely spelled out in confessional statements, could not do it. Presbyterians, in their liturgical astringency, could not do it. By no stretch of the imagination could I conceive of Methodists, Congregationalists, or Baptists, doing it. Anglicans alone *could* do it. And we *did* do it! I can think of a hundred other reasons why we have a special *raison d'être*, but this, I maintain, is one of them. To have opened the way for the return of a million and a half souls into fellowship with the Church at large, to have confirmed them in the Faith, to have validated their Orders, to be training all their future clergy, to have assisted them in preparing a revised Liturgy which is Catholic without being English, and to have exacted from them no price, no submission, no capitulation: *this*, I repeat, is what Anglicanism at its best can do. And did.

From the Philippine Independent Church we ourselves will in due course have much to gain. We may come, as I have already suggested, fully into their corporate life, in which case we will no longer be an "overseas missionary district", a Yankee importation. Already in the harmonious life together of the seminarians, Anglican and Independent, I see gigantic promise for the future. The bull sessions, the bickerings, the theological knock-down-and-drag-out fights, the friendships, the eating of the same Bread are the stuff of which Church Unity will be made.

Yet not one Anglican alive should be permitted the luxury of thinking that everything that should be done has already been done. I speak of a Philippine Independent Church desperately poor, a Church that in a lawsuit brought against it in 1906 by Rome lost all its properties. It is a Church whose major problem today is the lack of any schools of its own. In the absence of schools (and since the public schools are of inferior quality), Church members with means feel compelled to send their children to Roman schools, and that ends up with most of these children being won to Roman Catholicism. There are, of course, fates worse than that! But it is a tragic "blood-let" for the Philippine Independent Church, for in this way most of the young people who give promise of future leadership are lost to the Church of their parents.

Especially since the action taken by the General Convention meeting in Detroit in 1961, by which the Philippine Independent Church was taken into full intercommunion with us (an action that presumably will be ratified by other Provinces of the Anglican Communion in due course), our future in the Philippine Islands is irrevocably linked – and happily linked – with that of PIC.* But if PECUSA's future is linked with that of PIC and depends

* The Independent Church, by the way, stands in need of a better name as sorely as we do. Independent of what? Spain? Rome? Independence is achieved now. Times have changed. A name is needed which speaks less of ancient polemics and announces more persuasively what it has to offer.

upon our helping the latter to become thoroughly orthodox and evangelical, an outlay in money is called for which we have not yet remotely contemplated. This large but impoverished Church must have schools. It must have a great university on the scale of the one we once built in Shanghai. It will need the guidance of genuine *doctores* from the Older Churches. I raise my voice in a plea. When Anglican professors in universities and theological colleges approach the age of mandatory retirement, they should earnestly consider the possibility of dedicating themselves to the Philippines. It is impossible to overestimate the benefaction that would be conferred on a young and struggling Church by the arrival of a good historian or liturgiologist or any other competent teacher.

What better contribution could a man mature in scholarship and wisdom make than to spend what is euphemistically called the "sunset years" teaching in a school like St. Andrew's Seminary? The sun is often most splendid, most illuminating, just before it sets.

24

HONG KONG: Full-time Job by Part-time Priests

IT WAS A MAJOR DISAPPOINTMENT – MORE THAN THAT, A GRIEVOUS blow and the chief imperfection of my Grand Tour of Anglicanism – that I was not prospered to visit the Church in the Province of China, *Chung Hua Sheng Kung Hui*. I say "not prospered" rather than "not permitted", since, strictly speaking, nobody *refused* me permission. Except for a few hopeful and tentative efforts on my part, when I was first planning the itinerary, I soon gave it up, for I surmised that a visit would not be expedient.

Naturally, I made inquiries at first. I put out feelers to "old China hands". There was no point in my taking the matter up with the American State Department until I had had some sort of assurance, from the ecclesiastical side, that my visit would not be an embarrassment to the Chinese Church. At first I was encouraged to explore the possibilities. I was told that the Anglicans in China would be happy to welcome me and that the Chinese Government would have no objection. But having had some practice in the art of reading between the lines, I got the impression that the one possible source of difficulty might well be the local leaders of the Communist Party. Unless I misunderstood the signals altogether, the idea was that the smaller the community, the more a visit like mine might confirm local politicians in their *idée fixe*, that after all, Chinese Christians are nothing but agents and spies for the West. A person who at first had begged me to "allot two months to China, and I am sure we can get you in" suddenly called a halt by dispatching a letter in which he said, "I think I must now write to say that probably neither you nor anybody else connected with the Church should try to go in now. This," he continued, "is not based on any new information but rather on prolonged silence from the Chinese Bishops." These were the words of a man who had maintained frequent and friendly contacts with Chinese of all sorts, Christians or no, Communists or no, in spite of the Bamboo Curtain. But the day arrived when he received no replies to any of his letters.

After due consideration, it seemed to me wisest to desist. Why run the risk of making a difficult situation for Chinese Christians more difficult still? I want it to be understood, however, that the decision to stay out was my own doing. Neither Peiping nor Washington refused me, for I never applied to either.

But I went to Hong Kong. It is important in its own right, of course, but it had an added attraction for me because I thought it might be a good listening post. By putting my ear to the ground there I might be able to learn something about what was going on inside China. In this expectation I was disappointed. Perhaps I am deaf, or did not meet the right people. But my experience was that if people knew, they were not talking.

Since in this book I write only of what I have seen, there is nothing more I can tell of the Chinese Church, save to note that there is still an Anglican Church in China, with all the appurtenances that such a Church requires. The Chinese whom I met in Hong Kong told me, "If you have a Chinese Christian friend, do not send him as much as a postcard. He will know that you have not abandoned him. He will know that you are praying for him. He will know that the only outward way in which you can now express love is by leaving him severely alone. This is the best way to serve him now."

Anyone who has seen the motion picture called *Love is a Many-Splendoured Thing*, the locale for which was Hong Kong, knows that Hong Kong is itself a many-splendoured thing. The manifold beauties of its physical setting are matched only by the multiplicity of the problems that beset it.

The plight of Hong Kong, the great depot for persons fleeing from China, has been so much a matter of publicity and world concern that it is not necessary to say much more about it here. Our present interest is to find out what the Anglicans in this Crown Colony have done and are doing in an effort to meet a need of staggering, sickening proportions.

Surprisingly much, I would say – especially when it is remembered how few Anglicans there are. We number no more than fifteen thousand in a Colony crowded with three million inhabitants.* The Diocese decided it could make its best contribution by concentrating on schools. At the time

* Estimates vary, but the following figures cannot be far wrong. Counting Christians of all kinds, the number comes to about 300,000, i.e. 10 per cent of the total population. Of these, half are Roman Catholics. Anglicans have about thirty priests, one deaconess, and no religious. Compare that with Rome's 350 priests, 110 monks, and 600 nuns. I rejoice that Rome is so strong but lament the fact that we are so small. I wonder if we are big enough even to play the role in which we like to cast ourselves: that of serving as Rome's necessary *corrective*. At present, Anglican-Roman relations are those of mutual respect. But how on earth, or how under heaven, did the Church of England manage to lose out even in British Colonies?

of my visit (April, 1961), it could boast nine secondary schools, thirty-three primary schools, ten kindergartens, and nine night schools for adults – and more were in building. These are fine concrete structures, modern and efficient. Because of crushing need, most of the schools run three sessions: morning, afternoon, and evening.

It takes nothing away from the praise due to this energetic Diocese when one adds that such an achievement owes much to the liberality of the government which bears 50 per cent of the cost of building a new school and pays all of the teachers' salaries. Moreover, the government lends to the Church, interest-free, the other 50 per cent of the building costs. The Church has ten years to pay back the loan, and probably it would not be difficult to arrange an extension should the Church not yet be able to repay the government at the expiration of the ten-year period. Generous terms! In the long run, the schools cost the Diocese nothing, for the initial outlay is recovered through student fees. The Church surrenders little autonomy when it enters into such an arrangement. The teachers may all be Christians – if they can be found. All pupils attend daily prayers and receive instruction in the Scriptures from Anglican teachers. Non-Christian Chinese parents never object to this practice. After all, Confucius himself taught tolerance – and the great object is to get an education. Not Confucius but a student at one of our schools said, "To study is to store money in the brain." This reflects accurately the Chinese conception of (and passion for) education. The Chinese are a marvellously pragmatic people.

Church schools are so highly regarded in education-hungry Hong Kong that many a non-church school, when choosing a name for itself, prefixes the word "Saint" to a name appearing in no calendar of any branch of the Christian Church!

Our best known Church schools have as many as one thousand applications for every one hundred students who can be accepted. We are, moreover, deeply committed in the field of higher education. St. John's College, an Anglican residential hall at the University, is so splendid, modern, and beautifully situated that it could be made ready in fifteen minutes to serve as a luxury hotel. Its destinies are presided over by an Anglican priest, formerly a Danish Lutheran. And Chung Chi College, which will become a second university and under Christian auspices, has an American Anglican in charge of the department of the humanities. On a Sunday morning the Anglican Churches in Hong Kong are filled to overflowing, and the feature which chiefly strikes the Sunday visitor is that so many of the worshippers are young. They are the products of our schools.

There is but one worry about this whole splendid expansion of the school system. We have no freehold for the land on which we have built our schools.

So long as the administration of the Colony remains in British hands this is not a matter of too much concern. But under an entirely different type of political régime – always a possibility – all might be swept away. But this risk we must take. It is the *present* opportunity that must be grasped.

Not all the diocesan eggs are being put into one educational basket, however. The Chinese parishes thrive. New churches have been built since the war. The Cathedral, a big building, has a large multiracial congregation, although it is there – because of language – that British and Americans are mainly to be found. In co-operation with social service agencies, secular and religious, welfare work on an impressive scale is carried on. A brave new attempt has been made to grapple with the problem of drug addiction. Christianity, which in Marxist jargon is the opiate of the people, is deeply concerned about the opium eater.

Although the Hong Kong Government has done a heroic job in housing over 400,000 refugees in resettlement areas in the last ten years, and is actually beginning to get the problem under control, there are still more than 500,000 squatters living in squalid shacks up and down the steep hills of Hong Kong and some 75,000 dwelling miserably on the rooftops of tenement buildings. We have but thirty priests to do house-to-house calling! And even they, indeed, hardly have time for pastoral work, since most of them, in order to support themselves, must also serve as principals of schools. It takes a rugged kind of faith to keep going with courage and good cheer when the odds against success are so overwhelming. Yet the Diocese of Hong Kong seems to have a large measure of this kind of faith. Not without reason Hong Kong has been called the "Undaunted City".

To augment its ministerial staff, the Diocese has boldly experimented with the use of "auxiliary clergy". Laymen of good character, who are sound in the Faith and who have shown ability in some secular calling, are ordained to the priesthood after a short night course in theology; and then, without remuneration, they serve the Church while continuing their secular work. What they may lack in technical theological training they will make up for, it is hoped, by the maturity gained in their successful pursuit of some other field of endeavour. Thus there are lawyers and schoolteachers and accountants and shipping magnates in Holy Orders who devote their after-hours and their week-ends to the Church. Oriental psychology is such that men who have proved themselves in secular eyes as servants of the community get a better hearing and command more respect than someone who, from his youth, has known nothing but the Church.

If these auxiliary clergy are of the calibre of the one I met, a government-employed sanitation engineer (see Pl. 47) who drove me out to see his work among fisherfolk, I am sold on the idea. If there were no boarding schools like his for boys, education would be impossible. For these people have no settled home. The parents live on junks, and where the fish go, they must follow. The Church makes this possible, though on too small a scale. Wherever we stopped along the seashore, men, women, and children came running to greet their part-time priest, their faces beaming. Here was a friend. This man in the clerical collar, a sanitation engineer, had taught them hygiene, the benefits of which were so manifest that they were keen to hear whatever else he might have to teach them, and so he preached Jesus to them, "proving that this is very Christ". I cannot read the Chinese language, but I think I can read a little at least of what I see on Chinese faces. And what I read that afternoon, down among the bobbing junks, was love and gratitude.

25

TAIWAN AND OKINAWA: Island Hopping

JAPAN WAS THE NEXT GREAT SEGMENT OF THE ANGLICAN COMMUNION to engage my attention, but I could not forbear to make two intermediate stops *en route*: Taiwan and Okinawa.

I halted briefly on the beautiful but war-weary island which is better known to the world at large as Formosa, all that there is at the moment of Nationalist Free China. My treatment of Taiwan must be brief. Moreover, our work there, though of good quality, is infinitesimal. We have but five priests and eight organized congregations.

Over sixty denominations are at work on an island only 275 miles long and 75 miles wide, with a population of about 11,000,000 of whom more than 95 per cent are non-Christian. Christian witness is marred by intense competition between denominations. Instead of the comity of missions, there is enmity.

Credit must be given to the Roman Catholics and the Presbyterians for what they have accomplished, most of it in the short span of time that has elapsed since Taiwan, so recently a quiet backwater, was suddenly conspicuous on the front page of newspapers. There, in the rather dreary city of Taipei, the forces of Generalissimo Chiang Kai-shek took up their stand against the whole mainland mass of Communist China and their leaders proclaimed themselves the true Government, the only legitimate representatives of Free China. The swift inrush of troops and refugees caused the island to become swollen beyond recognition. Camps and camp followers brought unprecedented problems in their train. One can see the pinch of poverty in the lines of people's faces, and there has been enough bombardment and strafing from the hostile mainland to remind the populace that their position is perilous. In a situation like this, there is more than enough work for Christians of sixty denominations to do – if only they would pull together!

The Roman Catholics can claim the adherence of about two hundred thousand people. In 1948 they had but ten thousand. So all of this has been developed in the last fifteen years. A commendable feat! But then, Rome is wise. When forced out of the Chinese mainland, she strategically deployed many of her resources to Taiwan. *Here*, she said, is the place to train a vast company of priests, monks, and nuns so that we will have them in readiness to go in and rebuild the Church as soon as the mainland opens up. This is ecclesiastical statesmanship at its best. Anglicans have nothing comparable to offer, even on a greatly reduced scale.

Numerically, the Presbyterians are next in line with their one hundred and fifty thousand members. They have been zealous. The leadership is sound, solid. Eight hundred of their churches, carefully placed, cover the whole of Taiwan. They are well on their way to constituting an indigenous, independent, self-supporting Church.

This leaves about one hundred thousand Christians to be divided among fifty-seven varieties of other denominations. The Baptists, of many kinds, have the bulk of them. Anglicans come low on the list. We have about nineteen hundred, yet in 1961 the Church authorities were able to report an increase in communicant strength of 11.8 per cent.

With so many Christian bodies waging their campaigns, it may reasonably be asked why Anglicans entered the field at all. History, unfortunately, does not always follow a course of tidy logicality. Anglicanism came first to Taiwan from Japan. When the Japanese took over Taiwan in 1895, and ruled it for half a century, the Anglican Church in Japan went along to minister to Japanese Christians who were residing there, engaged in diplomacy or the military or commerce. It was not directly a mission to the Taiwanese but more of a chaplaincy to Christians of the occupying power. Quite naturally, however, some converts were made; and when the Japanese overlords were ousted, the Anglicans of Taiwan pleaded that they not be left orphans. Yet for political reasons it was inexpedient, indeed impossible, for Japanese clergy to remain. Clergy had to be imported from the mainland of China or Hong Kong, thereby maintaining a ministry to the few Taiwanese who were Anglicans. From a pastoral standpoint this was good. But to the present day our progress in Taiwan is retarded because, in the memory of people still living, we are too much the Japanese Church! We are associated in the public mind with a Nipponese sovereignty which the Taiwanese hated. If it were not tragic, it would certainly lend itself to comic treatment. A Church like ours that labours incessantly under the handicap of being "too English" or "too American" is in one place suspect as being "too Japanese". Here is a curious illustration of the fact that the Church, although it transcends nationality, never can escape from nationality. It is not easy to be a citizen of two worlds at once.

Refugees from the mainland after the Communist Revolution brought additional Anglican Christians to Taiwan, and today there are the many Americans, some of them Episcopalians, based there in connection with military and technical aid programmes.

These, then, are the several reasons for our presence in Taiwan today. I am thankful, therefore, that at the General Convention of the American Episcopal Church in September, 1961, the Bishop of Honolulu was given a Suffragan who will reside in Taipei and have episcopal jurisdiction over Taiwan and its neighbouring islands. We may never be very big there, but with a bishop in residence, we will grow. And, if ever the Chinese mainland opens up again, Taiwan is the Church's most logical springboard.

From the deck of an American man-of-war a young naval officer intending for Holy Orders took part in the terrific Easter Day bombardment of the island of Okinawa. He there and then made a vow: "If I live through this war, and if it should be God's will, I will come back to this place as a priest."

He did survive. He was ordained. He fulfilled his vow. And under the leadership of this American the small-scale work that the Japanese Church had begun in prewar days, but in the postwar situation could no longer maintain, was gently nursed back to life. The whole operation has been big in every sense except the numerical. One of the priests who has worked shoulder to shoulder with him in the task of reconstruction was a Japanese soldier who on that same Easter Day had stood on an Okinawan beach resisting the American naval attack.

Okinawa is part of an archipelago called the Ryukyus, sixty-three islands in all. The present political status of the island chain is not clearly defined. It has belonged to Japan and was never formally ceded at the end of World War II, yet it is now an American military base, though it does not rank as an American possession.

The Ryukyus should have a bishop of their own without delay. I am not unaware, however, of difficulties that stand in the way. Perhaps the political situation must first be clarified. If and when Japan resumes control of the islands, the bishop should be a Japanese, for most of his flock will be of that nation. Yet for the time being, when there are more American Episcopalians in the islands than there are Japanese Episcopalians, and as long as the Church has to be built virtually from the ground up, there is much to be said for having an American bishop. He would have, presumably, American "know-how" – which includes access to American funds. Most Americans would accept a Japanese bishop provided the right person could be found, but he has not loomed on the horizon yet, and it would appear, alas, that no Okinawan is quite ready for the task. And so we wait. How long we must wait is not known.

Meanwhile, the real administrator, the exerciser of discipline, the hirer and firer, the one who decides whether we buy and build or not, is a man *not* of episcopal rank, acting for the faraway Bishop of Honolulu, who in turn is acting for the still more remote Presiding Bishop of the United States. I am not making a criticism of the Presiding Bishop or of the Bishop of Honolulu. They do their job responsibly with respect to an outpost like Okinawa, but they can operate only from a distance and within the restrictions imposed upon them by their other concerns. Episcopal oversight by long distance is, as a policy, short sight.

Sooner or later – and the sooner the better, in my opinion – the work in the Ryukyus should come back under the wing of the Japanese Church, whatever the political status of those islands is to be. What I say would still hold true even if for a considerable period the mission to the Ryukyus should have to be subsidized from America. In Japan, however, I sensed a certain reluctance of the bishops to resume responsibility for these outer islands. They seemed to imply that they already had their hands full caring for the main islands. It is true that Nippon Sei Ko Kai is hard up and is only slowly recovering from the devastations and disruptions caused by the war in the Pacific. Even so, it is my judgement that it would do that Church good to be stretched a bit by assuming responsibility for a missionary field outside its present borders. But unless I am greatly mistaken, there is a timidity – almost a failure of nerve – on the part of Japanese Anglican leaders that holds them back, a fear that prevents them from venturing forth, and expresses itself, I think, in a too easy willingness to transfer jurisdiction over the Ryukyus to the American Church.

Be that as it may, something must be done. For the population of the Ryukyus grows rapidly. The American and Japanese Governments are encouraging people from Japan proper to settle on the islands in order to relieve the pressure on a Japan bursting at the seams. It is essential that the Church be *in* on the floor, ready to meet the new arrivals. The example of Brazil has demonstrated that Japanese who have gone to settle elsewhere are more open to the preaching of Christianity than those who remain in their homeland. And so it might well prove to be the case in the Ryukyus, too.

In Naha, the capital, there are three well-built and dignified church buildings, in two of which the services are in Japanese. The third congregation worships in English. American servicemen and their families, not all of them Episcopalians, come in great numbers and have made it a parish authentically alive. One Japanese priest runs a small student centre adjacent to the new university, and although he was just getting his project started when I saw it, it looked to me as if a good beginning had been made. A surprising number of students had already found their way to its doors, and friends from among the faculty were appearing too. At one of Naha's Okinawan churches we have an elementary school. The day I was there some of the world's most photogenic children were, one by one, sticking out their tongues at the visiting medical doctor who peered down their throats and thumped their chests. This was his offering to the Church.

To the north of Naha we minister to two leper colonies, with their neighbouring villages. In the city of Nago we have, in addition to a flourishing congregation, a Craft Centre. Here women, many of them war widows who were financially in desperate straits, have learned to support themselves because the Church came and taught them the skills required to produce many exquisite Okinawan arts and crafts. These were arts and crafts that had nearly died out. The Church has been instrumental in their recovery, both by teaching them and by finding for them a world market. The women workers receive a just recompense, which has been a lifesaver for most of them. When there are any profits left over, they are ploughed back into the Craft Centre and into the Parish Church in order that the operations of both may be expanded. All Nago takes pride in this centre – pride in the rediscovery of an ability distinctively Okinawan to produce beauty, pride in the fact that visitors from many nations motor many miles from Naha, even braving the rickety little ferry, in order to see and admire and buy. It is good when the Church can make a difference like this in the life of a town.

Though we have but a handful of clergy on Okinawa, they are prolific in thinking up new techniques. They are toying now with the idea of establishing a Christian township. It would provide a place for people who have been cured of their leprosy but who, because of ancient prejudice, are not readily accepted back into the communities of the healthy. The projected new township would also welcome reformed ex-convicts who, by reason of their once having been "moral lepers", face a similar difficulty when they seek readmission to normal life. The "arrested ones" – whether it was leprosy or the law that had been their problem – could support themselves by growing pandanus to be fashioned into the beautiful place mats made at the Craft Centre. The cultivation of coffee is also a possibility, and already experiments are under way to test its feasibility. Perhaps it is all a dream. It may come to naught. In that case we must dream anew. But at least there is a fulfilment of prophecy here. "Your young men shall see visions and your old men shall dream dreams." As long as there are Christians on Okinawa willing to dream, there is hope for the Ryukyus.

26

JAPAN: Seventeen-syllable Poems and Seventeen Years to Wait

JAPAN IS MY LOVE AND MY DESPAIR.

Did ever a conquered land so promptly win over its conquerors? Did ever a defeated nation so quickly stage a comeback? And was ever a country so beautiful, so attractive, and so baffling? Of all the countries I have ever seen, Japan remains to me the one most "foreign".

My first visit to the Land of the Rising Sun began on 28th April, 1952, the very day that Japan resumed her place among the sovereign nations of the world. The first postwar American ambassador to Japan sat beside me in the plane that carried me to Tokyo. My second visit began on 23rd April, 1961. The change that had taken place in less than a decade, the recuperative power of Japan, the prosperity and progress of the nation: these struck me first and with indescribable force (see Pl. 44). What struck me next was the fact that our Church in Japan has changed but little. It is almost as depressed, disconsolate, and discouraged as before.

Those of its bishops who were too old and tired in 1952 are older and still more tired today. But with few exceptions, they are still in the saddle. Saints they are. They have suffered much. Our debt to them is incalculable. By sacrifice they kept a Church alive which hell itself was intent upon destroying. But the plain and unadorned fact of today is that some of these men have not been able to readjust to the accelerated dynamics of postwar Japan. The gruesomeness of war broke their spirit. They are too aged to shift gears – and too poor to retire. Who can afford retirement? We did not make adequate provision.

And so these dear men sit, they meditate, they brew tea for interlopers like me, they compose seventeen-syllable poems – the most exacting of Japanese literary forms – as a salute to their visitors (it is the ultimate tribute), and they throw *sukiyaki* and *tempura* dinner parties for Episcopalians from America in the hope that they may raise the money that somehow will solve the problems that somehow have arisen.

I do not suggest that these men are idlers. On the contrary, they are industrious. *But they lack method.*

During the war years it was not possible to train men for the Ministry. The government saw to that. By no fault of Japanese Christians we lost a generation. Today, thanks to a topnotch seminary in Tokyo, we have a fine crop of youngsters ready to go. But the charge against them, in the Japanese way of thinking, is precisely their youth. The situation today is this: In the ranks of the clergy we have saintly old men, weary and wounded by war; no middle-aged men; a raft of young men, many ripe in promise, who need seasoning – especially in Oriental eyes where the veneration for age is such that the young men are not acceptable for advancement to positions of responsibility until their temples are grey.

It was indeed a revolutionary step when a few years ago a man of gigantic talent was made Bishop of Tokyo. It took twenty-two ballots to elect him. The chief reason against him was that he was too young. A mere fifty!

What is needed? Ten to fifteen years of patience. Anglo-American friends of Japan must wait for a decade or more and continue to be generous to its Church until some of the great saints of God have been called to their reward and until a new generation of clergy have acquired the age that will give them the needed "face" before they can succeed to high office.

Then, I am convinced, we shall make progress in the Land of the Rising Sun. At least there will be the chance of doing so. I could not fully document my reasons for this optimism, but I will name a few of them.

In spite of Japan's postwar prosperity and new-found self-confidence, there is still a substratum of despair; and despair, I believe, always provides a point of contact for the Christian message if the latter is presented properly. A despairing man may be able to hear the Christian message as Good News, as answer to ultimate questions, better than a man who is asking no ultimate questions and who lives on in an illusory sense of security. The same is true of entire cultures.

In spite of a resurgence of Buddhism – a Buddhism, by the way, which has taken a surprising number of leaves from the Christian book and which has been forced by the catastrophic character of recent history to rethink its own position in many respects – this great religion will, I think, find it increasingly difficult to answer the questions persistently being raised by the very intelligent Japanese mind. Buddhism is, of course, a profound system of thought, but I seriously question its capacity to grapple with the problems posed by contemporary society.

When I went to Japan nearly a decade ago to lecture on Kierkegaard in twenty-two Japanese universities and colleges – Christian, Buddhist, Shinto, and secular – I tried to arm myself for this first encounter with the East by reading all I could lay my hands on with respect to Buddhism and Shintoism. But what did I find? In the great universities it was not, for the most part, Buddhists and Shintoists I met. Largely, the professors were secularists. My hope is that the pattern we have witnessed in the West will repeat itself in the East – viz. that secularism, finally becoming conscious of its own inadequacy, will turn religious.

There is always the dire possibility that the religious quest of a shaken secularism may take a sinister turn. It might be a daemonic form of religion that revives. The West is not lacking in examples. It might be a saccharine form of religion that takes captive masses of the people. In this respect, too, the West has been sufficiently prolific in providing examples. For all the impassivity of a Japanese face, the Japanese are a highly emotional, even a sentimental people. I think that an eclectic, syncretistic, semi-psychological, half-Christian, half-Buddhist conglomeration, suffused with sentiment, might be what Japan will choose. I cannot believe that such a choice would be good for Japan, but I find it difficult to shake off the feeling that it is a genuine likelihood.

Equally I have the impression that Christianity is soon to have its first real chance in Japan for a breakthrough. If the bubble of prosperity should burst, if Buddhism cannot do a better job than it has done hitherto in showing its relevance to the problems of man in the contemporary world, and if a materialistic secularism should begin to ask some real questions about the meaning of existence, Christianity's *moment* will have arrived. These are big "ifs". But on these three "ifs" we who are Christians should stake everything. Japan is a nation of incomparable greatness. I believe it can be won for Christ if we will wait patiently for the opportune moment. In the language of Paul Tillich and the New Testament, we must wait for *kairos*, "the fulness of time", the moment at which eternity can intersect time with transforming effect.

By "waiting" I do not suggest inactivity. We must prepare for the *moment*. In addition to what the Japanese Anglicans are now doing, they ought to advance powerfully on two fronts – and to do so adequately will need outside help.

The first is rural evangelism. Up to now we have had scarcely any success outside the urban centres. It comforted me to discover that many Japanese Christian leaders, the Anglicans conspicuous among them, are racking their brains to find an effective method. Why not Folk High Schools and co-operative farms of the Grundtvigian type that transformed Denmark? A modest beginning has already been made under the imaginative leadership of the Japanese Presiding Bishop. There is also the American-sponsored programme known as KEEP (Kiyosato Educational Experiment Project) whose purpose is the development of rural Christian democratic centres. There is one community located on the slopes of Mt. Yatsu, seventy miles from Tokyo, which is successfully carrying Christianity and democracy to over 110,000 people by means of farm, hospital, clinic, and church services.

The second front on which advance should be made is that of an approach to Japanese intellectuals. Here we must not send a boy to do a man's work. The brightest Japanese Christians who show signs of apologetic gifts we should train, regardless of expense, to the full extent of their capacity. We need them as teachers, not only to staff our own Church schools and colleges, but also – and even more important – to occupy chairs in the great secular schools. Beyond that, we ought to build a student centre adjacent to the campus of every major Japanese university and provide it with a chaplain who is the intellectual equal of the best professor on campus.

A notable example of the kind of specialized ministry I have in mind is to be found at Sapporo in connection with the University of Hokkaido. I nearly froze to death in this northernmost of the main islands of Japan, and in token of my desire to identify myself with the people, I promptly came down with Asian flu – a small price to pay, however, for the thrill of seeing what the consecrated imagination of one man can accomplish. He is the Reverend William D. Eddy. Knowing the singular resistance of the Japanese student mind to Christianity when it is a matter of direct confrontation, he decided upon an oblique approach. Since the Japanese are insatiable devotees of Western classical music, he told the American National Council that the chief tool of evangelism he required was the best Hi-Fi set in the whole of Hokkaido.

When the set arrived and was installed in the very attractive student centre adjoining the campus, Mr. Eddy posted notices on the University bulletin boards, announcing that on the following Wednesday night he would play such and such recordings. A gratifying number of students turned up, including some members of the faculty as well. After all, in a place like Sapporo there are not many opportunities to hear a concert. He gave them a diversified programme. It was not an evening of "sacred" music, but he did include excerpts from *The St. Matthew Passion* of Bach. He prefaced the playing of each number with expert programme notes, describing the musical structure of the composition about to be heard and giving clues as to the intention of the composer.

The students were enraptured. The next week they were back for more, this time bringing many more students with them. Before long they were asking to hear the whole of *The St. Matthew Passion*. And in their enthusiasm for Bach, they wanted his B Minor Mass. Of Brahms, they wanted his Requiem as well as his symphonies; of Stravinsky, his controversial Mass as well as his controversial *Sacré du Printemps*. And thus it went. Without ever sermonizing, Mr. Eddy *preached* – by using his programme notes.

From this beginning developed new imaginative projects. Students came gladly to a series of lectures he offered on Dostoevski. Later he gave a series based on Pasternak's *Dr. Zhivago*. Kierkegaard came in for his turn. "Why," I asked the head of the Department of Philosophy of one of Japan's foremost universities, "are Japanese intellectuals so deeply interested in him?" The answer was: "Because he has understood us in our despair."

Mr. Eddy is not a man to run out of ideas. Next he added soirées on art. Here again he used the same indirect approach: not religious pictures alone were exhibited and analysed, but from time to time there would crop up something like the Avignon Pietà and the Isenheim Altar Piece of Matthias Grünewald. And then, by sudden inspiration, art and music would be combined. The students look at Grünewald's masterpiece and then listen to Hindemith's *Mathis der Maler*.

I submit that this is an inspired way of going about things. Although I do not suggest that such a method is capable of being transplanted to other parts of the world where the Church faces the campus, surely some adaptation of it would bring forth fruit, just as it has done in Hokkaido. Recognition of Mr. Eddy's efforts has now come in the form of his being asked to conduct seminars on theology and art within the university itself.

Japan is a land of universities and colleges – more than three hundred of them. Few countries in the world can match the Japanese hunger for learning. To build student centres at so many places is an obvious impossibility, but could we not set our sights on the major universities, particularly those that used to bear the title "imperial"?

As early as 1952 I found myself questioning the wisdom of the Church's maintaining an enormous university, St. Paul's, in Tokyo. More than ten thousand students are currently enrolled in its six colleges. There are six hundred members on its faculty. It is a great school and has done the Church incalculable good; but the Japanese, having learned from Christians the indispensability of universities, proceeded to build universities of their own. Having more money at their disposal, they have now beat us at our own game. The State universities excel ours in equipment and in scholarship. An ambitious young student *wants* to go to one of the imperial universities. In most cases, if he cannot gain admittance, he may settle for St. Paul's

as a second choice. He will receive a first-class education there, as well as
a kind of exposure to Christianity. But I wonder. Should the Church allow
itself to be associated in the public mind with something that is not topnotch?

How *Christian* is our St. Paul's? I asked the President what percentage
of his teaching staff were practising members of any Church. About 14
per cent, was his reply. He added that it was unfortunately impossible to
find enough Christians with academic qualifications to fill the various
chairs.

I would ask not to be misunderstood at this point. If we are looking for
someone to be professor of biology, what we want is the very best biologist
that can be found. It is devoutly to be hoped that this fine biologist will be
a Christian. But that cannot be the major consideration. Better a competent
biologist who is a Buddhist or a secularist or an agnostic than an inferior
biologist, no matter how orthodox and ardent he may be as a Christian.
Nor should we want a Christian biologist (historian, sociologist, etc.) to
exploit his professorial rostrum in the interests of Christian propaganda.
Anglicanism believes in intellectual integrity and is committed to the principle of the autonomy and objectivity of the sciences. On the other hand,
it would be hoped that when the biology or history lecture was over and
the teacher had asked what lessons might be deduced, his answer would be
informed by a Christian *Weltanschauung*. Can we say of a university that it
is Christian if most courses are taught from a nontheistic, secularist, or
even anti-Christian point of view – and then tack on to the curriculum, as
an optional addendum, a few courses in "Religion"?

I have to admit that the chapel programme at St. Paul's is excellent,
as are its well-attended courses in Christian thought. Many conversions, many
confirmations, result. And in the Law School, for example, we are producing
good friends for the Church among people who will be highly placed in
government. I do not forget that in the Gospel it is recommended to
Christians to make such friends. I am also reminded, by a shrewd American
observer of the Japanese scene, that a great institution like St. Paul's is
the one place "where the Anglican Church becomes visible and audible"
in Japan. In a land where "face" counts for much, every Japanese Anglican
takes heart from the fact that the Church can construct such impressive
edifices as St. Paul's University and St. Luke's Hospital.

It is now being argued that we should also have an imposing cathedral
in Tokyo, which has become, after all, the largest city in the world. Ten
per cent of the country's total population lives in the capital city. "What
we need," I was told, "is something big and magnificent." Land has been
purchased near the city's greatest tourist attraction, the incredible steel

Tokyo Tower that surpasses the Eiffel Tower in height but not in grace, and stunning plans for this new cathedral have been drawn up by one of the world's most prominent architects.

One thing that must be remembered is that after a century of missionary endeavour, less than one-half of 1 per cent of the Japanese people are Christian. Japan has a population of 90,000,000 and is increasing at the rate of 1,000,000 a year. All Christian forces combined can muster no more than a total of 450,000. Rome is far in the lead with its 242,000. The United Church (*Kyodan*: an amalgamation of Protestant Churches imposed by government order during the war years but living fairly happily together ever since) is in second place with some 176,000. We are a poor third with our approximately 43,000. The Orthodox lag not far behind with about 35,000 members. And then come the stragglers: seventy-six assorted denominations claiming an aggregate of 160,000.

We are thus in third place – a minority within a minority. Yet there can be no question that our past record and present performance in the fields of medicine and education have won for Christianity and for our form of it profound respect among the thinking people of the land. The government often seeks the opinion of our best leadership on many matters of public policy and hardly a week passes without our having an opportunity to address the people of Japan through the media of television and radio.

Whenever I am tempted to be pessimistic about the future of Christianity in Japan, I check the gathering gloom by reminding myself of three things.

The first is that the supposed impermeability of the Japanese mind to Christianity is a myth. Not only have countless Japanese of both high estate and low embraced Christianity; not only have Japanese Christian scholars made definite contributions to theology; but far more important: Japan has had more Christian martyrs, proportionately, than any other nation in history.

A second consideration: We must size up the opposition we face. As compared with the great successes Christianity has scored in Africa and in the islands of the South Pacific, the achievement in Japan (or India) seems paltry. In Africa and in the Pacific isles we were up against "low paganism". And so of course we made headway. In India and in Japan we encountered "high paganism" – sophisticated cultures, rich in artistic achievement and steeped in religio-philosophic traditions that should command our respect if not always our assent. Even with a deep bow to the dedicated missionaries of the late nineteenth and early twentieth centuries, it must be admitted that not many of them were intellectually equipped to grapple with paganism in its greatness. A new type of missionary must appear – and is in process of appearing – with this capacity. The new missionary will not always be a white man. He may come to Japan from Burma or Ceylon or Ghana. But in most cases, he will be a Japanese ministering to his own people. He will be acquainted with paganism at firsthand, appreciate its qualities, and will know unerringly how to engage it in dialogue. We are on our way in this direction. The Diocesan Bishops of *Nippon Sei Ko Kai* are all Japanese, as are two hundred and forty-four of its priests. The outbreak of World War II forced the Church to stand on its own feet. Only one American bishop, a Suffragan, remains from the old days. The thirty-four foreign priests currently serving in Japan are mainly engaged in teaching.

The third consideration is this: The Japan which, when finally opened to the West, became enamoured of the West, is now in flight from the West. The identification of Christianity with the Occident – with all its overtones of colonialism and imperialism and commercial exploitation and racial superiority – has set up in the Japanese mind a mental block against Christianity. I cannot believe that it will be anything more than a temporary feature of Japanese psychology. Why? Because Japan itself grows more Western by the minute. I am not sure that the Westernization of Japan is altogether a good thing. I am certain, however, that the more Japan is Westernized – or, better, internationalized – the more receptive it will be to the Christian message as an answer to its most urgent questions.

Towards midnight I met the Presiding Bishop of *Nippon Sei Ko Kai* on the platform of the railway station of Kobe. We sat up all night in a chair car. He travels third class to save the Church money. In the intervals between fitful dozing we discussed problems confronting the Church. We got out of the train in the cold grey light of early dawn at Hiroshima to attend services at the newly rebuilt and renamed Church of the Resurrection, which, phoenixlike, has arisen from the ashes of an older church destroyed by the atom bomb. Later in the day I sailed with this Kelham-trained son of a Samurai warrior in a small launch through the Inland Sea, whose mountainous islands have all the beautiful unreality of a jagged cardboard stage setting. Quite unself-consciously and without thought of appealing to American sympathies, the Bishop sighed to himself, "Island after island where the Gospel has never been preached."

Japan is not lost for Christ. Though it knows it not, it awaits him. But when he comes, as assuredly he will, he must not resemble too closely an American tourist.

How bluntly I have dealt with this mannered land of dwarfed trees, flower arrangements, tea ceremony, exquisite courtesy, intricate protocol – and occasional outbursts of savagery! In doing so I am afraid my own sun will have set in the Land of the Rising Sun. I shall no longer be welcome in a country that I love and would rejoice to see again.

27

KOREA: Unquiet Land of the Morning Calm

NOBODY HAD PREPARED ME FOR THE PHYSICAL BEAUTY OF KOREA. I had known the country only through the medium of newsreels flashed on our movie screens at home during the Korean War, at which time it had looked grim. But today, although the scars of war are still in evidence, the mountains, steep-pitched and green, remain in their theatrical magnificence. The summits command stunning views of islands, bays, and verdant valleys. The flooded rice paddies are silver in moonlight. By day they mirror perfectly the deep blue sky, or, when the sun is at the right angle, they shimmer like burnished gold. Dull gold are the roofs of woven palm fronds, a striking contrast in their smooth artistry to the scraggly thatches one sees in other lands. Trees, twisted and gnarled, make fascinating silhouettes against the sky.

Most arresting of all are the people. The women are beautiful and demure. Their costume is of a cut I know not how to describe, but it is lovely and is found nowhere else in the world. The colours they choose are pastels of an incredible delicacy, and the subtle ways in which they are combined would start whole new trends in women's fashions and interior decorating if only the outside world knew. And the chin-whiskered and top-knotted old men too are beautiful in their spotless white, with black slippers, strangely transparent black stovepipe hats, and walking sticks. All of these people, even those walking along a dusty road, look as if they had just stepped out of a bandbox (see Pl. 50, 51).

Most of the time I was too occupied with looking at these sights as we motored along or else with listening to the Bishop to have anything much to say myself. But during one stretch of the road which was of less interest I found myself musing about the whole extraordinary piece of good fortune that had befallen me: this journey to every country in which the Anglican Communion has work among the people of the land. And I remarked to the Bishop, "Something exciting or momentous has happened nearly every-where I've been so far. In one place a bishop died while I was there. . . . I reached another place where the bishop himself had assured me by cable only the day before that he was happily awaiting my arrival the next night; I arrived at the appointed hour; no bishop; then I learned that he had abandoned his diocese that morning, never to return! . . Revolution kept me out of Paraguay. . . . I arrived in Accra to find the Ghanaians up in arms, threatening to stone the French Embassy, put brickbats through the plate-glass windows of French stores, and freeze French assets. Why? Because the French were just about to explode their first atom bomb in the Sahara. But this was the season of the *harmattan*, when the hot, dry wind sweeping down from the desert causes the air over all of West Africa to be laden with grains of sand. Reflecting the sunlight, they shimmered so much that hardly any picture I took in West Africa is any good. 'You can understand why the people here are concerned about atomic explosions in the Sahara,' said one official, squinting his eyes against the wind-driven sand. . . . I arrived in Johannesburg the very night Mr. Macmillan made his celebrated 'Winds of Change' speech, and I left South Africa just shortly before the terrible blow-up at Sharpeville. That was a rocky time. . . . I came to Blantyre in Nyasaland in time to stand in the nervous crowd and see Dr. Hastings Banda, just released from prison, start on his famous journey to London. We did not know what might happen at any moment, and my companion implored me to keep my camera out of sight. . . . The Bishop of Uganda [now the Bishop of Namirembe], in spite of my pleading, would not permit me to accompany him on a visit to Ruanda-Urundi, for the Congo was just about to go up in flames."

As we jounced along in the Land Rover, I told all this to the Bishop in Korea, but in greater detail. When I had finished, he said, "Well, you can relax. Nothing happens here."

At three o'clock the very next morning bullets were whizzing over the Cathedral Close in Seoul! It was Tuesday, 16th May, 1961. The Cathedral lay in the direct line of fire between the former Imperial Palace where the revolutionary troops had garrisoned themselves, and the tele-communications centre which it was vital for them to capture. In a few hours of fierce fighting a revolutionary junta had ousted the government and had taken over, but the situation remained unclear the whole day, and an uneasy, ominous pall hung over a city that has had no little experience of this sort of misery.

At breakfast the Bishop, recalling my remarks of the previous day, said with a smile, "Johnson, you're a jinx! Get out!" But I could not obey his godly admonition, for the American Armed Forces radio barked out in peremptory tones that all Americans must keep indoors. Being a coward anyway, I was glad to remain under cover. And against the possibility of a new outbreak of shooting I put into the dry bathtub a pillow, a blanket, a tin of crackers, a bottle of water, and some back issues of *The Living Church*. I fondly hoped that the porcelain walls of the tub would provide some measure of armature. But nothing more happened, except that the crowds milling in the streets were cordoned off, and an early curfew imposed. I was a prisoner of the house for a day and a night in which I had hoped to have informative interviews with a number of people.

By the next day everything was still touch and go. The bullets had stopped, but rumours were flying. Some of them were ugly; all of them disquieting. A bishop visibly disturbed said to me, "There's no telling when the situation may worsen. If you can get a plane out of here, I think you had better go." He was smiling still, but serious. By adopting tactics faintly cloak and daggerish I got to the airport. All planes had been grounded the preceding day, but this day the new revolutionary government agreed to allow one Northwest Orient airliner to arrive from Tokyo and return, provided no Koreans were carried in either direction. It was this plane I was intent upon catching when it made its return flight to Tokyo. I did, but only after anxious delays. We would board and be on the point of taking off when suddenly we were ordered back. Clearance had not yet come through. It was a case of on again, off again for several hours. When at length we got the green light from the new government, we lost no time in making for the skies.

For such reasons my visit to Korea, short even as planned, was made even shorter. What I can tell you about Korea with the certainty of an eye-witness and the conviction of first-hand knowledge must, therefore, be brief indeed.

Numerically, Anglicanism was never very strong in the Land of Morning Calm – partly because this land has so seldom been calm. At our peak, which was in 1939, we had about ten thousand members with more than twenty Korean clergy as their pastors. It was in the North that the greatest missionary strides were made. In the thirties we were opening, on the average, six new churches a year. The future looked promising. Anglicans began to think hopefully of the day when it would be possible to subdivide the Diocese and create a Korean Province. Such a move would have been a great gain, for the Diocese dangles in lonely isolation, far too removed from distant Canterbury either to have adequate oversight or to be represented fully in the councils of the English Church. For it to be linked organically with the Church in China or the Church in Japan was not feasible. All manner of reasons blocked the way – historical, linguistic, racial – because the Koreans are neither Japanese nor Chinese. A Province of their own was something to be prayed for, worked for, hoped for.

War put an end to all this. The invaders from Nippon did not look with kindness upon the sort of resistance that all branches of the Christian Church engendered. But nobody can be more intractable than an Anglican when a matter of utmost importance is at stake. Much suffering was entailed. The Church's continuance was purchased by the shedding of blood.

Almost as soon as that particular tyranny could be spoken of in the past tense, the new blow fell: the Korean War that raged from 1950 to 1953. Five million Koreans died. Five million fled from the North to overtax the meagre resources of the South.

What of today? From all we can find out (which is not much, for the lines of communication have gone dead), the Church north of the 38th parallel is extinct. It was systematically exterminated. Undoubtedly there are Christians worshipping in secret, but, to the best of our knowledge, there is no sign of a Church above ground.

That the Church in North Korea should have been marked out for ferocious treatment at the hands of the new lords of the land permits of easy explanation. It was the Christian Church that had taken formal education to the North. The leaders of the people were almost exclusively products of Church Schools. As clergy, as church wardens, as vestrymen they had learned at least the rudiments of democratic processes, parliamentary law, and the rights of minorities. People so trained were almost the only leaders of any kind. *Ergo*, they had to be liquidated. And apparently they were. The only exceptions were the refugees who managed to escape to the South.

The more vigorous section of the Korean Church was thus lost to us, and our numbers were cut from ten thousand to five thousand. It will take a long time to recover, let alone forge ahead, although today twenty-seven gifted and dedicated men – Korean, English, and American – are giving themselves to the task. Of the seventeen priests at work in the Diocese when I was there, the Diocese itself was able to pay the stipends of only three. Our work is predominantly rural – and it is mostly women that we have been able to win (see Pl. 51 and 52) – with the result that self-support is entirely out of the question. How to get around this financial bend is the Bishop's chief headache. The problem is to secure enough assistance from abroad to enable us to carry out something more than a mere holding operation. Hold we must, but we must also effect an *advance* if ever the Korean Church is to grow large enough to come within sight, as it was in 1939, of the possibility of eventual self-support.

"Is it worth the struggle?" The question was put to me by a devout American Episcopalian. I stress the fact that he was *devout*. He was not the type who still, gropingly, asks the question, "Why missions?" He knows perfectly well the answer to that particular question. His question was of a different order: pragmatic. He wanted to know, from a strategic point of view, why Anglicans should continue to struggle in Korea when we have our hands full elsewhere, and Korea is already being "looked after" by large missions of the Roman Catholic, Presbyterian, and Methodist Churches. It is a fair question.*

My answer would be as follows. Yes, the struggle is worthwhile. Minute as we are, we have a role to play in a land where Christianity's headway among intellectuals is impeded by a backwash from fundamentalist preaching. I am not being uncharitable, merely candid. Vast numbers of missionaries from abroad and even larger numbers of native Korean Protestant ministers have not the educational qualifications to excite respect. And where such qualifications are present, their possessors are often men of such stiffness of manner as to render them incapable of entering into warm personal relationships with the people. Anglicans, at their best, score a better batting average when it comes to being both educated and affable. By reason of their culture (if they have it) they are appreciative of other cultures and can enter into conversation. (I would note that in Seoul the Diocese has opened a splendid four-story student centre facing the university. In charge of it is a brilliant young English priest who has a profound knowledge of Korean literature and life. Secular newspapers in Korea have syndicated the columns he writes on Korean affairs.)

Anglicanism's role in the Korean ecumenical scene may be to introduce a sparing pinch of Catholic salt into a land heavily invaded by Protestantism – and by a Romanism that will have nothing to do with the Protestants. In such a situation, unless we speak for ancient and apostolic Catholicism, nobody else will. Here lies our opportunity, for the vast majority of Koreans are still unchurched.

Even if considerations such as these carry no weight, there is one compelling reason for our continuing what we started. To feel the compulsion of it, all you have to do is spend a few days travelling by Land Rover with the Bishop to country towns with such intriguing names as Kangwha, Onsuri, Naeri, Chinchon, Chopyong, Kwanghyewon. Sit down with your hosts on rice mats in their houses, struggle with short steel chopsticks to convey to the mouth some of the best food ever set in front of you, then worship with these people in churches whose upswept eaves mark the

* Three groups of Presbyterians total 794,000 members; Rome has 452,000; Methodists, 237,000. Numerically the Anglicans are in ninth place.

buildings as belonging to the land. Discover by participation that the Lord's Supper on the Lord's Day is *the* event of the week. I am not the first person to comment on the "quality of supernatural beauty" that characterizes the worship and the lives of Korean country Christians. That quality is *there*, palpable and powerful. Not that these folk cannot also be difficult, given to parish quarrels, envy, and backbiting. As somebody once said, "The Koreans are the Irish of the Orient." Yet who can help loving the "Irish", even when they have a non-Hibernian slant to their eyes?

28

PANAMA, CENTRAL AMERICA, MEXICO:
Hoy, no Mañana

AFTER THE HASTY EXODUS FROM REVOLUTION-TORN SEOUL, I touched down briefly at Tokyo. Powerful spotlights glared at us as television cameras ground away and a battery of reporters took down every imperishable word we had to utter. It was a brief moment of feeling like a celebrity, for we were the first people to escape from a Korea on which strict censorship had clamped down but, alas, we were too weary to enjoy it much.

The following day, crossing the International Date Line, I gained for myself a second 18th May. Thus I came to Honolulu.

Within one hour of arrival, as I was going alongside St. Andrew's Cathedral, a sudden gust of wind brought a coconut hurtling earthward. I ducked only in the nick of time. The hard-shelled fruit, the size of a football, struck my shoulder a glancing blow and fell harmlessly on the lawn. "What an anticlimax that would have been!" I muttered to myself. "A nut dispatched by a nut!"

My hope had been to fly or sail from Hawaii to Panama. This proved to be impossible. Neither airlines nor shipping lines favour that route. The sole alternative was to fly to San Francisco and from there to take another plane bound for the Canal Zone. That is what I did.

Panama is best described as "the country cut in two". I refer, of course, to the Panama Canal, that remarkable forty-mile-long waterway begun in 1879 and completed, after much tribulation, in 1914. One man has the difficult task today of holding the two halves of the Republic together ecclesiastically, while at the same time standing with his feet firmly planted in the American soil of the Zone which bisects the sensitive Republic. This is the Bishop – Reginald Heber Gooden – California-born, Castilian-speaking, consecrated in 1945, and the third bishop to have jurisdiction over this missionary district of the American Church. To ensure that he will have problems enough, he is also expected to assume responsibility for Colombia and to expand our work down the west coast of South America.

Episcopalians from the United States are not exactly new-comers to the Isthmus of Panama, but we took our time before ordaining any Panamanians – a serious blunder. Even at the airport and during the drive into town I began to think about this. How could it be that this archdeacon who had come to welcome me – a man of distinguished countenance, intelligence, and charm, a man of West Indian origin, a man of no very great age – should be the *first* Panamanian we have ordained? Surely he was not the first likely candidate. From him I shifted my gaze to his companion, a fair-haired young Panamanian of European-American extraction, priested as recently as 1959. Yet this exceptionally gifted, completely bilingual man is the first clergyman we have set aside to work full time among Spanish-speaking people. Prior to his appointment, our ministry to this language group was sporadic.

Before going to the Isthmus I had not even begun to understand the differences between the Canal Zone and the Republic of Panama. I knew that there had been, on occasion, the flare of riots, the citizens of the Republic expressing resentment that a rich Uncle Sam should sit astride their country and grow richer by the day because of the ditch he had dug. This, I say, I knew, but not yet had I reflected on how these emotion-charged political realities would affect any Church whose earthly headquarters bore a New York postmark. Alas, there is a colour bar, a language bar, a nationality bar – and an awful lot of bars, on both sides of the border, at which people drink too much.

"Colour" is the biggest problem. Whites from "up north" are not greatly beloved. The United States Government pays them far more than it offers to its employees of Iberian or African derivation. When the ethnic and economic disparities are compounded by linguistic differences, no ingredient is lacking. The acids of discontent are all present for concocting a highly indigestible *olla podrida*. A Church like the Episcopal Church – supposedly both *Gringo* and *Protestante* – has already two strikes against it.

Anyone who has laboured thus far with me through so long a book will recognize, without my having to say it, that I regard this as an unmitigated tragedy. Obviously, I think that all people would be better off if they were Anglicans! But hope of this is small. A Christ who can speak only Hebrew, Aramaic, and perhaps also Greek would have a better chance of winning these people than a Christ who seemingly has only American English for a mother tongue and whose Spanish, if it exists at all, rests skimpily on a two-year high-school course with conjugations imperfectly mastered and with a cedilla not clearly distinguished from a tilde.

It is not alone the Iberian and African Panamanians who suffer from these dislocations. Yankees, straight from the States, are harmed by the whole setup. Remunerated out of all proportion to their neighbours, they live a protected life within the Canal Zone which has gained for itself the opprobrious name, "Golden Ghetto". It is not, generally, intolerance but timidity which prevents them from entering into genuine relationships with the Panamanians. Shyness more than arrogance keeps them a people apart. But the church to which they go – if indeed they go to church at all – is *our* church, an American church, and this divorces us all the more from life as it is really lived by the people whose land we have cut in two.

To the people who live within the "Golden Ghetto" great psychological damage is wrought by the ruling that no whites in the employ of the United States Government may buy and own property. This means that no one could retire here or continue to be a resident, however much he might enjoy the Panamanian climate and his Panamanian neighbour. Willy-nilly, Americans are imbued with an interim mentality: "We are just here for a time." (Many never ask for a letter of transfer from their "home parish" to a church within this Missionary District, for "We'll be going back home soon.") Their good pay and social position, their lack of Spanish and perhaps also their racial prejudice, and, above all, their awareness that they "won't be here for long" prevents them from identifying themselves with the people who surround them. Exclusion from the one side causes, of course, a reciprocal exclusion from the other side. Little love is lost. Hard, therefore, is the lot of a Church trying to minister to all these people.

I am sure the fluent Spanish-speaking Bishop would agree with me that a sign reading "*Aqui se habla Español*" should grace the bulletin board of every Episcopal Church in Latin America. Yet this part of the world will not permit us to speak Spanish exclusively, for in addition to the many North Americans who must be shepherded there are also the West Indians. For the most part their language is English and their religious background, Anglican.

Had not West Indians been brought to Central America to work the banana plantations, build the Isthmanian Railway, and dig the Canal, we would not have much of a church. These people deserve recognition as having been the chief missionaries of our Anglican understanding of Christianity in Central America from top to bottom. West Indians under English influence, far more than pale faces from north of the cactus curtain, have wrought the work.

Yet here again we are in difficulty. Anglicans have white faces or black faces, neither of which are in special favour with Central Americans beauti-fully bronze. Anglicans speak English, show little appreciation of Hispanic culture, and usually sound like dunderheads if they essay Spanish at all. Anglicans are either English – in which case they conjure up the bogies of Morgan and his men who sacked Panama Viejo, the oldest city on the Pacific Coast of the Americas – or else they are "niggers" – mere drawers of water and hewers of wood – or else they are Yankees, imperialists all – and all of them Protestants. And what Protestant, they say, can know any-thing about sacraments or apostolic succession?

The odds against us seem insurmountable. Yet, strangely enough, but too slowly for comfort, our numbers increase. Growth, despite the feebleness of our effort, is due to the inherent power of Anglicanism to commend itself to thoughtful persons in search of a Catholic form of Christianity which has neither political aspirations nor intellectual arrogance.

This is a debatable point. I have against me two people who know the ground far better than I do. One is the Bishop of Central America. "That we can make a great appeal to intellectuals in Central America," he writes, "is an attractive and charming theory but it is yet to be demonstrated." Perhaps I have misunderstood. However, I do not interpret that remark to mean that we have tried and failed but only that we have not yet properly tried. Next comes my friend, Gordon Charlton, who, deeply tanned by a long southern exposure, told me at lunch in Mexico City that he seeks to "dispose of a cherished fancy with which we Episcopalians fondly delude ourselves: that all Latin America is groaning and travailing in the hope and expectation of just such a 'middle way' as Anglicanism represents". Although a perfect host, Mr. Charlton laboured to disabuse me of one of my deepest convictions. "It is demonstrably untrue, and we must stop kidding ourselves with it," he said. He added to my discomfiture by going on to say, "There is no basis in fact to the notion that a reformed Catholicism which preserves the ancient faith and order of Christendom, free of the abuses of idolatry, superstition, and priestly domination, will immediately make an irresistible appeal to Latins."

With this I will not quarrel. I myself never used the words "immediately" or "irresistible". I would be the first to admit that all of this will take time, patience, and far more skill than we have manifested hitherto. *Of course* most of the people are not yet conscious of their need. Most of them, in fact, are not even conscious that there exists such a thing as Anglicanism. The fault isn't theirs. We have hardly given them a chance even to turn us down.

To escort my reader through Costa Rica, Nicaragua, El Salvador, Honduras, and Guatemala – country by country – would be to make a book already overlong intolerable, although I wish to insist on behalf of these republics that each is scenic and interesting in its own right. I pity, however, the bishop on whom has fallen the responsibility of serving five such diversified nations. Caroline Divines, who had frightful battles of their own to fight, would have regarded it as a weird and improbable task to lay upon one man the charge of so much diversity and difficulty. Which only goes to show that times have changed! We are no longer in neat and tidily organized Britain. We have come of age, although we are still adolescents. Anglicanism, I must maintain, stumbled into universality, prodded perhaps by Providence. I hope that we can grow into the job. Central America has an emerging middle class. There and among the intelligentsia lies our God-given task. Young people who must work their way through university will become the middle class and they will be open-minded enough to question the hierarchically-dominated Roman régime. These are the likely Episcopalians of the future.

From the Missionary District of Central America, a side excursion.

The Archbishop of the West Indies, writing from British Guiana, said, "I beg you not to exclude from your itinerary our little sister, British Honduras." Numerically, it is the smallest of the West Indian Dioceses. I complied with his request and was amply rewarded.

Belize, the capital city, is a somewhat ramshackle place, below sea level, and owes its existence to citrus fruits, sugar, chicory, hard wood, and mahogany. It is not without reason that the diocesan coat-of-arms displays four mahogany leaves. At certain times of the year Belize is a city of smells. The sea flushes back into the canals all that the citizens flushed out into the sea. Over the years, engineers from Britain, Holland, and the United States have been summoned to try to find a solution. Independently of each other they come up with the same answer: "The only solution is to move the city."

Yet let us be fair. Belize is a city much maligned. It is not as smelly and mosquito-infested as people in other parts of Central America had intimated. I found it picturesque. Its isolation from the rest of the world, however, is stultifying. The cathedral is the oldest non-Roman church building in Central America. It looked its age, too, like the well-worn but neatly pressed blue serge suit of a man in circumstances usually referred to as genteel poverty. The same could be said of the Episcopal residence, Bishopthorpe, which faced on the waterfront, exposed to the full blast of the salt sea spray. The Diocese had scrimped and saved for eleven years to paint the Bishop's house. In the tropics eleven years is a long time to go between coats of paint.

I was in Belize to share the people's pleasure as the painters set up their ladders to get rid of an eyesore. Only two months later Hurricane Hattie reduced the house to sodden splinters. Hardly a church in the Diocese went undamaged. Without a trace of histrionics or hysteria the Bishop wrote me, "We will be years in recovering." Every Caribbean diocese knows what it is to suffer some damage nearly every year from the violence of the West Indian wind.

It was with regret (as they say in travelogues) that I took leave of British Honduras, but no leave will be taken until we have made note of one more fact: this indigent, hurricane-battered, and almost unheard of Diocese can boast of possessing one of the most charming place names in the world – the Archdeaconry of Double Head Cabbage. (Other memorable names in British Honduras: Gallon Jug, Banana Bank, Orange Walk, Spanish Lookout, Dill Water, Monkey River, and Boom.) After inspecting the church and school at Double Head Cabbage, I munched on something indefinable but delectable which had been pummelled by a pestle in a mortar and cooked in an oven underground. As entertainment after luncheon, the schoolboys put on a cricket match, the brawny black Archdeacon serving simultaneously as coach to both sides and as impartial referee.

In one day I accomplished the following: Arose at 4.30 A.M. at Belize which is below sea level and terrifically hot . . . flew to Guatemala City to inspect our one and only church, St. George's, which is housed in a rented mansion and serves one hundred and thirty Americans and English, about thirty-five of whom deign to worship on an average Sunday. The recent appointment, however, of a gifted priest whose mother tongue is Spanish gives promise of the formation of a local congregation. There are inquirers enough, and he – in a good sense – knows the answers, having personally experienced this trajectory: from Romanism, to agnosticism, to secularism, and finally back to faith (but this time within our fold). . . . On this same day that I am describing an Army Major attached to the United States Embassy at Guatemala City put his wife and son and me into a station wagon and off we drove over the mountains to Antigua, former capital of this country. The extinct volcanoes with which the city is ringed lie dormant now, but the most stubborn of them refused to subside until in 1773 it had reduced Antigua to rubble. But even in its ruins there is impressive evidence here of how great was the Spanish effort to Christianize the people. Something great went, somehow, wrong. And then *we* have arrived – but so late, so late and armed with so little! . . . The Major and his family drove me back to the airport in Guatemala City, where they had picked me up a few hours before, and I took off for Mexico City, ending the day there at an altitude of nearly 8,000 feet, my teeth chattering. It was cold.

I am not certain how my constitution continued to stand such unremitting and drastic physical change. It requires a kind of nimbleness to undergo every few days (and sometimes within a single day) a change in altitude, climate, diet, water, customs, language, money. And because different countries drive on different sides of the road, I became a kerbstone coward, afraid to cross the street, not knowing *which* way the traffic would be moving. A journey like mine is destructive of all sense of time and location. The traveller expects breakfast but is confronted with a seven-course dinner. One is prepared for summer, but here it is winter! In the midst of these violent transitions I encountered two constant factors: the presence nearly everywhere of my Church, by which I was sustained and comforted; the second factor – greatly discomfiting – the universality of a human need which Anglicanism *could* supply but does *not*, except token-wise . . . because we as a Church are timid and tightfisted.

Mexico!

I had always wanted to go there, but except for a few "border raids" – incursions from San Diego to Tijuana and Agua Caliente for purposes of gambling and betting on the horses in preconversion days – I had never been there and certainly had had no comprehension of the real Mexico. Probably I don't know the "real" Mexico even yet. But I did pick up a few items which I will venture to call "facts", and I will share them with you.

The first fact is this. It has taken the Mexicans only twelve years to increase their numbers from twenty-four million to thirty-five million. It is already a big nation – and fast will be bigger. There is no country except the United States and Canada to the north and Brazil and Argentina to the south which will count so much for the future of the Western Hemisphere. Whatever your point of view, Mexico is important.

In spite of this, Mexico faces an uphill fight. Sixty per cent of the populace is ill housed. Forty per cent, illiterate. Yet, although Mexico has had a chequered past and has sometimes suffered, sometimes gained from bullet-ridden revolutions, it does seem to have learned some of the arts of self-government, and the elements of corruption from which no government is exempt are under control. I expect Mexico to go places.

But has Anglicanism any relevance to the Mexican scene? Potentially, more than a little. Actually, less than a little.

In an oblique manner I will try to substantiate these statements. Here we need recourse to a few rudiments of Mexican history.

In the 1860's there were ardent Catholics in Mexico who had no grudge against Rome but a huge hatred of Spain. In the polemical tensions of the moment it was, unfortunately, difficult to distinguish between the two. Apparently there was no way to be rid of the one without the other. Rome had come to savour of all the unpalatability of Madrid. Tragic! But of this confusion there was born in 1865 the *Iglesia de Jesus*. Its leaders bore Spanish names, but their zeal – and often their intelligence – was that of a very Germanic Martin Luther. Any impartial historian could testify that here was the inception of a genuine and significant religious reform movement. Mexico, at one moment in its history, might have had a Church of its own: catholic, biblical, reformed, evangelical, and Mexican. In the capital city it at once gathered to itself seven thousand supporters. Provincial towns and country districts were also attracted. But the vigorous infant had not long to live. It appealed to the Episcopal Church in the United States of America, not asking for money but for the Episcopate – but this we denied them. My faulty knowledge of history does not permit me to assert that this anguish for reform was entirely free from elements of oddity. It may have had eccentric features. But this much I do know. We are more liberal with our billions than we are with our bishops. I think we quenched a smoking flax. Would that American Episcopalians in the 1860's could have had the wisdom they showed a century later with the Philippine Independent Church! We let that Church wander for half a century into every manner of vagary, but finally we came to our senses and to its rescue. Mexico, however, we have lost except for a truncated remnant. The Mexican Episcopal Church has fewer members today than did the *Iglesia de Jesus* at its birth.

A point I wish to make will surely be contested, but it is always easy for me to be brave . . . on paper. Anglicanism's role, if only it would play it, is something far more than to pick up dissident and discouraged Roman Catholics, providing for them a spiritual home redolent of incense and orthodox enough to reduce the days they must spend in purgatory. Its far greater purpose, which only tangentially is in contest with Rome, is that of saving Latin America from the fates with which it is threatened: reversion to paganism, capitulation to Communism, engulfment in sectarian deviations. The greatest danger is a little further removed. And that is despair. Latin America is ripe for it. Perhaps it can be staved off for a while, but it will take more than Spanish Catholicism to cure it and, I think, more than American sects to prevent it.

The swing from papalism to pentecostalism is hardly to the advantage of Latin America. "What," I asked, "is the attraction of these sects?" The answer of those who had, in fact, been attracted in this direction was succinct and searing: "Because they make a difference in morals." Both Roman

Catholics and Anglicans might well take note of this and acknowledge that they have an occasion for humility.

It is a nomadic New Yorker's first Sunday in Mexico. Since he is an Episcopalian, he heads for his own cathedral and is thrilled to discover that his temple is colossal in size, embodying that harmonious balance between extension and ornament which was one of the singular achievements of Spanish colonial architecture. The stonework is massive; the portal, exquisitely carved; the lintel, a masterpiece. This is the Cathedral Church of San José de Gracia. To behold it even for a moment is to recognize that here is a building of considerable antiquity.

How came we into possession of so handsome an edifice, for Anglicans certainly did not arrive in time to build it by themselves! The answer is, of course, that originally it was a Roman Catholic house of worship – and eventually one of the many properties belonging to that Church which were confiscated by the new liberal government of Benito Juárez for return to public use. This was in 1857. Implicit in the new constitution, which enunciated the principle of the separation of Church and state, was the guarantee or at least the possibility of freedom of worship. Rome's three hundred years of uncontested monopoly was at an end. As might be expected, a desperate rear-guard action was fought. The Jesuits, in alliance with the aristocracy, drove President Juárez out and celebrated their victory by placing an imperial crown on the head of Maximilian. He had not long to wear it. By 1867 the ill-fated emperor had no further need of it. He was dead, having been executed by a firing squad carefully chosen for the excellence of its marksmanship. Juárez, reinstated as President, reintroduced his liberal ideas. In point of fact, much of the confiscated property was returned to the Roman Church, though certain buildings were retained and later handed over to various groups for charitable, educational, and religious purposes. One of these buildings, the dignified cathedral in which I worshipped on my first Mexican morning, finally was entrusted to us.*

If I rejoiced in our having an historic and noble building in which to practise our form of worship freely, I rejoiced too in the bold, multi-storied building under construction next door. I suppose it is completed by now. The reason for its several floors is that it will serve a multitude of purposes. Here will be – perhaps already are – diocesan offices, a parish hall of the cathedral congregation, Sunday School rooms, a bookstore, a clinic (if I remember rightly), and decent living quarters for the dean and his assistants.

* I wonder, by the way, if many Americans are aware that Abraham Lincoln, after California had been wrested from Mexico, was the person chiefly responsible for seeing to it that the beautiful Franciscan missions along El Camino Real were restored to the Roman Church which had been stripped of them by the Mexican Government.

For once in my life I climbed up unbalustraded staircases without trepida-
tion and balanced myself with unaccustomed insouciance on springy planks
connecting various parts of the building. There was nothing between me
and these heights and the ground below except the rarefied air of Mexico
City. Yet there was not a detail of the newly rising structure I was willing
to miss, for in the intelligent vigour of its design I thought I espied the possibility of Episcopalians amounting to something in Mexico after all.

One treasures every possible harbinger of a brighter future because, staring
you in the face, everywhere you turn, there are sufficient present-day reminders of doleful failures in the past. Returning to my hotel after the
cathedral service, I passed a church of sheer magnificence. Located on the
heavily travelled, brilliantly lighted Avenida Juárez, the Church of San
Francisco is no more than one city block from Alameda Park, and no rookie
ballplayer would be incapable of throwing a baseball from the church
which would splinter the window of the Palace of Fine Arts. In short, this
church is at the hub of the city. In New York, it would be like the location
enjoyed by St. Patrick's. In London, its location would combine the strategic
advantages of the placement both of St. Paul's and Westminster Abbey
and St. Martin-in-the-Fields too. This Church of San Francisco, a joy to
the eye, and a compelling indication of the Church's presence, once nearly
was ours. It was, in fact, offered to us by the Government. Anglicanism's
first bishop in Mexico, an Anglo-Chilean, turned down the offer, saying
he saw no need for it. Perhaps he meant no more than that he knew not
how to find the means of supporting it. This might well have been the crux
of the matter. It is not fair to quarrel with a dead man – especially one
who was conscientious and worked hard. Yet it was a mistake he made, an
error in judgement. Except for the Roman Catholic cathedral there is no
religious building in the city better designed, architecturally, for what the
Prayer Book calls "the exciting of piety", and not even the cathedral has a
location as advantageous. But the Church of San Francisco was lost to us.
What we did not want, the Romans did. In due course, they got it back.

Yet the loss of this one church at the heart of Mexico City is as nothing
compared to our virtual loss of the *Iglesia de Jesus*. Let us listen to Gordon
Charlton again, for he knows and he cares.

"In 1904, due to a recent influx of Americans in Mexico, our House of
Bishops made the country a Missionary District and sent a Bishop purely
for the development of English-speaking work. Bishop Aves was instructed
to give such oversight as he could to the *Iglesia de Jesus* as well, and the fact
that three Mexican Bishops-elect were waiting consecration (as they had
been at several times before) was ignored. Strange that Americans who had
to put up so long without bishops because of British tactlessness, timidity,

and tendentiousness, should have compounded the failure by behaving in much the same way in Mexico and the Philippines. In the face of this final disappointment, the remnant of the *Iglesia de Jesus* gave up its high hopes of becoming a genuine Mexican National Catholic Church and of reforming the entire Christianity of its country. It surrendered its autonomy and begged to be included as a part of the Missionary District of the American Episcopal Church. It was, by that time, down to a fraction of its former size, having lost congregation after congregation to sectarian Christianity through the lack of centralized authority, of organization, and of Episcopal oversight. The enthusiasm, zeal, and drive of its founders had been lost, through thirty-five years of trouble, disappointment, and fruitless waiting."

On a Sunday morning in mid-summer I found myself in the front seat of a car, squeezed in between Bishop Saucedo of Mexico and the visiting Bishop Swift of Puerto Rico. The highway leading southward from the capital rises to a height of 10,000 feet. By this scenic route one comes to Cuernavaca – the place where I am determined to spend my next holiday (or first convalescence!) – and then on to Alejandro, a rustic, rural village of eight hundred people. Waiting for us was a great concourse of Episcopalians from all over Mexico gathered to witness an event that happens all too infrequently in this land: the consecration of a new church, a big and handsome one too. That it was to be dedicated to *San Juan el Teólogo* further endeared the occasion to me, for that is also the name of the Cathedral where I am permitted to serve.*

For once we are the largest church and the only church! (A Roman church will doubtless follow soon!) The extraordinary thing was that all the villagers were friendly. There was not the slightest display of enmity. And the local *tienda* dispensing beer must have loved the advent of Anglicanism. On such a hot day, never had business been so good!

Present for the consecration of the new church were college students from three of our *internados*, augmented by a contingent of young women of the Girls' Friendly Society from the United States, plus a group of laymen from St. Barnabas' Church, Denver. These Colorado churchmen, accompanied by their rector, included thirteen attractive teenagers, motivated by a spirit of high adventure and concern about the mission of the Church. They came to live for a summer (mostly at their own expense, though the National Council had helped them) at the big *internado* at

---

* For a long time I have been rather uncomfortable about the formidable title I bear: Canon Theologian of the Cathedral Church of St. John the Divine. I have made representation to the Dean and Chapter that I would much prefer the style: Canon Divine of the Cathedral Church of St. John the Theologian.

Cuernavaca and to bend their backs to the task of building a laundry under the supervision of an American architect from the same Denver parish.

The day was unforgettable. People had come from everywhere to rejoice with those who rejoice: University people, *Norteamericanos*, a few British, rich Mexicans from Cuernavaca and the capital of Mexico, to worship and then to eat with simple countryfolk who, under the trees, while goats, cows, and untethered horses looked on, welcomed us with grace and quiet dignity and fed us bountifully with country fare, even while being a little overawed by perhaps the most momentous gathering in Alejandro's history.

Our Church, I maintain, could make history in Latin America – and change history. We have at least half a chance but will never make it with half measures. "*Hoy, no mañana*" – today, not tomorrow – is the proud motto on the coat-of-arms of the Diocese of British Honduras. But we will have no future in "*Mañana* Land" unless we act "*hoy*".

29

CANADA: Potential Unlimited

CANADA WAS THE LAST OF THE COUNTRIES ON MY GLOBAL ODYSSEY.
But it was the first of the countries where the Church has combined its
proud religious heritage with a strong sense of national identity, emerging
with a dignified and descriptive name for itself – the Anglican Church of
Canada.

After touching down briefly in my own country, I flew from San Francisco to Vancouver, British Columbia, in the south-west corner of Canada.
Vancouver is fairly Americanized, at least in superficial hustle-bustle, for
proximity to Seattle, Portland, and other cities of the Pacific North-west
has had a definite influence. It is an interesting contrast to Victoria, B.C.,
which has an archbishop, an unfinished cathedral, magnificent drives, a
profusion of rose gardens, and the quiet charm of an English provincial
town.

The Western dioceses of Canada are proud and independent. The Church
did not come to them by a mission from Eastern Canada but directly from
England by way of Cape Horn. Yet they keenly feel the leadership and
unity radiating from Toronto. Officials at Church House, Toronto – headquarters for the Church in Canada – are aware that some distrust of bureaucracy and centralization must be expected. Toronto treads carefully in its
valiant effort to pull the Church into one central force. By the sheer intelligence of its operations, Toronto is winning its way. Clear thinking and far-
sightedness are banishing the timorousness of people who were sceptical
because geographically they were separated. Canada, destined to become
a great nation, is on its way to having an Anglican Church that is united,
truly Canadian, yet loyal to the British Church from which it sprang.

Of course I had only an inkling of these happy conclusions when my plane
landed at Vancouver. Striding out to meet me was a priest who had literally

given his left arm for God. After I had known him for a while he casually remarked that his arm had been shattered while piloting a mission plane. But he did not go into the details of his brush with death; he was all for getting on with the business of showing me Anglican Canada. Although he is vicar of a church in a new suburb to the south of the city, he also makes himself responsible for part of Vancouver's teeming waterfront district. It really was not a parish in a formal sense. The docks and wharves were the aisles of the church and its parishioners were the seamen and the people who always follow seamen – from tattoo artists to prostitutes. My host laughingly said of the rather rough dockside hotel which is his headquarters, "It's the only rectory in the world equipped with three bars!"

From the waterfront I ventured into the rest of Vancouver, the See City of the Diocese of New Westminster. In Christ Church Cathedral (seven of Canada's twenty-one cathedrals are so named) American Episcopalians have no difficulty in following the service, even though Canadians have produced a Prayer Book of their own – and they are loyal to it. This loyalty is a major factor in unifying the Canadian Church in spite of the patchwork manner in which this Church came into being. One of their Prayer Book's unusual features is a Calendar which includes commemoration of persons (Laud, Latimer, Keble, and others) and events right down to the present century. It is not in any sense an attempt to canonize new saints along medieval lines, but rather an orderly way of giving thanks for significant people and happenings. The character of the Anglican Church in Canada is essentially a missionary one, and this national character is apparent in the new Calendar.

An interlude of three weeks in Alaska, a missionary district of the American Church, gave me an opportunity to mull over my initial impressions of Canada. Coming down from Alaskan villages above the Arctic Circle, I flew from Fairbanks and re-entered Canada at Whitehorse in the Yukon, a diocese so thoroughly Canadian that it has pine trees and a bear on its coat of arms. Diocesan heraldry in Canada often bespeaks the great outdoors – snow-capped mountains, the midnight sun, caribou heads, a beaver, a salmon, birchbark canoes with Indians, and the maple leaf which is the national emblem.

At Whitehorse, eight passengers alighted with me. I was third in line. The Customs official scrutinized minutely my passport, which by this time had grown to fantastic proportions with its many supplementary pages. He asked me please to step inside and seat myself. He quickly cleared the other arrivals. This done, he returned to me and asked gravely, for a second time, the purpose of my visit to Canada. In good faith I gave him the same

5. The Anglican Church of Canada

answer as before: "Tourism." Then, with all the pages of my accordion-pleated passport pulled out to their full length, he fixed me with a fishy stare and, pointing to the passport, he asked, "Now, Mr. Johnson, what is your real reason for coming to Canada? Nobody can be that interested simply in touring!"

But I finally convinced this vigilant official of my innocence. He let me in. And thus began a wonderful sweep across the whole width of this marvellous land – from Whitehorse to Edmonton, Regina, Winnipeg, Port Arthur, Sault Ste. Marie, Ottawa, Toronto, Montreal, Halifax, and St. John's, Newfoundland. With lightning speed, moving too fast to be fully informed, I cut a swath across a whole continent, from west to east, receiving at every point a reception both cordial and intelligent.

My chief impression is this: Anglicanism in Canada, as in Australia, got off to a slow start. It laboured under similar disabilities – geographical isolation and provincialism. Regional pride caused the various sections of the country to hang on stubbornly to their own theological seminaries and their own autonomy. Extremes of Churchmanship bred distrust and divisiveness. Canada is yet to complete her escape from these entrapments, but her progress in this direction (perhaps stimulated in part by the Episcopal Church to the south) has been so remarkable that the Australian Church suffers by comparison. What once was a disorganized "clump of churches" in Canada is best described today as a unified Church with "potential unlimited".

Sure of making enemies at every turn, I will go on record as saying that the Canadian Church is only fifteen years behind the times; the Australian Church, forty. It is inevitable that a foreign observer should compare and contrast the Canadian and Australian Churches. Each must serve an enormous, sparsely populated country. Canada, however, exceeds Australia both in terms of geographical size (Canada consists of 3,851,809 square miles; Australia 2,974,581) and in terms of population strength. The Canadian population was in 1961 estimated to stand at 18,085,000; the Australian population in the same year was in the neighbourhood of 10,398,200. Yet, Anglicans "down under" are still in the majority (almost 40 per cent) – however threatened this numerical superiority may be. The Anglicans of Canada, by contrast, are definitely in the minority. They do not constitute more than 8 per cent of the total population. It is commonly forgotten that nearly one half of the Canadian population belongs to the Roman Catholic Church. Yet I will bet my bottom Canadian dollar and, into the bargain, my few remaining Australian pounds that the Anglican 8 per cent in Canada has a far profounder impact on the culture of Canada than does the Anglican 40 per cent on the culture of Australia. For the Canadian Church is more vital, more imaginative, more up to date. Its clergy are, on the whole, better educated; its people tend to be more prosperous, for Canada is rich in natural resources; and, may an American be forgiven for such boasting, it has received impetus of a generally beneficent sort from the aggressive Church which percolates so furiously south of the three-thousand-mile unfortified American-Canadian border.

Canada won my heart because I see in it a synthesis of that which is best about Britain and best about the United States. But this synthesis, imperfectly realized as yet, has come to the fore only of late. It was an unexpected by-product of World War II. Canadian Anglicans, second to none in their loyalty to the British Commonwealth of Nations, perceived that war-beleaguered Britain and the British Church should no longer be looked to for "mothering". The time had come for the Anglicans of Canada to stand on their own feet, to raise their own funds for the work of the Church, and to rear their own sons for the Ministry. This was no American-style "Declaration of Independence" from England. It was, rather, the mature decision of a very English daughter, steadfast and grateful, who saw that "Mother" already had her hands full and that the moment had arrived for the daughter, out of love for the Mother, to make her own way in the world.

This involved – in spite of war and the economic depression which preceded it – a determined and largely successful effort to achieve self-support. It meant also an intensified search to recruit her clergy from among her own children. It was a call upon her to summon the courage, without disloyalty, to produce a Prayer Book of her own, better suited to her needs and more consonant with the best contemporary scholarship. It entailed, supremely, the choice of a new name for herself. It is impossible sufficiently to admire her decision in 1955 to call herself "The Anglican Church of Canada". By a single stroke, a very English Canadian Church accomplished two things. The heavy immigration in the postwar period, with its growing diversification of national backgrounds in the Canadian population, had taught her that to be called "The Church of England in Canada" was evangelistically a drawback. So she dropped it. At the same time, she was rightly unashamed of the fact that this particular formation of the Christian tradition had its provenance in the British Isles, and for this reason she had no hesitation in acknowledging parentage. She called herself "Anglican" – and thus became the first member of the Anglican Communion to lift this word to legal status. But note well: it is the Anglican Church of Canada – and the accent is as much on "Canada" as it is on "Anglican".

The size of Canada is staggering even to Australians and Americans who are not exactly unacquainted with the phenomenon of distance. But persons who have never budged from the British Isles can hardly believe their ears when they hear Dr. Carrington, sometime Archbishop of Quebec, tell them that a Londoner bound for Vancouver has accomplished less than half of his journey on his arrival in Quebec.* We are talking about a country which faces on three oceans: the Atlantic, the Pacific, and the Arctic. Newfoundland was no part of it before 1949. It did not even become a country until 1867, and so far as the Anglican Church is concerned, the General Synod was not formed on a national basis until 1893. Europeans are blameless for not being able to grasp things so large and so new. (I remember how I startled Danes in 1946 by telling them that the first white woman to be born in the State of Arizona was still alive.) The scattered colonies which were to become Canada were held together, for many decades, by nothing more binding than the steel rails of the Canadian Pacific and Canadian National Railways. Indeed, until fifteen years ago, Canadian motorists who wanted to cross the continent by car drove south of the border to avail themselves of American highways. To this very day, the Trans-Canada Highway has some rough stretches.

The Canadian Church, in short, must still address itself to frontier life. On both the east and west coasts the Church's work among fisherfolk and isolated settlers is done by ships, there being no other way to reach them. In the north, the Church arrives by sled.

My generalizations on Canada are reflected in the individual dioceses I visited. After entering Canada at Whitehorse†, I flew to Edmonton, the See City of the Diocese of the same name. It has doubled in size since the discovery of oil in 1947. The population has soared to three hundred thousand, a growth watched with apprehensive interest because the Anglo-Saxon population of the Province of Alberta is only just big enough to swing the provincial vote. Despite the Anglo-Saxon majority, Anglicans comprise no more than a mere 10 per cent of the population. But such estimates are misleading, for a 10 per cent slice of the numerical count would mean that the city of Edmonton alone could claim thirty-six thousand Anglicans – and there are not that many in all of Alberta.

Alberta has large groups of Ukrainians and Germans, as well as a sizeable

---

* Canadians chuckled when a London newspaper, reporting on heavy rains in Canada, ran the headline: CANADA FLOODED.

† Whitehorse, a jumping-off place for the gold rush, has a cathedral of logs (built in 1900) well known to American servicemen based there in wartime and during the construction of the Alaska Highway. The old building stands near the starkly modern Christ Church Cathedral completed in 1960.

number of Hungarians. One readily realizes that the old name, the Church of England in Canada, was a real handicap.* The immigrants, for the most part, founded their own churches. (There are twenty-one churches on one street in Edmonton.) But as children grow up and forsake the old language they are largely lost to their churches, though some are finding their way to us. The intermarriage of Anglo-Saxons with persons of other national backgrounds brings many to the Church.

The Orthodox priests seem bent on holding to the old ethnic and linguistic ties, a devotion that does not best serve those of Russian and Ukrainian descent who are third-generation Canadians.

But to go back to Edmonton, a city that is at least 50 per cent Central European. You can travel for twenty miles in any direction outside Edmonton and not meet a soul whose native language is English. The French element, which is large, is heavily Roman Catholic, of course, and often their priests are scandalously misinformed, not to say malicious, in what they allege about Anglicans. In speaking of the clergy I should add that the most encouraging feature of Western Canada is the great growth of an indigenous Anglican Ministry.

Like most Americans, when I thought at all of Canada, I thought of it as a nation of Empire Loyalists. I imagined runaway Englishmen who were often more British than the British. What a surprise to discover that a good one-third (if not one-half) of the people I passed on the streets of Edmonton spoke English with a variety of charming accents.

At the end of a happy week-end in Edmonton I flew to Regina, Cathedral city of the Diocese of Qu'Appelle, situated on the seemingly limitless prairies of Saskatchewan. Its church population, spread over a large area, is seventy-six thousand. I immediately began to hear bits and pieces of one of the most curious diocesan histories in all my travels – indeed, in the whole Anglican Communion. Occasionally I have spoken in this book of organizations in England called "Friends of the Diocese of Such-and-Such", which have from afar exerted influences of tremendous good – and, let us be frank, of tremendous harm. The "Friends" back in Mother England, however basically good their intentions may have been, often had the same smothering influence which the novelist Philip Wylie has so bitterly attributed to that form of American motherhood he calls "Momism".

The Qu'Appelle Association in England, prior to World War II, thought of itself as *being* the Diocese of Qu'Appelle. In a real sense it *was*. It heavily

* One well-named denomination is the United Church of Canada. The United Church, according to Dr. Carrington, was "formed some forty years ago, out of the old Methodist Church, and a substantial part of the old Presbyterian Church, with the few Congregationalist churches which had been formed in Canada". I was told that most non-Roman Catholics gravitate to the United Church because it has clergy who also speak the European languages.

subsidized the Diocese, met its annual deficits, provided its clergy (Englishmen and a few Irish), and presided over its destinies from abroad. Everybody conceived of it primarily as a British Chaplaincy. It built its churches, but not, alas, its parish houses. Since parish houses had never been customary in England, it was reasoned, why in the world should they be necessary in Canada. In short, England did everything and the Canadian Anglicans out West did almost nothing for themselves. Then came 1940 and the stoppage of funds from the United Kingdom. The Qu'Appelle Association dried up as a source of revenue. Naturally this precipitated a financial crisis for the Diocese – one from which it has not yet fully recovered.*

One has to keep in mind the newness of Regina, the seat of the Diocese of Qu'Appelle. When the first Bishop acquired twenty acres of land as a building site for his cathedral, for his Synod Office, girls' school, theological college, and Bishop's Court, the property was eccentric, located on the outskirts of town. Not a tree was to be seen in any direction. The Provincial Parliament, built even farther out of town, stood in handsome isolation on a treeless prairie. Today both the ecclesiastical and provincial buildings are well shaded and surrounded by a city which has more than doubled its population since 1945.

The Bishop drove me to see a church in a new housing area. The site was well chosen. The Church, for a change, got in on the ground floor. It was the first in the field. A large new school has been erected just across the street. And, in the words of the Bishop, "bungalows burgeoned as fast as bunnies." Approximately four hundred new houses had gone up in the past year – yet the Church had not grown at all. What *is* it that we fail to do, or else do wrong?

On my first evening in Regina the Bishop and his wife took me to dine at a hotel where I found the headwaiter was Danish, while one of the waitresses was German and another, Dutch. All were extremely friendly. I talked with them all, thinking to myself that this little group was a living reminder of how cosmopolitan Canada has become. Yet we go on acting as if we had a ministry only to people of British origin.

The Bishop of Qu'Appelle was, I found, fully aware of our unfortunate tendency to cater solely to people of British origin. He was fighting against it furiously. But he told me the sickening story of an entire congregation of Ukrainian Orthodox (in a town where there was no church of their own)

---

* The American Church is repeating the same mistake in Brazil, the Philippines, and in Mexico. It is not that there should be fewer American dollars for missions. On the contrary, there should be more. But they should be dollars for *extension*, not for subsidizing existing work which could be trained to support itself.

who approached the local Anglican Church, asking to be admitted and were turned away. So they said, "Go to . . . We'll build a church of our own." This happened only a few years ago. Today their church stands – large, well-built, gleaming – with a resident Ukrainian priest and a congregation three times as large as the Anglican one.

How difficult it is to report such an incident without appearing to be unappreciative of, and ungrateful towards, the Church of England! May I affirm once again that I am an Anglophile and that I, like many other critical outsiders, realize that all Anglicans everywhere owe more than they can possibly realize, or ever repay, to *Ecclesia Anglicana*, the Mother of us all. Yet it *is* a fact that the very Englishness of Anglicanism has often been as much a hindrance and a handicap as it has been a help. The Anglican Communion came into being at a time when England was top nation, king of the walk, and Englishmen thought of themselves as the lords of creation. To their credit was their concern, their deep, genuine, authentic, sincere concern for their Empire. To their discredit was their hauteur, an unconscious arrogance which in part remains to this day, even though their Empire has largely disappeared. I glory not in the dissolution of that Empire. I do not think that it has been to the advantage of the world that that Empire no longer exists. Nor can I sufficiently admire the skill and sagacity with which the English, faced with the facts and forces of history, relinquished their claims and gradually withdrew from hegemony.

I have read the arguments of Gore, Temple, Fisher, and others, but I still feel that the Establishment ought to go. The Church of England, exploited even from pre-Reformation days, would have been a far stronger entity if it could have been freed from its connection with the State. Only as a free Church can it really be in fact free to become what it now likes to claim it is – the conscience of a nation.

During my stay in Qu'Appelle I realized that I was in a Province which has *three* theological colleges, not one of them first class – and this is true of all Canada with a few glorious exceptions. The colleges were founded and maintained through the years because of the partisan strife of bishops who were not on speaking terms with each other! The bishops of the Province had not even sat down with each other to discuss mutual problems until recent years. But now – happy augury of a new age – we have a Bishop of Qu'Appelle, reputedly High Church, though trained at Wycliffe, and a Bishop of Saskatchewan, something of a Low Churchman in spite of his training at traditionally High Church Trinity College, who confer periodically. The future, I repeat, is bright with promise. Only a pessimist lacking historical perspective could think otherwise. I am not of that school.

Since many Americans think of totem poles and red-coated Royal

Canadian Mounted Police as symbols of Canada, I was interested to learn that the Bishop of Qu'Appelle was Chaplain to the Mounties' Central Training School at Regina. The picturesque chapel is the oldest building on the campus.

While I found that the Diocese of Qu'Appelle had once been regarded as a British chaplaincy in Canada, I was to learn that Winnipeg, my next stop after Regina, is, in many ways, like a British chaplaincy in Europe. The main reason for this impression is the presence of so many ethnic groups among Winnipeg's four hundred and fifty thousand people. Its fifty thousand Ukrainians constitute the largest group of Ukrainians outside the Ukraine. Golden "onion" domes, surmounted by the crosses of the Eastern Orthodox Church, are typical of the internationalism of Winnipeg and the surrounding country. I heard many tongues. English is not taken for granted – not by any means, as evidenced by a sign I spotted in a shop window, "English spoken here."

In the ecclesiastical province of Rupert's Land – particularly in Winnipeg, its See City – the Church is slow, once again, to recognize that many of the newcomers would be happy as Anglicans. But if the people are not yet uniting in religion, at least they are in some of the arts. Winnipeg is forced to create its own theatre, ballet, and music. After all, there is nothing to the north except the North Pole, no city to the south until you reach Minneapolis, no cities to the east or to the west for five hundred miles. Many of the surrounding towns with their wide, unpaved main streets look ready-made for the shooting of a Western film.

Winnipeg was the fourth major Canadian city I had visited. By this time I began to see that the Canadian Church is fairly slow in taking up newer features of the Liturgical Movement. Either the service remains unchanged, or no attempt is made to explain the introduction of such innovations as the Gospel procession, the bringing of the elements, as well as the alms at the offertory, and the Westward Position at the altar. As a consequence, some ceremonial observances often appear to be little more than "gimmicks".

My chief architectural interest in Winnipeg was not in the handsome old chapel but in the inspired renovation of a downtown church. The entire wall behind the altar had been replaced by stained glass of contemporary design in soft colours into which the old, traditional window has been reset.

The Diocese of Rupert's Land had large numbers of Scottish Presbyterians who had scant choice but to become Anglicans because for a long time the Hudson's Bay Company would permit only the ministrations of Anglican priests.

Not only Rupert's Land, but the whole Canadian Church, suffers from Victorian *Cathedralesque Chancelitis*. It goes on singing the psalms, no matter how unmelodious or unedifying they may be. Often this is detrimental to public worship. In brief, the Canadian Church is hobbled by tradition. In playing out its self-appointed role as *Chaplaincy to the Faithful* it encounters pious people who *want the whole service* – and imagine it is not Anglicanism unless everything is chanted. They get what they want. But almost no thought is given to devising worship that would reach outside the narrow circle of the traditionalists. We cannot expect people to tolerate protracted services nor can we become sacrament-centred if we refuse to authorize laymen to administer the chalice.

One of the finest aspects of the Anglican Church in Canada are the Diocesan Councils of Social Services. No diocese lacks one. Most of them are wide-awake and hard-hitting. Their task is to stimulate in the parishes a social concern that in turn inspires long-range planning for such undertakings as hospital chaplaincies, Indian chaplaincies, and other activities. Despite their presence in every diocese, we still must wait for planning on a national scale. The councils are too confined to diocesan autonomy. Moreover, there should be in Ottawa, the national capital, a liaison between the Church and the government, especially in such matters as Indian work. I found it difficult to learn the Anglican attitude on specific social problems. As yet, there is nobody who can speak for the Church as a whole.

"Social concern" is something quite new to the Anglican Church in Canada. Yes, there has been concern for the Indians on the reservations. ("Up on the reservation where they belong" is the phrase usually heard.) Solicitude for the Indian frequently amounts to nothing more than that shown by a lady who may be prepared to take an Indian girl as a maid for the summer – if the lady is feeling especially Christian.

There are more Indians, or people of Indian extraction, in Winnipeg than on any one of the reservations in Manitoba. The Church has behaved exactly like the government in handling the Indians, perpetuating a psychology of permanent dependence and irresponsibility. More than one diocese gives the impression that it will supply missionaries *ad infinitum* without any expense to Indians. The diocese thus unconsciously emulates the example of those English societies which once had helped to support the Church in Canada.

The Indians have been under extreme pressure to move to labour centres because the trapping and hunting industries are about finished. But the Indians have not been trained to cope with the city. Nor does the Indian, when he comes to town, have a friend at court. That much-needed friend might be supplied in the person of the Anglican priest, if only there were more celibate priests who could live in the depressed areas of the city where the Indian finds himself.

In other words, the Church must go to the Indian whether he is on a reservation or in a slum. It cannot build great ghetto-like institutions, such as orphanages, hospitals, and homes for the aged. The Church did this in the last century, but now the government has the money for such projects and it is up to the Church to work *through* the government facilities.*

With the decline of traditional activities such as hunting and trapping the Indians in urban areas have to do the most menial tasks and unskilled work, much of it seasonal. In the off-seasons many Indians go back to the reservations. It is a migratory existence and one that gives them the feeling of not belonging anywhere. It is a rootlessness that reminds me of the Australian "walkabout".

The situation is much relieved by an institution such as the Indian and Métis Friendship Centre in Winnipeg. Happily co-operating in its support are Roman Catholics, Anglicans, Presbyterians, and the United Church.

One of the principal problems recognized at the Friendship Centre is that people who have always been hunters or trappers find it difficult to adjust to an eight-hour day. Indian men on trek were accompanied by their wives. But in the jobs they are offered today – bush clearing for a hydro-electric plant is an example – wives cannot go along and consequently there is the temptation to marital infidelity.

The total Indian population of Canada is estimated to be one hundred and eighty thousand.† This does not include the métis – those of mixed blood. The various tribes are at very different levels of development. Some have the feeling that the world owes them a living.

If the Anglicans do not take over Indian welfare right now, with serious intent and redoubled vigour, the Romans and the Pentecostals will. We must move far beyond the idea, summed up in the words "the Church and Old Clothes" – the feeling that everything is all right as long as the women of the Church keep up the supply of old clothes to the Indians.

When I was delving into the Indian problem I visited St. Andrew's-on-the-Red River, a few miles north of Winnipeg. Erected in 1849, St. Andrew's is the oldest stone church continuously in use in Western Canada. It held

* Regretfully I must say that the Roman Catholic Church is a big stumbling block in the way of integration. Rome wants to keep its own schools; it does not want to abandon the Indian schools it already has on the reservation.

† The problem of people and changing populations is not confined to the Indians. The Gordon Commission estimated that by 1970 there will be a concentration of 57 per cent of the Canadian population in fifteen urban centres. This points up the importance of studying the Church's role and proper *modus operandi* in large cities.

within its venerable walls an unusual surprise in my tour of Anglicanism – hassocks covered with buffalo hide.

And I remember St. Andrew's, too, for the story I heard of an Indian boy who, emerging with his father from a Wild West movie, said, "Dad, don't we ever win?"

An ancient but comfortable steamer, puffing asthmatically across Lake Superior, conveyed me from Port Arthur to Sault Ste. Marie. When I saw under construction the mighty bridge which will link Canada with Michigan and the United States I could not help but reflect how important it is to have an ecclesiastical bridge of understanding and exchange between the United States and Canada.

In Toronto (where the Cathedral Church of St. James raises the tallest spire in Canada) I found lively interest in many aspects of Anglicanism because of the long preparation for the Anglican Congress of 1963. A dozen years ago the Anglican population was largest, with the Roman Catholics next, and the United Church in third place. In the census of 1961 the Romans were the biggest because of the huge immigration from Europe. As a whole the Anglican Church in Canada is not girded to meet the challenge, but the Diocese of Toronto is trying. There is, for instance, an Anglican congregation of two hundred Japanese families. Segregated only because of language, they have no building of their own but meet in existing churches. Their young people already identify themselves with other Canadians. An admirable relationship exists with the Orthodox and, in an outlying area where they have not yet built a church, the Orthodox children attend the Anglican Sunday Schools.

Toronto reminded me of Chicago and Philadelphia, mixed in equal proportions. The pattern of its downtown churches is like that of any large city. The diocese wants to keep these churches open for the people who still reside in the changing neighbourhoods. Toronto has come as far as really *knowing* the pattern of the Inner City. The integration of many races has been fairly well achieved in these downtown parishes – although this has not been accomplished in suburban parishes.

It was in Toronto that I discovered there is not so much feeling in Canada as in the United States that the Church must stay out of politics. Yet it is in Canada that the Church's political utterances often seem too liberal for the laity and especially to the big businessmen from Montreal.

My stay in Toronto also offered more insight into the missionary role of the Anglican Church in Canada. The truth is that it has not made up its mind, particularly in the West, as to *what* its mission should be and to whom it ought to be directed. While its missionary objectives are not always clearly defined, it reaches out with a large and generous heart: there has been a spurt of workers – sixty-seven in all – going overseas recently; there is a total of twenty-two Indian and Eskimo clergy, the largest of any religious body in North America; and 28 per cent of the Church's missionary budget is spent in Canada. Certainly there is a lot of ecclesiastical paternalism. It is always the Man from the East or from the West who swoops in by aeroplane to administer the sacraments, shakes hands, beams, looks at his watch – and flies away. This is "the Church" to many people in the remote reaches of Canada. What, then, should the Church be in these places? Is it the people headed by the local catechist who has shared their joys and sorrows – or is it the airborne missionary from headquarters? The equation of education with ordination is an Anglican heresy. Why do we contend that only a man theologically educated may be ordained? It strikes me as far more practical to have the theologically educated man come in periodically to teach, and let him who lives among the people be the one who gives them the sacraments.

Confronted with the vast expanses of Canada we are reminded of the blessings of radio and television. In these media we do not make sufficient use of the laity. A clergyman must always do the "churchy" and "preachy" things. But a priest does not necessarily become the best spokesman on television by simply bringing him into a studio and plastering him with light pancake make-up and handing him a blue-dyed clerical collar. (A white collar gives us on the television screen a halo that is not always an appealing, nor particularly deserved, embellishment of our appearance.)

The director of radio and television work in the Diocese of Toronto takes encouragement from the excellent co-operation between various Churches, Rome included, and the Canadian Broadcasting Corporation. I regard television as one of the great sources of security in a mobile society. And, at least in Canada, it is not difficult to gain an audience's attention, because the same "Westerns" are used every week – hence *even* a religious programme is welcomed! Finally, there is the enormously stimulating statistical report revealing that 90 per cent of the Canadian people might have television in their homes if they wished.

When Canada's particular problems and solutions were poured out to me I thought immediately of the need for all of our radio and television specialists to meet together. They are not always clergy – in fact, Toronto's supervisor is an articulate, knowledgeable lady, Mrs. Gordon Montizambert. But clergy or not, they have a mission and a ministry of great significance and potential. Why not let all the Mrs. Montizamberts confer? We are wasting much time and money by needless duplication.

As for formal education, the clergy does not have the right to enter the secular schools, where courses in moral and spiritual values are taught by their own teachers. In a few localities the children may be released for religious instruction by their pastors – "released time", as Americans call it – but not many take advantage of it. No one appears much disposed to increase the number of Anglican parochial schools.

There is at least one bright spot in my findings on Canadian education, and that is the loyal adherence throughout Canada to the same set of Sunday School lesson materials. This has been an important factor in creating nation-wide unity in the Canadian Church.

A close look at the Diocese of Toronto presents some interesting facts. The most striking is the concentration of population in metropolitan Toronto and the existence outside it of about seven urban communities of considerable size. The diocese has bought future sites in all of them. The rest of the work is rural, carried on by a total of fifty priests.

Toronto is the marketing, distributing, and industrial centre of Canada, and consequently land values are extremely high. Its present population of one and three-quarter million is expected to increase to a total of three million. There is the typically Canadian range of various cultures – for instance, there are two hundred and fifty thousand Italians, which means that one out of every ten persons in Toronto is an Italian. I was still pondering these staggering figures when I saw Thorncliffe Park and learned that it was the only all-apartment development in Canada – an indication of what remains to be done suitably to accommodate future residents. In this new housing area the diocese has bought a two-acre site on which one of its nine "portable" chapels can be situated. The chapels-on-wheels are but one of the innovations in the Toronto diocese. Another is the Anglican Information Centre, which interviews more than three thousand people a year who inquire about the Church. And the diocese can be unusually proud of its monthly newspaper, *The Anglican*, which has a paid circulation of over thirty-five thousand.

Ottawa was the last world capital I visited on my long journey. Its chief landmark is the grey stone government building where the changing of the guard is the most English ceremony anywhere – England included. Ottawa, as one might expect, is also a See City. Seventeen per cent of the population is Anglican – a figure slightly higher than the Anglican percentage for all of Canada (nationally, the country is 44 per cent Roman Catholic, 25 per cent United Church, and 18 per cent Anglican).

In Ottawa I heard one of those disconcerting little stories (perhaps discouraging is a more appropriate word!) that came to me now and then throughout my tour of Anglicanism – a story which, I suppose, might be encountered in any church, although that does not make it any easier to bear. The report concerned a Jew who wanted to join forces with us and be ordained to the priesthood. He was an educated man of eminent talent. He was rejected. Why? "Where could we use him?" asked the authorities. Of course I inquired about his eventual fate. The answer was that having become a convinced Christian he could hardly be daunted by being turned away by the Anglicans, and so he went into the United Church. He became one of its most distinguished leaders.

Montreal was the last of the large cities I visited. It was my misfortune to arrive just prior to Labour Day – the holiday that traditionally falls on the first Monday in September and makes up the last of the long summer week-ends. It is observed in Canada as in the United States, though perhaps even more scrupulously in Canada where, of course, the Fourth of July Independence Day celebration is hardly an occasion for shutting up shop!

So I missed meeting people who might have helped me in my exploration of the Church's work in Montreal. I did not see the Archbishop, who with many other bishops and archbishops was, I am sure, having his final short vacation before beginning a busy season of confirmations, ordinations, and other episcopal duties. Nor did I meet the Reverend Eric Jay, who had come to the Montreal Theological College after serving as Chaplain to Dr. Fisher. But his presence in Montreal gave me cause for reflecting on some of the unusual ways in which the Church has enabled a few of its priests to observe its workings at its very heart – Lambeth Palace – and then has sent them to a variety of posts. I recalled, for instance, that the amiable Scotsman, Alan Don, brought a great deal to his post as Dean of Westminster because of his many years of devoted service as chaplain to the ninety-seventh Archbishop of Canterbury, Cosmo Gordon Lang.

My trip was drawing to its close. But my itinerary still called for several days in Quebec and Newfoundland. I noted in my diary at the time, "The farther East I go, the more English everything becomes. That is to say, the less hospitable people become and the less they understand what I am after."

On Newfoundland I brought to bear all the powers of observation that had been sharpened by my visits to eighty countries. I found that it was only gradually learning, both politically and ecclesiastically, to be a part of Canada. Everyone spoke of the swift and tremendous social changes. Yet if things are greatly changed, greatly modernized *now*, one wonders what Newfoundland must have been like twenty-five years ago. St. John's, though looked upon by people in the outposts as the last word and the very hotbed of modernity, has an outward appearance of the 1920's and earlier.

The last question to ask in St. John's is, "Where were you born?" Redundant query! Nearly everybody in St. John's was born in St. John's. By contrast, in the two new pulp and paper towns on the west coast, almost the first question to be asked is, "Where do you come from?" A whole new cosmopolitan element is moving in.

Gander is a similar place. Prior to World War II, only the caribou lived there. Now it is an international airport. So also Goose Bay. And in the interior of Labrador there are the new mines – with miners from the world over.

The mines, the industries, the aeroplane, the new roads, the automobiles, the radio and now television are jolting Newfoundland out of its isolation and inbreeding. Union with Canada has made and will continue to make momentous differences. Government is being greatly expanded, all manner of new governmental workers have moved to the island. New houses have gone up everywhere.

But the Church is slow in adjusting itself to changing conditions. As evidence of this, let me mention the notice board outside the Cathedral of St. John the Baptist. Although freshly painted, it still declares that this is none other than "The Church of England" (presumably the gate of heaven) – not that it is "The Anglican Church of Canada", whatever *that* might lead to. And the Cathedral did not have a sufficient quantity of the new Canadian Prayer Book to enable its congregation to follow the prescribed order of worship. The explanation was economics and a short supply of the new books from the printers. It was hardly the whole story. The real reason was that people were in no hurry to change.

It is greatly to Newfoundland's credit that 90 per cent of its clergy are "local talent". To meet clergy that are Newfoundland born and bred is a refreshing discovery. Yet there is the need to face up realistically to what it reflects – a fear of the outside, a distrust of Canada, and of Toronto in particular.

In St. John's the population is 42 per cent Roman to 22 per cent Anglican. The so-called "Irish Invasion" accounts for the predominance. We are still important in the community, and we hold our own in the professions. But in the financial field our position is weaker. The situation reminded me of my findings in Quebec and Montreal where Anglicans protect themselves from the French by clinging, with some desperation, to English ways of thought and behaviour. This is truer of Montreal than of Quebec, because there are enough Anglicans in Montreal to enable them to band together as a clique. In Quebec City there are so few Anglicans that they have to fraternize with the French Canadians, and they do so very affably.

It is pleasant to note that Roman-Anglican cordiality dates from the arrival of the first Anglican Bishop in Quebec. That courageous pioneer was met at the wharf by the Roman Catholic Archbishop who kissed him on both cheeks, in proper French fashion, and said with a broad smile, "Thank God you have arrived. It's high time you got here to shepherd your sheep!"

At last I arrived in Nova Scotia. An impressive Vocational Conference in the See City of Halifax indicated Nova Scotia's awareness that shore-fishing and small farming are dwindling. Only the big mechanized farms are self-supporting; the smaller farmers are coming into town. The best rural leadership is constantly drained off and, too, there are fewer country lads who seek Holy Orders. The result is that city boys must be persuaded to minister in the country – and most of them want little part of it. If they go at all, they undertake a country parish as a stepping stone to a better position back in town.

"The Church of England in Nova Scotia still suffers from being too English," said a young man seated next to me as we flew to Halifax. That ruggedly built Canadian, who pilots a plane in the summer in order to finance his studies in dentistry, added with more insight than he knew: "One would prefer a nasal accent, even if one abominates a nasal accent, if it comes to a choice between that and the assumed English accent of too many of the clergy."

On that negative note, which is, nonetheless, a telling truth, I finished my final observations in the last of dozens of small notebooks that I had filled as I encircled the globe. Yet this chance remark had its positive value, for I was reminded of the many accents and tongues in which the entire Anglican Communion raises its single and universal invitation, "Let us pray for the whole state of Christ's Church. . . ."

30

UNITED STATES: A Tour de Force

IT MIGHT WELL BE WONDERED WHY IT IS THAT A BOOK OF THIS SORT contains no discussion of Hawaii and Alaska – which were among the most interesting places I visited.

Each has a fascinating history. Each, in its own way, is spectacularly scenic. Both have been missionary concerns of the American Episcopal Church for a long time and, from an ecclesiastical point of view, give us reason for rejoicing.

But they are omitted from this book for the simple reason that they have achieved Statehood in the American Union of States. This occurred in 1959. To be neglected by me is part of the heavy price they must pay for Statehood! For I have made up my mind to write *nothing* about the Episcopal Church in my own country. A drastic decision, I admit, for we *are* part of the Anglican Communion – and by no means an uninteresting part. Why my silence? There are two reasons.

One, if I were to praise my Church in my own country – as I certainly would have to do – non-American Anglicans (some of whose knuckles I have rapped rather hard) might accuse me of bias and boasting.

Two, if I were to criticize my Church in my own country – as I certainly would have to do – I would get myself in hot water with many of my fellow churchmen. After all, I have to *live* here! In the case of other countries, I could drop my dynamite and run. But here in the United States I have to stay.

Accordingly, I beg leave to submit the United States by title only.

Now it is necessary for some Anglican to come from Brazil or Japan or Ireland or Burma – someone as brash as I am, someone as willing to trust snap judgements as I have been, someone as little deterred by his possession of nothing more than superficial knowledge, someone who shares my talent for being rude: Let this someone pay a fleeting visit to the United States and then let him write a chapter *ad modum* Johnson that can be appended as a supplementary chapter to a possible second edition of this book.

Meanwhile PECUSA need have no fear. Its secrets are safe with me. I will take them with me to my grave.

31

WHAT'S IN A NAME?

SUPPOSE THAT AFTER A SLEEPLESS NIGHT ON THE MIDNIGHT EXPRESS
from Gaya, followed by a long bus ride, you have alighted at a place called
Ranchi, in the State of Bihar and the Diocese of Chota Nagpur. You are
dust-covered and gaunt. Because a letter announcing your arrival went
astray there is no one to meet you. You cannot remember the dedication
of the Cathedral Church, and the only means of transportation available is a
pedicab. What do you ask for? Do you say to the cyclist, "Take me, please,
to the Church of India, Pakistan, Burma and Ceylon"? That is a mouthful
that could be chewed only in places like Lambeth Palace. So you say,
hopefully, "The Anglican Church?" Faced with a friendly but uncompre-
hending stare, you are forced to say, reluctantly, "The Church of England?"
Still you get nowhere. At last you break down and say, "Take me, please,
to the S.P.G. Church" . . . and as fast as his legs can pedal, you are there.
S.P.G. he knows. The others he has never heard of.

Elsewhere in the world the dialogue between you and the driver would
follow much the same pattern except that you would end by asking for
C.M.S. or U.M.C.A. or B.C.M.S. instead of S.P.G.* To houses of worship
so initialled he can take you. Otherwise you never pull away from the kerb,
unless he is an enterprising and perhaps unscrupulous man, in which case
you are taken on an expensive city tour to each church until you find the
one you are seeking.

The word "Anglican" has not yet won general currency. We fool ourselves if we think it has. In the United States of America it is commonly
thought to mean "Anglo-Catholic" – "Oh, yes! he's *Anglican*, you know!"
In mission fields that owe their existence, humanly speaking, to the missionary endeavours of the Protestant Episcopal Church in the United States

* Some American Episcopalians may need to be told that these initials stand, respectively,
for Church Missionary Society, Universities Mission to Central Africa, Bible Churchmen's
Missionary Society, and Society for the Propagation of the Gospel.

of America, Anglican Christians think of themselves as Episcopalians, and it is by the same designation that their neighbours know them. You would have a difficult time finding your way if in Cuba, the Philippines, or Liberia you inquired for directions to the Anglican Church or the Church of England. And your difficulty would be just as great if in New Zealand, Kenya, or Hong Kong you asked for the Episcopal Church.

The situation is worse in places deriving from the great labours of the English missionary societies. I have taken snapshots of billboards in front of churches which imperturbably bear the notice that this is "S.P.G. Church" or "C.M.S. Church". It is almost as if we had developed loyalty to particular societies within the Church instead of to the Church itself. That was nobody's intention, naturally, but such was the not unnatural result of our peculiar way of going about things.

I happened to be in Zanzibar, Tanganyika, and Kenya at the time negotiations were in progress leading up to the formation of the new ecclesiastical Province of the Church in East Africa. The problems involved in creating a Province loomed larger in the minds of many an African Anglican than they ought to have done because he thought that this was somehow a matter of Church unity. Were the officials trying to merge two *Churches*, the U.M.C.A. Church and the C.M.S. Church? The fact that all of them were Anglicans already, members of the same fellowship, had not been clear to them, and it had seemed a huge and daring step for two such disparate groups to "get together".

One thinks of the Anglican from Nigeria who in Parliament Square pointed to Westminster Abbey and inquired of the London bobby, "Can you tell me? Is that a C.M.S. Church or an S.P.G. Church?"

A new day is coming, I am grateful to report. Gradually the offending old billboards are being repainted and relettered in proper style, and when new stationery is ordered from the printer the letterhead is worded less misleadingly.

But consider by how many names our Church is known. My list may be incomplete, but I count at least eighteen of them.

> The Church of England
> The Church in Wales
> The Church of Ireland
> The Episcopal Church in Scotland
> The Protestant Episcopal Church in the U.S.A.
> The Anglican Church of Canada
> The Church of India, Pakistan, Burma and Ceylon
> The Church of England in Australia and Tasmania
> The Church of the Province of New Zealand

The Church of the Province of South Africa
The Church of the Province of the West Indies
Nippon Sei Ko Kai
Chung Hua Sheng Kung Hui
The Church of the Province of West Africa
The Church of the Province of Central Africa
The Archbishopric in Jerusalem
The Church of the Province of East Africa
The Church of the Province of Uganda

One would have to add to this list many variations in detail whenever the name is translated: e.g. *Église Episcopal d'Haiti*, *Igreja Episcopal Brasileira*, *Chosen Sung Kung Whai* (Korea), *Eklesia Episkopaly Malagasy*. Other names also appear, e.g. the Arab Evangelical Episcopal Church, Episcopal Church in the Sudan, The English Episcopal Church, and N.A.C. – Native Anglican Church.

Is it not fantastic for one visible entity to go by so many different names? And am I guilty of pettiness in taking exception to most of these names? We rightly complain against Rome's tendency to monopolize for itself the word "Catholic", but then we turn right around and with even greater hauteur arrogate to ourselves, without any qualifying adjective at all, the title "*The* Church": "The Church of England", "The Church in Wales" – almost as if there were no others. Perhaps geographical designations of this sort were inevitable in the case of Churches established by law – but I am not among the defenders of the principle of establishment.

Particularly offensive to me is the name we have given ourselves in China and Japan. "The Holy Catholic Church of China" and "The Holy Catholic Church of Japan" sound arrogant to me, but Christian friends from the Orient try to assuage my anger by assuring me that the title has not the same force in the Eastern languages that it has when translated into English. In Chinese and Japanese there is no definite article; hence a Church can call itself "Holy Catholic Church" without claiming that it is the *only* Catholic Church. If this be true, I withdraw my objections. The difficulties of translation are notorious, especially from Occidental to Oriental languages. I chuckled when I learned that every endeavour to translate "The Protestant Episcopal Church" into Japanese invariably ended up with something sounding like "The Assembly of the Bickering Overseers".

What are we to think of a name like "The Church of England in Australia and Tasmania"? It is an improvement upon the old name, "The United Church of England and Ireland in Australia and Tasmania". But it seems not yet to have occurred to many Australian Anglicans that even the new name might be cumbersome and a handicap to our Church "down under" as it begins to approach hundreds of thousands of new Australians, immigrants from Europe, who have no connection whatsoever with things English and Irish. When diffidently I raised the question, I received for the most part blank stares by way of answer. Whatever could have prompted such a question?

We ought not to conceal the fact that the Church in a particular locality had its life in history mediated to it through the labours of the Church based in another land. Daughter churches do well to honour their Mother. But need the *name* of a church read like the pedigree of a thoroughbred horse?

Anglicana, though a venerable name, is proving a hindrance and disadvantage to us as we extend our mission to people of non-British cultures. If I had my will, we would do away with all restrictive, nationalistic, limiting, geographical designations. The Church of God, though intimately, disturbingly, and therapeutically related to the life of every nation, transcends all nationality.

In the United States why do we persist in having an agency of the Church called The National Council? The agency must of course be there. I object only to the name. Every working day this Council makes decisions affecting nations other than our own – Liberia, Panama, Costa Rica, Brazil, the Philippines, the Dominican Republic, to mention but a few. I doubt, therefore, the appropriateness of calling it a *national* council, unless it is in fact a council in which one national Church imposes its will upon the Church in other nations. Doesn't our very terminology reflect a bygone age of empire? Despite all the dangers of bureaucracy, I am a great believer in "headquarters". Elsewhere in this book I argue as persuasively as I can for far greater centralization than we now have. But I yearn for the day when the councils of the Church will be as international and transnational as the Church itself has become. Our geographical universality should be reflected in our polity *and* in our nomenclature.

The sad reality of a divided Christendom forces upon us the necessity of giving to each part of the Church a name (and often a long name if it is to be accurate). And what is a denomination if not precisely a name? Accordingly, I hereby go on record as having contended that the word "North" be added to the already wordy title of our Church in the United States. I hold no brief for our present legal name, but so long as we retain it, we must make it more precise by adding to it. Especially now. For these are the days in which we are instructing our children to give up chewing gum for Lent in order to stuff their Mite Boxes with pennies for the peons "south of the border". I do not mean to sound more scornful than I actually am. It is high time for American Episcopalians to wake up to their missionary responsibilities in this hemisphere. I welcome every effort in this direction.

Even a fleeting visit to Central and South America is sufficient to convince me that there, inescapably, the next great missionary effort should be made. Of this I had much to say in an earlier chapter. I content myself now with making two obvious remarks, although they seem not to be obvious to most American Episcopalians.

Two strikes against us already is the name of our Church. Latin Americans are passionately *American*. They do not take kindly to our having laid exclusive claim to this noble name. They are Americans too! Perhaps they are excessively touchy about it, but this we can understand, and on the whole they are not to be blamed for it. It does us good to have them issue such a reminder. Just as Anglicans do not like to have Roman Catholics claim to be the only Catholics, Peruvians and Chileans object to having "Americans" claim to be the only Americans! We are *North* Americans. For this reason, if the Protestant Episcopal Church in the United States of America, operating with this name, is to have any success with Latin Americans one requisite is to add to our title the word "North". We should be PECUSNA. It is, at any rate, still pronounceable.

After this sum in addition, the next step is an exercise in subtraction. The word "Protestant" in our title has to go. Here I reverse myself radically. For years I have fought to retain "Protestant" as part of our title. From one point of view the Reformation was a tragedy. It is true that the Church had so far strayed in the Middle Ages from its moorings in Holy Scripture and in the traditions and Councils of the ancient and undivided Church that at last a reformation was an imperative necessity. But given this necessity, there is occasion for solemn jubilation in the realization that there still remained within the medieval Church elements of health, sanity, and plain Christianity equal to the task of putting through a reformation. It took heroism, self-denial, and martyrdom to achieve it. But the Reformers were willing to pay the cost. Thank God for them!

Mistakes were made, of course. How might it have been otherwise? In Britain it went better than on the Continent – there was more moderation, more reasonableness, less fanaticism, less extremism – but even in Britain the task was not perfectly accomplished. It remained for later centuries to complete the task. The Evangelical Revival, the Oxford Movement, the stirrings of social concern, the passion for missionary outreach – these were some of the contributions of the nineteenth century. Such heady elements, effecting as they did a "Second Reformation", are still not in perfect accord. Imbalances remain. The future, however, is rich in promise, provided that we can take in stride "the great new fact of our age", i.e., the Ecumenical Movement, and provided, moreover, that we can really get it into our heads that the time is short.

I am ashamed, therefore, only of Episcopalians who are ashamed to call themselves *Protestant* Episcopalians. What does it mean to belong to a Protestant Episcopal Church? It means to associate yourself with those *episkopoi*, those Catholic Bishops (for there are no other bishops entitled to the name) who at a particular point in history rose up to protest the errors of the Bishop of Rome. It was a protest *for* Catholicism not *against* Catholicism. What was needed in Britain was a Reformed Catholic Church, and that was precisely what Britain got.

I stand, therefore, with the Reformation, and by temperament I have been polemical enough to resist all efforts to delete the word "Protestant" from our official title. My opposition was dictated by the fact that the champions of this deletion were, almost exclusively, the highest of High Churchmen. Yet "spikes" are not always wrong. They happen to be quite right in wanting to be quit of the word "Protestant". But in this instance they are right for the wrong reasons.

But why then have I reversed myself? Why do I now campaign to get rid of "Protestant"? It is because I have lately been to Central and South America. There I learned that the word has such negative connotations in Latin ears that no Protestant sect ventures to use it. *Protestante* is the kiss of death. Recognizing this the sects call themselves *evangelista*. Many Latins have little love for the Spanish Catholicism on which they were brought up, but their early conditioning is such that they could not possibly swing to something calling itself Protestant. The word sets off unconscious mechanisms. If something is "Protestant" it is anti-Christian. Someone has pointed out that a Mexican is as much attracted to a Protestant Church as a Mississippian would be to a Yankee Church.

The prime function of Anglicanism in Latin America should be to demonstrate to those who are disaffected by the Church of Rome that there is an alternative way of being a Catholic Christian. But those who oppose us have an effective way of vitiating our efforts. All they have to do – and they do it – is circulate photostatic copies of the title page of our Prayer Book. "You see!" they cry. "Whatever these Episcopalians may tell you, they are Protestants after all. Just look at their official publication!"

A hardy perennial at the General Convention of the Protestant Episcopal Church is the debate about changing the name of the Church. Some of the new names proposed are ridiculous. The chief focus of interest, however, is not so much on getting a new name as it is on getting rid of "Protestant" in the old name. Most of those urging a change would be satisfied to be known simply as "The Episcopal Church". Unfortunately the debate is carried on almost exclusively along Churchmanship lines. "Evangelicals", feeling that much is at issue, fight to retain the word "Protestant". "Catholics", with feelings just as strong, are convinced the word must be struck out.

Suddenly I see the irrelevance of what, after all, is a purely American (I beg your pardon – North American!) discussion. The terms of reference are provincial only; the dimensions of the debate, strictly regional. Untouched is the vastly larger question: What is the whole Anglican Communion to call itself? It still is of importance, no doubt, that the one and only member of the Communion which officially, legally, and publicly calls itself "Protestant" should take steps to call itself something else. Low Church (and other) opponents of a change might find their resistance to change lessened if they were to reflect on our obligations to Latin America and on our involvement in a Communion much larger than the fifty sovereign states comprising the United States of North America. If the battleground on which the fight about the name were to be shifted from party strife to consideration of the missionary strategy of a world-wide Church, both sides might lay down their arms and work together to find the right name. It is to be noted that the General Convention meeting in Detroit in 1961 did give permission for overseas missionary Districts of PECUSA to drop the word "Protestant" from their formularies and from the title page of the Prayer Book in translation. A good step forward but the problem however remains. Photostatic copies can still be produced – and then it looks as if we were doubly guilty of duplicity.

The time will come, let us hope, when an Archbishop of Canterbury will have something a little less ambivalent to say as he crowns a future King or Queen of England. How typically English, how typically Anglican, that hitherto he has had to pledge the Monarch to do his or her utmost to maintain "the Protestant Reformed Religion established by law" and then to place upon the Monarch's finger a ring while saying, "Receive this Ring, the ensign of kingly dignity, and of defence of the Catholic Faith." There is genius in this, I cannot say how much I admire it. But it is specifically *English* genius, this delicate balance, this fruitful compromise, this skilful piece of dialectical thinking. As such, it suits the English admirably and in a providential way has sustained and set forward the life of the Church of England. But to the rest of the world it sounds like double talk. If the Church of England, moving out beyond the borders of that island kingdom, is ever to be more than an English exportation, an English extension of the British Empire, an English imposition upon cultures of non-British antecedents, in sum, if it is ever to be more than an English chaplaincy abroad, it will have to be more plain-spoken. Its ancient formularies will have to be updated to correspond with its present understanding of itself and of its vocation.

Let us hope, too, that the next time a Queen of England pays a visit to the Pope she will go attired in white, which is the privilege of a Catholic Queen. If a Fabiola goes in white, no Elizabeth need go in black.

In the course of my Grand Tour of Anglicanism I canvassed hundreds of bishops, priests, deacons, religious, and laymen on the question: What should we call ourselves?

The answers are not without interest.

The two chief contenders, the two favourites, are: THE ANGLICAN CHURCH and THE EPISCOPAL CHURCH. The people of whom I inquired around the world seem about equally divided in preferring the one name or the other. Agreement, however, was general on one point: the shorter the name the better. Let us be done with adjectives. And everybody feels the need of a single name common to us all.

Neither name is perfect – which should not dismay us since all the perfect names have already been pre-empted (and often corrupted) by other Christian bodies. Fault is found with "The Anglican Church" because the adjective ties us still to England. In most languages "Anglican" can be translated only by words which really mean "English". Fault is found with "The Episcopal Church" partly because it is an unfamiliar designation to the majority of Anglicans and partly because it names us after a particular form of ecclesiastical polity whereas (so the argument goes) it is the peculiar genius of Anglicanism to have developed a polity in which government by bishops has been enriched by the infusion of presbyteral and congregational elements.

I take no sides here. I am merely reporting what I have found.

At the Lambeth Conference of 1958 the then Archbishop of Canterbury, in a mood half-joking and half-serious, said he would offer a prize if anybody could come up with a really good name for our Church. So far as I am aware, no prize has yet been awarded. Nor is one likely to be in the foreseeable future. But veritably we are, or else ought to be, a Church in search of a name.

Alas, I myself have no prize-winning name to propose. My own proposal is far more modest: I propose only that the forthcoming Anglican Congress and the next Lambeth Conference put this problem on the agenda.

As long as Christendom is hobbled by denominationalism, we ought to do our best to see to it that our own denomination is denominated properly. That is, accurately, modestly, invitingly.

"What's in a name?" The implication behind the question is that names do not matter very much. This, however, is not a Hebraic and Biblical way of thinking. The important thing about Abram, Jacob, Simon, and Saul is that God saw to it that they were given new names. Think, too, of the extraordinary pains the Almighty took to ensure that John the Baptist and the Saviour of the world should have appropriate names. To Moses it was of the utmost urgency to learn the Proper Name of God.* Jesus himself could sum up his Ministry by saying, "I have made known to them thy Name."

Catechisms and Confessions of Faith usually begin with powerful, heaven-storming, world-shaking affirmations. One thinks, for example, of the Westminster Confession's splendid opening blast: "What is the chief end of man?" and of its magnificent answer. By contrast, it has been suggested, the Prayer Book Catechism gets off to a lame start. No! On the contrary! "What is your Christian Name?" "Who gave you this Name?" In Holy Baptism you were given the Name by which you will be named and known throughout all eternity.

Names matter.

* For a tremendous meditation on this subject, see the chapter entitled "The Name Which Is Above Every Name", in Walter Lowrie's *What is Christianity?* (New York: Pantheon).

32

PROBLEMS AND PROSPECTS

THE JOURNEY WAS COMING TO AN END. AS THE TWO HUNDRED AND tenth aeroplane required by my Odyssey was speeding me towards my final destination, New York, I tried to jot down, as succinctly as possible, a list of the things I chiefly learned during my two years abroad.

You may think it absurd that it should have taken me so long to learn so little, but – for whatever it's worth – here are my principal findings, neatly tabulated.

1. In spite of the jet plane, the world is still big.

2. Nevertheless, this big world is what Wendell Willkie said of it: "One World." So interlocked, so intertwined is it, that whatever happens in any part of it has immediate repercussions, for good or ill, in every other part.

3. A quotation (whose source I cannot trace) states the case precisely when it issues the stern reminder that "Most of God's world is not Christian, not white, and not American." These are elemental facts which Christians, Caucasians, and Americans had better learn fast!

4. Formidable adversaries have reasserted themselves. Ancient religions, such as Buddhism and Islam, resurgent and often riding on the flood tide of nationalism, have turned missionary and are making a powerful bid for the allegiance of mankind. Another great rival is the religion that has appeared of late: Communism. I think I understand its menace even better than does the Extreme Right. But I do not for *this* reason urge a rush to Christianity. No, Berdyaev was right: we have no right to struggle spiritually against Communism unless we are also prepared to struggle spiritually against problems to which Communism is an attempted – though mistaken – answer.

5. When we combine the factors briefly sketched in Points 3 and 4, we understand then that *the time is short*. A journey around the world has thrown me into an eschatological mood. Unless counterfactors are set in

motion it may be that, proportionally, Christianity will shrink more and more and become a minority movement with diminishing capacity for influencing culture. I am sorry if I have sounded gloomy. The facts do not entitle me, I fear, to speak in any other way.

6. Yet something within me – a kind of stubborn cheerfulness – compels me to add that, short as the time is, the situation can still be redeemed. At least there is a chance, provided that enough people, moved by love of God and love of man, will get down to business.

7. "Getting down to business" involves many things. I shall not try to make an exhaustive list, but here are a few tasks which seem to me the most urgent.

(a) The quality of preaching and teaching must be improved. Without that there will never be enough recruits for the Ministry and the Religious Life and the other types of Church work, nor will there be that vast increase in giving which the situation absolutely demands.

(b) Every effort must be made to restore the Church to visible unity. The divisions of Christendom constitute the chief impediment to the progress of Christianity.

(c) What used to be called "foreign missions" must be multiplied a thousandfold. No place in the world is "foreign" any more.

The points made above apply to all who profess and call themselves Christians. Now I wish to make a new series of points which deal more specifically with the people called Anglicans.

1. Not nearly enough Anglicans are instructed about the size and scope of the world-wide Communion of which they are members. Lacking instructions, which is the fault of their clergy, they have little lively awareness of their participation in a goodly fellowship far larger than their regional church – and little concern for it.

2. Those Anglicans who do think about the Anglican Communion have, in general, a somewhat idealized and romanticized notion of its extension and strength. We are big, but we are not everywhere. We get around, but often we are thin on the ground. I have complained before and will complain again about the mendacity of showing our children coloured maps of the world and telling them, "Now, children, this is the world and all those countries coloured pink form the Anglican Communion." Any child can see that the only parts of the world *not* coloured pink are Greenland, which is all ice, the Sahara, which is mostly sand, and Siberia, where not even Communists care to go. In this way we simply confirm our children in the illusion that already we live in the Church Triumphant!

3. My impression is that Anglicanism has somewhat overextended itself. It is good for a Church to be stretched, but actually we are straitened.

With the present level of missionary giving (although in many countries –
and in England notably – it is higher than ever before) we cannot support
adequately the work we undertook. Endlessly and monotonously, we are
short on manpower and money.

4. Anglicanism suffers from still another kind of shortness: we are short-
sighted. We have no long-range plans, no over-all strategy. We live from
hand to mouth. My own branch of the Anglican Communion once launched
a Ten Year Plan, but nobody knew from year to year what the plan for
the following year was to be; and before the ten years were over, we heard
nothing more of any Ten Year Plan. By contrast, certain other religious
bodies are thinking and planning with a view to the future. They buy up
real estate for a song and are content to let the land lie fallow for thirty
or forty years – until the people arrive. When the people do put in their
appearance, these religious bodies are on hand to meet them. Then, when
the price of property has soared so high that *we* can scarcely afford to purchase any of it, *we* create a committee and have a special fund drive in
order to buy at vast expense what once we could have had for a pittance.

5. From this follows another point: we imperatively need greater centralization and co-ordination. Not many Anglicans would desire a pyramidi-
cal structure like that of the great Church of Rome. Yet more and more it
becomes apparent that the few existing means of inter-Anglican communication and joint consultation must be augmented. A Lambeth Conference
held once a decade is not frequent enough in a world where you have to
run twice as fast just to stand in the same place. Moreover, Lambeth is
not enough, indispensable as it is, because *bishops* are not enough. The
priests and the people must also have a say. Anglican Congresses are a
step in that direction – but too timid a step. As a tentative first step, however,
these Congresses have a rightful claim upon our support. Another right
move was the transforming of Canterbury's ancient College of St. Augustine
into a Central College of the Anglican Communion. By the decision of the
Lambeth Conference of 1948 it was no longer to be a missionary college
where young Britishers were trained and sent out to the four corners of the
earth. Under its new constitution it was to be, instead, a Centre to which
promising young men, after five to ten years of practical experience, would
come in from the four corners to drink the pure waters of Anglicanism at
its wellspring under the shadows cast by the soaring Bell Harry Tower of
Canterbury Cathedral. A noble idea. Already its beneficent effects are felt.
St. Augustine's helps to produce a new generation of prospective leaders –
whether in the episcopate or in theological education or in any other branch
of the Church's endeavour – who know each other and are friends as a
result of having worshipped together, studied together, fought out disputed

points in seminars and over coffee in the Common Room. Against this excellent College, however, I have two objections. It is still conducted much in the manner of an ordinary theological college: there is too much lecturing, too little colloquy. I speak feelingly and remorsefully, because I myself lectured my head off when I had the honour of being a Visiting Fellow at the College in its infancy (1953–54); I lectured and lectured – and did very little listening. What a pity not to listen more when, sitting before me, were mature students from eighteen different countries!

A question much bruited about in these days is: Can it be the destiny of the Anglican Communion to disappear? This anxious query is prompted, no doubt, by the fact that a large portion of Indian Anglicans left our Communion to form part of the Church of South India. Now it seems likely that many more Anglicans will be assimilated into the emerging new Churches of North India, Pakistan, and Ceylon. Nigerian interest in the formation of a United Church for West Africa runs high, and there are Anglicans in Singapore and Malaya who have shown themselves hesitant about the creation of a Province of the Church in South-east Asia because their foremost concern is Church Union in Malaya itself. There is also the instance of the Philippines. As we have noted, the Episcopal Church in those islands may decide, in time, to become absorbed into the Philippine Independent Church. Even in staid Britain and proud America, ecumenical discussions have done little to allay the fears of some members of our Communion.

A Winston Churchill who once announced himself discontent and unwilling to preside over the dissolution of the British Empire has many Anglican counterparts, grieving over the thought that they shall witness the whittling away of the world-wide Anglican Communion. Bit by bit, one component member after the other submerges its separate identity, in order to emerge as part of a new united Church.

I have nothing fresh to contribute to this discussion, but of points already made by others I would insist that two especially are in need of underscoring. To begin with, it is *of course* Anglicanism's destiny to disappear –ultimately. We ought not to forget that the *whole* Church, quite as much as any part of it, exists for the sole reason of finally becoming superfluous. Already Socrates knew that a teacher's function is, as it were, to talk himself out of a job – i.e., so to stimulate his pupil into self-activity that there would eventually be no more need of the teacher. Of heaven St. John the Divine said, "I saw no temple therein." Eternity requires no special place marked off as "sacred", for when the world has come to an end the whole of the "profane" will have been sanctified. The Church is a necessity only in sin-riddled historical time.

In heaven there will be as little place for the Church as for sin. Both will have been superseded – and good riddance!

But if we must wait until the *eschaton*, the end of time, before we are delivered both from sin *and* the Church, it might well be the case that Anglicanism should not be hasty in planning its own demise. I hope that even within historical time we will disappear as a particular denomination, having lost our life in order to find it, having died to self so that a resurrection to a new and larger life became possible. Yet Anglicanism must not "die" prematurely. I am convinced that God has given us a special *raison d'être*. We are, at this juncture, needed for certain tasks for which I believe God and the accidents of history have given us unique equipment. Through no merit of our own, we find entrusted to ourselves functions we can perform better than any other Christian body. The chief of these functions is in the realm of ecumenics. Paradoxical as it may sound, we must for the time being maintain our separate existence as Anglicans precisely in order to speed the day when the Church will have regained visible unity.

This I believe with all my heart – and it frightens the life out of me that several friends have suggested that, the moment this book is published, I shall no longer be welcomed in Anglican circles and will have to seek Christian fellowship elsewhere! To state the truth baldly: I do not know where I would turn should the necessity arise of my having to change Churches. Without unchurching the others, this is the only Church *for me*.

Yet having made that declaration of love, I must add something else. *My* Church – if I may venture so to claim it – is like every other Church in Christendom in that it suffers from separation and schism.

Let me explain.

Anglicanism looks at the Reformation and says, "What a tragedy!" Yes, with that I agree. That a reformation of Christ's own Church should have been necessary is the height of tragedy. Thank God the Reformation finally broke through! Yet the very effort to recapture Christianity's purity was carried out by finite men, themselves not totally pure. The result was a new reading of Christianity, closer to the ancient understanding than the medieval, yet somewhat distorted. The pendulum swung too far. In a polemical situation, men always overstate the case. This is what happened in the sixteenth century. Continental Protestantism, both in its Lutheran and Calvinist forms, went to extremes. Exaggeration marred the truths newly rewon and emphasized. And this Reformation produced, in turn, a Counter-Reformation. Here again the pendulum swung too far – but now in the opposite direction. The Council of Trent, sincerely meaning to do right, ended up by making matters worse. As a result, Christianity now is transmitted to posterity in two somewhat distorted forms: the Protestant and the Post-Tridentine. This is the tragedy of the Reformation and Counter-Reformation.

Now, Anglicanism likes to think that somehow Anglicanism was totally immune to this tragedy and that no germ of this disease found lodging in its veins. But this is vainglory and a delusion. We cannot boast that we alone escaped from the calamity. Had we not come through the crisis better than the others I would not be an Anglican. But I want the truth to be told. Anglicanism does not emerge unscathed.

One example will suffice to show what I am driving at. Protestant theologians talk most movingly about the "Word". Anglicans have not a clue to what the Protestants are talking about. Roman theologians, on the other hand, talk movingly about "sacraments". Once again the Anglicans are in the dark. In our own formularies it comes easily to Anglicans to trip easily off the tongue the phrase "Word and Sacraments". Yet, though we speak of both and commend ourselves on having achieved a perfect synthesis, perhaps now we must face the fact that we are mouthing realities of which we have but limited experiential knowledge. We say both but understand neither, in the depths.

A non-Anglican friend of mine, who happens to love us, has said, "You call yourselves a 'Bridge Church'; but what is a bridge that does not really touch land on either side?"

This is not a question unworthy of our consideration. It hurts. It might minister to our healing.

Bishop Stephen Neill has said that "Anglicanism is not compromise for the sake of peace but comprehensiveness for the sake of truth." I happen to agree with him wholeheartedly. Yet I do not overlook the dread possibility that sometimes we may be comprehensive at the expense of depth.

To win first prize for uttering something stupid, one has only to say, "Well, after all, aren't all religions basically the same? Aren't they just climbing the same mountain from different sides? Aren't they all out for the same thing?" In a sense, Yes. They're are all out – and they *go* "all out" – to win the allegiance of men. But they seek humanity's devotion for very different ends.

The best story I know illustrating this point was told me by the best teacher I ever had: A. T. Mollegen of Virginia Theological Seminary. Towards the end of the last century, an Indian rajah was in conversation with one of our bishops from America.

"What we want from the West," said the rajah, "is not your Christ and your Church. What we want is your Baldwin locomotives and your McCormick reapers."

The bishop had the sagacity to reply quickly, "But you cannot have our locomotives and our reapers without Christ and his Church. Don't you see that our Baldwin locomotives would run over and kill your sacred cows, and that McCormick reapers would snip off the head of the sacred cobra?"

Without Christ, nature is either too sacred to touch or else too daemonic to touch. In either case, tampering with nature is taboo. And for this reason, a polluted Ganges flows on. People on holy pilgrimage bathe in it – and in its filth they both contract and spread disease.

Mr. Nehru himself has pointed to the fact that in the East people worship the cow but do not care for it, whereas the peoples of the West, though not worshipping the cow, do care for it.

One is glad that some of the leaders of the world have turned secularist. Mr. Nehru is an example. He disavows all religion. Secularism is at least one step closer – albeit a dialectically negative step – to true religion than is enchantment with false religion. Conversions from agnosticism or even atheism are more likely than conversions from those who are "in the know" about the "gods many, and lords many", who are, in Christian thinking, not deities.

Having spoken so heatedly on this point, I have no intention of softening the blow. Yet my position would be misunderstood if I did not add another consideration.

It has never occurred to me to suppose that non-Christians are all bound for hell. This is the absurd supposition of certain "Biblical" sects. Certainly those who are not Christians for the sole reason that they have never heard of Christ – or have never heard of him in such reasonable and persuasive accents as to be won by him – are not consigned to hellfire. In the justice of God, let alone his mercy, it is unthinkable that people should perish who never had the chance to become Christians.

Nor would I think of condemning all non-Christian religions of the world. Some of them are beneficent. We must, I think, take our stand with the second-century Apologists. These Christian Fathers, mindful of the text that God has nowhere "left himself without witness", taught that all religions, all philosophies, have grasped part of the truth (fragments of what in Greek is called *logos*; in English, the Word). But since only a part was grasped – and the part was made into the whole – that partial glimpse of truth was somehow distorted, put out of focus. And where only the part is known, it comes to be overlaid with human conjecture and human error.

To the Christians, on the contrary (and through no merit of their own), there has been granted a revelation of *holos logos* – the whole truth.

Christians find in Jesus of Nazareth their absolute clue to the identification of the Power which set us in being. By the same token, they find in him a definition of our present duty under God and the guarantee that the Power which awaits us at the end of history, our fulfilment and consummation, is none other than the Power which initiated the whole process. When Christians confess that "Jesus Christ is the same yesterday, and to-day, and for ever," they are saying, "as it was in the beginning, is now, and every shall be," glory be to God; for if the Deity be perfectly self-defined in Christ Jesus, we know that we have a God who is utterly trustworthy. It is not for nothing that Christians place Alpha and Omega on their altars with a cross between the α and the Ω. This is ecclesiastical shorthand for the most revolutionary of all declarations. It is saying that a cross planted in the midst of history makes clear the mystery of our origin before history and the mystery of our destiny when history comes to an end. From the very humanity of Jesus we know how godly is God. Underneath are the everlasting arms. We know something of these arms. They are arms stretched out on the cross, fixed there by nails which humanity pounded into place. Yet, even as we drove the nails, our victimized Victor prayed, "Father, forgive them, for they know not what they do." *This*, say the Christians, reveals the nature of God, a love which accepts even when we reject.

Such an understanding puts Christians in a peculiar position. Uniquely placed, they are both tolerant and intolerant of other religions. Through sheer gift, they have been given the whole truth and are therefore able to espy in other religions corresponding elements of truth, congruent ideas, concordant verities. Thus – if we know what we are about – it is possible for us to begin conversation with the others. Standing within the whole truth, we catch glimpses of truth wherever we find them. We rejoice over this, for we discern in these shared perceptions of truth points of contact which open the door to genuine dialogue.

At the same time, however, instructed Christian thinking does not fall into the trap of relativism. From the perspective of standing within the whole truth, we have the criteria for detecting where other religions and philosophies have gone astray. They have taken a fraction of the truth and exalted it into the whole. Etymologically, this is the very meaning of the word "heresy". *Hairesis* is a taking, a choice. One picks up part of the truth, makes it the whole of the truth, and thereby distorts even that measure of truth one has.

Now my reasoning comes full circle. Two points need underscoring. Christians can be, and by their own convictions should be, generous in their estimation of other religions, other world views. We rejoice in the truth, wherever it is found. But not for this reason do we sit at home. Our generosity needs to be matched by our aggressiveness. I do not mean pugnaciousness. I mean getting out and giving out – latching on to the talking points we have in common, and trying to demonstrate how partial truth already recognized comes into its own when the totality stands free and clear.

Accordingly, Christians are both proud and humble. Proud in that – all unworthily – they are permitted to be bearers of the truth. Humble in that, as recipients and bearers of the truth, they have sometimes diminished its radiance by confusing Christianity with culture, Atonement with Anglo-Americanism.

A bishop of my acquaintance, who would have to be characterized, I think, as a rather rigid Anglo-Catholic, recently made a trip around the world. The journey left a profound impression upon him. He will never be the same. Having seen for the first time the shrines and temples with their great outpourings of devotion, and after having studied the countenances of devout men and women at prayer, he said to me, "But these people cannot be lost eternally! God must be working through these religions." And he continued to speak along the lines of what I have just recounted.

Then I commented : "Bishop, when I was teaching in one of our seminaries several years ago, I nearly got run out of town on a rail for voicing similar sentiments."

"Yes, I know," he replied, "and ten years ago I would have helped to run you out. But now I think that way no longer."

People in all ages say that travel is an education in itself. I have reason to believe this.

I remember one afternoon in Nuku'alofa when, in the course of the saunterings to which I am partial in order to get the feel of a new place, I passed an employment centre. A great many men, desirous of work but disappointed in their need, were loitering in the shade of the few available trees. Here was willingness, here was readiness. But in economically depressed Tonga there was no one to employ them.

The Gospel for Septuagesima, which strikes many as offensive and unjust, hit me as it had never hit me before. "Why stand ye here all the day idle? They say unto him, Because no man hath hired us."

Why are billions of men and women not yet employed as labourers in the Lord's vineyard? It is because nobody has yet hired them. This means, no Christian missionary has gone out to engage them. And surely it is for *this* reason – namely, the failure of Christians to recruit the workers – that those who were called only at the eleventh hour and responded, will get the same wage as those who have "borne the burden and the heat of the day".

It is not to rescue people from the brink of eternal damnation that the Christian missionary moves out. He goes, rather, because he is in receipt of Good News. News too sensational, too good, to be hugged to himself in a monopolistic way. This is news which *has* to be shared. The "other-directed", the divine-directed "ought" about the missionary endeavour, finds its wholehearted "Amen" in an inner-directed "I *must*, and by God in heaven, I *will*."

This is as close as I have come in this book to dealing with the theology – the why and wherefore – of missions. Closer to it I will not come, although I regard it as the paramount question before the house. In all that I have written, I simply assume the veridity of the Christian Faith, from which follows, by every test of logic, the imperative necessity of missions. If Christ be the Captain of our Salvation, to question his orders is to be guilty of insubordination.

Don't get yourself baptized, don't bring your child to Holy Baptism, unless you are willing to go the whole way. To accept Baptism is to acknowledge that Christ has the right to command. But remember: if you once submit yourself to a tribunal of law, you thereby bind yourself to *all* the laws of that court. There is no ambiguity about the law in this case. "Go ye into all the world . . ." reads the law. It would be difficult for even the most dimwitted to misunderstand. And would even a dullard dare to disobey?

Who said it first? I do not know. But some inspired soul put the truth into words: "The Church doesn't *have* missions; it *is* Mission."

Three concluding points – short and sharp:

1. Our dioceses are too big. If the work load is so heavy that the Ordinary needs episcopal assistance, the time has come to divide the diocese. Even from a theological standpoint, a suffragan or assistant bishop is a dubious entity; for what, after all, is a bishop without a *cathedra*? If support of the episcopate is a problem, let the bishop of a small diocese double as dean and rector of the cathedral, and give him a curate and a lay administrator so that the bishop himself can go on his rounds. We profess to be Episcopalians, but we do not have enough *episcopi*.

2. Much Anglican work falls short of maximum success because it is not, strictly speaking, *Anglican*. It is either hyper-Anglican or sub-Anglican. I pray God that we can continue to be a comprehensive church, but I also pray that extremity and eccentricity will be surmounted.

3. Our consciousness of ourselves as a church has not yet caught up with the reality of ourselves. We Anglicans are, in fact, an international church, but we have not yet learned to tap our international resources. If in Mexico, for example, we are suspect because we are too Yankee, pull out the Yanks. Bring in missionaries from Australia or Brazil. If in Kenya we are too English, pull out the British. Replace them with Mexicans or Pakistani. Anglicans have at least one talent: the talent of universal appeal. Why bury it?

33

AS OTHERS SEE US

IN ALL EARLIER PARTS OF THIS BOOK I HAVE LUXURIATED IN THE personal pronoun. I have spoken of what *I* have seen, known, and experienced of the Church of which I am a member. In this my conclusion, however, I would like to summon the testimony of two witnesses, both of them "outsiders". That is, neither of them Anglicans.

One is Reinhold Niebuhr.

This profoundly learned man has said, "At its worst Anglican thought is a compound of liberalistic moralism and traditional piety. At its best it manages to combine all facets of the Christian doctrine of Grace more truly than other churches." Succinct, incisive, and accurate. In two sentences he has hit the nail precisely on the head and driven it home. He knows us better than most of us Anglicans know ourselves.

The second witness is Dr. Chaim Wardi. This extraordinary man when I met him in Jerusalem in 1957 played and still plays the role of Adviser to the Minister on Christian Affairs of the Government of Israel. A more civilized human being I have never met. He is urbane, brilliant, sensitive, perceptive. I may not have remembered all the details of his biography perfectly, but I can convey a more or less correct impression if I say that he had a Scottish Jew as his father and a Norwegian Jewess as his mother. From his boyhood he knew both English and Norwegian. Then as a youth he went to stay with his grandfather in Poland. So there he learned Polish. In the course of his schooling he gained fluency in Hebrew, Yiddish, and Russian. Then, while earning several doctorates in a variety of European universities, he added to the list of languages in which he is proficient, German, French, Spanish, and Italian.

He is thoroughly versed in Judaism, his own religion. Islam he knows like the back of his hand. His specialty is Christianity. He can tell you, in minute detail, the history of every holy place in Palestine. The ins and outs of the Ethiopic or Greek or Russian or Armenian or Roman connections with each sacred site are at his fingertips. Art, music, drama, philosophy, religion, politics – whatever you like – he is prepared to discuss intelligently. The man of whom I speak is, in short, a twentieth-century version of the all-round savant whom we admiringly hail as a "Renaissance man".

When he made his first visit to New York, it fell to me to show him the Cathedral Church of St. John the Divine. To express myself more accurately, I was privileged to see the Cathedral through the eyes of this man. Attentively he watched as I pointed out to him the details of the Cathedral's iconography. For example, I showed him St. Luke's Bay, which honours the medical profession. In the windows the healing miracles recorded in the Bible are depicted. But displayed also are Pasteur inoculating a sheep, a country doctor in his buggy, Madame Curie discovering radium, a hospital bed which we like to think could double as a psychoanalyst's couch.*

I showed the visitor from Israel St. Ives' Bay, honouring judges and lawyers. Here is memorialized man's agelong struggle for equity and justice. Both in the reredos and in the windows above can be seen Moses the Law-Giver, and St. Paul who radically reassessed the Law, and Christ who himself is the New Law. But there is also shown Hammurabi and the Magna Carta and every other great person and moment figuring in the fight for law and order against the tyrannies that threaten human dignity.

My guest took all this in, intently interested but silent. His trained eye missed nothing. The windows depicting Industry, Management, Labour, and Communications he studied for a long time. An appreciative grin illumined his face when we came to St. Hubert's Bay. Here, in a window given by athletes, was every sport mentioned in the Bible: Jacob wrestling with an angel, David with his slingshot, Esau hunting, Samson killing the lion, and St. Paul's injunction to run a good race and to put on the armour of God. But in addition to these ancient pastimes were the modern:

* In 1956, the 100th Anniversary of the birth of Freud, we held in Cathedral House a colloquium to which came by invitation thirty Christian theologians and ministers with clinical experience, and thirty psychologists, psychiatrists, and psychoanalysts to consider Freud's contribution and to deal with the question: "Christianity and Psychoanalysis. Are we friends or foes, rivals or allies?" The members of this colloquium represented many different religious traditions – and some who eschewed all religions. The papers read were brilliant. By their sparks a fiery dialogue was kindled. For holding a colloquium of this sort the Cathedral was roundly criticized by a few religious zealots – and I am reminded that a zealot is a person who is unable to listen to anybody else. One Anglo-Catholic periodical made snide remarks about "the spirit of St. Sigmund wafting over the altars on Cathedral Heights", and an Evangelical pamphlet joined the excoriating chorus by asking if the Cathedral authorities were unaware that Sigmund Freud was an atheist. To this kind of carping criticism, the then Dean made answer by a single trenchant sentence: "Well, Sigmund Freud is not an atheist *now*!"

baseball, boxing, football, hockey, lacrosse, archery, fencing, and many others.

Our tour completed, we went to my office. And there, at last, my friend from Jerusalem broke silence. "All religions reject, reject – exclude, exclude. But I come to your Cathedral – the first Anglican House of Worship I have ever visited – and what do I find? In statuary and in glass I find Labour and Management, athletics and psychiatry, Moses and Maimonides, Athanasius and Augustine, Aquinas and Averroës, Luther and Calvin and Wesley. And suddenly I find that you Anglicans aren't religious like the others, for you Anglicans leave *nothing* to Satan."

We do not fully deserve this tribute. But this is what we aspire to be – and in part, by the mercy of God, are.

APPENDIX

How to Pronounce and Address every Anglican Diocese*

PROBABLY NOT ONE EPISCOPALIAN IN TEN THOUSAND WILL EVER have occasion to dispatch a cablegram to, let us say, the Bishop of Keewatin or the Archbishop of Sydney. Yet the need *might* arise, and to a few people, at least, the following list could prove helpful. Certainly it would save money, for I give the registered cable address of every diocese of the Anglican Communion or, if there be none, I specify the shortest form of address which is certain of reaching the destination intended.

But if not many will be burning up the wires with telegrams, radiograms, and cablegrams, every Episcopalian will be – or should be – storming heaven with intercessory prayer for each of these dioceses; and, although it doubtless makes little difference to the Almighty, it *might* make a difference on earth if we knew how to pronounce each other's names!

A romantic lover dotes on the name of his beloved. It often inspires him to poetry. Think how many sonnets and sonatas are based on a meditation on the name of the person he loves. Christians, who in a far deeper sense love each other and have solicitude for each other, might be glad for the opportunity to pronounce correctly the name of a diocese which they are concerned to take up into their God-relationship.

It is said of our Master that he "calleth his own sheep by name". Would it, therefore, be wrong of us, who profess to follow him, that we endeavour to pronounce, as best we can, the names of his "other sheep"?

Merriam-Webster Pronunciation Key.

ā āle: ă chăotic: â câre: ă ădd: *ă ă*ccount: ä ärm: ȧ ȧsk: *ȧ* sof*ȧ*: b but: ch chair: d day: dū̬ verdū̬re: ē ēve: ȩ hȩre: ĕ evênt: ĕ ĕnd: *ĕ* silĕnt: ẽ makẽr: f fill: g go: h hat: ī īce: ĭ ĭll: *ĭ* charĭty: j joke: k keep: к ...ch in German ich: l late: m man: n nod: ɴ bon (French bon): ng sing: ō ōld: ŏ ŏbey: ô ôrb: ŏ ŏdd: ŏ̤ sŏ̤ft: *ŏ* cŏnnect: oi oil: o͞o fo͞od: o͝o fo͝ot: ou out: p pen: r rat: s sit: sh she: t to: th thin: ~~th then~~: tū̬ natū̬re: ū cūbe: ü ünite: û ûrn ŭ ŭ?: *ŭ* circ*ŭ*s: u German grün: v van: w wĭn: y yet: z zone: zhz – in azure.

---

* Key for use of list:
Capital letters signify cable address.
Asterisk (*) denotes that the diocese should be addressed in care of the Archbishop of Canterbury, Lambeth Palace, London, S.E.1, England.

PROVINCES AND DIOCESES OF THE ANGLICAN COMMUNION

Name	Cable Address (or other)	Pronunciation (of Diocese)
Aberdeen and Orkney	The Bishop, 46 Queen's Rd., Aberdeen, Scotland	ăb'ȧr·dēn ôrk'nĭ
Accra	ANGLICAN CHURCH, ACCRA, GHANA	ȧ·krä'
Adelaide	Bishop's Court, North Adelaide, South Australia	ăd'l·ād
Alabama	Episcopal Bishop, Birmingham 3, Ala.	ăl'ȧ·băm'ȧ
Alaska	The Bishop, District Office, Box 441, Fairbanks, Alaska	ȧ·lăs'kȧ
Albany	Diocesan Office, 62 So. Swan St., Albany 10, N.Y., U.S.A.	ôl'bȧ·nĭ
Algoma	Bishophurst, 134 Simpson St., Sault Ste. Marie, Ontario, Canada	ăl·gō'mȧ
Amritsar	Bishop's House, Taylor Rd., Amritsar, Punjab, India	ŭm·rĭt'sĕr
Anglican Diocese in Argentina and Eastern South America with the Falkland Islands	The Bishop, 25 de Mayo, 282, Buenos Aires, Argentina	är'jĕn·tē'nȧ ēs'tĕrn sou ȧ·mĕr'ĭcȧ fôk'lǎnd
Anhwei & Kiangsi	*	än'hwā & jĭ·äng'sē'
Ankole-Kigezi	P.O. BOX 14, MBARARA, UGANDA, AFRICA	ang·kō'lā Kĭ·gā'zē
Antigua	Bishop's Lodge, Antigua, British West Indies	ăn·tē'gȧ
The Arctic	ARCTICUS, TORONTO, ONTARIO, CANADA	ärk'tĭk
Argyll and the Isles	The Bishop, St. Bride's Rectory, Onich, Inverness-shire, Scotland	är·gīl'īlz
Arizona	Diocesan Office, Box 676, Phoenix, Ari., U.S.A.	ăr'ĭ zō'nȧ
Arkansas	Diocese of Arkansas, 300 West 17th St., Little Rock, Ark., U.S.A.	är'kǎn·sô

Name	*Cable Address (or other)*	*Pronunciation (of Diocese)*
Armagh	The Archbishop, The Palace, Armagh, N. Ireland	är·mä′
Armidale	Bishopscourt, Armidale, N.S.W., Australia	ä′mĭ·dāl
Assam	KUTI, SHILLONG, ASSAM, INDIA	ă·săm′
Athabasca	ANGLICAN SYNOD OF-FICE, PEACE RIVER, ALBERTA, CANADA	ăth·á·bās′kà
Atlanta	Diocesan Office, 2744 Peachtree Rd. N.E., Atlanta 5, Ga., U.S.A.	ăt·lăn′tà
Auckland	DIOSEC, AUCKLAND, AUSTRALIA	ôk′lănd
Ballarat	BISHOP'S REGISTRY, BALLARAT, VICTORIA, AUSTRALIA	băl′à·răt
Bangor	BISHOP, BANGOR, CAER-NARVONSHIRE, WALES, U.K.	băng′gĕr
Barbados	Bishopscourt, St. Michael, Barbados, British West Indies	bär·bā′dōz
Barrackpore	Bishop's Lodge, Barrackpore, W. Bengal, India	băr′răck·pōor
Basutoland	BOX 87, MASERU, BASU-TOLAND, S. AFRICA	bà·sōo′tō·lănd′
Bath and Wells	Bishop's Palace, Wells, Somerset, England	bàth wĕlz
Bathurst	DIOCESAN REGISTRY, BATHURST, AUSTRALIA	băth′ûrst
Bendigo	THE BISHOP, BENDIGO, VICTORIA, AUSTRALIA	bĕn′dĭ·gō
Benin	The Bishop, Benin, Nigeria, W. Africa	bĕ·nĭn′
Bermuda	BISHOP: BERMUDA	bĕr·mū′dà
Bethlehem	The Diocese of Bethlehem, 826 Delaware Ave., Bethlehem, Pa., U.S.A.	bĕth′lē·ĕm
Bhagalpur	The Bishop, Champanagar, Bhagalpur 4, Bihar, India	bhä·găl·pūr′
Birmingham	Bishop's Croft, Birmingham 17, England	bûr′mĭng·hăm

Name	Cable Address (or other)	Pronunciation (of Diocese)
Blackburn	Bishop's House, Clayton-le-dale, Blackburn, England	blăk′bẽrn
Bloemfontein	THE BISHOP, P.O. BOX 200, BLOEMFONTEIN, S. AFRICA	blōōm′fôn·tän′
Bombay	FELICITY, BOMBAY, INDIA	bŏm·bā′
Bradford	Bishopcroft, Ashwell Road, Bradford 9, England	brăd′fẽrd
Brandon	The Bishop, Brandon, Manitoba, Canada	brăn′dŭn
Brechin	Forbescourt, Broughty Ferry, Scotland, U.K.	brē′kĭn
Brisbane	Bishopsbourne, Brisbane, Queensland, Australia	brĭz′bán
Bristol	Bishop's House, Clifton Hill, Bristol 8, England	brĭs′t′l
British Columbia	Bishop's Close, Victoria, B.C., Canada	brĭt′ĭsh ko·lŭm′bĭà
British Honduras	The Bishop, St. Mary's Rectory, Belize, British Honduras	brĭt′ĭsh hŏn·dōōr′ăs
Bunbury	Bishopscourt, Bunbury, S.W. Australia	bŭn′bẽr·ĭ
Calcutta	COIBAC, CALCUTTA, INDIA	kăl·kŭt′à
Caledonia	ANGLICAN SYNOD OFFICE, PRINCE RUPERT, B.C., CANADA	kăl′ĕ·dō′nĭ·a
Calgary	The Bishop, 1029 Hillcrest Ave., Calgary, Alberta, Canada	kăl′gà·rĭ
California	Diocese of California, 1055 Taylor St., San Francisco 8, Calif., U.S.A.	kăl′ĭ·fôrn′yà
Canberra & Goulburn	Diocesan Register, Church House P.O. Box 189, Goulburn, Australia	kăn′bĕrà gōl′bẽrn
Canterbury	Lambeth Palace, London, S.E. 1, England; or Diocesan House, Lady Wooton's Green, Canterbury, Kent, England	kăn′tẽr·bẽr·ĭ

Name	Cable Address (or other)	Pronunciation (of Diocese)
Cape Town	The Archbishop, Bishopscourt, Claremont, S. Africa	kāp'toun'
Cariboo	The Bishop, 171 Nicola St., W., Kamloops, B.C., Canada	kăr'ĭboo̅
Carlisle	ROSE CASTLE, CAR-LISLE, ENGLAND	kär·līl'
Carpentaria	CHURCH OFFICE, THURS-DAY ISLAND, AUS-TRALIA	kär'pĕn·târ'ĭ·à
Cashel and Emly, Waterford and Lismore	Bishopsgrove, Waterford, Ireland	kăsh'ĕl ĕm'lĭ wô'tĕr·fĕrd lĭz·mōr'
Central America	EPICAM, SAN JOSE, COSTA RICA	sĕn'trăl à·mĕr'ĭ·kà
Central Brazil, Missionary District of	PECUSAM, RIO DE JAN-EIRO, G.B., BRAZIL	sĕn'trăl brà·zĭl'
Central New York	Diocese of Central New York, 935 James Street, Syracuse 3, N.Y., U.S.A.	sĕn'trăl nū yôrk'
Central Tanganyika	TESTIMONY, DODOMA, TANGANYIKA, AFRICA	sĕn'trăl tăn'găn·yē'kà
Chekiang	*	jŭ'jĭ·äng'
Chelmsford	Bishopscourt, Chelmsford, England	chĕlms'fĕrd
Chester	BISHOP'S HOUSE, CHES-TER, ENGLAND	chĕs'tĕr
Chicago	The Diocese of Chicago, 65 East Huron St., Chicago 11, Ill., U.S.A.	shĭ·kä'gō
Chichester	Diocese, Hove, England	chĭch'ĭs·tĕr
Chota Nagpur	P.O. BOX 1, RANCHI, BIHAR, INDIA	chōtà năg'poŏr
Christchurch	Bishopscourt, 100 Park Terrace, Christchurch, New Zealand	krīs [t] 'chûrch
Clogher	Thornfield, Fivemiletown, Co. Fermanagh, N. Ireland	klŏk'ĕr
Colombo	Bishop's House, Steuart Place, Colombo, Ceylon	kō·lŭm'bō
Colorado	Diocese of Colorado, 1313 Clarkson St., Denver 18, Colo., U.S.A.	kŏl'o·rä'dō

Name	Cable Address (or other)	Pronunciation (of Diocese)
Connecticut	EPISCON, HARTFORD, CONNECTICUT	kŏ·nĕt′ĭ·kŭt
Connor	CONNOR, CO. ANTRIM, N. IRELAND	kŏn′ēr
Cork, Cloyne and Ross	Diocesan Office, 52 South Mall, Cork, Ireland	kôrk kloin rŏs
Coventry	BISHOP'S HOUSE, COVENTRY, ENGLAND	kŏv′ĕn·trĭ
Cuba, Missionary District of	The Bishop, Calle 13. No. 876, esq. a.6, Vedado, Havana, Cuba	kū′bȧ
Dacca	The Bishop, Victoria Park, Dacca 1, East Pakistan	dăk′ȧ
Dallas	Diocese of Dallas, 2220 Main St., Dallas, Tex., U.S.A.	dăl′ăs
Damaraland	Bishop's House Windhoek, S.W. Africa	dăm′ȧ·rȧ·lănd′
Delaware	Diocese of Delaware, 2020 Tatnall St., Wilmington 2, Del., U.S.A.	dĕl′ȧwār
Delhi	Bishop's House, 1 Church Lane, New Delhi, India	dĕl′ĭ
Derby	DIOCESAN HOUSE, DERBY, ENGLAND	där′bĭ
Derry and Raphoe	DIOCESAN OFFICE, LONDON STREET, LONDONDERRY, N. IRELAND	dĕr′ĭ rä·fō′
Dominican Republic	EPISCOPAL, SANTO DOMINGO, R.D.	dō·mĭn′ĭ·kăn rē·pŭb′lĭk
Down and Dromore	The See House, Knockdene Park, Belfast, N. Ireland	doun drō·mōr′
Dublin and Glendalough and Kildare	The See House, 4 Burlington Rd., Dublin, Ireland	dŭb′lĭn glĕn′dȧ·lŏk′ kĭl·där′
Dunedin	Bishop's House, 10 Claremont St., Dunettar, Dunedin, New Zealand	dŭn·ē′d′n
Durham	The Bishop, Auckland Castle, Co. Durham, England	dûr′ăm
East Carolina	Episcopal Diocese, Wilmington, N.C., U.S.A.	ēst kăr′ō lĭ′nȧ

Name	Cable Address (or other)	Pronunciation (of Diocese)
Eastern Oregon, Missionary District of	Missionary District of Eastern Oregon, Box 951, Bend, Oregon, U.S.A.	ēs′tẽrn ŏr′ē·gŏn
East Szechwan	*	ēst sŭ′chwän′
Easton	Episcopal Diocese of Easton, Box 1027, Easton, Md., U.S.A.	ēs′tŭn
Eau Claire	Diocese of Eau Claire, 510 S. Farwell St., Eau Claire, Wis., U.S.A.	ō′klār′
Edinburgh	Bishop's House, 4 Lansdowne Crescent, Edinburgh, Scotland	ed′n·bŭr·ŭ
Edmonton	Synod Office, 9707 107th St., Edmonton, Canada	ĕd′mŭn·tŭn
Egypt and Libya	ALL SAINTS' CATHEDRAL, CAIRO, EGYPT	ē′jĭpt lĭb′ĭ à
Ely	BISHOP'S HOUSE, ELY, CAMBS., ENGLAND	ē′lĭ
Erie	Episcopal Diocese, Erie, Pa., U.S.A.	ēr′ĭ
Europe: Convocation of American Churches in	COMPASROSE, LONDON, S.W.1, ENGLAND	ū′rŭp
Exeter	BISHOP, EXETER, ENGLAND	ĕk′sĕ·tẽr
Florida	Episcopal Diocese of Florida, 325 Market St., Jacksonville, Fla., U.S.A.	flŏr′ĭ·dà
Fond du Lac	FONDULAC, WISCONSIN, U.S.A.	fŏn′dŭ·lăk′
Fort Hall	The Bishop, P.O. Box 121, Fort Hall, Kenya, E. Africa	fôrt hôl
Fredericton	The Bishop, Fredericton, N.B., Canada	frĕd′rĭk·tŭn
Fukien	*	f′ōōkyĕn′
Gambia and the Rio Pongas	The Bishop, P.O. Box 51, Bathurst, Gambia, W. Africa	găm′bĭ·à rē′ō pŏng′ŭs
George	The Bishop, Box 126, George, S. Africa	jôrj′

Name	Cable Address (or other)	Pronunciation (of Diocese)
Georgia	Diocese of Georgia, 611 East Bay St., Savannah, Ga., U.S.A.	jôr'jȧ
Gibraltar	DIOGBRA, LONDON, ENGLAND	jĭ·brôl'tēr
Gippsland	Bishopscourt, Sale, Australia	gĭps'lănd
Glasgow and Galloway	C/O THE BISHOP IN GLASGOW, SCOTLAND	glăs'kō găl'ŏ·wā
Gloucester	Church House, Gloucester, England	glŏs'tēr
Grafton	BISHOPSHOLME GRAF-TON, N.S.W., AUSTRALIA	grăhf'tŭn
Grahamstown	AERARIUM, GRAHAMS-TOWN, S. AFRICA	grā'ȧmz·toun
Guiana	ARCHBISHOP, GEORGE-TOWN, BRITISH GUIANA	gī'ä·nȧ
Guildford	DIOCESAN HOUSE, GUILDFORD, ENGLAND	gĭl'fērd
Haiti	VOEGELI PORT-AU-PRINCE, HAITI	hā'tĭ
Harrisburg	Episcopal Diocese of Harris-burg Harrisburg, Pa., U.S.A.	hăr'ĭs·bûrg
Hereford	THE PALACE, HEREFORD, ENGLAND	hĕr'ĕ·fērd
Hokkaido	The Bishop, 1507 Nishi 17-chome, Minami, 14-jo, Sap-poro, Japan	hŏ·kī'dō
Honan	*	hŏ'nän'
Hong Kong and Macao	BISHOPRIC, HONG KONG	hŏng'kŏng & mȧ·kou'
Honolulu, Mission-ary District of	PECUSAM, HONOLULU, HAWAII	hŏn"l·o͞o'lo͞o
Huron	THE BISHOP, HURON, LONDON, CANADA	hūr'ŭn
Hupeh & Hunan	*	ho͞o'pä'& ho͞o'nän'
Ibadan	The Bishop, P.O. Box 21, Ibadan, Nigeria, W. Africa	ē·bä'dän
Idaho, Missionary District of	Episcopal District Office, 107 E. Fort St., Boise, Idaho, U.S.A.	i'dȧ·hō

Name	Cable Address (or other)	Pronunciation (of Diocese)
Indianapolis	Episcopal Diocese of Indianapolis, 2847 N. Meridian St., Indianapolis 8, Ind., U.S.A.	ĭn'dĭ·ăn·ăp'ō·lĭs
Iowa	Episcopal Diocese of Iowa, 225 37th St., Des Moines 12, Iowa, U.S.A.	ī'ō·wȧ
Iran	TESTIMONY, ISFAHAN, IRAN	ē·rän'
Jamaica	CHURCH OFFICES, KINGSTON, JAMAICA, B.WI.	jȧ·mā'kȧ
Jesselton	The Bishop, Jesselton, North Bornea	jĕs''l·tŭn
Jerusalem	ANGLEPS, JERUSALEM, JORDAN	jĕ·rōo'sȧ·lĕm
Johannesburg	DIOCESAN, JOHANNESBURG, S. AFRICA	j·ōhăn'ĭs·bûrg
Jordan, Lebanon, and Syria	ST. GEORGE'S CLOSE, JERUSALEM, JORDAN	jôr'd'n lĕb'ȧnŭn sĭr'ĭ·ȧ
Kalgoorlie	BISHOP, KALGOORLIE, W. AUSTRALIA	kăl·gōor'lē
Kansas	Diocese of Kansas, Bethany Place, 9th and Polk, Topeka, Kan., U.S.A.	kan'zȧs
Karachi	Bishop's House, Lawrence Rd., Karachi, Pakistan	kȧrä'chĭ
Keewatin	KEEWASTOWE, KENORA, ONTARIO, CANADA	kē·wā't'n
Kentucky	Episcopal Diocese of Kentucky, 421 S. 2nd St., Louisville 2, Ky., U.S.A.	kĕn·tŭk'ĭ
Kaingsu	*	jĭ·äng'sōo'
Killaloe, Kilfenora, Clonfert, and Kilmacduagh	Diocesan Secretary, Deanery, Killaloe, Ireland	k;'l'·a·lōo kĭl·fĕn·ō'rȧ klŏn'fĕrt kĭl·măc·dōo·'ȧ
Kilmore and Elphin and Ardagh	The See House, Kilmore, Cavan, Ireland	kĭl'mōr ĕl fĭn är'dĕ
Kimberley and Kuruman	Bishopsgarth, Kimberley, S. Africa	kĭm'bĕr·lĭ
Kobe	The Bishop, 5, 3-chome, Nakayamate-dori, Ikuta-ku, Kobe-shi, Japan	kō'bē

Name	Cable Address (or other)	Pronunciation (of Diocese)
Kootenay	Bishop's House, 2136 Abbott St., Kelowna, B.C., Canada	kōo't' n·ā
Korea	The Bishop, Anglican Church, Seoul, Korea	ko·rē'a̤
Kuching	Bishop's House, Kuching, Sarawak (via Singapore)	kōo'chĭng
Kurunagala	BISHOP'S HOUSE, KURU-NAGALA, CEYLON	kōor'oo·nâg'a̤·la̤
Kwangsi & Hunan	*	gwäng'sē'& hōo'nän'
Kyoto	The Bishop, Karasumaru-dori, Shima Tachiuri Agaru, Kamkyo-ku, Kyoto-shi, Japan	kyō'tō̄
Kyushu	The Bishop, 107, 8-chome, Kaji-machi, Kokura-shi, Kyushu, Japan	kyōo'shōo
Lagos	Bishopscourt, Lagos, Nigeria, W. Africa	lä'gŭs
Lahore	TESTIMONY, LAHORE, PAKISTAN	la̤·hōr'
Lebombo	LIBOMBOS LOURENCO MARQUES, PORTU-GUESE E. AFRICA	lĕ·bŏm'bō
Leicester	Bishop's Lodge, Leicester, England	lĕs'tẽr
Lexington	Episcopal Diocese of Lexington, 544 Sayre Ave., Lexington, Ky., U.S.A.	lĕk'sĭng·tŭn
Liberia	PECUSAM, MONROVIA, LIBERIA	lī·bēr'ĭ·a̤
Lichfield	The Close, Lichfield, England	lĭch'fēld
Limerick, Ardfert, and Aghadoe	Bishop's House, Limerick, Ireland	lĭm'rĭck ärd'fẽrt ä·ä·dō'
Lincoln	Bishop's House, Eastgate, Lincoln, England	lĭng'kŭn
Liverpool	CHURCH HOUSE, LIVER-POOL, ENGLAND	lĭv'ẽr·pool
Llandaff	Llys Esgob, The Green, Llandaff, Cardiff, Wales, U.K.	lăn'dăf

Name	*Cable Address (or other)*	*Pronunciation (of Diocese)*
London	FULHAM PALACE, LON-DON, ENGLAND	lŭn'dŭn
Long Island	The Diocese of Long Island, 65 Fourth St., Garden City, N.Y., U.S.A.	lōng ī'land
Los Angeles	Episcopal Diocese, 617 West 7th St., Los Angeles 17, Calif., U.S.A.	lŏs ăn'jĕ·lĕs
Louisiana	Episcopal Diocese of Louisiana, 2265 St. Charles Ave., New Orleans 13, La., U.S.A.	loo'ĭ·zĭ·ăn'à
Lucknow	11 CANNING ROAD, AL-LAHABAD, INDIA	lŭk'nou
Madagascar	La Mission Anglicane, Tana-narive, Madagascar, Africa	măd'à·găs'kĕr
Maine	Bishop's Office, 143 State St., Portland 3, Me., U.S.A.	mān
Manchester	BISHOP OF MANCHESTER, MANCHESTER, ENGLAND	măn'chĕs'tĕr
Maryland	Episcopal Diocese of Mary-land, 105 W. Monument St., Baltimore, Md., U.S.A.	mĕr'ĭ·lănd
Masasi	The Bishop, Masasi, S.P., Tanganyika, E. Africa	mă·sā'sī
Maseno	The Bishop, P.O. Box 1, Maseno, Kenya, E. Africa	mă·sā'nō
Mashonaland	BOX 7, SALISBURY, S. RHODESIA	mà·shō'nà·lănd
Massachusetts	Episcopal Diocese of Massa-chusetts, 1 Joy St., Boston 8, Mass., U.S.A.	măs'àchoo'sĕts
Matabeleland	Bishop's House, Bulawayo, S. Rhodesia	mătà·bē'lē·lănd
Mauritius	The Bishop, Phoenix, Mauri-tius, Africa	mô·rĭsh'ĭ·ŭs
Mbale	Bishop's House, P.O. Box 473, Mbale, Uganda, Africa	m·bä'lē
Meath	BISHOP'S HOUSE, KILLU-CAN, WEST MEATH, IRELAND	mēth

Name	Cable Address (or other)	Pronunciation (of Diocese)
Melanesia	MELANESIA, HONIARA, BRITISH SOLOMON ISLANDS	měl·à nē′zhà
Melbourne	Bishopscourt, Melbourne, Victoria, Australia	měl′bĕrn
Mexico, Missionary District of	The Bishop, Calle de la Otra Banda, 40 San Anguel, Mexico 20, D.F. Mexico	měk′sĭ·kō
Michigan	Diocese of Michigan, 4800 Woodward Ave., Detroit 1, Mich., U.S.A.	mĭsh′ĭ·găn
Mid-Japan	The Bishop, 11-chome, Yamawaki-Cho, Showa-ku, Nagoya, Japan	mĭd jà·pǎn′
Milwaukee	Episcopal Diocese of Milwaukee, 804 E. Juneau Ave., Milwaukee 2, Wis., U.S.A.	mĭl·wô′ke
Minnesota	Episcopal Diocese of Minnesota, 309 Clifton Ave., Minneapolis 3, Minn., U.S.A.	mĭn′ĕ·sō′tà
Mississippi	Diocese of Mississippi, 112 South West St., Jackson 5, Miss., U.S.A.	mĭs′ĭ·sĭp′ĭ
Missouri	Episcopal Diocese of Missouri, 1210 Locust St., St. Louis 3, Mo., U.S.A.	mĭ·zoor′ĭ
Mombasa	Bishopsbourne, P.O. Box 502, Nairobi, Kenya, E. Africa	mŏm·bä′sà
Monmouth	BISHOPSTOW, MONMOUTH, U.K.	mŏn′mŭth
Montana	Episcopal Diocese of Montana, Last Chance Gulch, Helena, Mont., U.S.A.	mŏn·tăn′à
Montreal	The Bishop, Synod Office, 1444 Union Ave., Montreal, Quebec, Canada	mŏn′trĕ·ôl′
Moosonee	DIOCESE OF MOOSONEE, SCHUMACHER, ONTARIO, CANADA	mo͞os′ŏ·nē
Moray, Ross and Caithness	Bishop's House, 43 Fairfield Rd., Inverness, Scotland	mûr′ ĭ rŏs kāth′nĕs
Nagpur	Cathedral House, Nagpur 1, Maharastra, India	năg′po͞or

Name	Cable Address (or other)	Pronunciation (of Diocese)
Nakuru	BOX 54, NAKURU, KEN-YA, E. AFRICA	nä·kōō′rōō
Namirembe	TESTIMONY, KAMPALA, UGANDA, AFRICA	nă·mĭ·rĕm′bĕ
Nasik	Bishop's House, Sharanpur, Nasik, India	nä′sĭk
Nassau and the Bahamas	The Bishop, Addington House, Nassau, British West Indies.	năs′ô bà·hä′máz
Natal	Bishop's House, Pietermaritz-burg, Natal, S. Africa	nà·tăl′
Nebraska	Episcopal Diocese of Nebraska 1008 W.O.W. Bldg., Omaha 2, Neb., U.S.A.	nĕ·brăs′kà
Nelson	DIOCESAN OFFICE, NEL-SON, NEW ZEALAND	nĕl′s′n
Nevada	Diocesan Office, P.O. Box 1590, Reno, Nev., U.S.A.	nĕ·văd′a
Newark	Episcopal Diocese, Newark, N.J., U.S.A.	nū′ĕrk
Newcastle	BISHOP'S REGISTRY, NEWCASTLE, N.S.W., AUSTRALIA	nū′kas″l
Newcastle	The Bishop, Newcastle, Eng-land	nū′kas″l
Newfoundland	THE BISHOP OF NEW-FOUNDLAND, ST. JOHN'S, NEWFOUNDLAND, CANADA	nū′fŭn [d]·lănd′
New Guinea	Anglican Mission, Samarai, Papau, N.G.	nū gĭ′nē
New Hampshire	Episcopal Diocese of New Hampshire, 63 Green St., Concord, N.H., U.S.A.	nū hăm [p]′shĕr
New Jersey	Diocese of New Jersey, 808 West State St., Trenton 8, N.J., U.S.A.	nū jûr′zĭ
New Mexico and South-west Texas	PECUSA, SANTA FE, N.M., U.S.A.	nū mĕk′sĭ·kō southwĕst tĕk′săs
New Westminster	The Bishop, 329 Seymour St., Vancouver 2, B.C., Canada	nū wĕs [t]′mĭn·stĕr

Name	*Cable Address (or other)*	*Pronunciation (of Diocese)*
New York	CATHJOHN, NEW YORK, U.S.A.	nū yôrk′
Niagara	Niagara Church House, Hamilton, Ontario, Canada	nĭ·ăg′á·rȧ
The Niger	TESTIMONY, ONITSHA-NIGERIA, W. AFRICA	nī′jĕr
The Niger Delta	Bishop's House, Aba, Nigeria, W. Africa	nī′jĕr dĕl′tȧ
North Africa	(Temp under jurisdiction of the Bishop of Gibraltar, 35 Great Peter St., London, S.W.1, England)	nôrth ăf′rĭ kȧ
North and Central Europe, Jurisdiction of	COOTE, BYFLEET 42127, LONDON, ENGLAND	nôrth and sĕn′trȧl ū′rŭp
North Carolina	Episcopal Diocese, Raleigh, N.C., U.S.A.	nôrth kăr′ō·lĭ′nȧ
North China	*	nôrth chī′nȧ
North Dakota, Missionary District of	Episcopal Diocese of North Dakota, 809 8th Ave., S., Fargo, N.D., U.S.A.	nôrth dȧ·kō′tȧ
North Kanto	The Bishop, 2 Irifune Cho, Tochigi, Japan	nôrth kăn′tō
Northern California	DIOCNORCAL, SACRAMENTO, CALIF., U.S.A.	northern kăl′ĭfôrn′yȧ
Northern Indiana	Episcopal Diocese of Northern Indiana, 117 No. Lafayette Blvd., South Bend 1, Ind., U.S.A.	northern ĭn′dĭ·ăn′ȧ
Northern Michigan	Episcopal Diocese of Northern Michigan, 922 10th Ave., Menominee, Mich., U.S.A.	northern mĭsh′ĭ·găn
Northern Provinces of Nigeria	Bishopscourt, P.O. Box 72, Kaduna, Nigeria, W. Africa	northern prŏv′ĭnsĕz nī·jĕr′ĭ·ȧ
Northern Rhodesia	Bishop's Lodge, Box 183, Lusaka, N.R., C. Africa	northern rō·dē′zhȧ
North Queensland	BISHOPSLODGE, TOWNSVILLE, AUSTRALIA	nôrth kwēnz′lănd
North Uganda	THE BISHOP, GULU, UGANDA, AFRICA	nôrth ū·găn′dȧ
North-West Australia	THE BISHOP, NORTHWEST AUSTRALIA	nôrth-wĕst ôs·trāl′yȧ

Name	*Cable Address (or other)*	*Pronunciation (of Diocese)*
North-West Texas	Episcopal Diocese of North-West Texas, 1520 Bryan St., Amarillo, Tex., U.S.A.	nôrth wĕst tĕk'săs
Norwich	DIOCESAN OFFICES, NORWICH, ENGLAND	nŏr'ĭj
Nova Scotia	Anglican Diocesan Centre, Halifax, N.S., Canada	nō'và skō'shà
Nyasaland	ULEMA, FORT JOHN-STON, NYASALAND, C. AFRICA	nĭ·ăs'á·lănd
Ohio	Episcopal Diocese of Ohio, Church House, Cleveland, Ohio, U.S.A.	ō·hī'ō
Oklahoma	Diocesan Office, 608 N.E. 18th St., Oklahoma City 1, Okla., U.S.A.	ō'klà·hō'mȧ
Olympia	Diocese of Olympia, 1551 10th Ave., E., Seattle 2, Wash., U.S.A.	ō·lĭm'pĭ·à
Ondo	TESTIMONY, ONDO, NIGERIA, W. AFRICA	ŏn'dō
Ontario	Synod Office, 87 Clarence St., Kingston, Ontario, Canada	ŏn·târ'ĭ·ō
Oregon	Episcopal Diocese of Oregon, 11800 S.W. Military Lane, Portland 19, Ore., U.S.A.	ŏr'e·gŏn
Osaka	The Bishop, 175 Matsuzakicho 2-chome, Abenoku, Osaka, Japan	ō'sä·kä
Ossory, Ferns, and Leighlin	The Bishop's Palace, Kilkenny, Ireland	ŏs'ō·rĭ fûrnz lē'lĭn
Ottawa	Bishop's Court, Ottawa, Canada	ŏt'à·wà
Owerri	BISHOP, EGBU, OWERRI, NIGERIA	ō'wĕr·ĭ
Oxford	THE BISHOP, OXFORD, ENGLAND	ŏks'fĕrd
Panama Canal Zone	PECUSA, BALBOA, CANAL ZONE	păn'ă·mô kà·năl'zōn
Pennsylvania	Episcopal Diocese of Pennsylvania, 202 W. Rittenhouse Sq., Philadelphia 3, Pa., U.S.A.	pĕn'sĭl·vān'yà

Name	*Cable Address (or other)*	*Pronunciation (of Diocese)*
Perth	DIOPERTH, AUSTRALIA	pûrth
Peterborough	PALACE, PETERBOR-OUGH, ENGLAND	pē'tĕr·bûr'ȧ
Philippines	BISHOPSTED, MANILA, PHILIPPINES	fĭl'ĭ·pēnz
Pittsburgh	Episcopal Diocese, Trinity House, 325 Oliver Ave., Pittsburgh 22, Pa., U.S.A.	pĭts'bûrg
Polynesia	BISHOP, POLYNESIA, SUVA, FIJI IS.	pŏl'ĭ·nē'zhȧ
Portsmouth	CATHEDRAL, PORTS-MOUTH, ENGLAND	pōrts'mŭth
Pretoria	EPISCOPUS, PRETORIA, S. AFRICA	prē̆·tōr'·ĭ·ȧ
Puerto Rico	PECUSAM, SAN JUAN, P.R.	pwĕr'tŭ rē'kō
Qu'Appelle	Bishop's Court, Regina, Sask., Canada	kȧ'pĕl'
Quebec	CHURCH HOUSE, 36 GARDEN ST., QUEBEC, CANADA	kwe·bĕk'
Quincy	Episcopal Diocese of Quincy, 3900 Hawthorne Pl., Peoria, Ill., U.S.A.	kwĭn'sĭ
Rangoon	Bishop's Court, 140 Halpin Rd., Rangoon, Burma	răng·gōōn'
Rhode Island	Diocese of Rhode Island, 101 Benefit St., Providence 3, R.I., U.S.A.	rōd ī'lănd
Ripon	Bishop Mount, Ripon, England	rĭp'ŭn
Riverina	The Bishop, P.O. Box 10, Narrandera, N.S.W., Australia	rĭ·vē̆·rē'nȧ
Rochester	Diocesan Office, 935 East Ave., Rochester 7, N.Y., U.S.A.	rŏch'ĕs'tĕr
Rochester	Bishopscourt, Rochester, England	rŏc'ĭ'ĕs'tĕr
Rockhampton	Phone 2339, Rockhampton, Queensland, Australia	rŏk·hăm [p]'tŭn
Ruanda-Urundi	NGOZI, RUANDA-URUNDI, E. AFRICA	rōō·än'dä ōō·rōōn'dĕ̆

Name	*Cable Address (or other)*	*Pronunciation (of Diocese)*
Rupert's Land	Trinity Hall, Winnipeg, Man., Canada	rū′pĕrts lănd
Ruwenzori	BOX 37, FORT-PORTAL, UGANDA, AFRICA	roō [w] ĕn·zō′re
St. Albans	The Bishop, Abbey Gate House, St. Albans, England	ôl′bănz
St. Andrew's, Dunkeld, and Dunblane	Bishop's House, Fairmount Rd., Perth, Scotland	ăn′droōz dŭn·kĕld′ dūn·blăn′
St. Arnaud	REGISTRY, ST. ARNAUD, AUSTRALIA	ärn′ō
St. Asaph	The Bishop's Palace, St. Asaph, N. Wales, U.K.	ā′săf
St. David's	ABERGWILI PALACE, CARMARTHEN, WALES, U.K.	dă′vĭdz
St. Edmundsbury and Ipswich	Bishop's House, Ipswich, Suffolk, England	ĕd′mŭnz·bĕr·ĭ ĭps′wĭch
St. Helena	Bishopsholme, Island of St. Helena, S. Africa	′l·ē′nȧ
St. John's	Bishopsmead, Umtata, C.P.S., Africa	jŏnz′
Salisbury	BISHOP OF SALISBURY, WILTSHIRE, ENGLAND	sôlz′bĕr′ĭ
San Joaquin, Missionary District of	Episcopal Diocesan Office 1617 N. Hunter St., Stockton 4, Calif., U.S.A.	săn wŏ kēn′
Saskatchewan	DIOCESE OF SASKAT-CHEWAN, PRINCE ALBERT, SASK., CANDA	săs·kăch′ĕ·wŏn
Saskatoon	The Bishop, 334 5th Ave., N., Saskatoon, Canada	săs′kȧ·toōn
Shantung	*	shăn′tŭng′
Sheffield	The Bishop, Ranmoor Grange, Sheffield 10, England	shĕf′ēld
Shensi	*	shĕn′sē′
Sierra Leone	Bishopscourt, P.O. Box 128, Freetown, Sierra Leone, W. Africa	sĭ·ĕr′ȧ lē̄·ōn′
Singapore and Malaya	EPISCOPOS, SINGAPORE	sĭng′gȧ pōr mȧ lā′ȧ

Name	Cable Address (or other)	Pronunciation (of Diocese)
Sodor and Man	Bishop's Court, Isle of Man, England	sŏ'dōr and măn
Soroti	TOMUSANGE SOROTI, UGANDA, AFRICA	sō·rō'tĭ
South Carolina	Diocese of South Carolina, 138 Wentworth St., Charleston 6, S.C., U.S.A.	south kăr'ŏ lĭ'nȧ
South China	*	south chĭ'nȧ
South Dakota, Missionary District of	Episcopal District Office, 200 W. 18th St., Sioux Falls, S.D., U.S.A.	south dȧ·kō'tȧ
South Florida	Diocese of South Florida, 324 N. Interlachen Ave., Winter Park, Fla., U.S.A.	south flŏr'ĭ·dȧ
Southern Brazil, Missionary District of	The Missionary Bishop, Caiza 2684, Porto Alegre, R.G.S., Brazil	sŭ'thẽrn brȧ·zĭl'
Southern Ohio	Diocese of Southern Ohio, 412 Sycamore St., Cincinnati 1, Ohio, U.S.A.	sŭ'thẽrn ŏ·hī'ō
Southern Virginia	Diocese of Southern Virginia, 618 Stockley Gardens, Norfolk 7, Va., U.S.A.	sŭ'thẽrn vẽr·jĭn'yȧ
Southwark	THE BISHOP OF SOUTH-WARK, LONDON, ENGLAND	sŭth'ẽrk
Southwell	CHURCH HOUSE, PARK ROW, NOTTS. ENGLAND	sŭth'ẽl
South-West Tanganyika	BOX 32, NJOMBE TANGANYIKA, E. AFRICA	south wĕst tăn'gȧn·yē'kȧ
Southwestern Brazil, Missionary District of	The Missionary Bishop, Rua Vale Machado, Caixa Postal 98, Santa Maria, R.G.S., Brazil	south wĕs'tẽrn brȧ·zĭl'
Southwestern Virginia	Diocese Episcopal, Roanoke, Va., U.S.A.	south wĕs'tẽrn vẽr·jĭn'yȧ
Spokane, Missionary District of	HUBBARD, EPISCOPAL CHURCH, SPOKANE, WASH., U.S.A.	spō·kăn'
Springfield	Episcopal Diocese of Springfield, 821 S. 2nd St., Springfield, Ill., U.S.A.	sprĭng'fēld

Name	*Cable Address (or other)*	*Pronunciation (of Diocese)*
The Sudan	The Bishop, The Clergy House, Khartoum, The Sudan	sōo·dăn′
Swansea and Brecon	ELY TOWER, BRECON, S. WALES, U.K.	swŏn′zē brĕ′kŭn
Sydney	EPISTRALIA, SYDNEY, AUSTRALIA	sĭd′nĭ
Taiwan	PECUSAM, TAIPEI, TAIWAN	tī′wän′
Tasmania	Registrar, Box 250 C, Hobart, Tasmania, Australia	tăz·mā′nĭ·a̸
Tennessee	Episcopal Diocese of Tennessee, 692 Poplar Ave., Memphis 5, Tenn., U.S.A.	tĕn′ĕ·sē′
Texas	Episcopal Diocese, Houston, Tex., U.S.A.	tĕk′săs
Tohoku	The Bishop, Odawara Chomei Saka, Hara Machi, Sendai, Japan	tō·hō′kōo
Tokyo	The Bishop, 23 Tokiwamatsu, Shibuya-Ku, Tokyo, Japan	tō′kĭ·ō
Toronto	The Bishop, Synod House, 135 Adelaide St., E., Toronto, Ont., Canada	tŭ·rŏn′tō
Trinidad and Tobago	The Bishop, Hayes Court, Port of Spain, Trinidad, British West Indies	trĭn′ĭ·dăd to·bā′gō
Truro	Lis Escop, Truro, England	trū′rō
Tuam, Killala, and Achonry	THE SEE HOUSE, TUAM, IRELAND	tū′a̸m kĭl·lăl′a̸ ă·kŏn·rē
Upper South Carolina	Diocese of Upper South Carolina, Senate and Barnwell Sts., Box 1705, Columbia, S.C., U.S.A.	ŭp′ĕr south kăr′ō·līna̸
Utah, Missionary District of	Episcopal District Office, 231 E. 1st St., Salt Lake City 11, Utah, U.S.A.	ū′tô
Vermont	Diocese of Vermont, Burlington, Vt., U.S.A.	vĕr·mŏnt′
Virgin Islands, Missionary District of	PECUSAM, SAN JUAN, P.R.	vûr′jĭn ī′lăndz

Name	Cable Address (or other)	Pronunciation (of Diocese)
Virginia	Episcopal Diocese of Virginia, 110 W. Franklin St., Richmond 20, Va., U.S.A.	vẽr·jǐn'yả
Waiapu	ECCLESIA, NAPIER, NEW ZEALAND	wī'ả·pú
Waikato	DIOCESAN OFFICE, HAMILTON, NEW ZEALAND	wī·kä'tō
Wakefield	THE BISHOP, WAKEFIELD, YORKS., ENGLAND	wāk'fēld
Wangaratta	BISHOP'S LODGE, WANGARATTA, AUSTRALIA	wǒng·ảt·ả
Washington	Episcopal Church House, Washington 16, D.C., U.S.A.	wōsh'ǐng·tǔn
Wellington	Bishopscourt, Wellington, New Zealand	wěl'ǐng·tǔn
West Buganda	The Bishop, P.O. Box 242, Masaka, Buganda, Africa	wěst bǔ·gǎn'dả
West Missouri	Diocese of West Missouri, Kansas City, Mo., U.S.A.	wěst mǐ·zr'ooï
West Texas	Diocese of West Texas, Cathedral House, 111 Torcido Dr., San Antonio 9, Teā., U.S.A.	wěst tek'sǎs
West Virginia	Diocese of West Virginia, 1608 Virginia St., Charleston, W. Va. U.S.A.	wěst vẽr·jǐn'yả
Western Kansas, Missionary District of	Episcopal Church, Western Kansas, P.O. Box 345, Salina, Kan., U.S.A.	wěs'tẽrn kǎn'zǎs
Western Massachusetts	Diocese of Western Massachusetts, 37 Chestnut St., Springfield 3, Mass., U.S.A.	wěs'tẽrn mas'ả·choo'sĕts
Western Michigan	Diocese of Western Michigan, 855 28th St., S.E., Grand Rapids, Mich., U.S.A.	wěs'tẽrn mǐsh'ǐ gǎn
Western New York	Bishop, Western New York, 1114, Delaware, Buffalo 9, N.Y., U.S.A.	wěs'tẽrn nū yôrk'
Western North Carolina	Diocese of Western North Carolina, 46 Macon Ave., Asheville, N.C., U.S.A.	wěs'tẽrn nôrth kǎr'o·lǐ'nả
West Szechwan	*	wěst sǔ'chwän'

Name	Cable Address (or other)	Pronunciation (of Diocese)
Willochra	The Bishop of Willochra, Gladstone, S. Australia	wĭl·ō·krā′
Winchester	Church House, Winchester, England	wĭn′chĕs′tẽr
Windward Islands	Bishop's House, St. Vincent, British West Indies	wĭnd′wẽrd ī′lăndz
Worcester	The Bishop, Froxmere Court, Crowle, Worcester, England	wŏŏs′tẽr
Wyoming, Missionary District of	District Office, Box 17, Laramie, Wyo., U.S.A.	wi·ō′mĭng
Yokohama	NOSSE 49, SHIMOCHO, MITSUZAWA, JAPAN	yō′kŏ·hä′má
York	Bishopthorpe, York, England	yôrk
Yukon	Box 547, Whitehorse, Yukon Territory, Canada	yōō′kŏn
Yunnan & Kweichow	*	yōō′năn′& gwä′jō′
Zanzibar	Bishop's Lodge, Muheza, Tanga, Tanganyika, E. Africa	zăn′zĭ·bär
Zululand and Swaziland	BOX 147, ESHOWE, ZULULAND	zōō′lōō·lănd′ swä′zẽ·lănd′

WHERE CREDIT IS DUE

Hardly anybody reads acknowledgements, I am told. If this is so, I am heartily sorry, for I should like to give a prominent place to some of the many people who abetted me in my Grand Tour of Anglicanism.

At the top of the list, absolutely without a peer, stands Edith Neftel, the best secretary a man ever had. *I* had all the fun of exploring Anglicanism. *She* had all the work of it – before, during, and after.

The Presiding Bishop of the Protestant Episcopal Church in the United States of America gave me his approbation and encouragement and smoothed my way with letters of introduction, while his Advisory Committee on Anglican Relations helped to find financial support for my expedition and promised to bring me home if it should collapse in midstream – a service which was happily not required. This assistance and moral support I appreciated all the more because I was in no sense an official representative or spokesman for either the Presiding Bishop or his Committee.

My ecclesiastical superior, the Bishop of New York, together with the Trustees of the Cathedral Church of St. John the Divine and my brothers of the Cathedral Chapter, showed both patience and generosity in tolerating my prolonged absence and paying the major part of my secretary's salary.

Certain laymen and voluntary organizations within the Church, their imagination stirred by the audacity of my project, put up most of the money for the trip. The identity of most of these individuals and groups has been kept concealed from me. I have, therefore, no way to thank them by name. They gave me the great adventure of my life – an experience of such magnitude that the rest of my life is doomed to be anticlimax.

It should be understood that I travelled at little expense to the Church. No part of the Church's regular work was shortchanged in order to make room for me. Of course, the people who made me welcome along the way were put to expense which, although I should never have guessed it from their ungrudging hospitality, I knew some of them could ill afford. In each case I tried to find hidden means of reimbursement.

This brings me to the subject of my hundreds of hosts. These are the people who met me at airports, docks, and railway stations, often at unreasonable hours; the people who fed and housed me; the people who drove me around; the people who patiently answered my thousands of questions; the people who were liberal with their time. I only wish it were in my power to thank them all by name and to tell about them all in the book itself. Space precludes it. It implies no disparagement of a person I visited if I do not mention him. No more does it imply disparagement that there were whole dioceses that I felt obliged to skip.

Not only to fellow Anglicans am I indebted for great kindness and hospitality. Roman Catholic bishops received me warmly. Lutherans flew me. Methodists made available to me their cars. More than once, Presbyterians prayed with me and for me. With a delightful Baptist missionary couple I "gathered at the river" while they helped me do my laundry. In all these contacts I was able to learn how Anglicans look to non-Anglican eyes, and I realized anew that the kindred with whom Christ has enriched us, although divided into different folds, are all members of one flock.

For the mechanics involved in a journey of such dimensions I owe more than I can say to D. George Adams, Assistant Treasurer of the Diocese of New York, to A. Leonard Gustafson, a valuable member of our Cathedral family, to my travel agents extraordinary, Else Petersen, William B. Parkinson, and Fred Fulgieri, to the friendly people at the Leica Camera Company in New York, who instructed me in photography, and to the magicians of Modernage Custom Darkrooms and Tcholak Laboratories, both of New York, who made presentable pictures even out of my less successful attempts. My friends, Mr. and Mrs. Noel T. Arnold, talented non-professional photographers, gave me further helpful instruction in camera artistry. Then Sam Holmes, gifted picture editor, came mightily to my aid by helping me to select and arrange the pictures for exhibition in this book.

To Mr. and Mrs. William A. Weech and to Mrs. Walter Lowrie, who at various times offered me havens of quiet in which to write undisturbed, I am also deeply grateful.

My best thanks to James B. Simpson, talented author of *The Hundredth Archbishop of Canterbury*, who heard my despairing plea for help after I had exhausted the patience of my long-suffering publishers. When the deadline for my manuscript was passed, he came to my rescue and put words into my mouth, and here and there he did for me a fine bit of literary hemstitching. "Invisible mending" is a sign I have seen in the show windows of many tailor shops. Mr. Simpson, and also Eleanor Jordan of Harper & Row, are chief among the invisible menders who have been of service to me. Wherever there are gaps in that seam, it is attributable solely to the fact that sometimes, overruling these counsellors arbitrarily, I have ripped out the stitches which they, painstakingly and invisibly, had sewn in.

In conclusion I would like to mention by name the people who have helped me by reading and criticizing my manuscript: Nadene Goff, Eric James, Mrs. D. George Adams, Carolyn S. Joy, the Reverend Basil G. Law, the Reverend Bruce M. Williams, Victor Zitani, and, severest critic of them all, my mother, Jessie Howard Johnson.

I am also indebted to Lisa McGaw, who prepared the index with unfailing intelligence and tenacity despite the pressures of time and the complexities of Anglican nomenclature.

Without the help of many persons, neither the journey would have been possible nor the book that describes it.

BIBLIOGRAPHY

THE FOLLOWING LIST OF BOOKS IS FAR FROM CONSTITUTING AN exhaustive bibliography. Nor can it claim to be selective – that is, it is not restricted, in every instance, to the very best books. Certain titles find a place here not so much on merit as for the reason that no other book on the subject exists.

I do not pretend that I have read from cover to cover every book listed, although I have read enough of them all to know that it would not be a waste of any interested person's time to read them entire.

Many of the volumes are included at the urging of one or more bishops. I asked each of my episcopal hosts to recommend three to five books that would best help to shed light on the Church's situation in his particular jurisdiction. Often the answers I received were disappointing. Occasionally no books were suggested. Some bishops are kept so busy that they have not been able to keep up with their reading. And there are a few of our Fathers in God who have not, I think, voluntarily opened a book for years. One bishop, himself an erudite man, charmingly described his situation in these words: "There is no good book about my corner of the globe. I haven't had time to write it yet!"

Although of the making of many books there is no end, there is still a tremendous poverty when it comes to accurate and up to date accounts.

For the most part I have left unmentioned small pieces, occasional literature, pamphlets, brochures, and the like, for no matter how excellent they are, it is an ephemeral sort of literature, most of it now hard to obtain.

Not often have I included older works, some of which have attained the status of Anglican classics. They are indispensable as background reading, but they leave us in the lurch when it comes to the present day. It suffices, therefore, if I point to Bishop Neill's *Anglicanism*, Bishop Wand's *The Anglican Communion*, and Bishop Higgins' *One Faith and Fellowship*, for in these volumes are to be found comprehensive bibliographies covering the earlier periods.

My own book will have failed of its purpose if it does not serve as an *apéritif* to whet the appetites of my readers for at least some of the books listed below.

GENERAL READING

Church Assembly Overseas Council. *The Moving Spirit: A Survey of the Life and Work of the Churches of the Anglican Communion.* London: The Church Information Board, Church House, Westminster, 1958.

Ellison, G. A., *The Anglican Communion, Past and Future.* London: S.P.C.K., 1960.

Gray, G. F. S. *The Anglican Communion.* London: S.P.C.K., 1958.

Higgins, John Seville. *One Faith and Fellowship.* Greenwich, Conn.: Seabury Press, 1958. (Bibliography included.)

Jefferson, P.C., ed. *The Church in the 60s.* Greenwich, Conn.: Seabury Press, 1962.

Johnson, H. A. ed. *This Church of Ours.* Greenwich, Conn.: Seabury Press, 1958.

Latourette, K.S. *A History of the Expansion of Christianity.* New York: Harper & Brothers, Vol. IV, 1941.

Leidt, William, ed. *Anglican Mosaic.* Toronto: Anglican Book Centre; Greenwich: Seabury Press, 1962.

Morgan, Dewi, ed. *They Became Anglicans.* London: Mowbray, 1959.

Morgan, E. R., and Lloyd, R. B. *The Mission of the Anglican Communion.* London: S.P.C.K. and S.P.G., 1948.

Neill, Stephen. *Anglicanism.* New York: Penguin, 1958. (Bibliography included.)

———. *The Christian Faith Today.* New York: Penguin, 1955.

———. *The Unfinished Task.* London: Edinburgh House, 1958.

Pike, James Albert, ed. *Modern Canterbury Pilgrims.* New York: Morehouse-Gorham, 1956; London: Mowbray, 1956.

Rawlinson, A. E. J. *The Anglican Communion in Christendom.* London: S.P.C.K., 1960.

Rouse, Ruth, and Neill, Stephen. *History of the Ecumenical Movement.* Philadelphia: Westminster, 1954.

Simpson, James B. *The Hundredth Archbishop of Canterbury.* New York: Harper & Row, 1962.

Wand, J. W. C. *The Anglican Communion.* New York: Morehouse-Gorham, 1948. (Bibliography included.)

———. *Anglicanism in History and Today.* London: Weidenfeld and Nicolson, 1961. (Bibliography included.)

Warren, Max. *Challenge and Response.* New York: Morehouse-Gorham, 1959.

RECOMMENDED GENERAL PERIODICALS

Anglican World. London: Church Illustrated Ltd., 29 Tufton Street, S.W.1.

Pan-Anglican. Hartford, Conn.: Church Mission Publishing Co., 207 Farmington Avenue.

The East and West Review. London: S.P.C.K.

BOOKS ABOUT INDIVIDUAL MISSIONARY SOCIETIES

Clarke, W. K. Lowther. *History of the S.P.C.K.* London: S.P.C.K., 1959.

Lancaster, Violet B. *A Short History of the Mothers' Union.* London: Mothers' Union, 1958.

Literature for the Anglican Communion. London: S.P.C.K., 1960.

Pascoe, C. F. *Two Hundred Years of the S.P.G.* London: S.P.G., 1901.

Reffold, A. E. *Wilson Carlile and the Church Army.* London: Church Army Press, 1956.

Stock, Eugene. *History of the Church Missionary Society.* London: C.M.S., 1899. Supplementary volume the fourth, London: C.M.S., 1916.

Strong, L. A. G. *The Flying Angel.* London: Methuen, 1956.

Thompson, H. P. *Into All Lands: The History of the S.P.G.* London: S.P.C.K., 1951.

Waddy, R. P. Stacy. *A Ship under Sail.* London: S.P.G., 1951.

Williams, John G. *Hungry World.* London: S.P.C.K., 1960.

CHAPTER 1. WEST INDIES: THE TOPSY-TURVY PROVINCE

Bennett, J. H. *Bondsmen and Bishops.* University of California Publications in History, vol. 62. Berkeley: University of California Press, 1958.

Burns, Sir Alan C. *History of the British West Indies.* London: Allen and Unwin, 1954.

Cave, Hugh, *Haiti: High Road to Adventure.* New York: Henry Holt, 1952.

Roberts, Mrs. B. C. *Mrs. Roberts Visits the West Indies.* London: S.P.G., 1955.

Rodman, Selden. *Haiti: The Black Republic.* New York: Devin-Adair, 1961.

CHAPTER 2. SOUTH AMERICA: THE NEGLECTED CONTINENT

Dawley, Powel Mills. *Brazilian Destiny.* New York: National Council, 1951.

Every, E. F. *The Anglican Church in South America.* London: S.P.C.K., 1915.

Rycroft, W. Stanley. *Religion and Faith in Latin America.* Philadelphia: Westminster, 1958.

CHAPTER 3. WEST AFRICA: COASTING ON INHERITED CAPITAL

Laughton, John. *Gambia.* London: S.P.G., 1949.

The Sierra Leone Church. London: S.P.C.K., 1961.

CHAPTER 4. SOUTH AFRICA: A LAND TURNED IN UPON ITSELF

Barker, Anthony. *The Man Next to Me: An Adventure in African Medical Practice.* New York: Harper & Brothers, 1959. (*Giving and Receiving.* London: Faith Press, 1959.)

Brading, Barbara, and Brading, Richard. *Basutoland: Portrait of a Protectorate.* London: S.P.G., 1961.

Broomfield, G. W. *Colour Conflict.* London: Edinburgh House Press, 1943.

Clayton, Geoffrey F. *Where We Stand.* New York: Oxford University Press, 1960.

Kruger, D. W. *South African Parties and Policies 1910–1960.* New York: International Public Service, 1960.

Lee, A. W. *Once Dark Country.* London: S.P.C.K., 1949.

Mayer, Philip. *Townsmen or Tribesmen.* Cape Town: Oxford University Press, 1961.

Paton, David M., ed. *Church and Race in South Africa.* London: S.C.M., 1958.

———. *Christian Unity: A South African View.* Grahamstown: Rhodes University Press, 1951.

Pollock, J. C. *Earth's Remotest End.* New York: Macmillan, 1961.

Rubin, Leslie. *This Is Apartheid.* London: Victor Gollancz, 1959.

CHAPTER 5. CENTRAL AFRICA: TOO LITTLE TIME

Broomfield, G. W. *Towards Freedom.* London, U.M.C.A., 1957.

McCulloch, Mary. *A Time to Remember.* London, U.M.C.A., n.d.

Taylor, J. V., and Lehmann, Dorothea. *Christians of the Copperbelt.* Napiersville, Ill.: Alec Allenson, 1961.

Waldron, D. *Bechuanaland: The Church Says Yes.* London: S.P.G., 1961.

Wilson, G. H. *The History of the Universities Mission to Central Africa.* London: U.M.C.A., 1936.

CHAPTER 6. EAST AFRICA: A PROVINCE IS BORN

Oliver, R. A. *Missionary Factor in East Africa.* London: Longmans, Green, 1952.

Stradling, L. E. *A Bishop on Safari.* London: S.P.C.K., 1960.

Stuart, Mary. *Land of Promise.* London: C.M.S., 1959.

Sundkler, B. G. *The Christian Ministry in Africa.* Uppsala: Swedish Institute of Missionary Research, 1960.

Warren, Max. *Revival: An Enquiry.* London, S.C.M., 1954.

Welbourn, F. B. *East African Rebels.* London: S.C.M., 1961.

CHAPTER 7. UGANDA: OUR BEST FOOT FORWARD

Carpenter, G. W. *The Way in Africa.* New York: Friendship Press, 1959.

Mission Unlimited in Africa. New York: National Council, 1959.

CHAPTER 9. ENGLAND: SECOND REFORMATION IN PROGRESS

Garbett, C. *The Claims of the Church of England.* London: Hodder and Stoughton, 1947.

Moorman, J. R. H. *A History of the Church in England*. New York: Morehouse-Gorham, 1954.

The Official Yearbook of the Church of England. London: S.P.C.K., 1961.

Welsby, P. A. *How the Church of England Works*. London: S.P.C.K., 1960.

CHAPTER 10. WALES: "THE OLD MOTHER"

Green, C. A. H. *The Setting of the Constitution of the Church in Wales*. London: Sweet and Maxwell, 1937.

James, J. W. *A Church History of Wales*. Stockwell, 1945.

Lewis, E. D. *The Rhondda Valleys*. London: Phoenix House, 1959.

Lewis, Ewart. *Prayer Book Revision in the Church in Wales*. Penarth, Glamorgan: Llandoff House, 1958.

Rees, Sir James Frederick. *Studies in Welsh History*. Cardiff: University of Wales Press, 1947.

Williams, A. H. *Introduction to the History of Modern Wales*. London: John Murray, 1950.

CHAPTER 11. IRELAND: SANCTITY, SCHOLARSHIP AND SHRINKAGE

Phillips, W. A. *History of the Church of Ireland*, 3 vols. London: Oxford University Press, 1933.

CHAPTER 12. SCOTLAND: CHURCH AND KIRK

Don, Alan Campbell. *The Scottish Book of Common Prayer*. London: S.P.C.K., 1949.

Donaldson, Gordon. *Scotland: Church and Nation through Sixteen Centuries*. London: S.C.M., 1960.

Goldie, F. *Short History of the Episcopal Church in Scotland*. London: S.P.C.K., 1951.

CHAPTER 13. THE MEDITERRANEAN: MISSION TO THE MILITARY

Axton, J. T., Jr. *Brief History of the Churches in the U.S. Army*. Fort Leavenworth: 1925.

Drury, C. M. *The History of the Chaplain Corps USN, Vol. 1: 1778-1939*. Washington: Bureau of Naval Personnel, 1948.

Vol 2: 1939-1949. Washington, D.C.: Bureau of Naval Personnel, 1949.

Frank, E. L. *The Chaplaincy in the Armed Services: a Preliminary Bibliography*. Oberlin: 1945.

Honeywell, R. J. *History, Chaplains of the U.S. Army*. Washington, D.C.: The Superintendent of Documents, U.S.G.P.O., 1958.

Jorgensen, D. F. *A History of the United States Air Force Chaplaincy, Vol. 1: The Service of Chaplains to Army Air Units 1917-1946*. Washington, D.C.: Office, Chief of Air Force Chaplains, n.d.

Thompson, D. A. *American Army Chaplaincy: A Brief History.* Washington, D.C.: War Department Pam 16–1, 1946.

CHAPTER 14. THE MIDDLE EAST: BUILDING ON OLD FOUNDATIONS

Barclay, *Biography of Bishop.* London: S. W. Partridge & Co.

Bridgeman, C. T. *The Episcopal Church and the Middle East.* New York: Morehouse-Gorham, 1958.

Cragg, Kenneth. *Call of the Minaret.* New York: Oxford University Press, 1956.

——. *Sandals at the Mosque: Christian Presence Amid Islam.* New York: Oxford University Press, 1959.

Dehqani-Tafti, H. B. *Design of My World.* New York: Association Press, 1959.

Gobat, M. *T. D. Gobat: His Life, Work, and Teaching.* Letchworth: G. W. Wardman, 1938.

Upton, Joseph. *History of Modern Iran.* Cambridge, Mass.: Harvard University Press, 1960.

CHAPTER 15. INDIA, PAKISTAN, BURMA AND CEYLON: A "PECULIAR VINEYARD"

Bayne, S. F. *Ceylon, North India, Pakistan: A Study in Ecumenical Decision.* London: S.P.C.K., 1961.

Bookless, Guy. *Spotlight on India.* London: C.M.S., 1959.

Brown, Ashley W. *On Bombay Coast and Deccan.* London: Deccan, 1937.

Bryan, R. W. *All in a Day's Work.* London: Highway Press, 1954.

Campbell, Alexander. *The Heart of India.* New York: Knopf, 1958.

Chatterton, Eyre. *A History of the Church of England in India.* London: S.P.C.K., 1929.

Ferguson, J. P. *Kashmir.* New York: International Publications Service, 1961.

Garrett, T. S. *Worship in the Church of South India.* Richmond, Va.: John Knox Press, 1958.

Grant, J. W. *God's People in India.* London: Christian Literature Society, 1959.

Hervat, E. V. S. *Christianity in Western India.* London: S.P.C.K., 1937.

Holland, Sir Henry. *Frontier Doctor.* London: C.M.S., 1959.

Paul, R. D. *The First Decade.* Madras: Christian Literature Society, 1958.

Sundkler, B. G. *The Church of South India.* London: Lutterworth Press, 1954.

Survey Report: A Study of the Economic, Educational, and Religious Condition of the Church. Lahore: West Pakistan Christian Council.

West, Grace. *Car Nicobar.* London: S.P.G., 1950.

Winslow, J. C. *Christian Approach to the Hindu.* London: Edinburgh House, 1958.

CHAPTER 17. BORNEO: MIRACLES OUT OF MUD

Cornwall, Nigel. *Borneo: Past and Future.* London: S.P.G., 1952.

Runciman, Steven. *White Rajahs: a History of Sarawak from 1841 to 1946.* Cambridge University Press, 1960.

CHAPTER 18. AUSTRALIA: GROWING PAINS DOWN UNDER

Elkin, A. P. *The Diocese of Newcastle.* Glebe, N.S.W.: Australian Medical Publication, 1955. (Bibliography included.)

Grattan, C. H. *Australia.* Berkeley, Calif.: Berkeley University Press, 1947.

Rowland, E. S. *The Tropics for Christ.* North Queensland, Australia: Diocesan Offices, 1960.

CHAPTER 19. NEW ZEALAND: ENGLAND TRANSPLANTED

McCall, T. B. *Blood and Race.* Christchurch, New Zealand: Anglican Truth Society, 1957.

————. *Is the Church of England Changing?* Christchurch, New Zealand: Anglican Truth Society, 1959.

Purchas, H. T. *History of the New Zealand Church.* Christchurch, New Zealand: Simpson and Williams, 1914.

CHAPTER 20. POLYNESIA: A CINDERELLA STORY

Whonsbon-Aston, C. W. *Challenge in Polynesia.* Sydney: Australian Board of Missions, n.d.

————. *Polynesia Patchwork.* London: S.P.G., 1948.

————. *The Moon and Polynesia.* London: S.P.G., 1961.

CHAPTER 22. MELANESIA: THE "DO-IT-YOURSELF" DIOCESE,

Artless, S. W. *Story of the Melanesian Mission.* London: Church Army, 1955.

Fox, C. E. *Lord of the Southern Isles.* London: Mowbray, 1958.

CHAPTER 23. PHILIPPINES: A GREAT DAY AHEAD

Roberts, W. N. *Survey Report on Theological Education in the Philippines.* New York: National Council of Churches, Far Eastern Office, Philippine Federation of Christian Churches, 1962.

Whittemore, Lewis Bliss. *Struggle for Freedom.* Greenwich, Conn.: Seabury Press, 1961.

Zabriskie, Alexander. *Bishop Brent.* Philadelphia: Westminster Press, 1948.

CHAPTER 24. HONG KONG: FULL-TIME JOB BY PART-TIME PRIESTS

Endacott, G. B., and She, D. E. *The Diocese of Victoria, Hong Kong.* Hong Kong: Standard Press, 1949.

Murray, J. L. *The Problem of the People.* Hong Kong: Information Service, 1960.

CHAPTER 25. TAIWAN AND OKINAWA: ISLAND HOPPING

Tong, Hollington. *History of Christianity in Taiwan.*

Kerr, George A. *Okinawa: The History of an Island People.* Rutland and Tokyo: Charles E. Tuttle, 1958.

CHAPTER 26. JAPAN: SEVENTEEN-SYLLABLE POEMS AND SEVEN-TEEN YEARS TO WAIT

Campbell, Alexander. *The Heart of Japan.* New York: Knopf, 1961.

Robbins, H. C., and MacNaught, G. K. *Dr. Rudolf Bolling Teusler: an Adventure in Christianity.* New York: Scribner's, 1942.

Sansbury, C. K. *Japan.* London: S.P.G., 1947.

Tucker, B. D. *God Gave the Increase.* Sapporo, Japan: St. Michael's Church.

Tucker, H. St. G. *The History of the Episcopal Church in Japan.* New York: Scribner's, 1938.

CHAPTER 27. KOREA: UNQUIET LAND OF THE MORNING CALM

Morning Calm, A Quarterly Magazine. London: Secretary to the Korean Mission, 55 Bedford Garden, W.8.

Rutt, Richard. *The Church Serves Korea.* London: S.P.G., 1956.

———. *Korean Works and Days.* Rutland and Tokyo: Charles E. Tuttle.

Osgood, Cornelius. *The Koreans and their Culture.* New York: The Ronald Press, 1951.

CHAPTER 28. PANAMA, CENTRAL AMERICA, MEXICO: *Hoy, No Mañana*

Albarnoz, A. F. Carillo de. *Roman Catholicism and Religious Liberty.* Geneva, Switzerland: World Council of Churches, 1959.

Barbieri, S. U. *Land of Eldorado.* New York: Friendship Press, 1961.

———. *Christians and Social Change in Latin America.* Latin America Commission on Church and Society, Montevideo, Uruguay, and the Department on Church and Society of the World Council of Churches, Geneva, Switzerland.

Coleman, William J. *Latin-American Catholicism. A Self Evaluation.* New York: Mary Knoll Publications.

Luckhardt, Mildred. *Mission in Mexico.* Greenwich: Seabury Press, 1960.

MacKay, John A. *The Other Spanish Christ.* New York. Student Christian Movement Press, 1933.

McCorkle, Henry L. *The Quiet Crusaders.* New York: Friendship Press, 1961.

CHAPTER 29. CANADA: POTENTIAL UNLIMITED

Fleming, A. L. *Archibald: the Arctic.* New York: Appleton, 1956.

Mann, W. E. *Church, Sect and Cult in Alberta*. Toronto: University of Toronto Press, 1955.

Vernon, C. W. *The Old Church in the New Dominion*. London: S.P.C.K., 1929.

Walsh, H. H. *The Christian Church in Canada*. Toronto: Ryerson, 1956.

CHAPTER 30. UNITED STATES: A TOUR DE FORCE

Addison, J. T. *The Episcopal Church in the United States: 1789–1931*. New York: Scribner's, 1951.

Dawley, P. M. *The Episcopal Church and Its Work*. Greenwich, Conn.: Seabury Press, 1955.

Manross, W. W. *A History of the American Episcopal Church*, 2nd ed. New York: Morehouse-Gorham, 1950.

Shepherd, M. H., Jr. *The Oxford American Prayer Book Commentary*. New York: Oxford University Press, 1950.

Shoemaker, R. W. *The Origin and Meaning of the Name Protestant Episcopal*. New York: American Publications, 1959.

INDEX

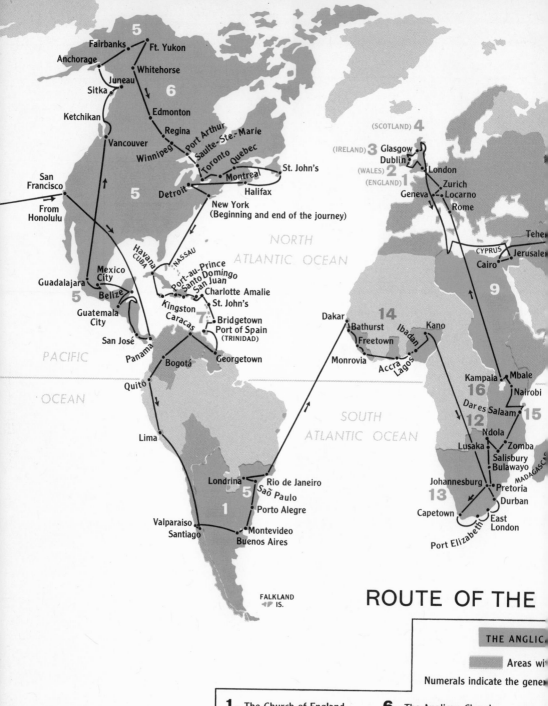

ROUTE OF THE

1. The Church of England

2. The Church in Wales

3. The Church of Ireland

4. The Episcopal Church in Scotland

5. The Protestant Episcopal Church in the United States of America

6. The Anglican Church of Canada

7. The Church of the Province of the West Indies

8. The Church of India, Pakistan, Burma and Ceylon

9. Jurisdiction of the Archbishop in Jerusalem

Lilli Mautner